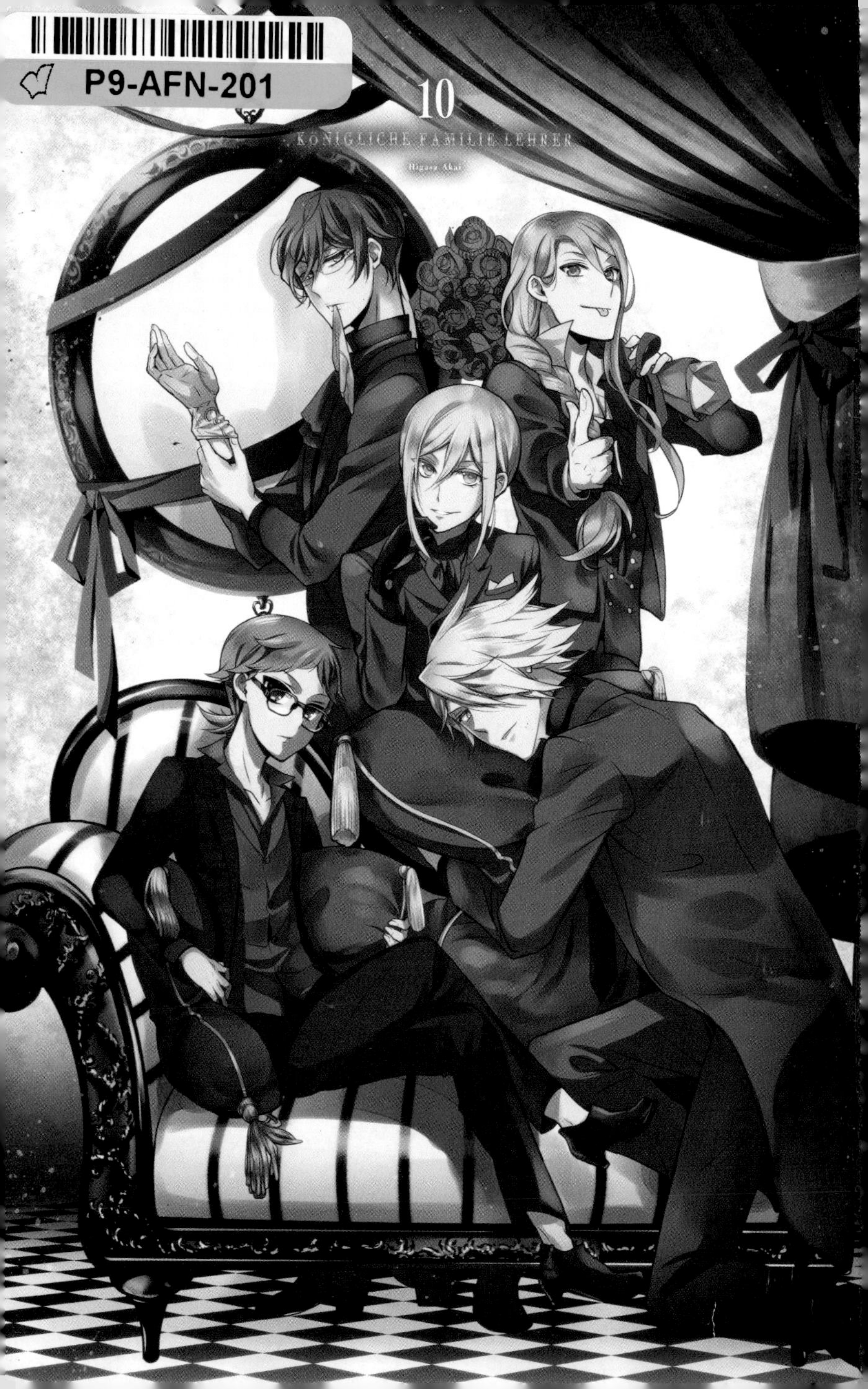
10
KÖNIGLICHE FAMILIE LEHRER
Higasa Akai

CONTENTS

KÖNIGLICHE FAMILIE HEER

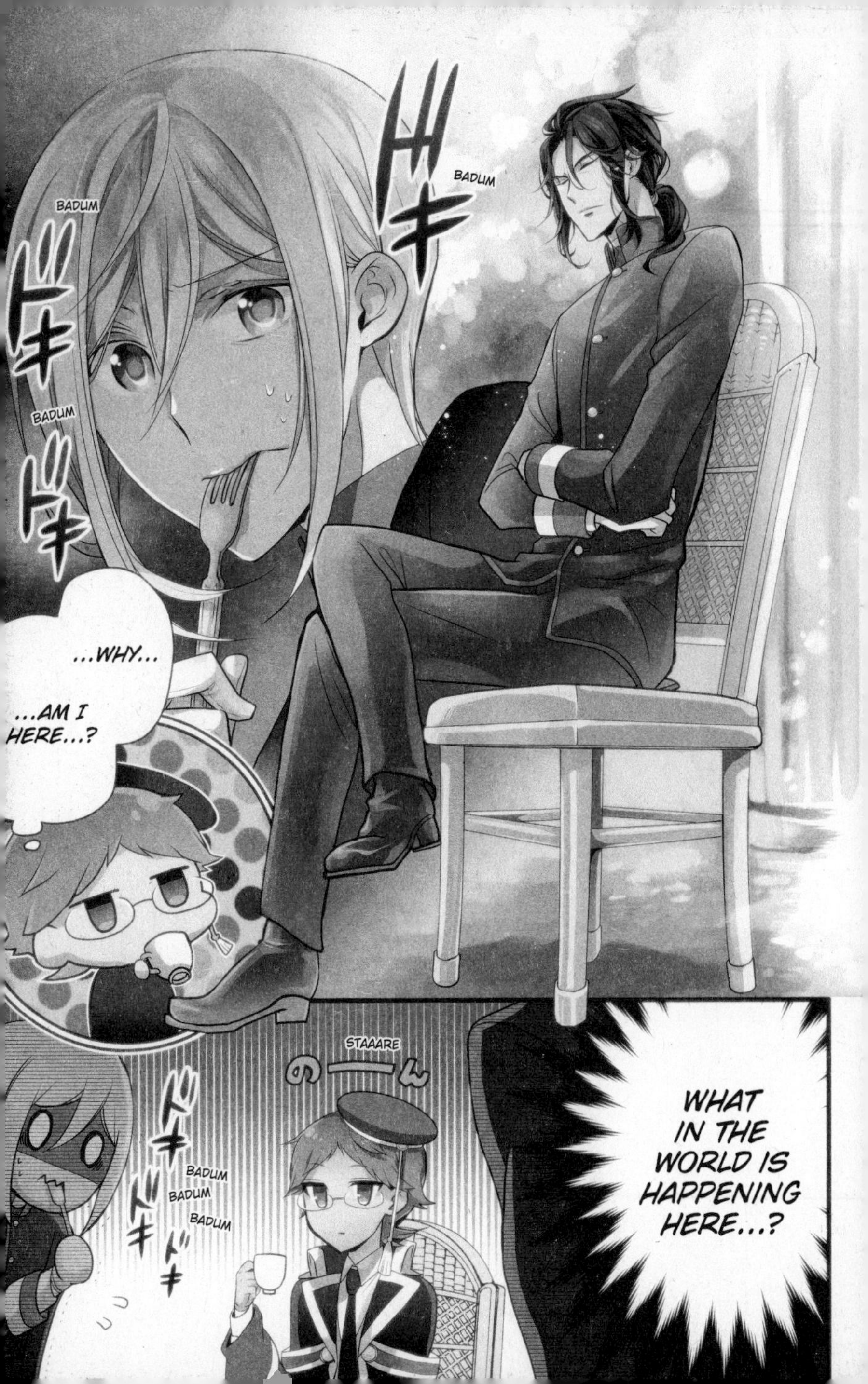
BADUM
BADUM
BADUM
...WHY...
...AM I HERE...?
WHAT IN THE WORLD IS HAPPENING HERE...?
STAAARE
BADUM
BADUM
BADUM

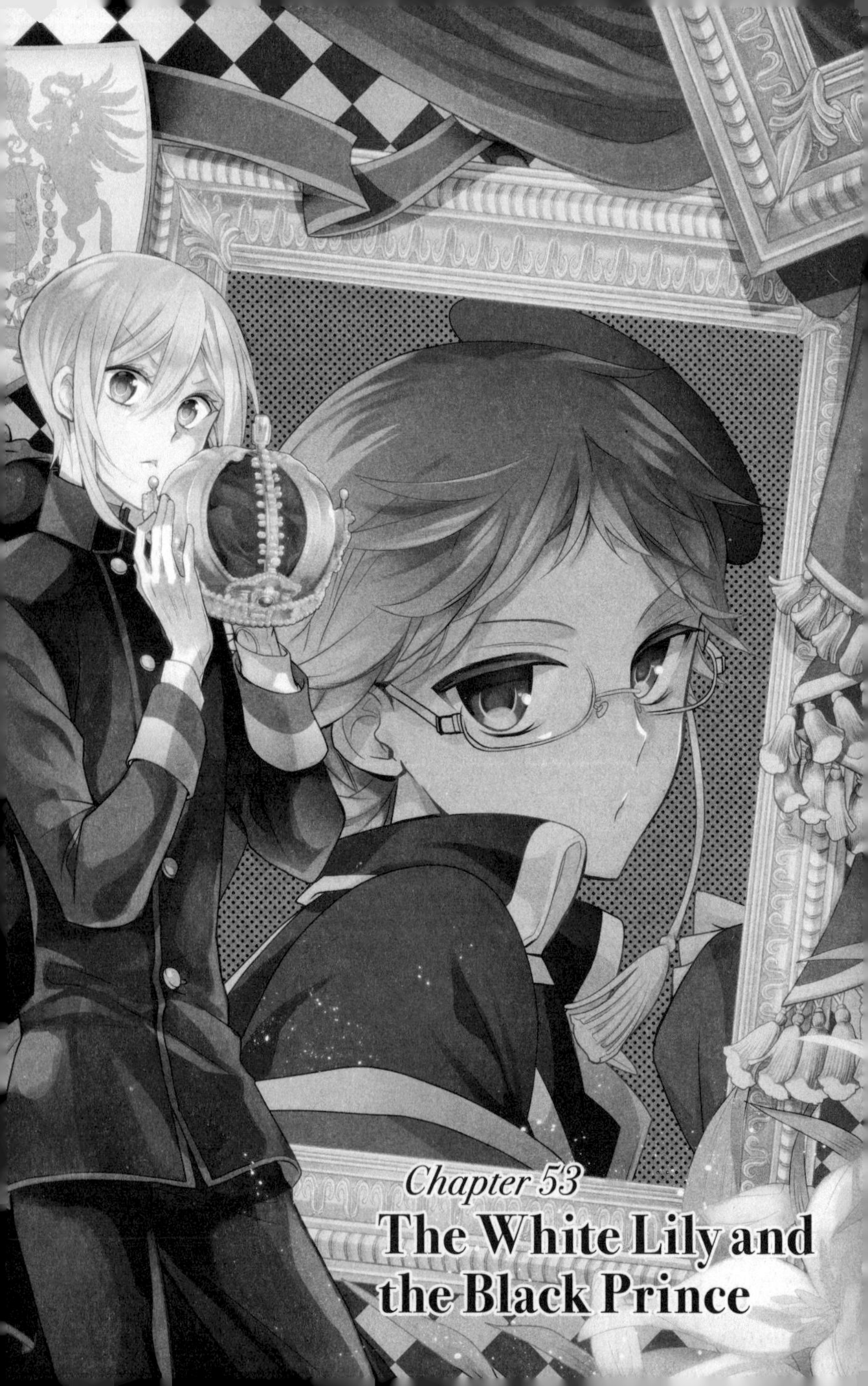
Chapter 53
The White Lily and the Black Prince

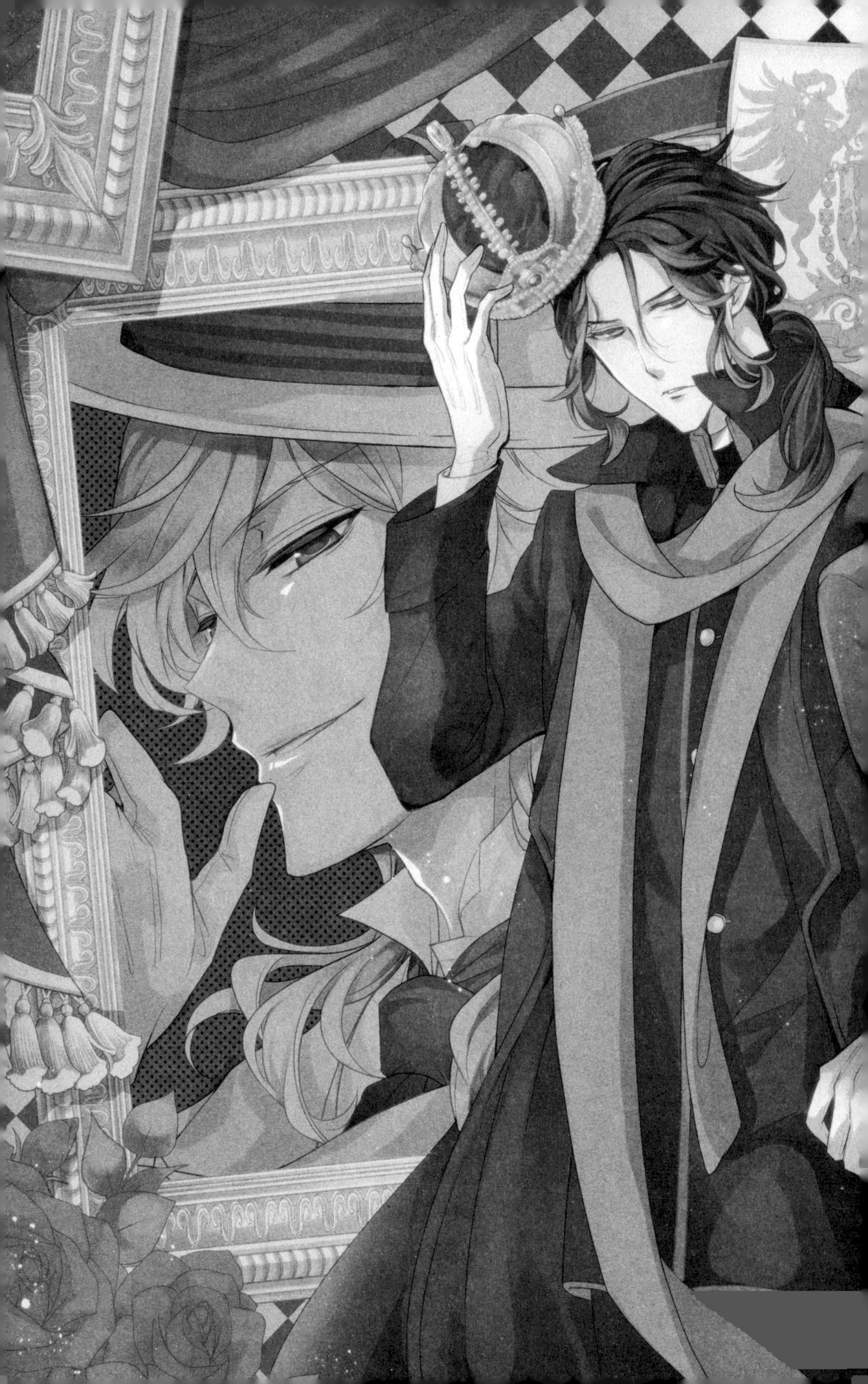

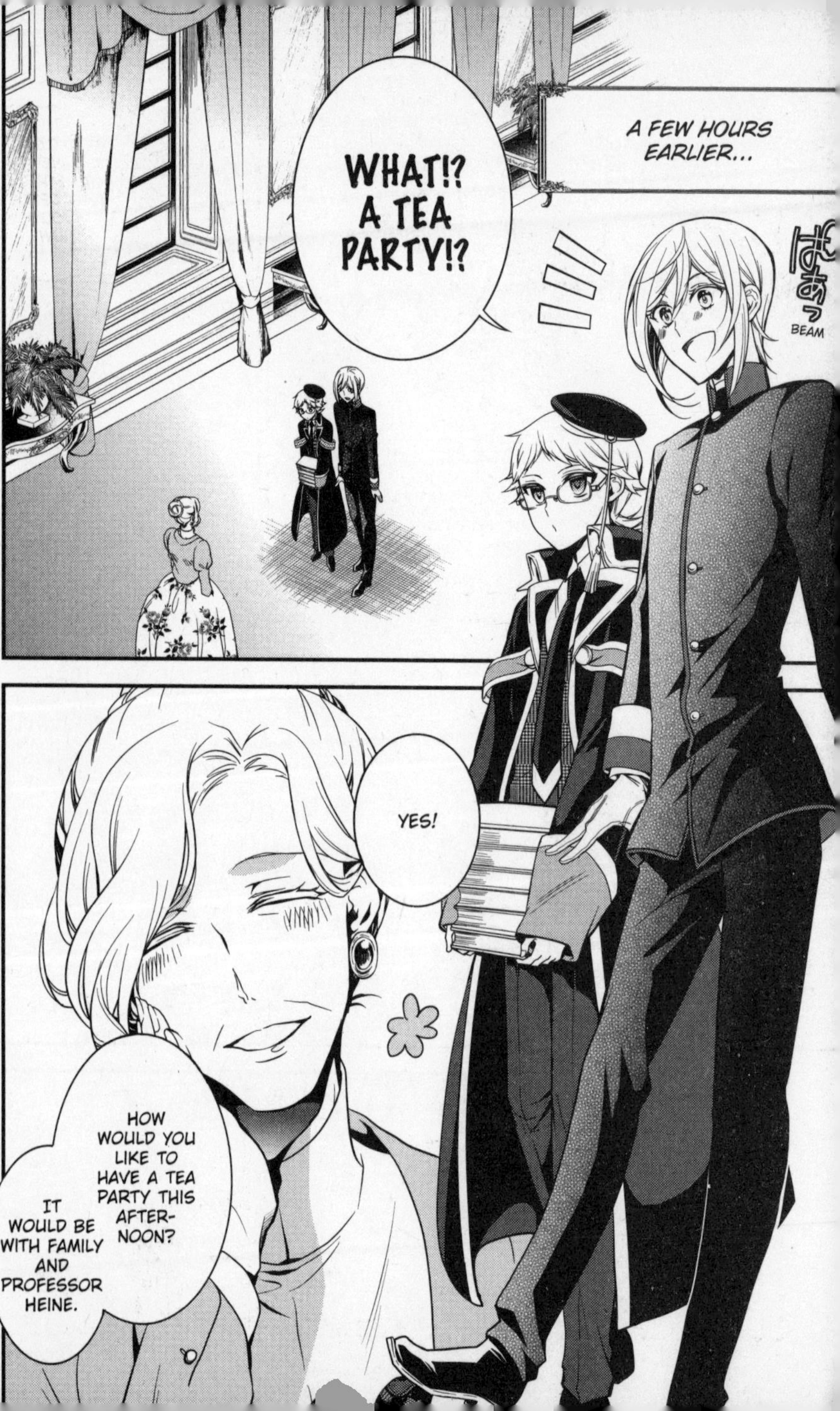

A FEW HOURS EARLIER...
WHAT!? A TEA PARTY!?
ぱあっ
BEAM
YES!
HOW WOULD YOU LIKE TO HAVE A TEA PARTY THIS AFTER-NOON?
IT WOULD BE WITH FAMILY AND PROFESSOR HEINE.

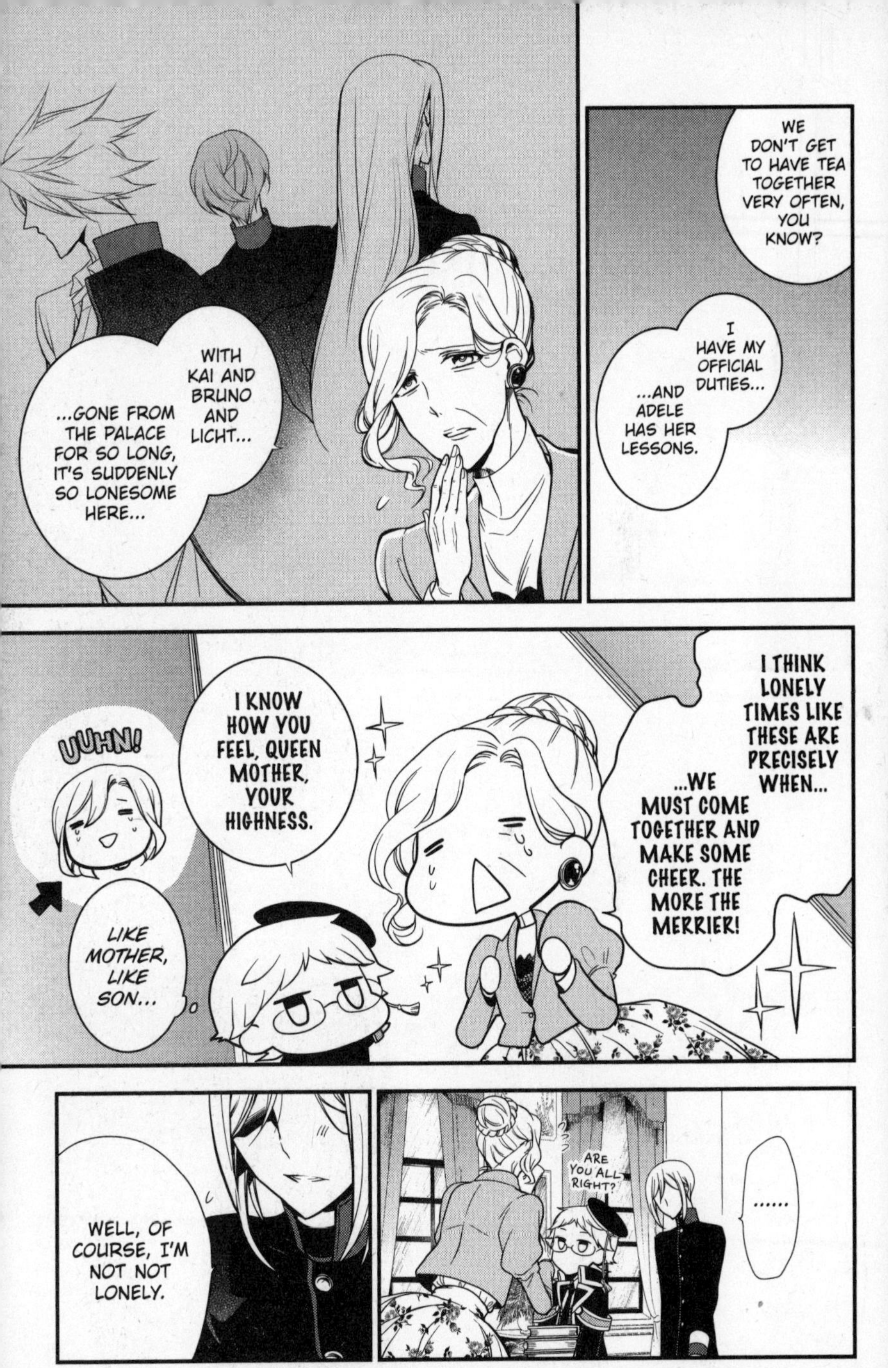
WE DON'T GET TO HAVE TEA TOGETHER VERY OFTEN, YOU KNOW?
I HAVE MY OFFICIAL DUTIES...
...AND ADELE HAS HER LESSONS.
WITH KAI AND BRUNO AND LICHT...
...GONE FROM THE PALACE FOR SO LONG, IT'S SUDDENLY SO LONESOME HERE...
I THINK LONELY TIMES LIKE THESE ARE PRECISELY WHEN...
...WE MUST COME TOGETHER AND MAKE SOME CHEER. THE MORE THE MERRIER!
I KNOW HOW YOU FEEL, QUEEN MOTHER, YOUR HIGHNESS.
UUHN!
LIKE MOTHER, LIKE SON...
......
ARE YOU ALL RIGHT?
WELL, OF COURSE, I'M NOT NOT LONELY.

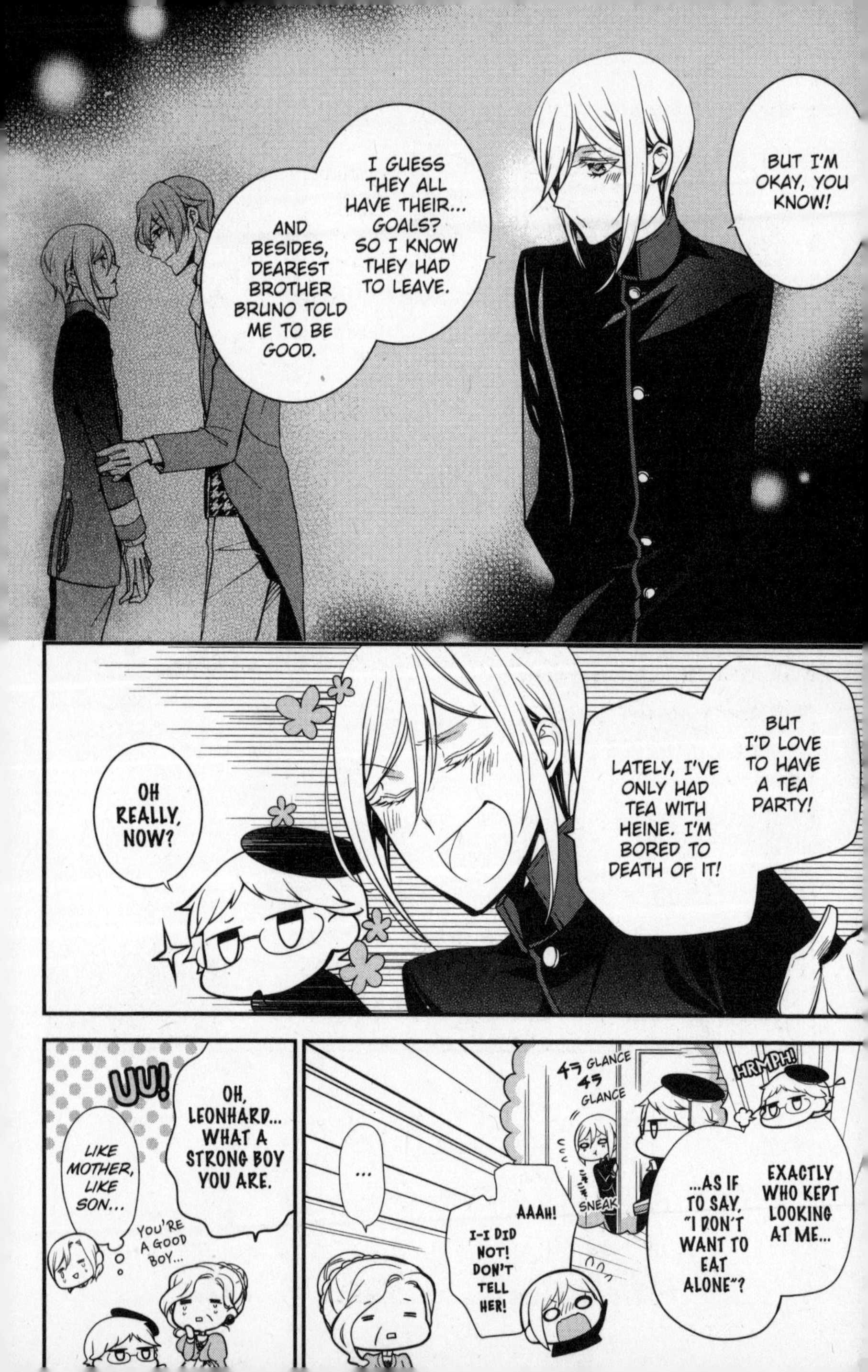
BUT I'M OKAY, YOU KNOW!
I GUESS THEY ALL HAVE THEIR... GOALS? SO I KNOW THEY HAD TO LEAVE.
AND BESIDES, DEAREST BROTHER BRUNO TOLD ME TO BE GOOD.
BUT I'D LOVE TO HAVE A TEA PARTY!
LATELY, I'VE ONLY HAD TEA WITH HEINE. I'M BORED TO DEATH OF IT!
OH REALLY, NOW?
HRMPH!
EXACTLY WHO KEPT LOOKING AT ME...
...AS IF TO SAY, "I DON'T WANT TO EAT ALONE"?
GLANCE
GLANCE
SNEAK
...
AAAH!
I-I DID NOT! DON'T TELL HER!
OH, LEONHARD... WHAT A STRONG BOY YOU ARE.
UU!
LIKE MOTHER, LIKE SON...
YOU'RE A GOOD BOY...

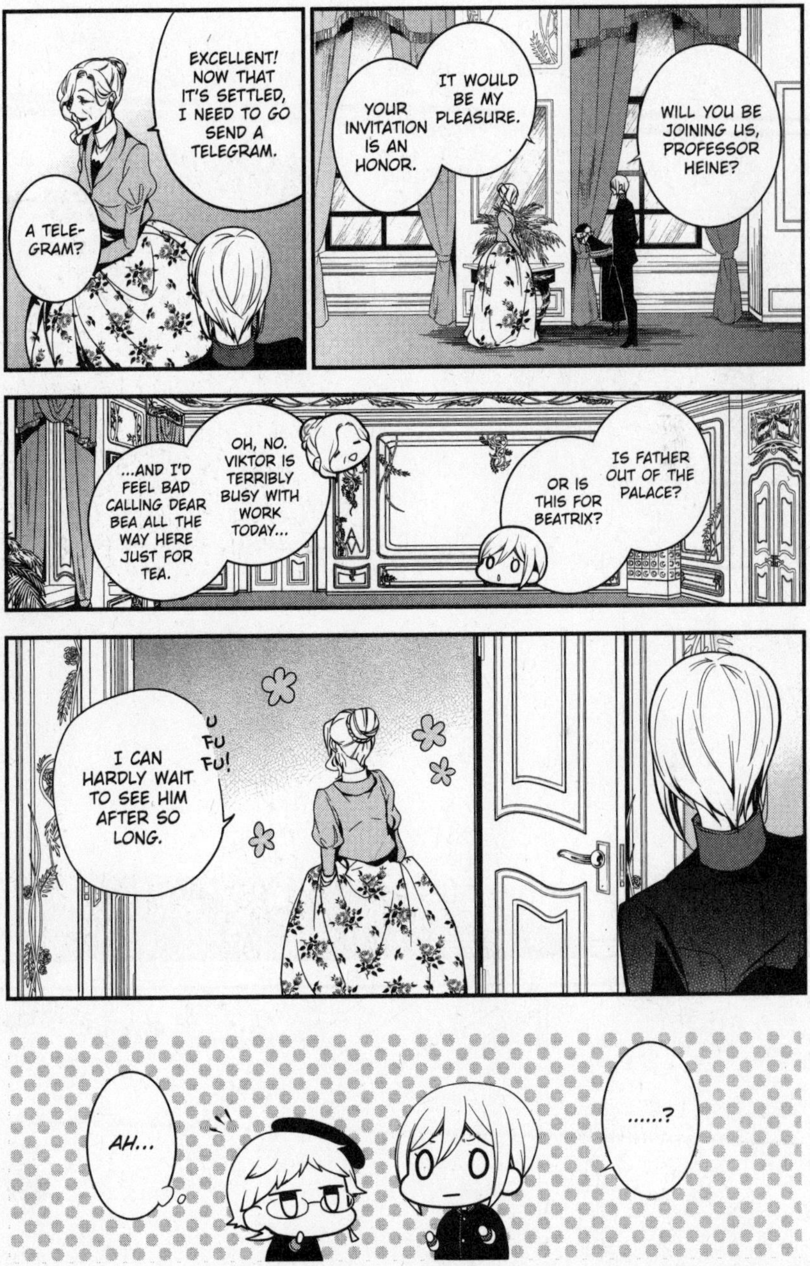
WILL YOU BE JOINING US, PROFESSOR HEINE?
IT WOULD BE MY PLEASURE.
YOUR INVITATION IS AN HONOR.
EXCELLENT! NOW THAT IT'S SETTLED, I NEED TO GO SEND A TELEGRAM.
A TELE-GRAM?
IS FATHER OUT OF THE PALACE?
OR IS THIS FOR BEATRIX?
OH, NO. VIKTOR IS TERRIBLY BUSY WITH WORK TODAY...
...AND I'D FEEL BAD CALLING DEAR BEA ALL THE WAY HERE JUST FOR TEA.
U FU FU!
I CAN HARDLY WAIT TO SEE HIM AFTER SO LONG.
......?
AH...

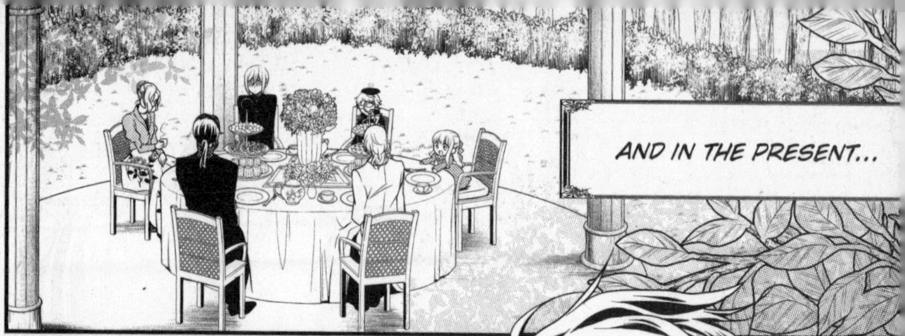
AND IN THE PRESENT...

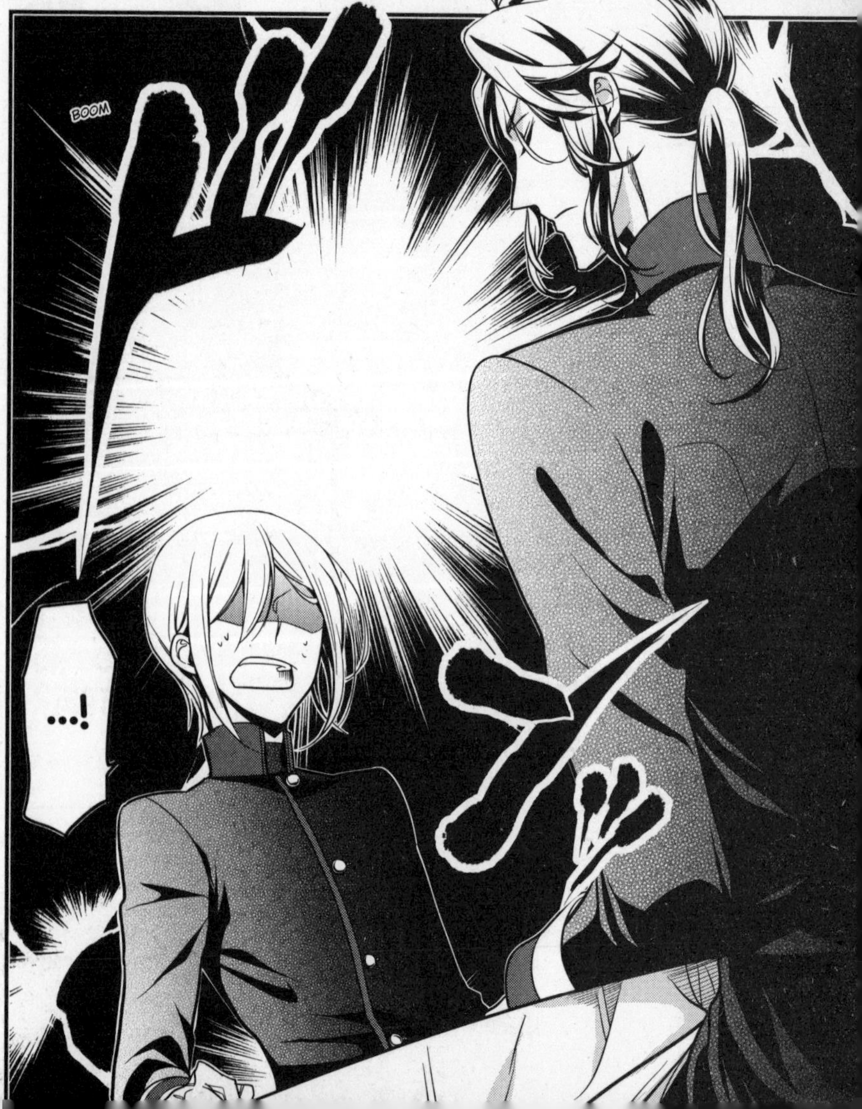
BOOM
...!

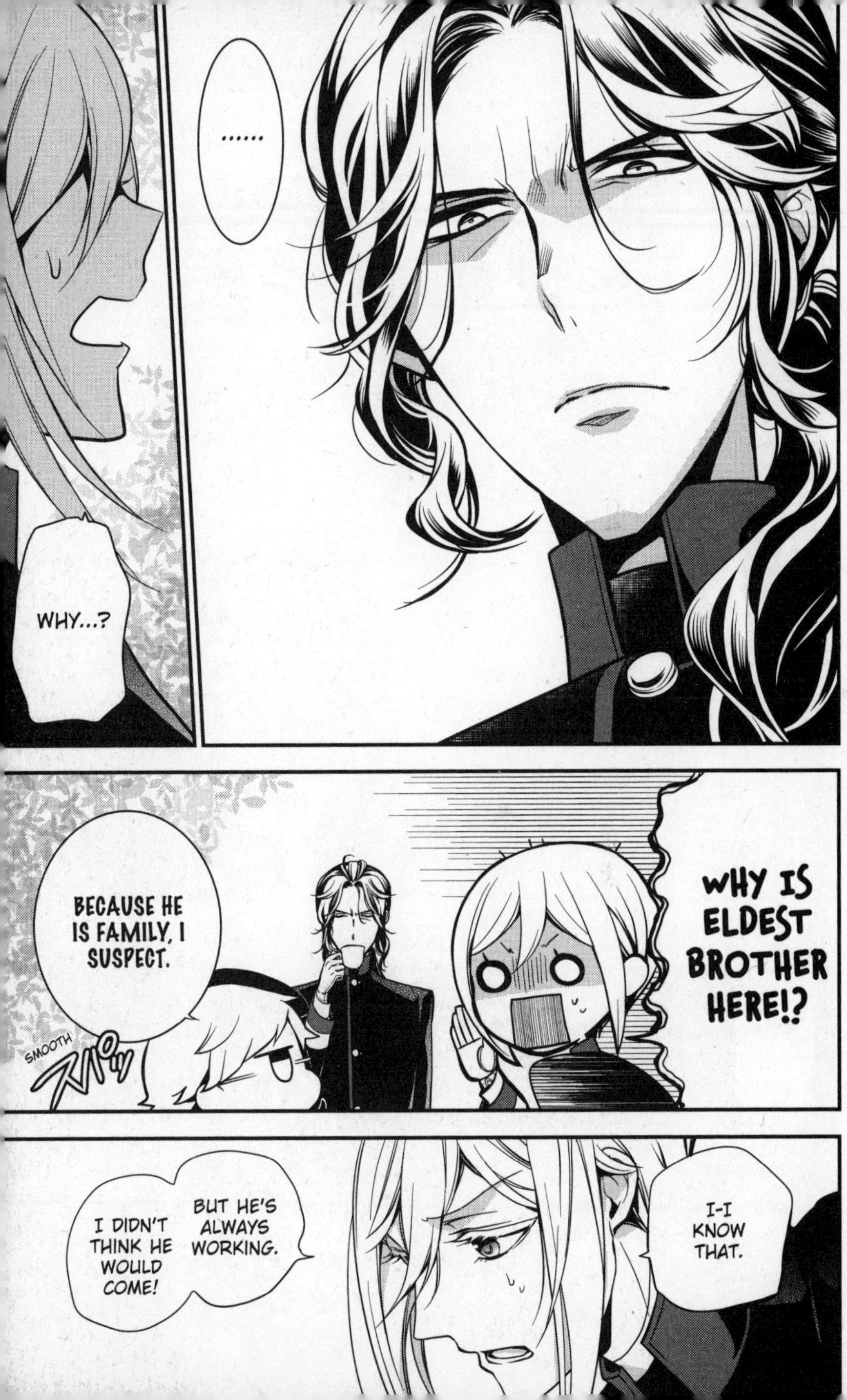
......
WHY...?
WHY IS ELDEST BROTHER HERE!?
BECAUSE HE IS FAMILY, I SUSPECT.
SMOOTH
I-I KNOW THAT.
BUT HE'S ALWAYS WORKING.
I DIDN'T THINK HE WOULD COME!

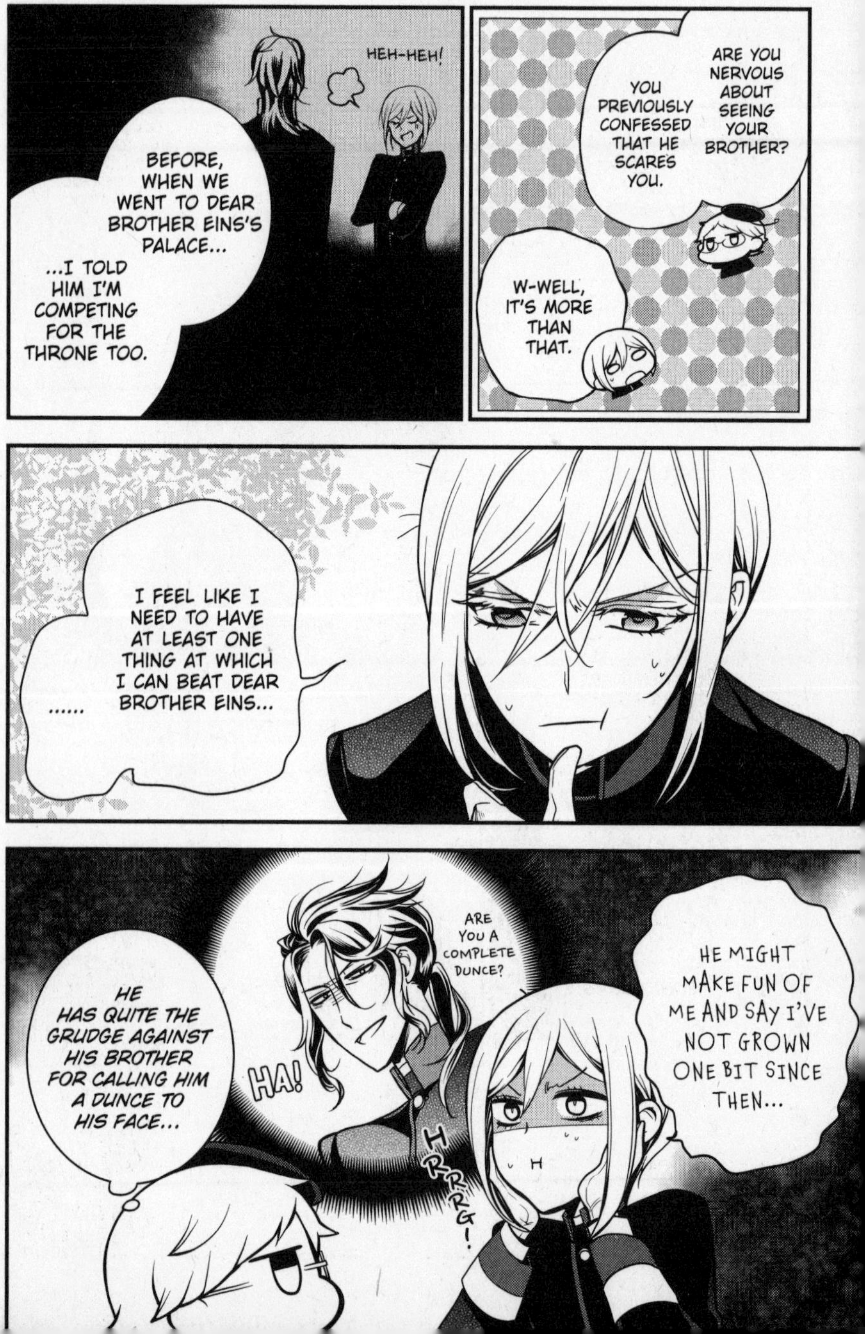
ARE YOU NERVOUS ABOUT SEEING YOUR BROTHER?
YOU PREVIOUSLY CONFESSED THAT HE SCARES YOU.
W-WELL, IT'S MORE THAN THAT.
HEH-HEH!
BEFORE, WHEN WE WENT TO DEAR BROTHER EINS'S PALACE...
...I TOLD HIM I'M COMPETING FOR THE THRONE TOO.
I FEEL LIKE I NEED TO HAVE AT LEAST ONE THING AT WHICH I CAN BEAT DEAR BROTHER EINS...
......
HE MIGHT MAKE FUN OF ME AND SAY I'VE NOT GROWN ONE BIT SINCE THEN...
ARE YOU A COMPLETE DUNCE?
HE HAS QUITE THE GRUDGE AGAINST HIS BROTHER FOR CALLING HIM A DUNCE TO HIS FACE...
HA!
HRRRG!

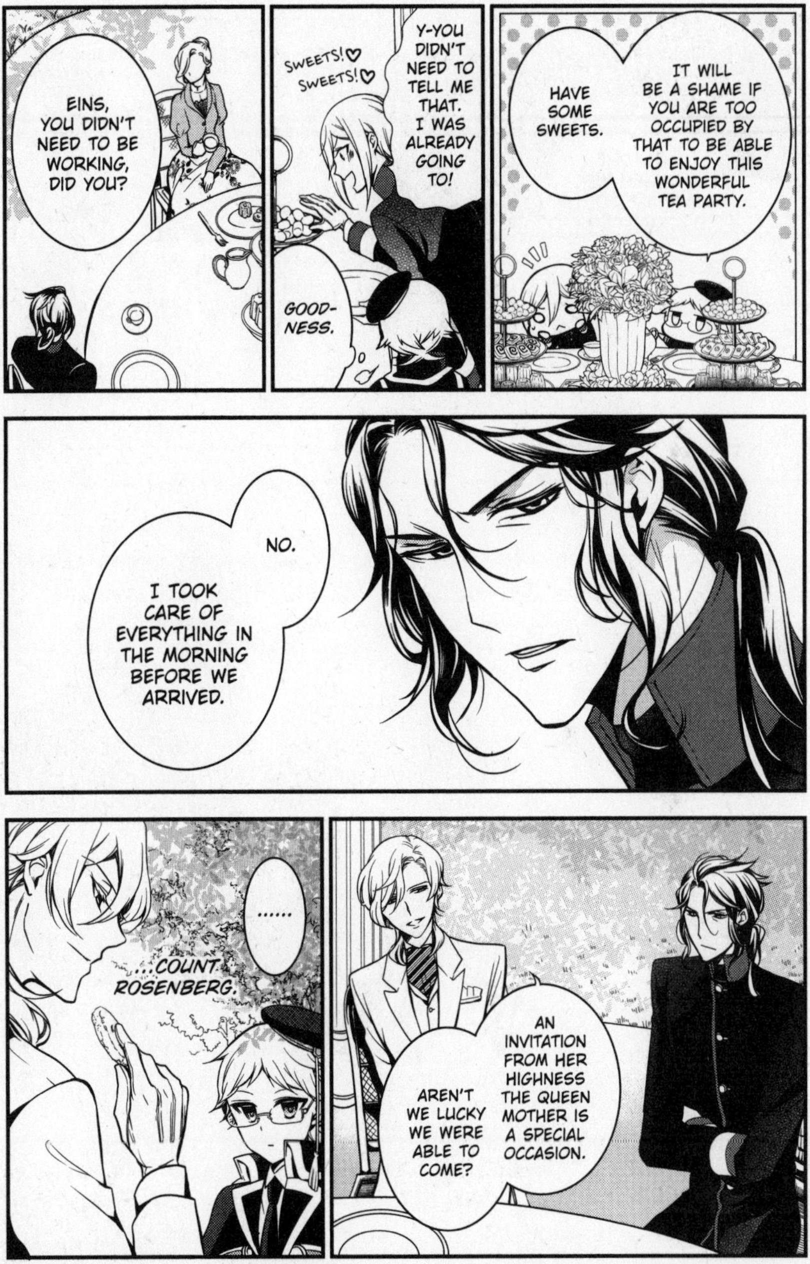
IT WILL BE A SHAME IF YOU ARE TOO OCCUPIED BY THAT TO BE ABLE TO ENJOY THIS WONDERFUL TEA PARTY.
HAVE SOME SWEETS.
Y-YOU DIDN'T NEED TO TELL ME THAT. I WAS ALREADY GOING TO!
SWEETS! SWEETS!
GOODNESS.
EINS, YOU DIDN'T NEED TO BE WORKING, DID YOU?
NO.
I TOOK CARE OF EVERYTHING IN THE MORNING BEFORE WE ARRIVED.
AN INVITATION FROM HER HIGHNESS THE QUEEN MOTHER IS A SPECIAL OCCASION.
AREN'T WE LUCKY WE WERE ABLE TO COME?
......
...COUNT ROSENBERG.

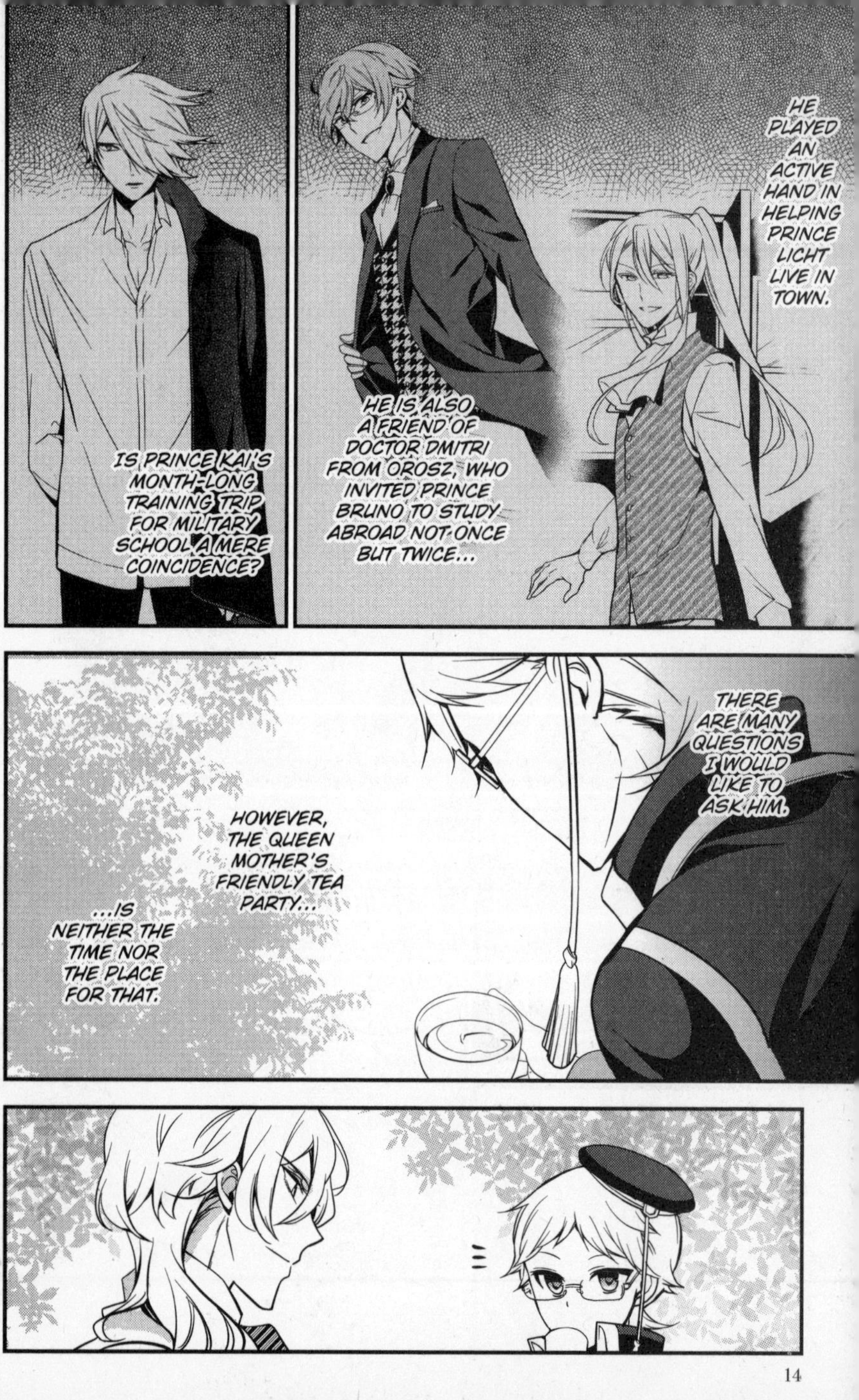
HE PLAYED AN ACTIVE HAND IN HELPING PRINCE LICHT LIVE IN TOWN.
HE IS ALSO A FRIEND OF DOCTOR DMITRI FROM OROSZ, WHO INVITED PRINCE BRUNO TO STUDY ABROAD NOT ONCE BUT TWICE...
IS PRINCE KAI'S MONTH-LONG TRAINING TRIP FOR MILITARY SCHOOL A MERE COINCIDENCE?
THERE ARE MANY QUESTIONS I WOULD LIKE TO ASK HIM.
HOWEVER, THE QUEEN MOTHER'S FRIENDLY TEA PARTY...
...IS NEITHER THE TIME NOR THE PLACE FOR THAT.

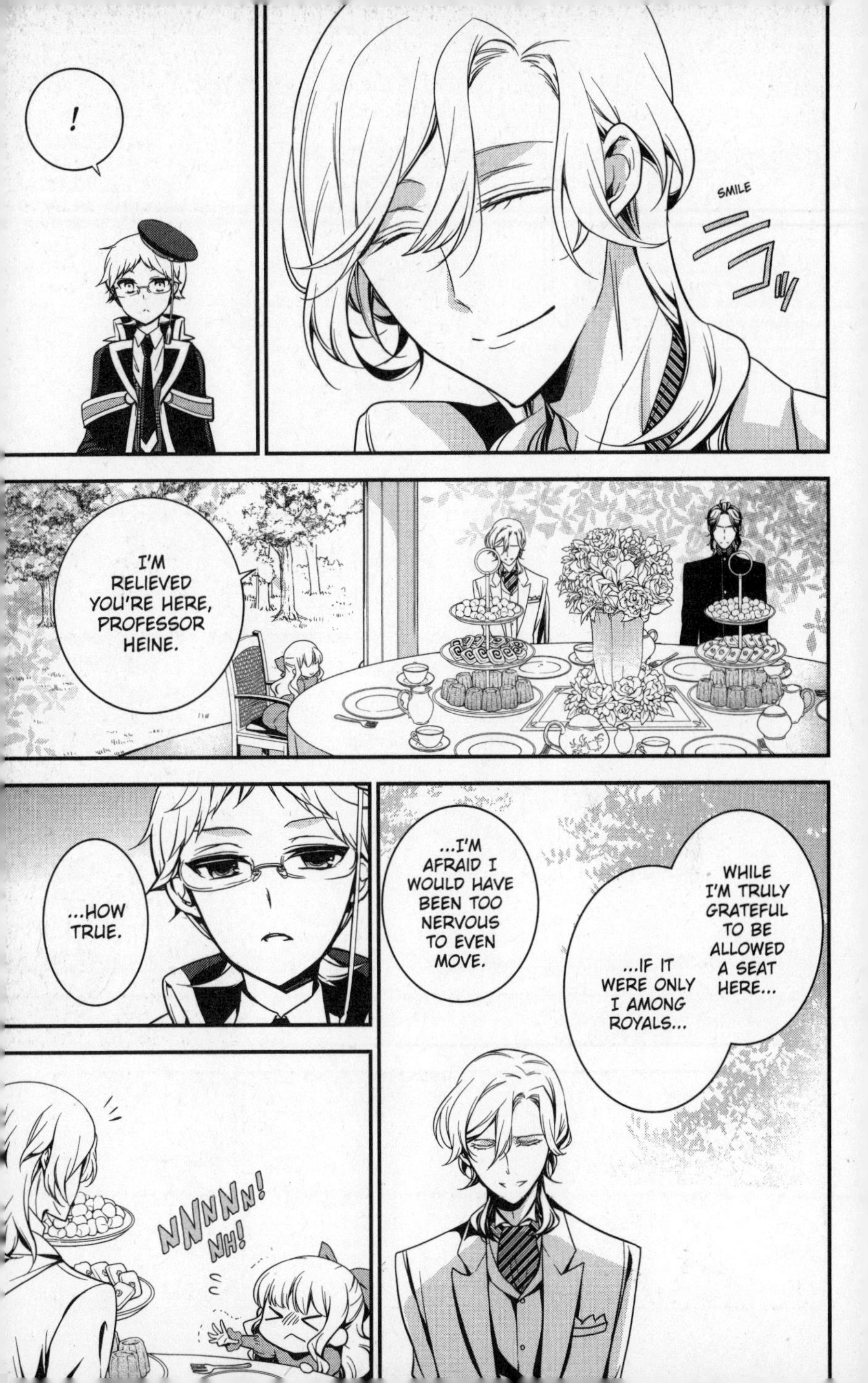
SMILE
!
I'M RELIEVED YOU'RE HERE, PROFESSOR HEINE.
WHILE I'M TRULY GRATEFUL TO BE ALLOWED A SEAT HERE...
...IF IT WERE ONLY I AMONG ROYALS...
...I'M AFRAID I WOULD HAVE BEEN TOO NERVOUS TO EVEN MOVE.
...HOW TRUE.
NNNNN! NH!

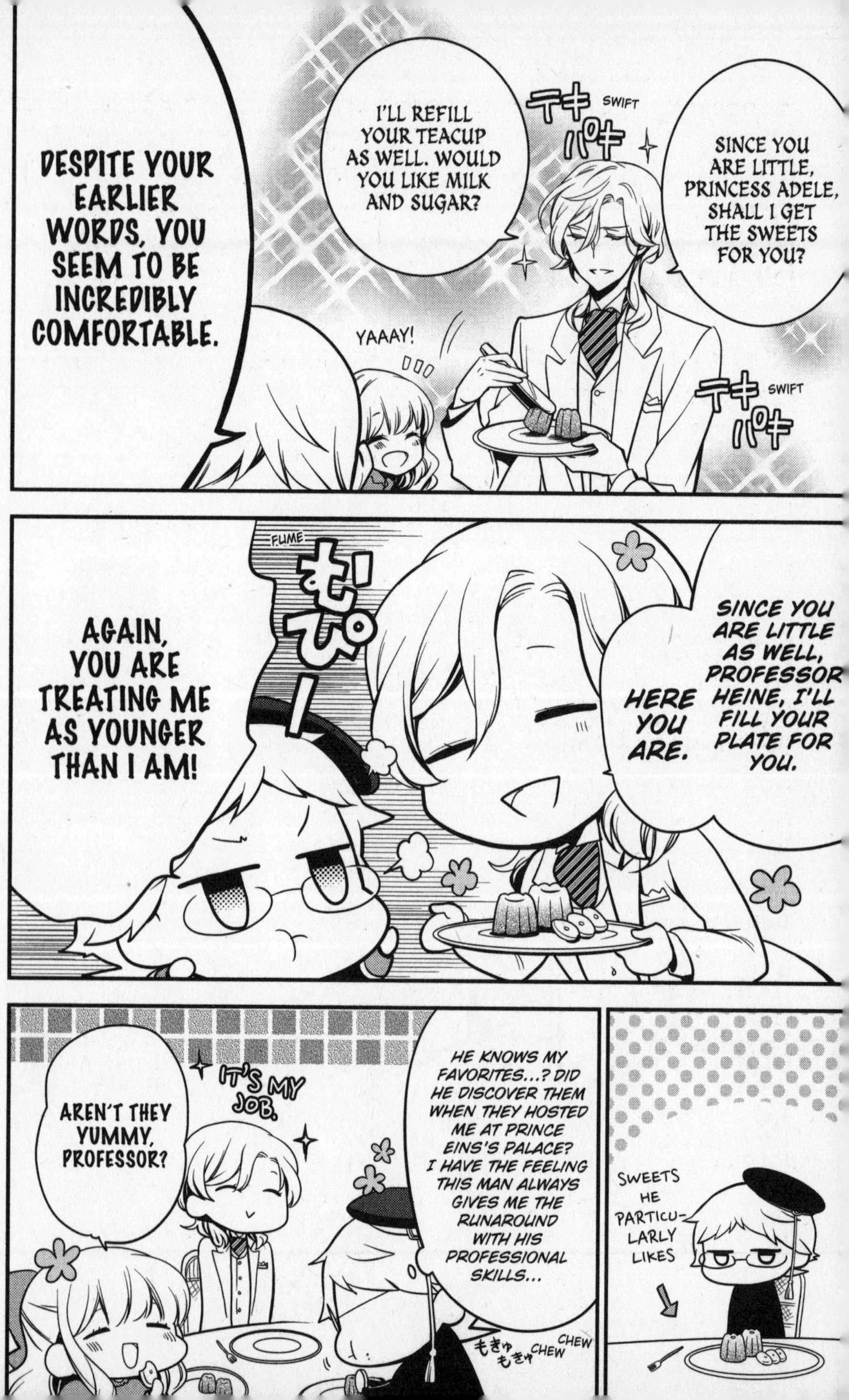
SINCE YOU ARE LITTLE, PRINCESS ADELE, SHALL I GET THE SWEETS FOR YOU?
テキパキ SWIFT
I'LL REFILL YOUR TEACUP AS WELL. WOULD YOU LIKE MILK AND SUGAR?
テキパキ SWIFT
YAAAY!
DESPITE YOUR EARLIER WORDS, YOU SEEM TO BE INCREDIBLY COMFORTABLE.
SINCE YOU ARE LITTLE AS WELL, PROFESSOR HEINE, I'LL FILL YOUR PLATE FOR YOU.
HERE YOU ARE.
むぴー FUME
AGAIN, YOU ARE TREATING ME AS YOUNGER THAN I AM!
SWEETS HE PARTICULARLY LIKES
HE KNOWS MY FAVORITES...? DID HE DISCOVER THEM WHEN THEY HOSTED ME AT PRINCE EINS'S PALACE? I HAVE THE FEELING THIS MAN ALWAYS GIVES ME THE RUNAROUND WITH HIS PROFESSIONAL SKILLS...
もきゅもきゅ CHEW CHEW
IT'S MY JOB.
AREN'T THEY YUMMY, PROFESSOR?

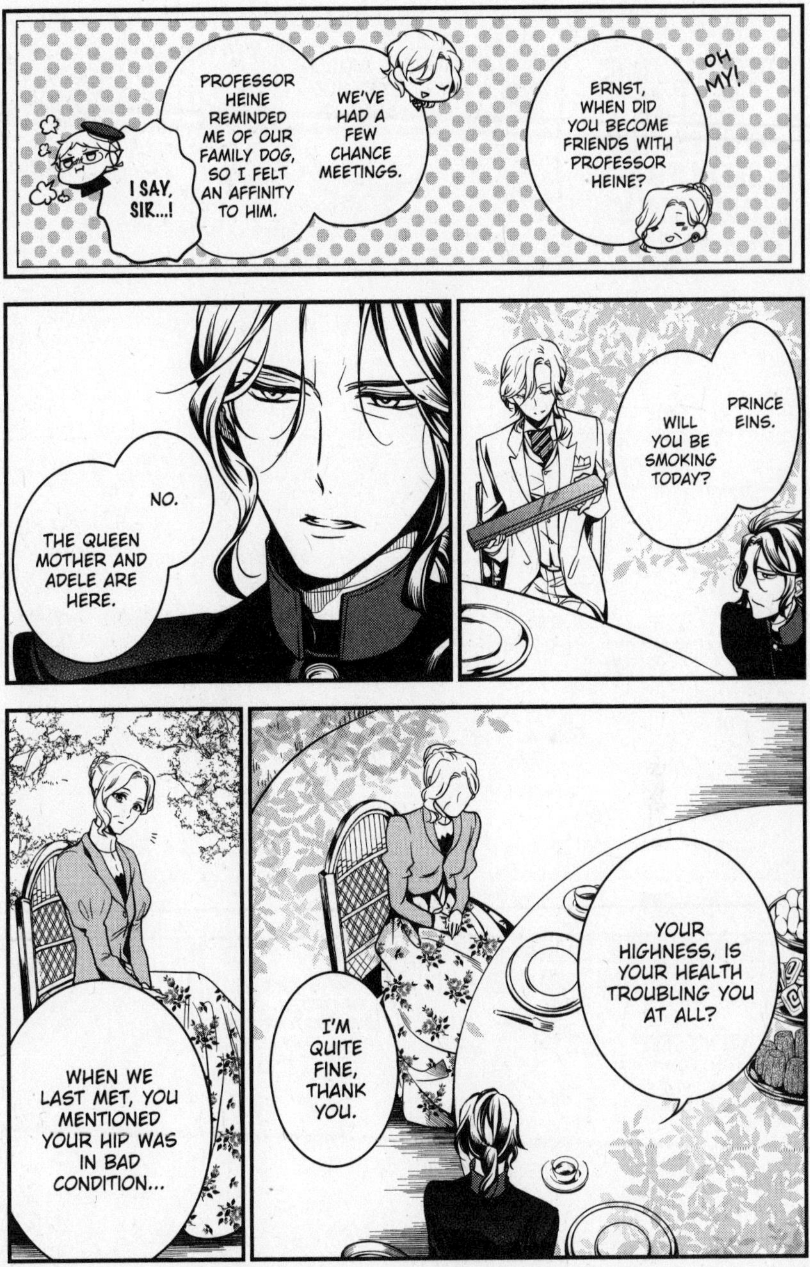
OH MY!
ERNST, WHEN DID YOU BECOME FRIENDS WITH PROFESSOR HEINE?
WE'VE HAD A FEW CHANCE MEETINGS.
PROFESSOR HEINE REMINDED ME OF OUR FAMILY DOG, SO I FELT AN AFFINITY TO HIM.
I SAY, SIR...!
PRINCE EINS.
WILL YOU BE SMOKING TODAY?
NO.
THE QUEEN MOTHER AND ADELE ARE HERE.
YOUR HIGHNESS, IS YOUR HEALTH TROUBLING YOU AT ALL?
I'M QUITE FINE, THANK YOU.
WHEN WE LAST MET, YOU MENTIONED YOUR HIP WAS IN BAD CONDITION...

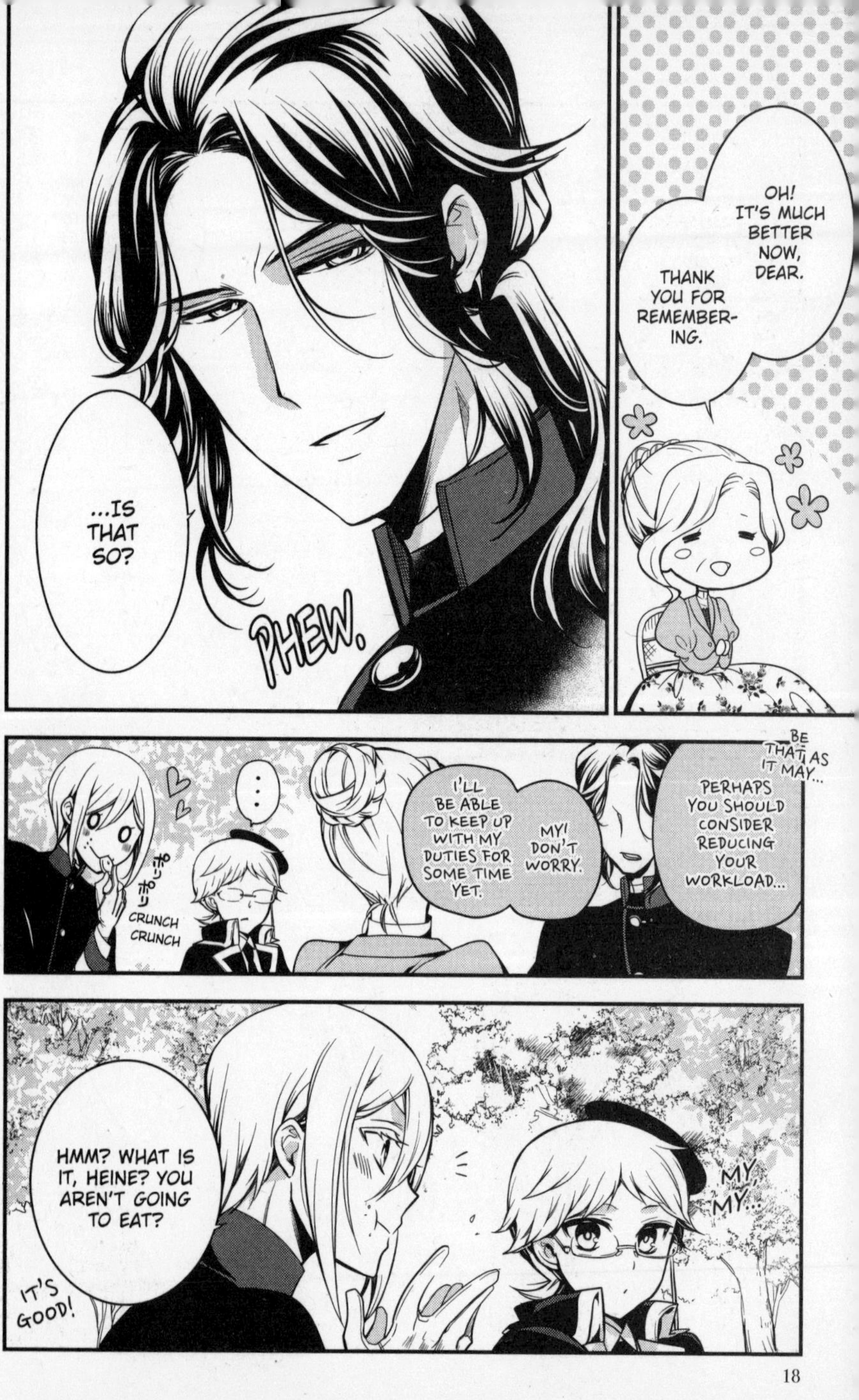
OH! IT'S MUCH BETTER NOW, DEAR.
THANK YOU FOR REMEMBER-ING.
...IS THAT SO?
PHEW.
BE THAT AS IT MAY...
PERHAPS YOU SHOULD CONSIDER REDUCING YOUR WORKLOAD...
MY! DON'T WORRY.
I'LL BE ABLE TO KEEP UP WITH MY DUTIES FOR SOME TIME YET.
...
CRUNCH CRUNCH
MY, MY...
HMM? WHAT IS IT, HEINE? YOU AREN'T GOING TO EAT?
IT'S GOOD!

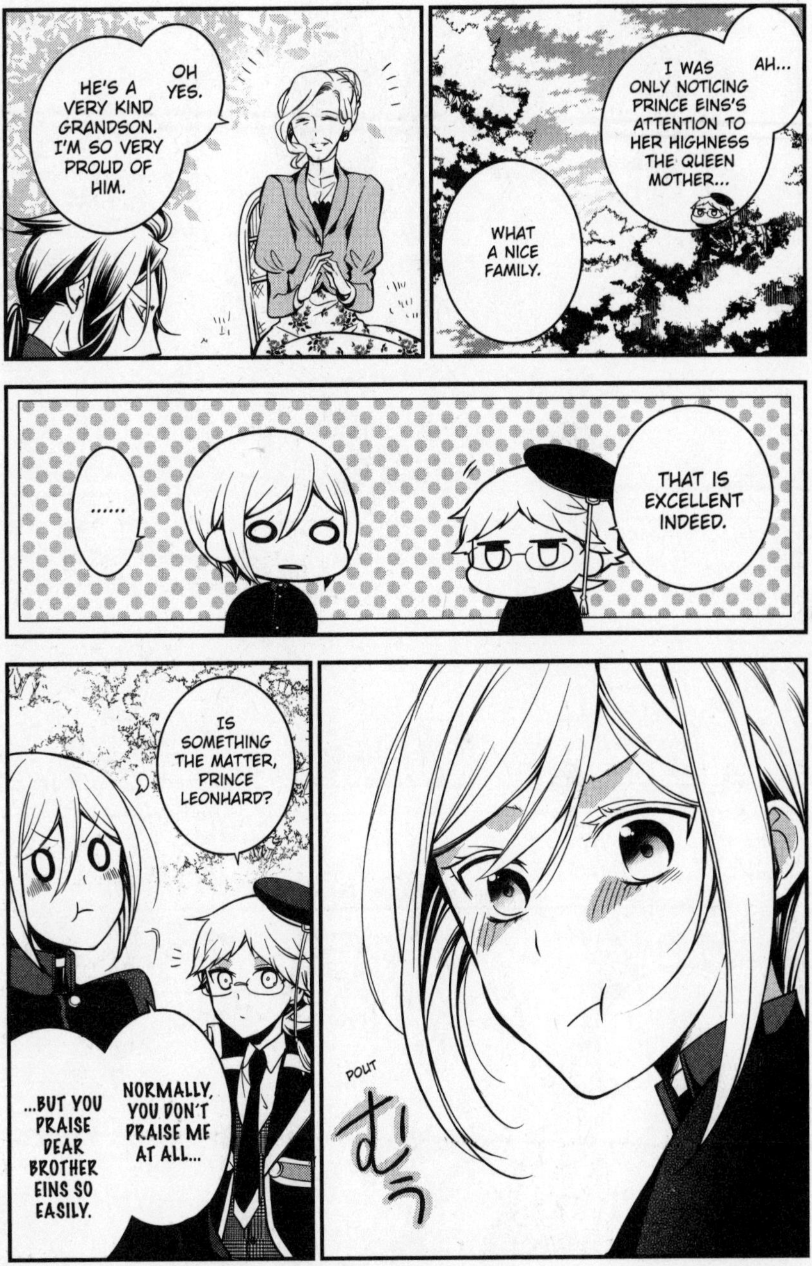
AH...
I WAS ONLY NOTICING PRINCE EINS'S ATTENTION TO HER HIGHNESS THE QUEEN MOTHER...
WHAT A NICE FAMILY.
OH YES.
HE'S A VERY KIND GRANDSON. I'M SO VERY PROUD OF HIM.
THAT IS EXCELLENT INDEED.
......
POUT
むぅ
IS SOMETHING THE MATTER, PRINCE LEONHARD?
NORMALLY, YOU DON'T PRAISE ME AT ALL...
...BUT YOU PRAISE DEAR BROTHER EINS SO EASILY.

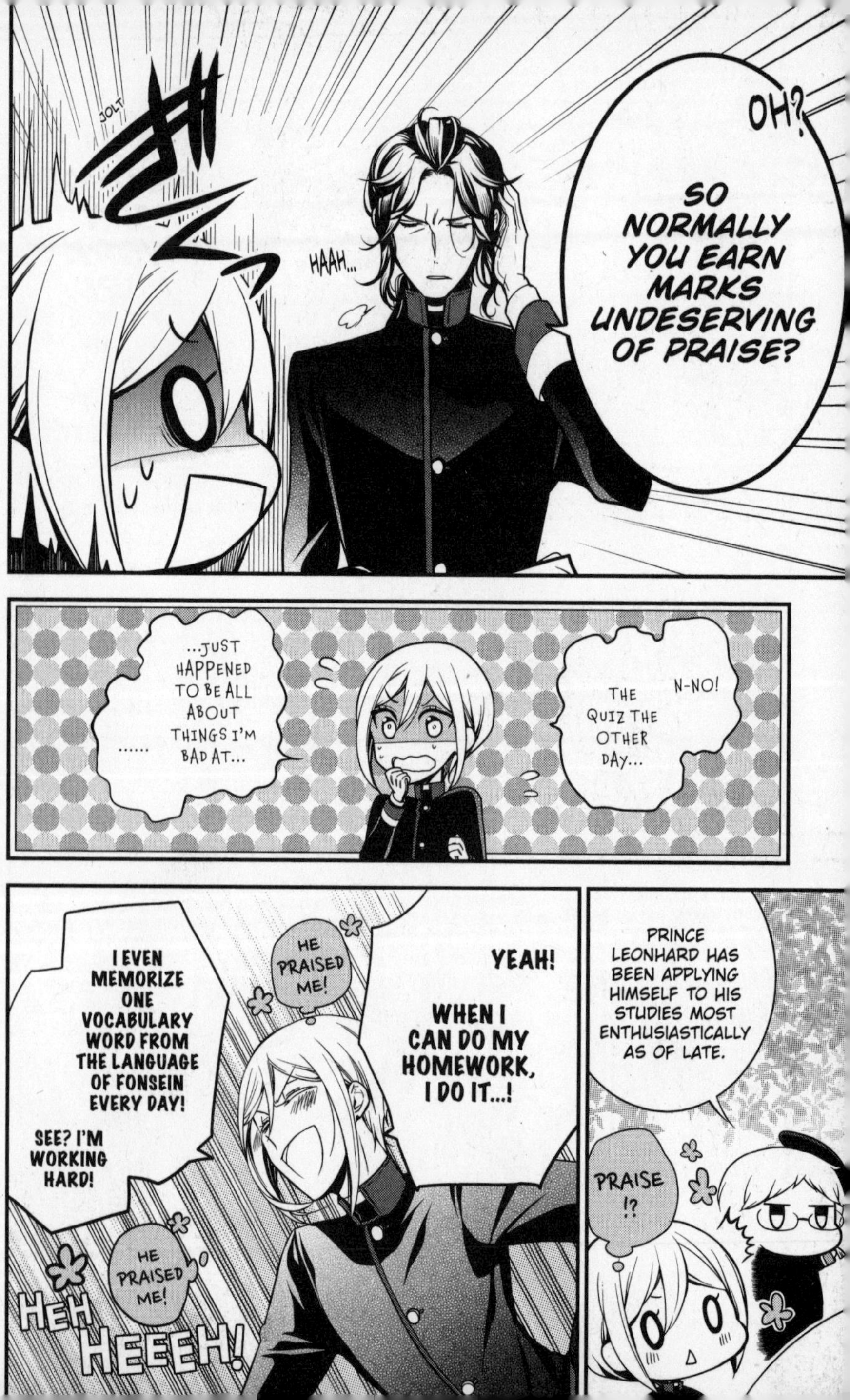
OH? SO NORMALLY YOU EARN MARKS UNDESERVING OF PRAISE?
HAAH...
JOLT
N-NO! THE QUIZ THE OTHER DAY...
...JUST HAPPENED TO BE ALL ABOUT THINGS I'M BAD AT... ......
PRINCE LEONHARD HAS BEEN APPLYING HIMSELF TO HIS STUDIES MOST ENTHUSIASTICALLY AS OF LATE.
PRAISE!?
YEAH! WHEN I CAN DO MY HOMEWORK, I DO IT...!
HE PRAISED ME!
I EVEN MEMORIZE ONE VOCABULARY WORD FROM THE LANGUAGE OF FONSEIN EVERY DAY!
SEE? I'M WORKING HARD!
HE PRAISED ME!
HEH HEEEEH!

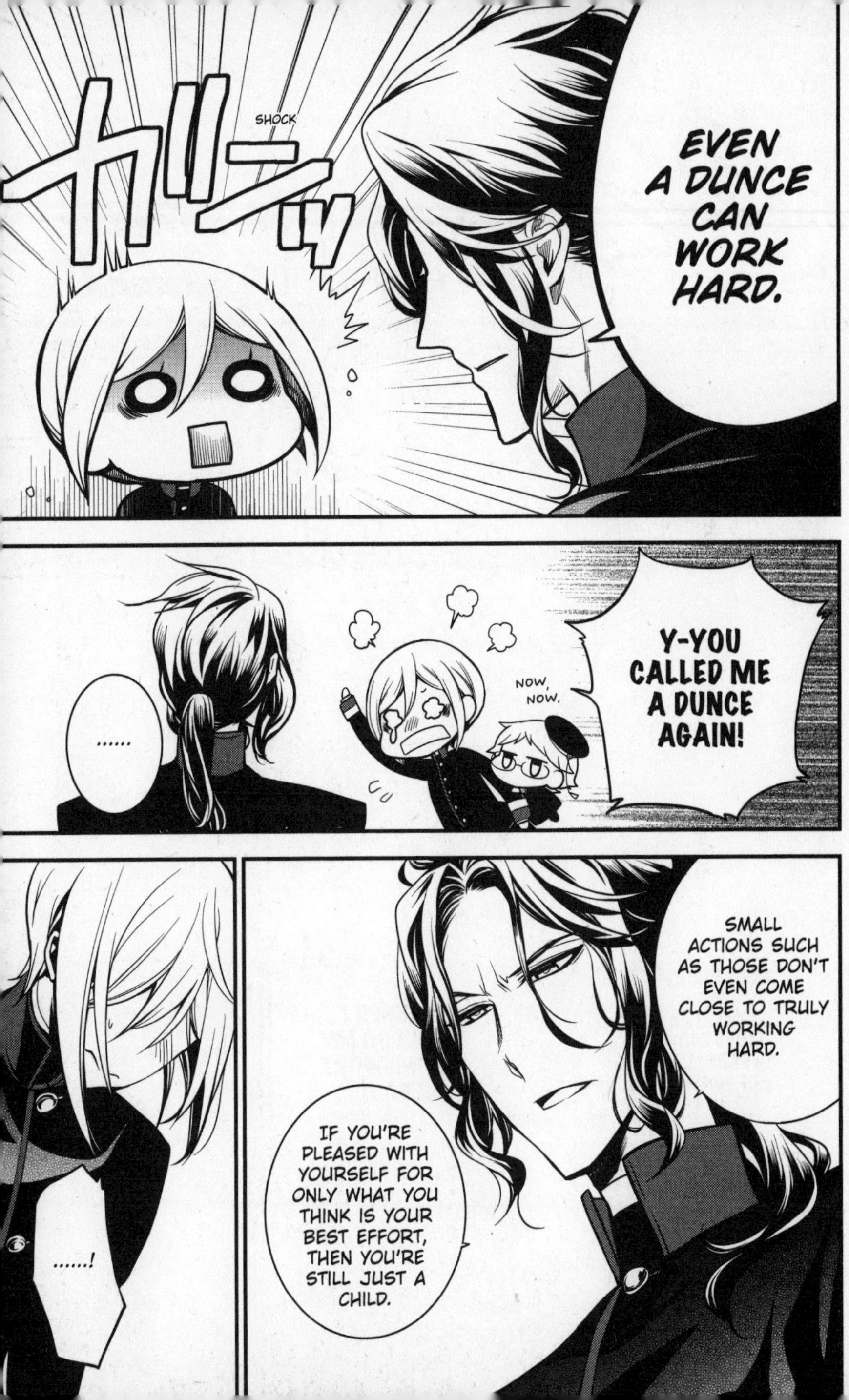
EVEN A DUNCE CAN WORK HARD.
SHOCK
Y-YOU CALLED ME A DUNCE AGAIN!
NOW, NOW.
......
SMALL ACTIONS SUCH AS THOSE DON'T EVEN COME CLOSE TO TRULY WORKING HARD.
IF YOU'RE PLEASED WITH YOURSELF FOR ONLY WHAT YOU THINK IS YOUR BEST EFFORT, THEN YOU'RE STILL JUST A CHILD.
......!

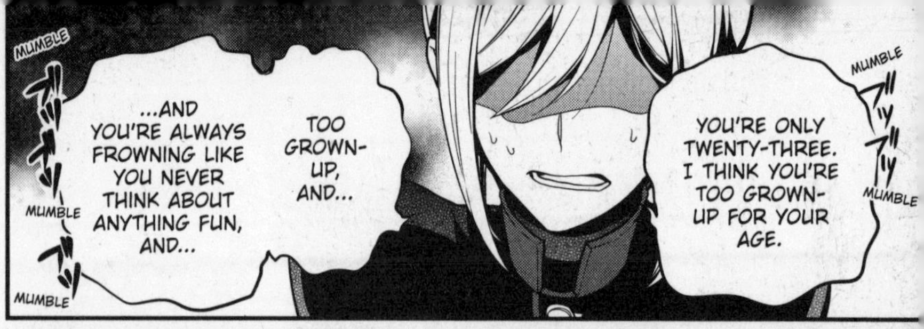
MUMBLE
MUMBLE
YOU'RE ONLY TWENTY-THREE. I THINK YOU'RE TOO GROWN-UP FOR YOUR AGE.
TOO GROWN-UP, AND...
...AND YOU'RE ALWAYS FROWNING LIKE YOU NEVER THINK ABOUT ANYTHING FUN, AND...
MUMBLE
MUMBLE
MUMBLE

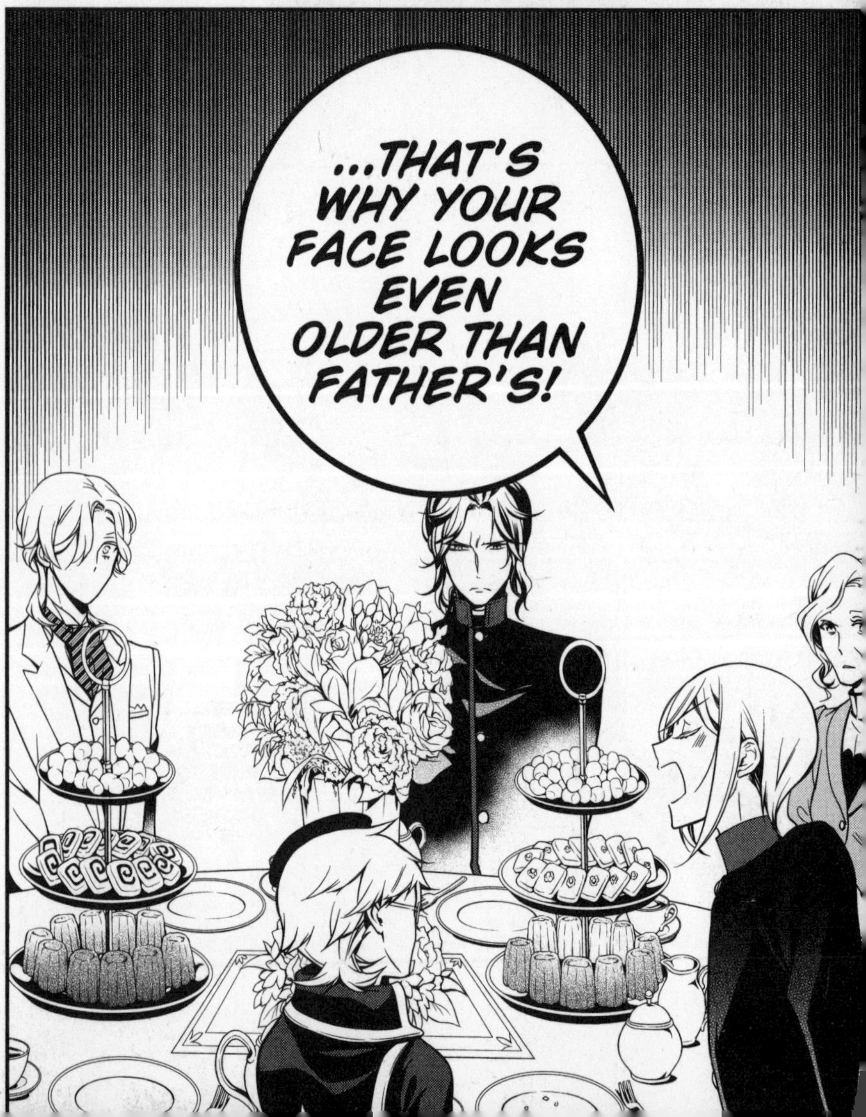
...THAT'S WHY YOUR FACE LOOKS EVEN OLDER THAN FATHER'S!

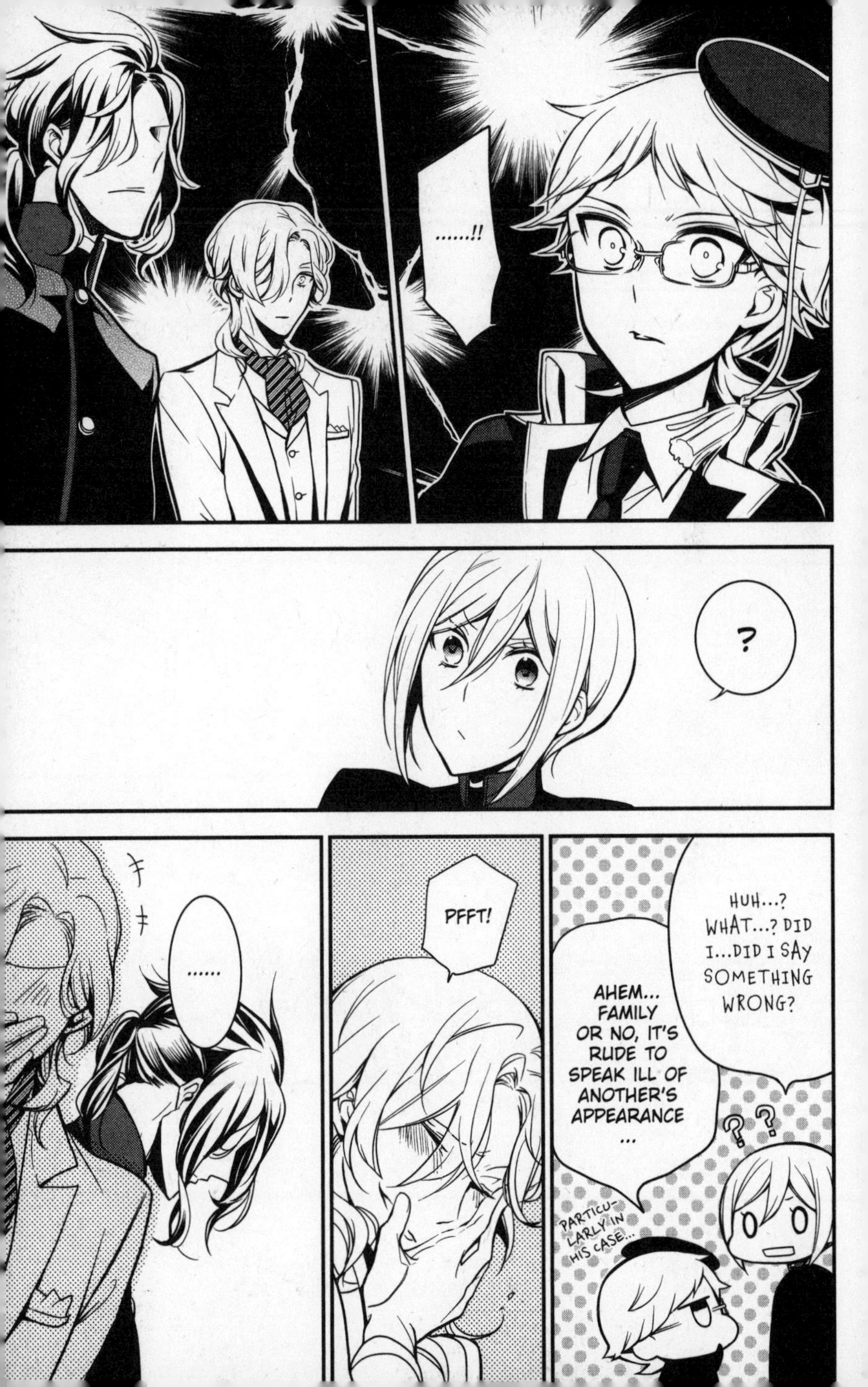
......!!
?
HUH...? WHAT...? DID I...DID I SAY SOMETHING WRONG?
AHEM... FAMILY OR NO, IT'S RUDE TO SPEAK ILL OF ANOTHER'S APPEARANCE ...
PARTICU-LARLY IN HIS CASE...
PFFT!
......

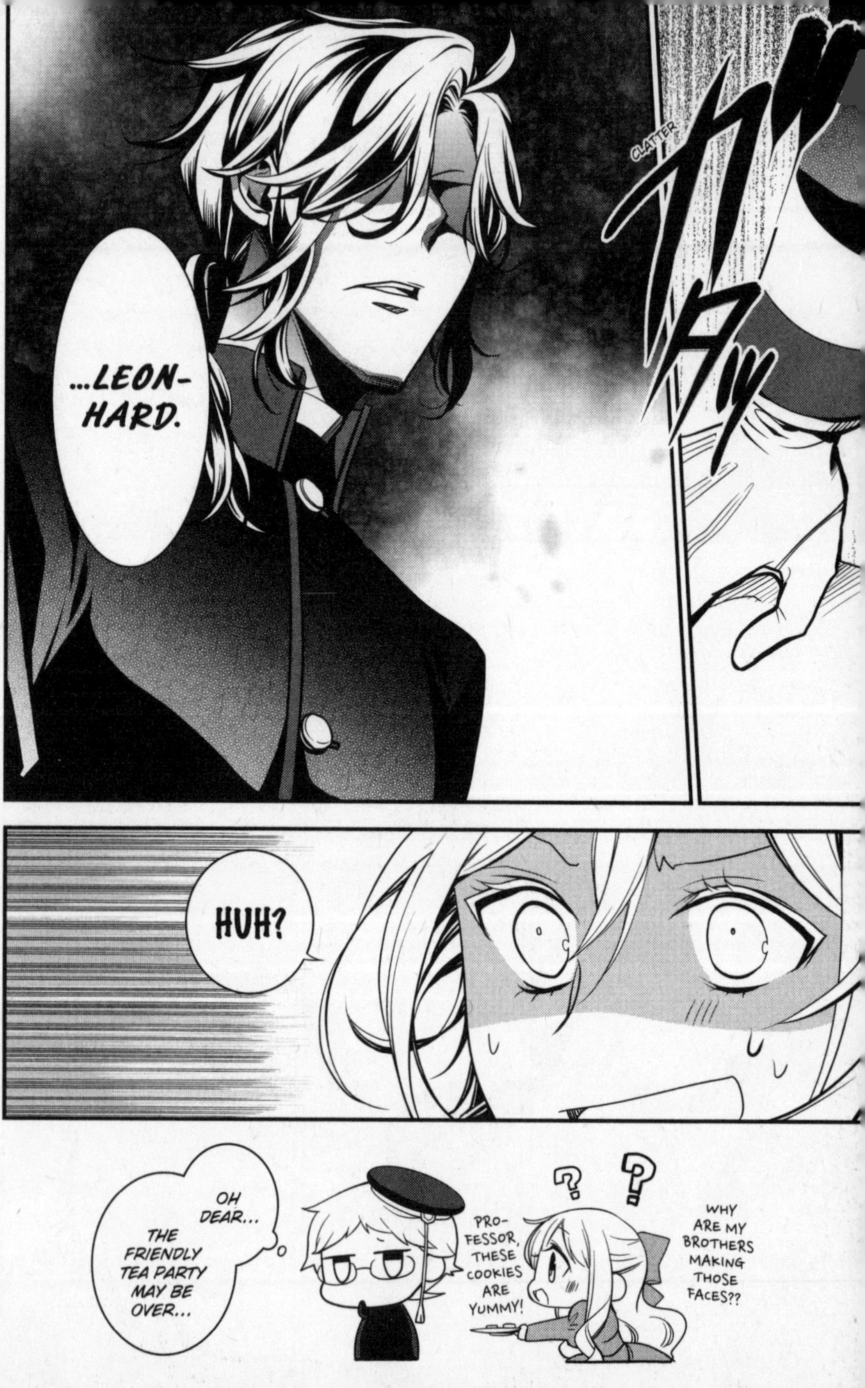
CLATTER
...LEON-HARD.
HUH?
WHY ARE MY BROTHERS MAKING THOSE FACES??
PROFESSOR, THESE COOKIES ARE YUMMY!
OH DEAR...
THE FRIENDLY TEA PARTY MAY BE OVER...

Chapter 54

Potential of the White Lily

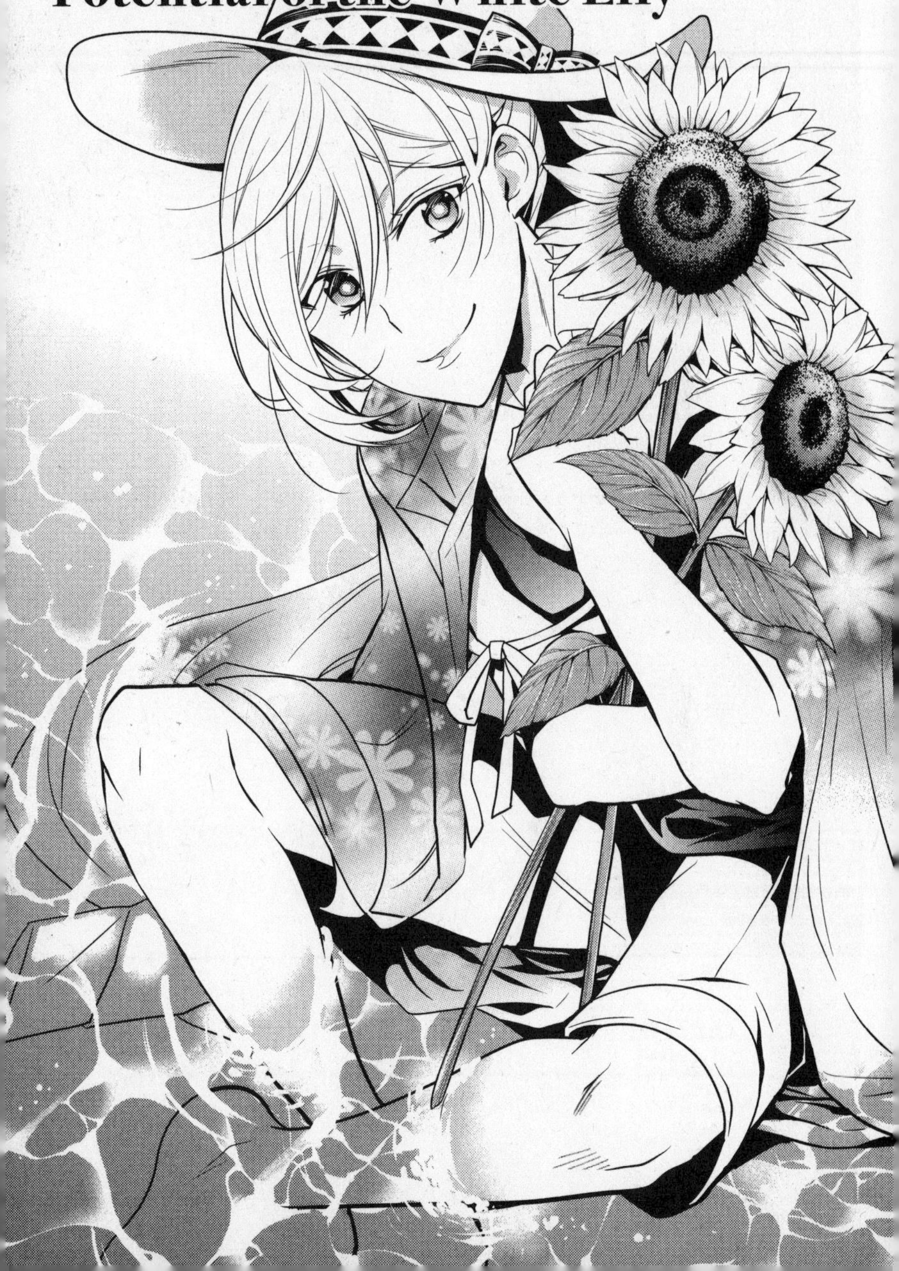

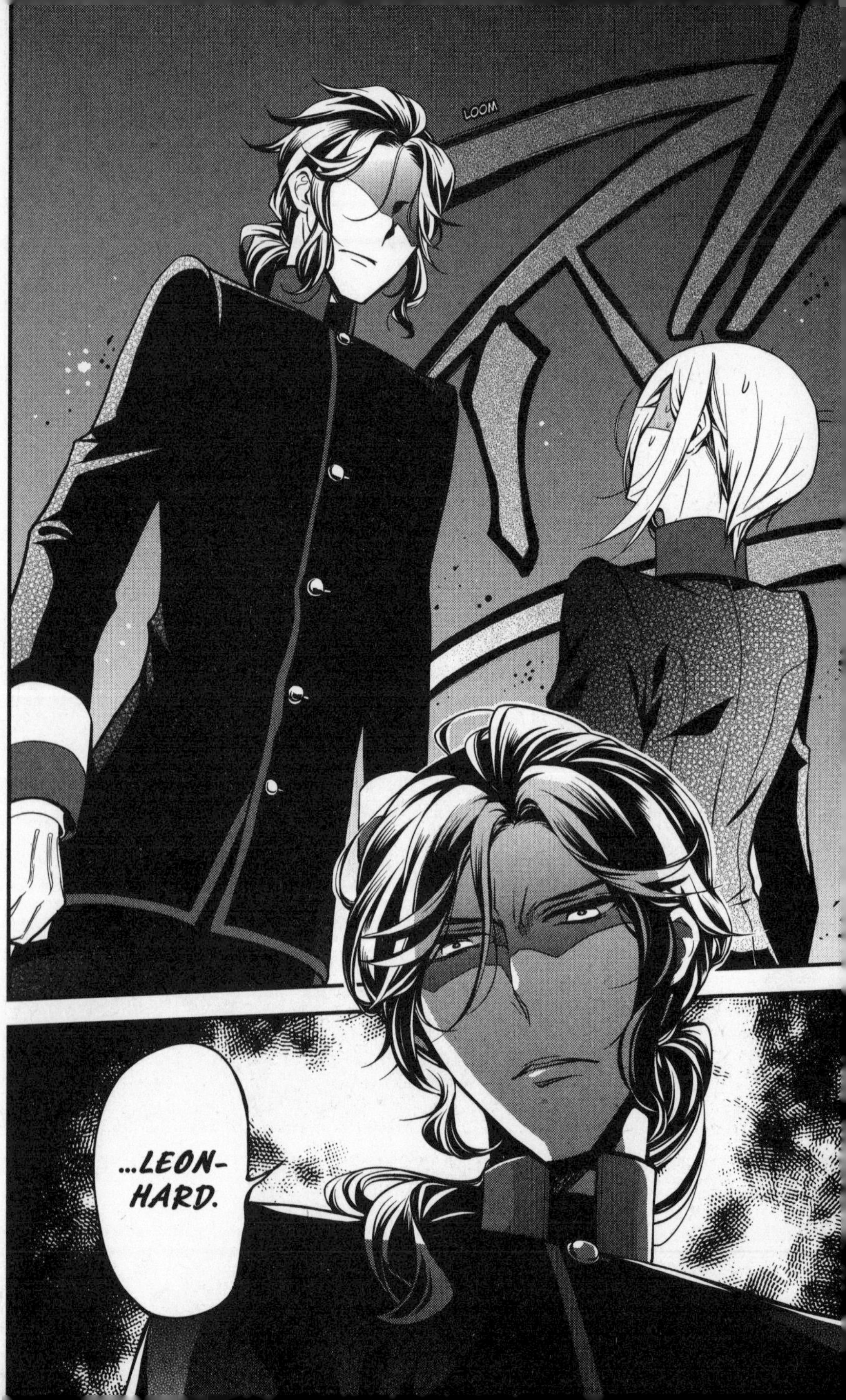
LOOM
...LEON-
HARD.

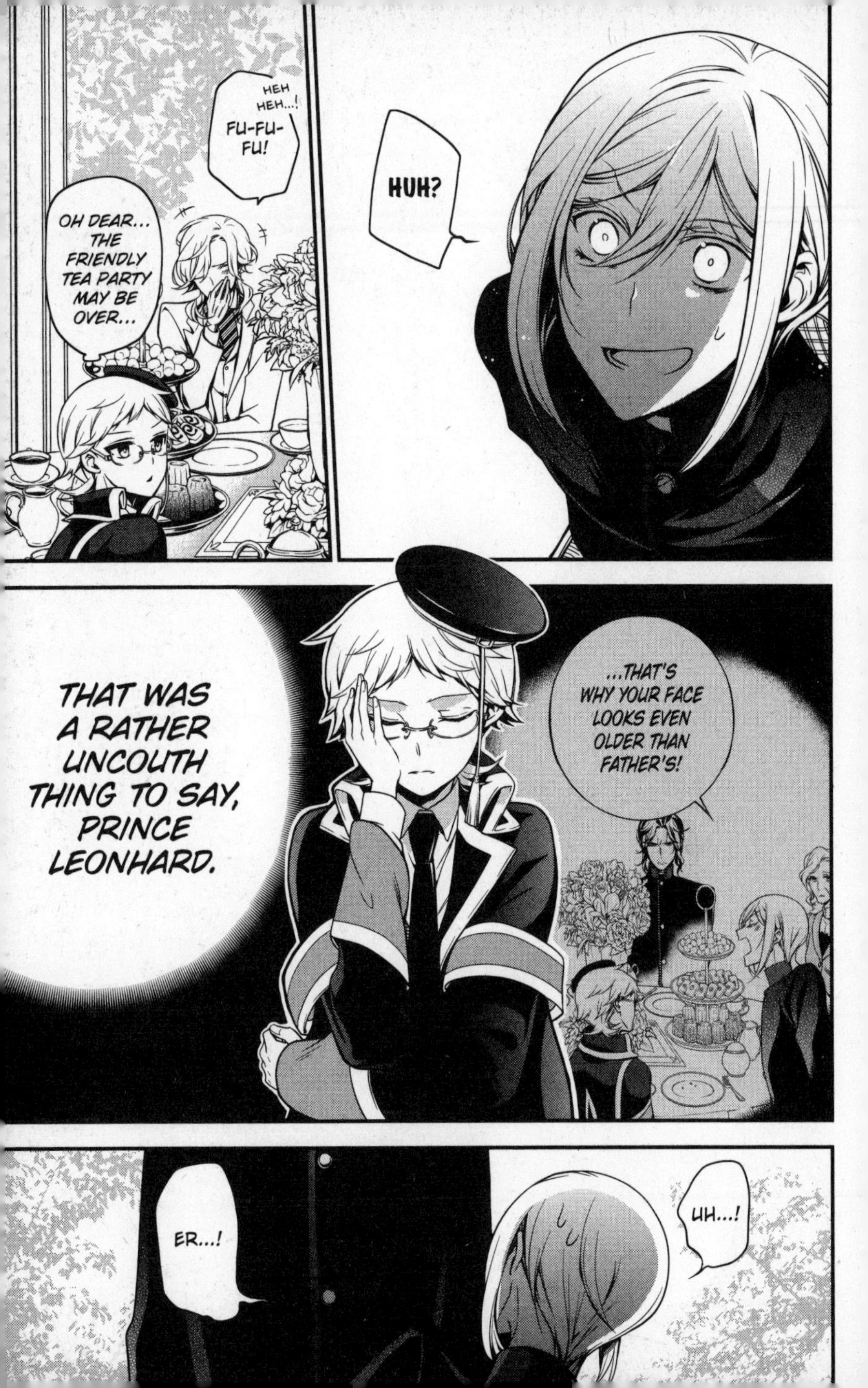
HUH?
HEH HEH...! FU-FU-FU!
OH DEAR... THE FRIENDLY TEA PARTY MAY BE OVER...
...THAT'S WHY YOUR FACE LOOKS EVEN OLDER THAN FATHER'S!
THAT WAS A RATHER UNCOUTH THING TO SAY, PRINCE LEONHARD.
UH...!
ER...!

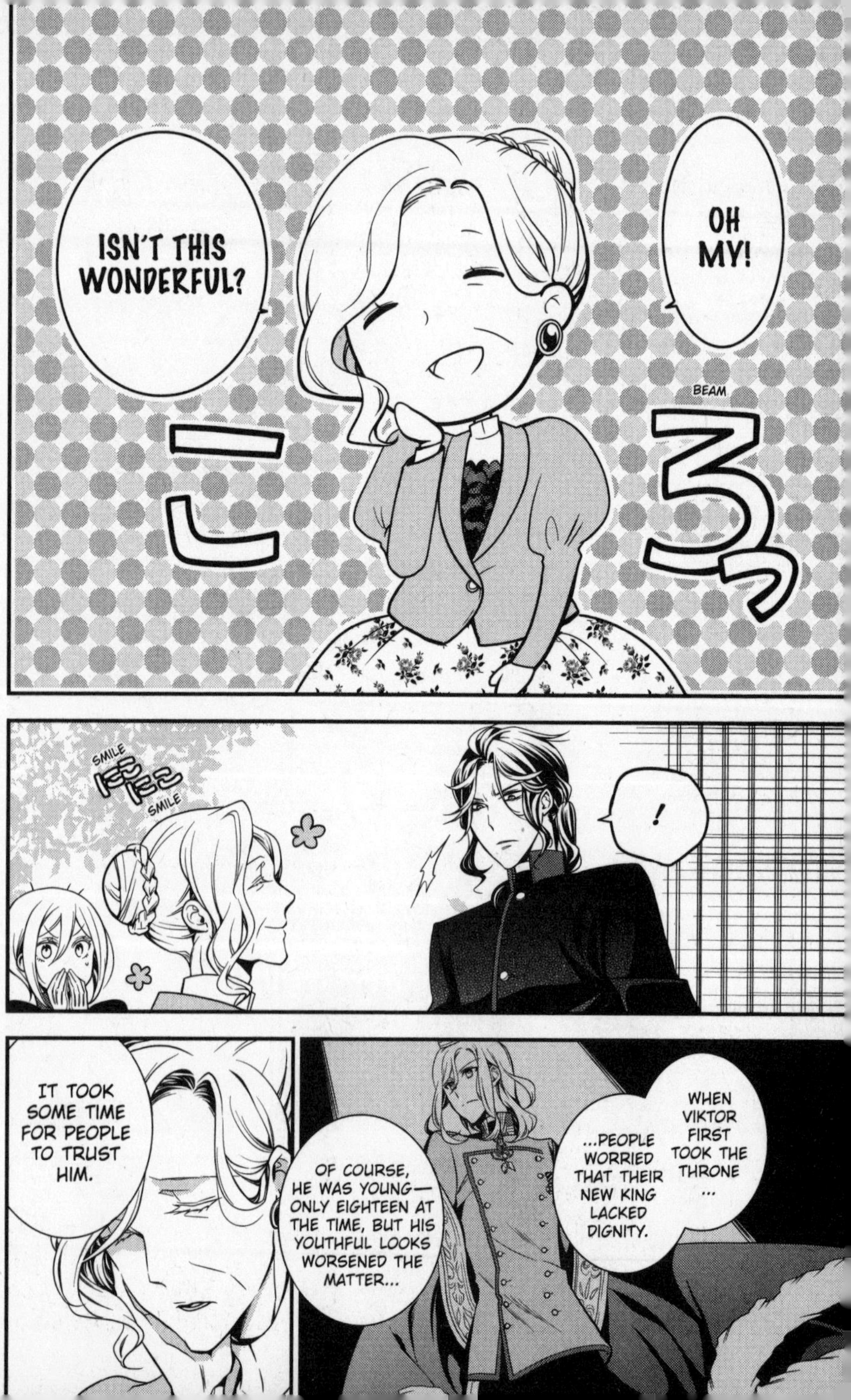

OH MY!
BEAM
ころっ
ISN'T THIS WONDERFUL?
!
SMILE
にこにこ
SMILE
WHEN VIKTOR FIRST TOOK THE THRONE ...
...PEOPLE WORRIED THAT THEIR NEW KING LACKED DIGNITY.
OF COURSE, HE WAS YOUNG—ONLY EIGHTEEN AT THE TIME, BUT HIS YOUTHFUL LOOKS WORSENED THE MATTER...
IT TOOK SOME TIME FOR PEOPLE TO TRUST HIM.

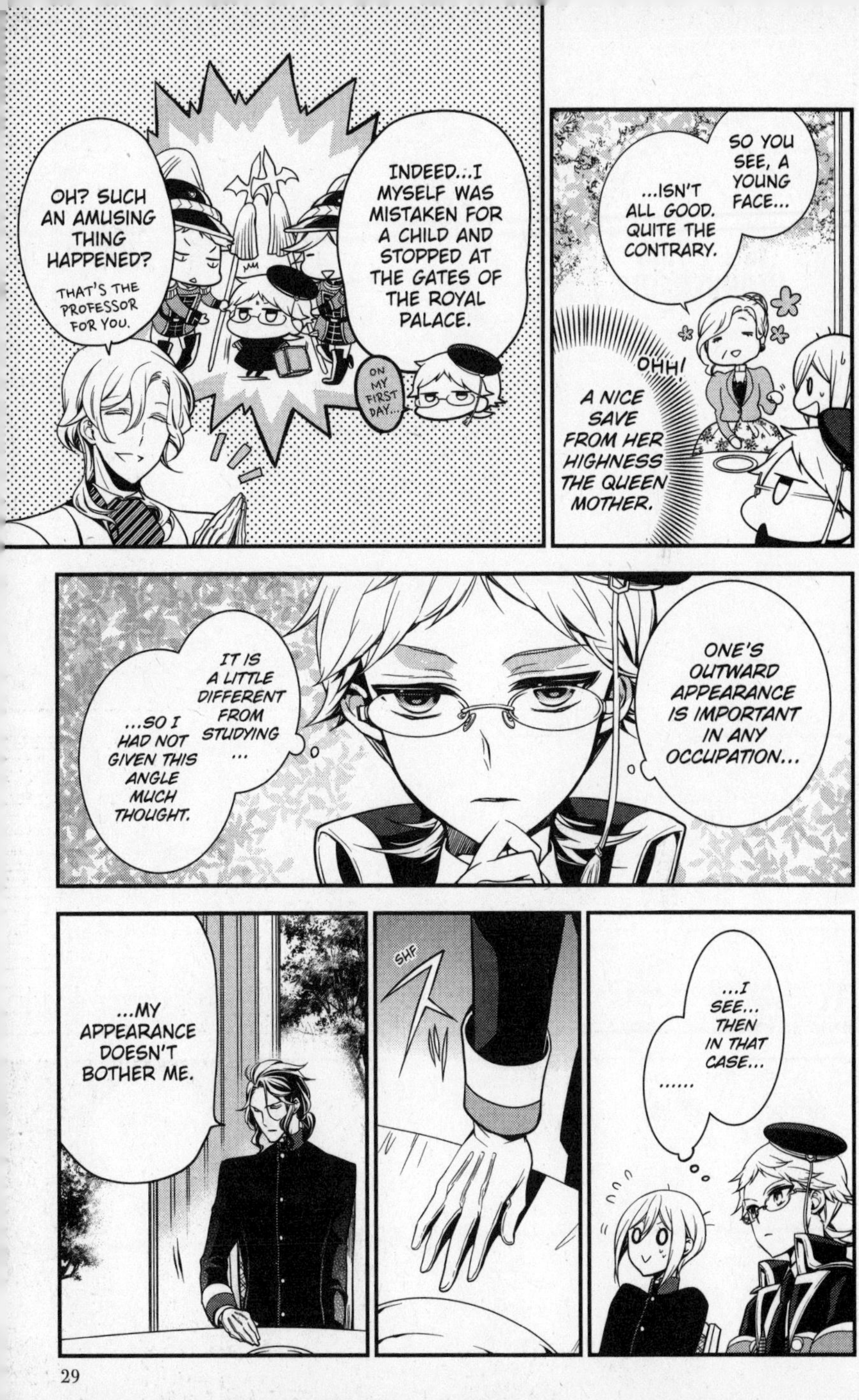
SO YOU SEE, A YOUNG FACE...
...ISN'T ALL GOOD. QUITE THE CONTRARY.
OHH!
A NICE SAVE FROM HER HIGHNESS THE QUEEN MOTHER.
INDEED...I MYSELF WAS MISTAKEN FOR A CHILD AND STOPPED AT THE GATES OF THE ROYAL PALACE.
ON MY FIRST DAY...
OH? SUCH AN AMUSING THING HAPPENED?
THAT'S THE PROFESSOR FOR YOU.
ONE'S OUTWARD APPEARANCE IS IMPORTANT IN ANY OCCUPATION...
IT IS A LITTLE DIFFERENT FROM STUDYING...
...SO I HAD NOT GIVEN THIS ANGLE MUCH THOUGHT.
...I SEE... THEN IN THAT CASE...
......
SHF
...MY APPEARANCE DOESN'T BOTHER ME.

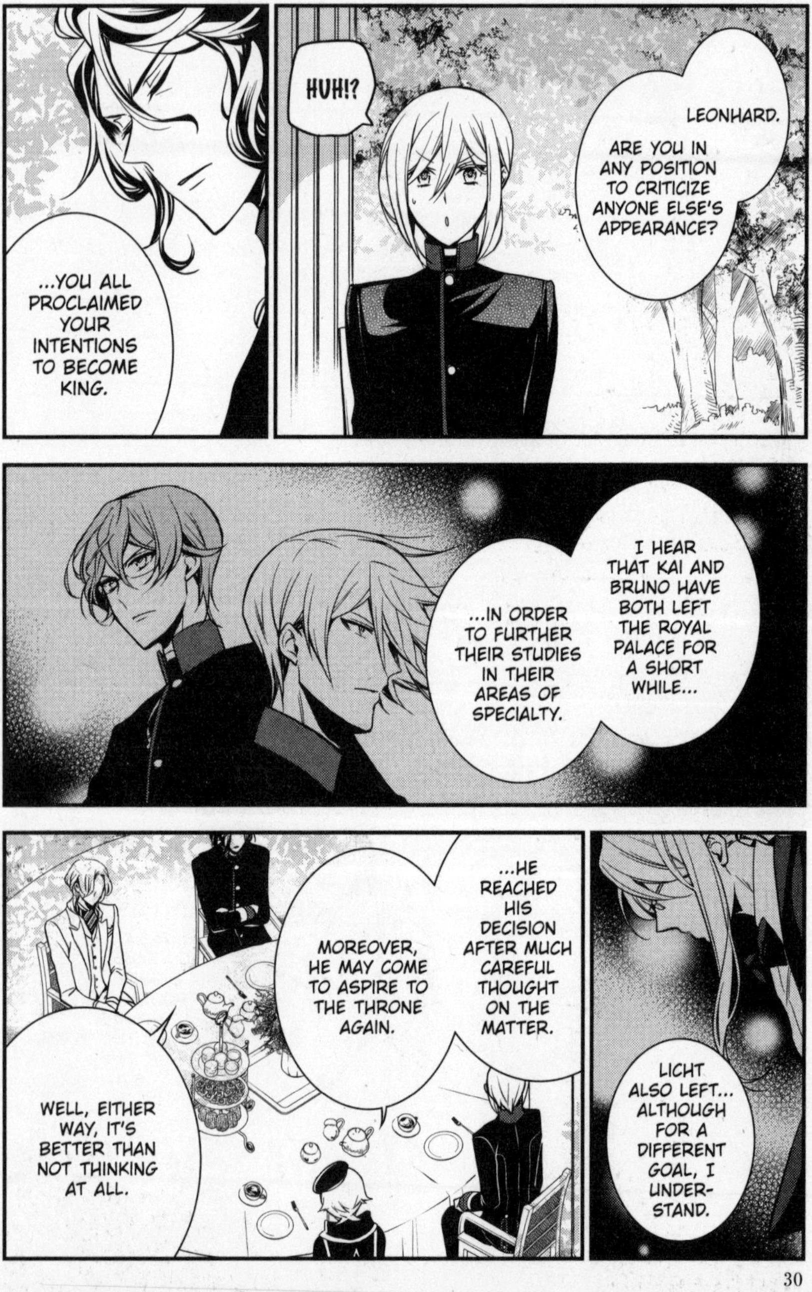
LEONHARD.
ARE YOU IN ANY POSITION TO CRITICIZE ANYONE ELSE'S APPEARANCE?
HUH!?
...YOU ALL PROCLAIMED YOUR INTENTIONS TO BECOME KING.
I HEAR THAT KAI AND BRUNO HAVE BOTH LEFT THE ROYAL PALACE FOR A SHORT WHILE...
...IN ORDER TO FURTHER THEIR STUDIES IN THEIR AREAS OF SPECIALTY.
LICHT ALSO LEFT... ALTHOUGH FOR A DIFFERENT GOAL, I UNDER-STAND.
...HE REACHED HIS DECISION AFTER MUCH CAREFUL THOUGHT ON THE MATTER.
MOREOVER, HE MAY COME TO ASPIRE TO THE THRONE AGAIN.
WELL, EITHER WAY, IT'S BETTER THAN NOT THINKING AT ALL.

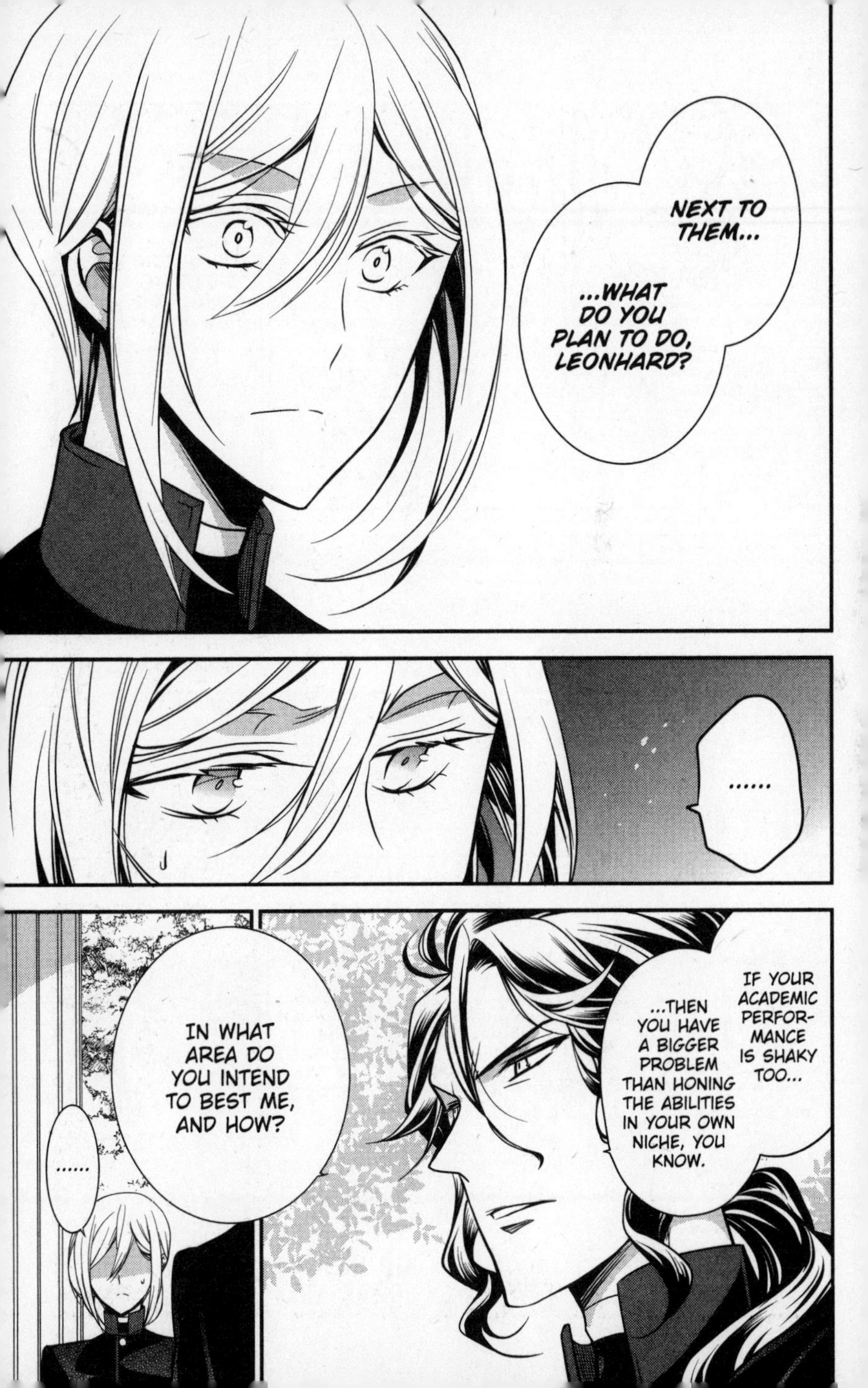
NEXT TO THEM...
...WHAT DO YOU PLAN TO DO, LEONHARD?
......
IF YOUR ACADEMIC PERFORMANCE IS SHAKY TOO...
...THEN YOU HAVE A BIGGER PROBLEM THAN HONING THE ABILITIES IN YOUR OWN NICHE, YOU KNOW.
IN WHAT AREA DO YOU INTEND TO BEST ME, AND HOW?
......

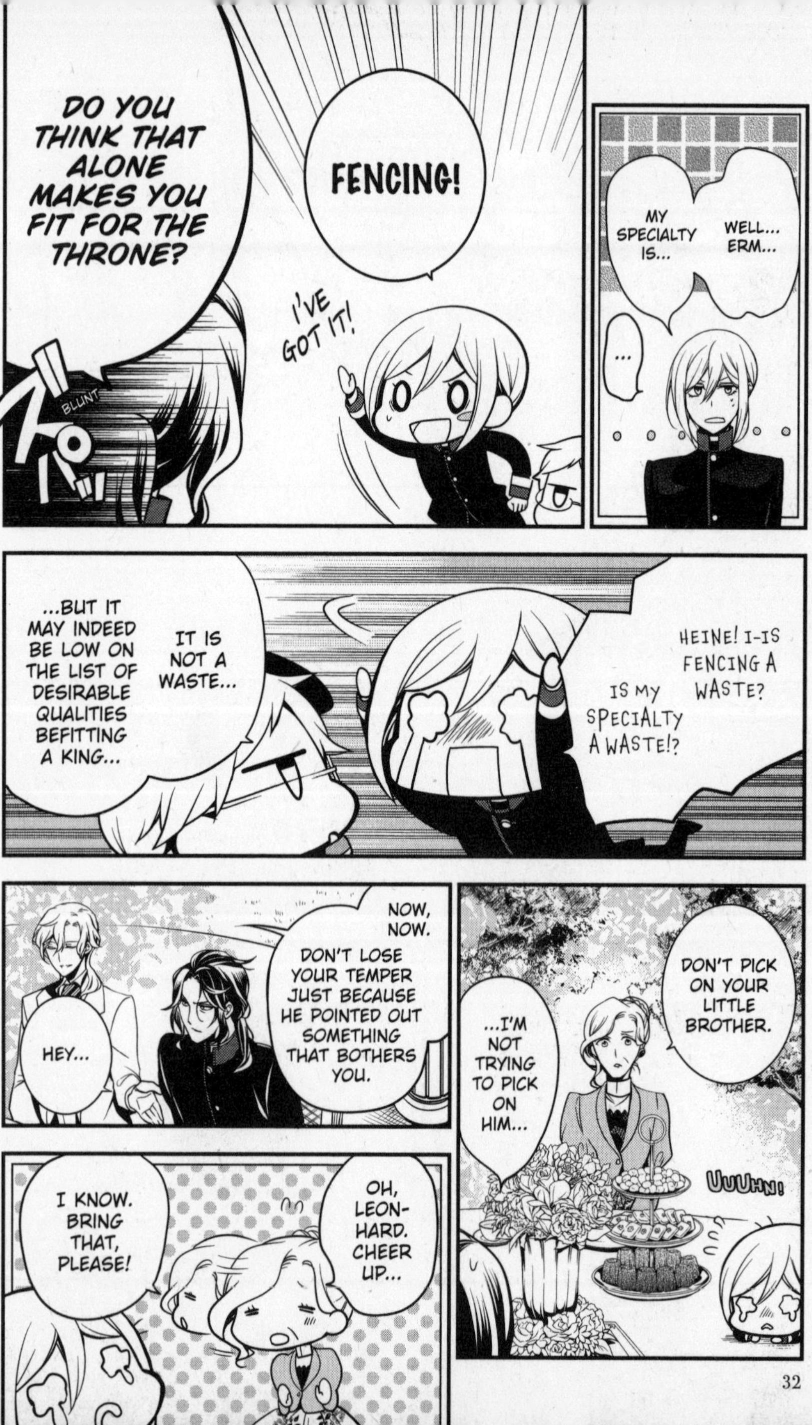
MY SPECIALTY IS... WELL... ERM...
...
I'VE GOT IT!
FENCING!
DO YOU THINK THAT ALONE MAKES YOU FIT FOR THE THRONE?
BLUNT
HEINE! I-IS FENCING A WASTE?
IS MY SPECIALTY A WASTE!?
IT IS NOT A WASTE...
...BUT IT MAY INDEED BE LOW ON THE LIST OF DESIRABLE QUALITIES BEFITTING A KING...
DON'T PICK ON YOUR LITTLE BROTHER.
...I'M NOT TRYING TO PICK ON HIM...
UUUHN!
NOW, NOW. DON'T LOSE YOUR TEMPER JUST BECAUSE HE POINTED OUT SOMETHING THAT BOTHERS YOU.
HEY...
OH, LEONHARD. CHEER UP...
I KNOW. BRING THAT, PLEASE!

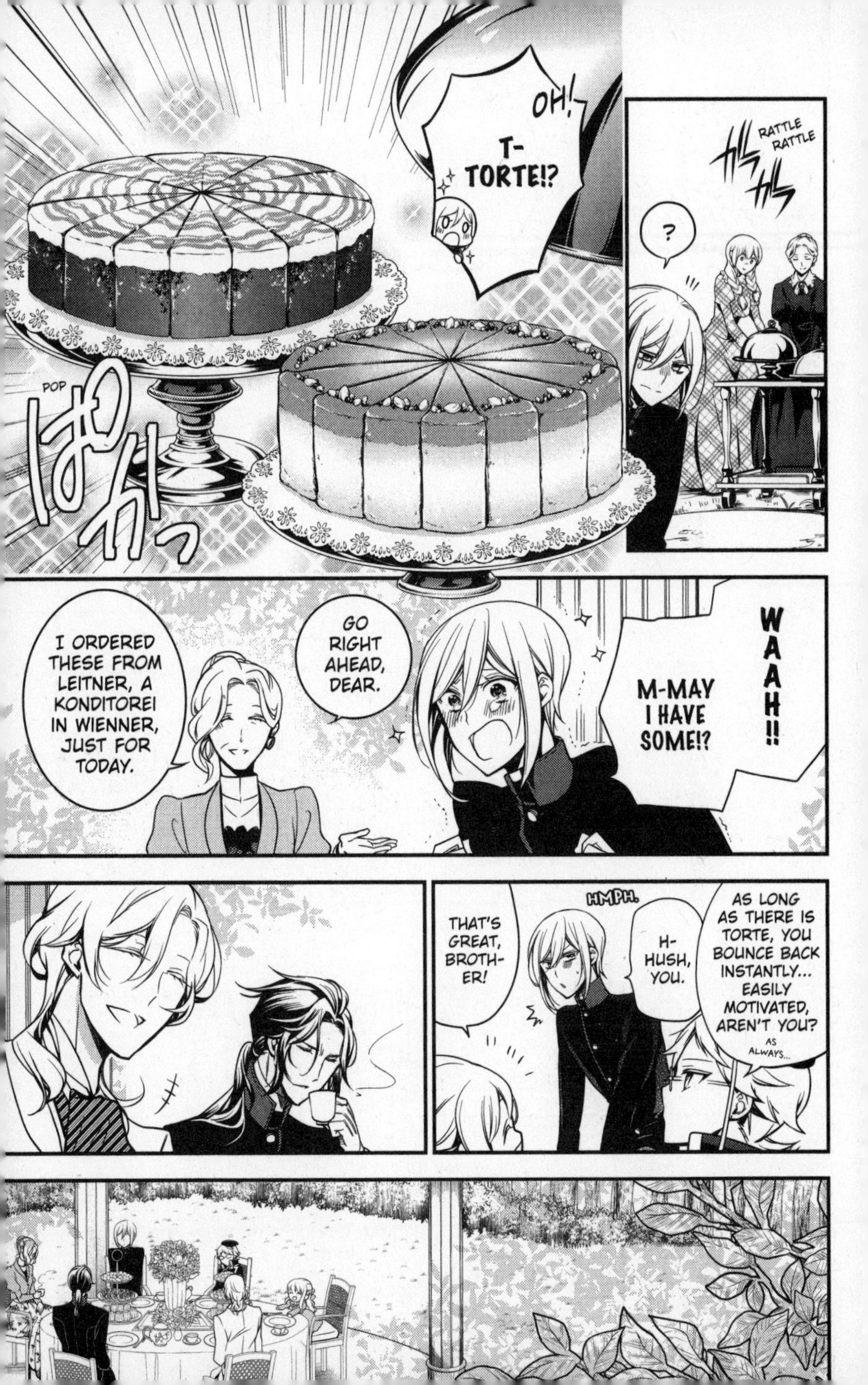

RATTLE RATTLE
?
OH!
T- TORTE!?
POP
ぱわっ
WAAAH!!
M-MAY I HAVE SOME!?
GO RIGHT AHEAD, DEAR.
I ORDERED THESE FROM LEITNER, A KONDITOREI IN WIENNER, JUST FOR TODAY.
AS LONG AS THERE IS TORTE, YOU BOUNCE BACK INSTANTLY... EASILY MOTIVATED, AREN'T YOU?
AS ALWAYS...
HMPH.
H-HUSH, YOU.
THAT'S GREAT, BROTHER!

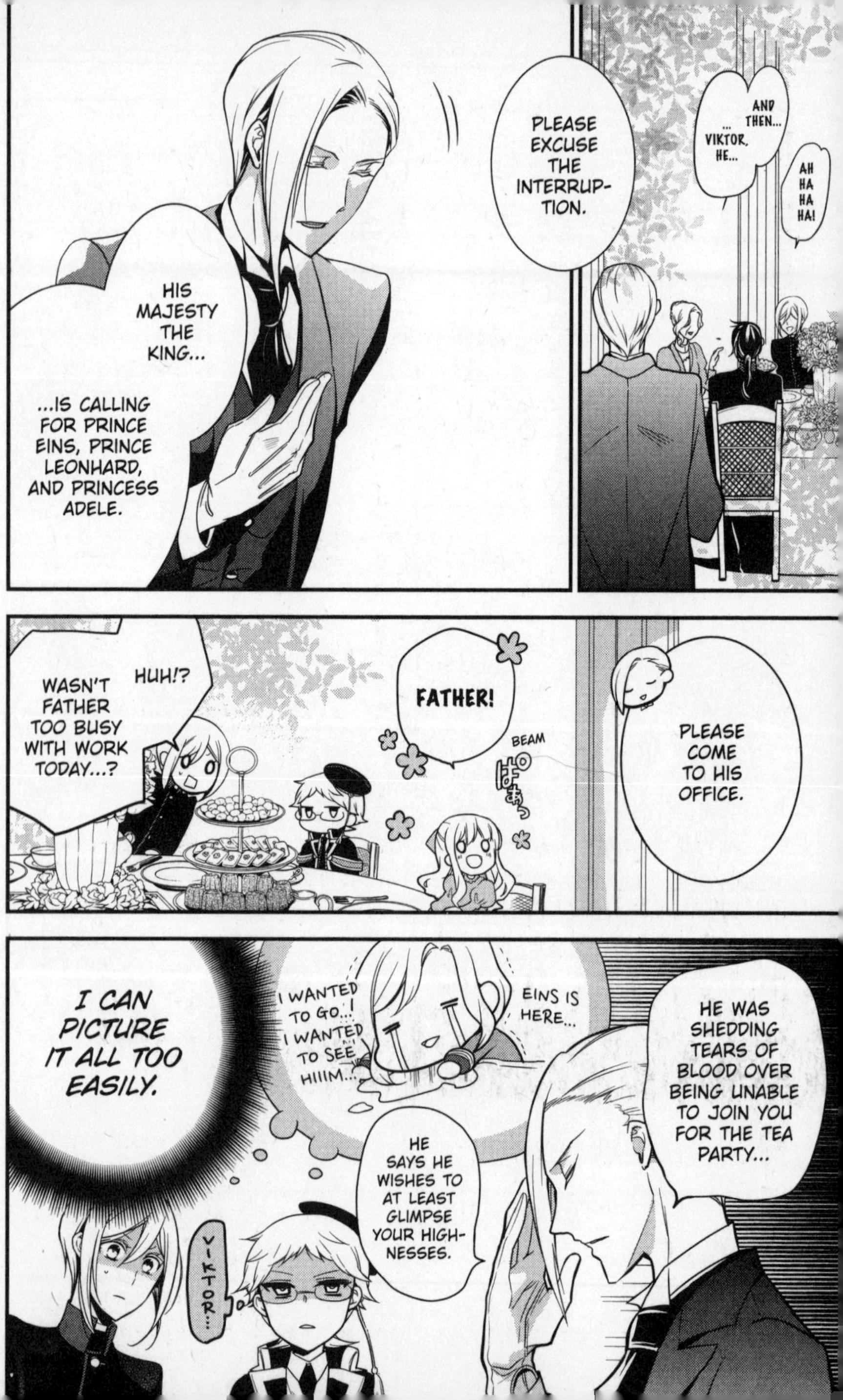
AND THEN... ...VIKTOR, HE...
AH HA HA HA!
PLEASE EXCUSE THE INTERRUPTION.
HIS MAJESTY THE KING...
...IS CALLING FOR PRINCE EINS, PRINCE LEONHARD, AND PRINCESS ADELE.
PLEASE COME TO HIS OFFICE.
FATHER!
BEAM
ぱぁっ
HUH!?
WASN'T FATHER TOO BUSY WITH WORK TODAY...?
HE WAS SHEDDING TEARS OF BLOOD OVER BEING UNABLE TO JOIN YOU FOR THE TEA PARTY...
EINS IS HERE...
I WANTED TO GO...! I WANTED TO SEE HIIIM...
HE SAYS HE WISHES TO AT LEAST GLIMPSE YOUR HIGHNESSES.
VIKTOR...
I CAN PICTURE IT ALL TOO EASILY.

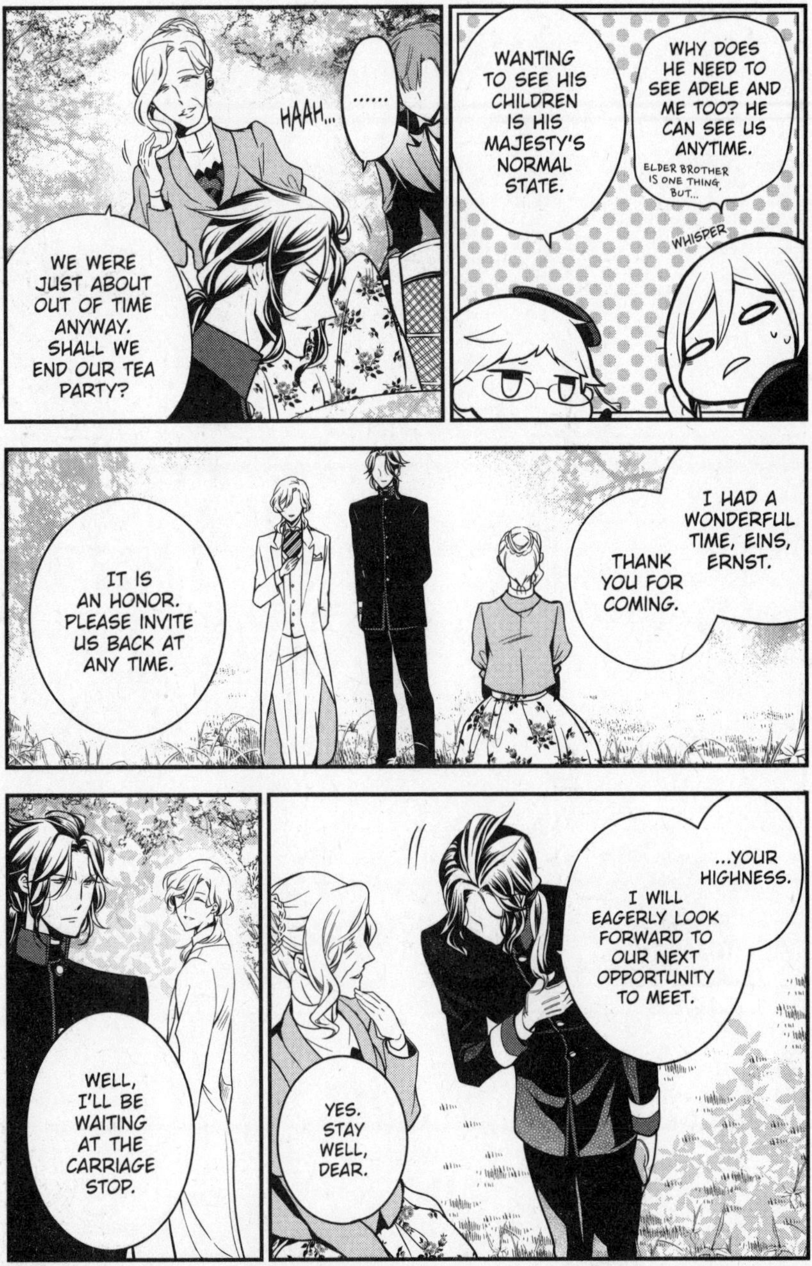
WHY DOES HE NEED TO SEE ADELE AND ME TOO? HE CAN SEE US ANYTIME.
ELDER BROTHER IS ONE THING, BUT...
WHISPER
WANTING TO SEE HIS CHILDREN IS HIS MAJESTY'S NORMAL STATE.
......
HAAH...
WE WERE JUST ABOUT OUT OF TIME ANYWAY. SHALL WE END OUR TEA PARTY?
I HAD A WONDERFUL TIME, EINS, ERNST. THANK YOU FOR COMING.
IT IS AN HONOR. PLEASE INVITE US BACK AT ANY TIME.
...YOUR HIGHNESS. I WILL EAGERLY LOOK FORWARD TO OUR NEXT OPPORTUNITY TO MEET.
YES. STAY WELL, DEAR.
WELL, I'LL BE WAITING AT THE CARRIAGE STOP.

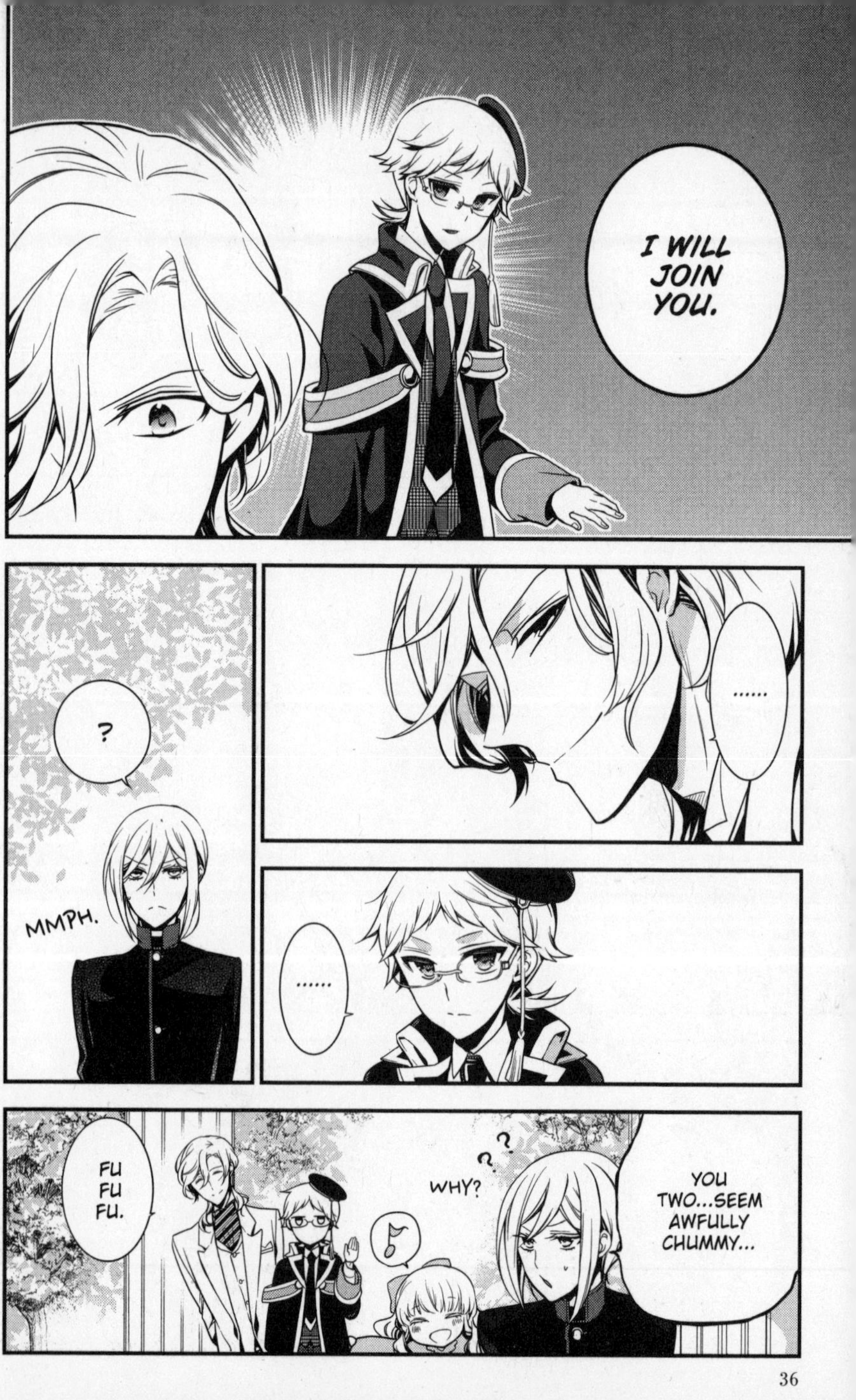
I WILL JOIN YOU.
......
....
?
MMPH.
YOU TWO...SEEM AWFULLY CHUMMY...
? ?
WHY?
♪
FU FU FU.

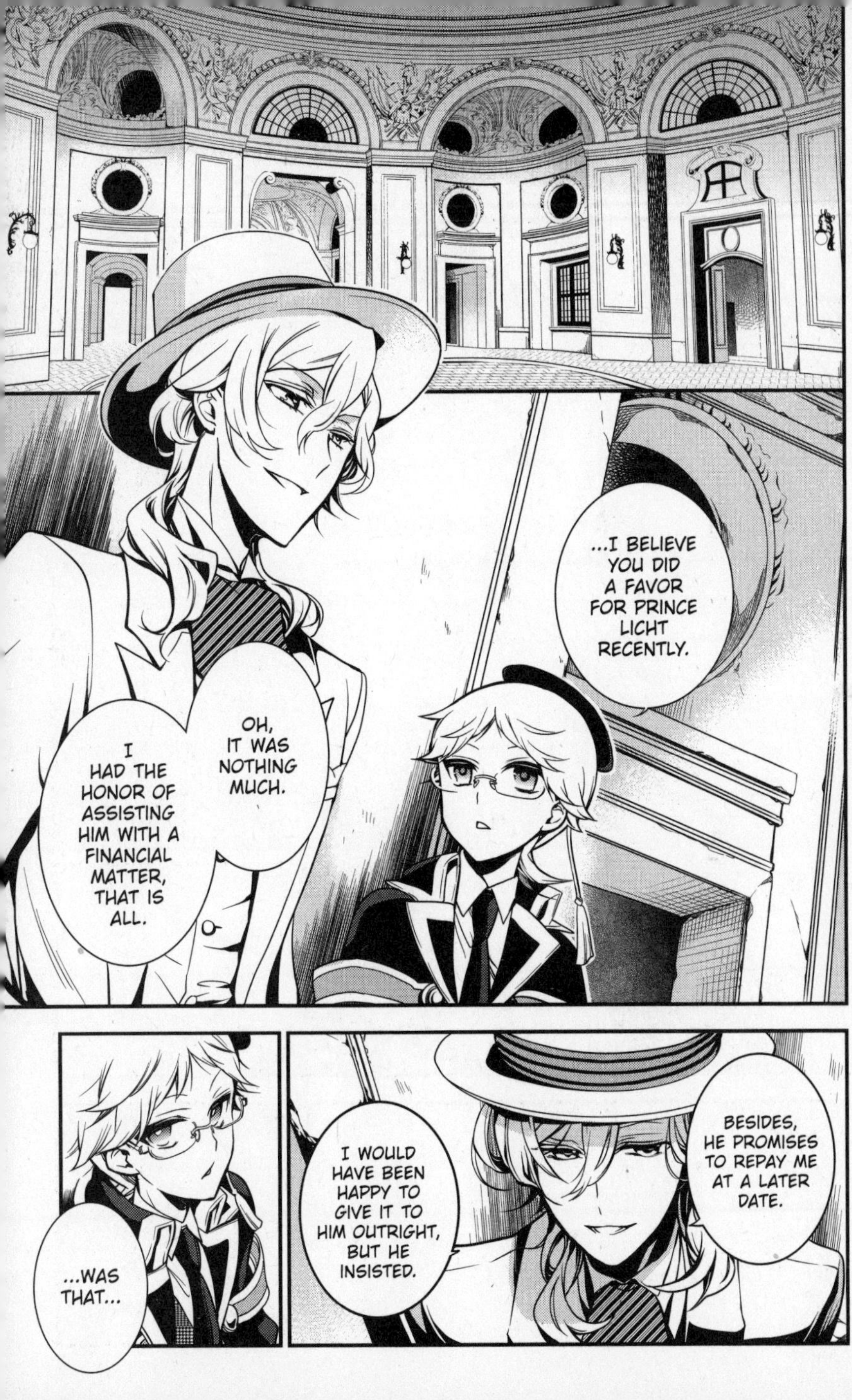
...I BELIEVE YOU DID A FAVOR FOR PRINCE LICHT RECENTLY.
OH, IT WAS NOTHING MUCH.
I HAD THE HONOR OF ASSISTING HIM WITH A FINANCIAL MATTER, THAT IS ALL.
BESIDES, HE PROMISES TO REPAY ME AT A LATER DATE.
I WOULD HAVE BEEN HAPPY TO GIVE IT TO HIM OUTRIGHT, BUT HE INSISTED.
...WAS THAT...

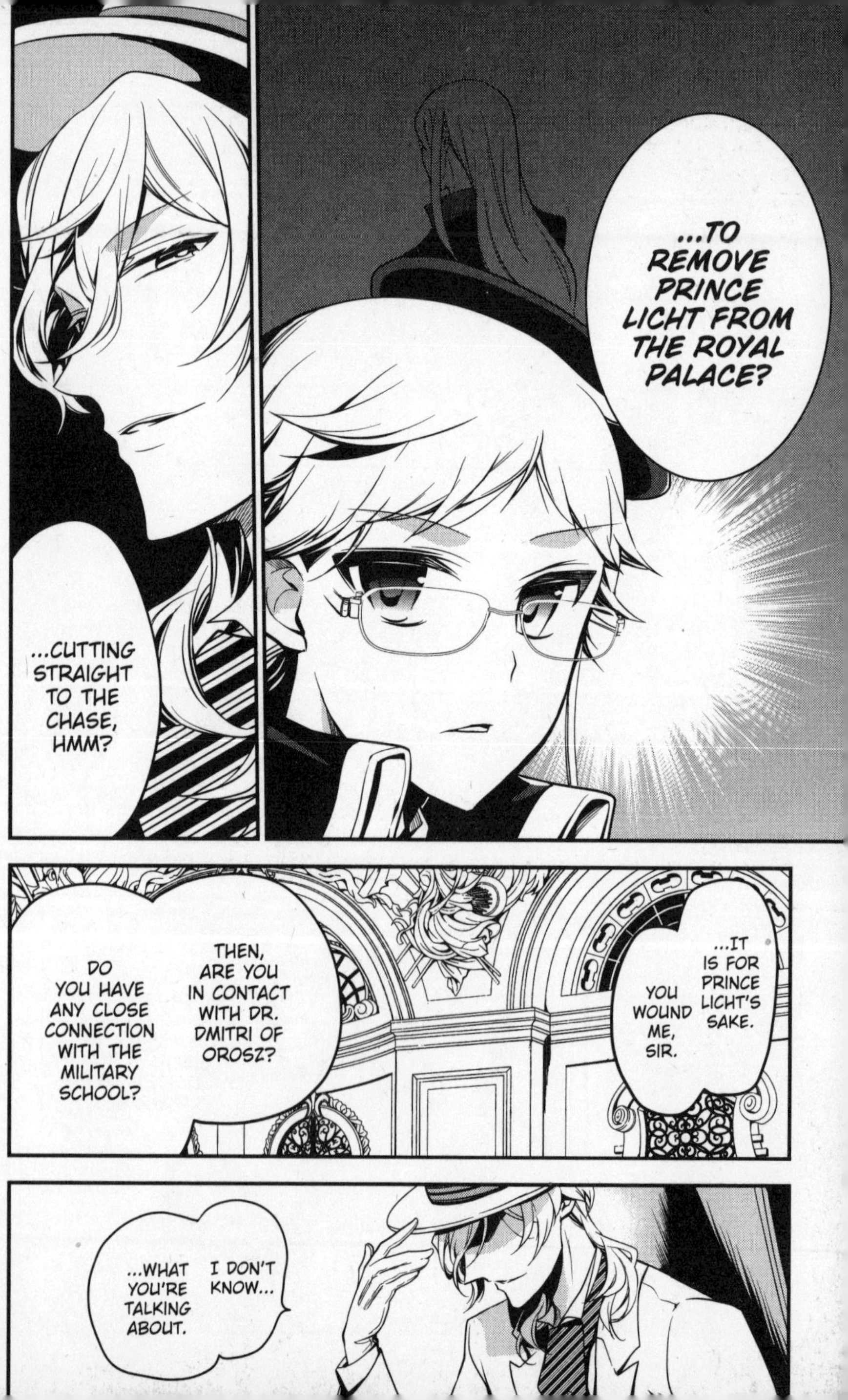
...TO REMOVE PRINCE LICHT FROM THE ROYAL PALACE?
...CUTTING STRAIGHT TO THE CHASE, HMM?
...IT IS FOR PRINCE LICHT'S SAKE.
YOU WOUND ME, SIR.
THEN, ARE YOU IN CONTACT WITH DR. DMITRI OF OROSZ?
DO YOU HAVE ANY CLOSE CONNECTION WITH THE MILITARY SCHOOL?
I DON'T KNOW...
...WHAT YOU'RE TALKING ABOUT.

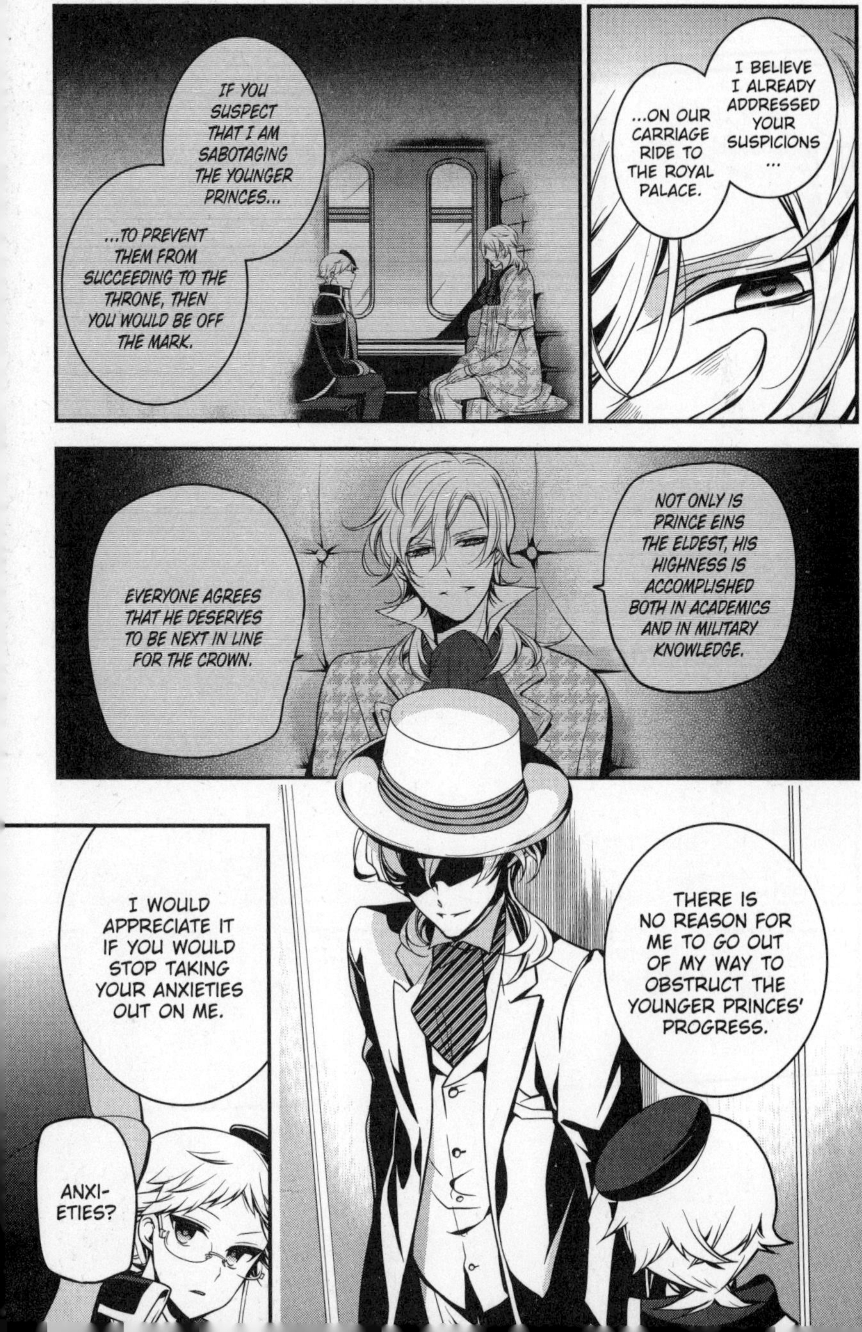
I BELIEVE I ALREADY ADDRESSED YOUR SUSPICIONS ...
...ON OUR CARRIAGE RIDE TO THE ROYAL PALACE.
IF YOU SUSPECT THAT I AM SABOTAGING THE YOUNGER PRINCES...
...TO PREVENT THEM FROM SUCCEEDING TO THE THRONE, THEN YOU WOULD BE OFF THE MARK.
NOT ONLY IS PRINCE EINS THE ELDEST, HIS HIGHNESS IS ACCOMPLISHED BOTH IN ACADEMICS AND IN MILITARY KNOWLEDGE.
EVERYONE AGREES THAT HE DESERVES TO BE NEXT IN LINE FOR THE CROWN.
THERE IS NO REASON FOR ME TO GO OUT OF MY WAY TO OBSTRUCT THE YOUNGER PRINCES' PROGRESS.
I WOULD APPRECIATE IT IF YOU WOULD STOP TAKING YOUR ANXIETIES OUT ON ME.
ANXI- ETIES?

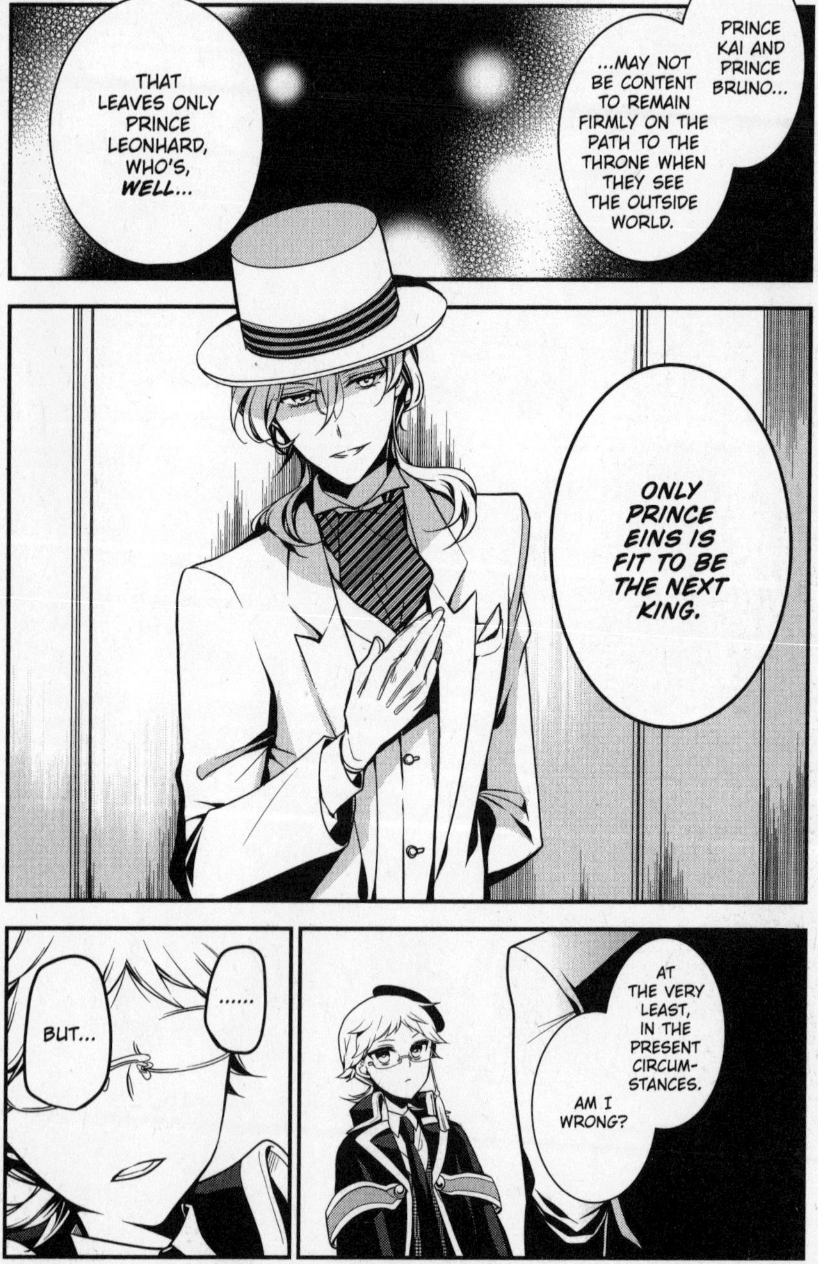
PRINCE KAI AND PRINCE BRUNO...
...MAY NOT BE CONTENT TO REMAIN FIRMLY ON THE PATH TO THE THRONE WHEN THEY SEE THE OUTSIDE WORLD.
THAT LEAVES ONLY PRINCE LEONHARD, WHO'S, *WELL...*
ONLY PRINCE EINS IS FIT TO BE THE NEXT KING.
AT THE VERY LEAST, IN THE PRESENT CIRCUMSTANCES.
AM I WRONG?
......
BUT...

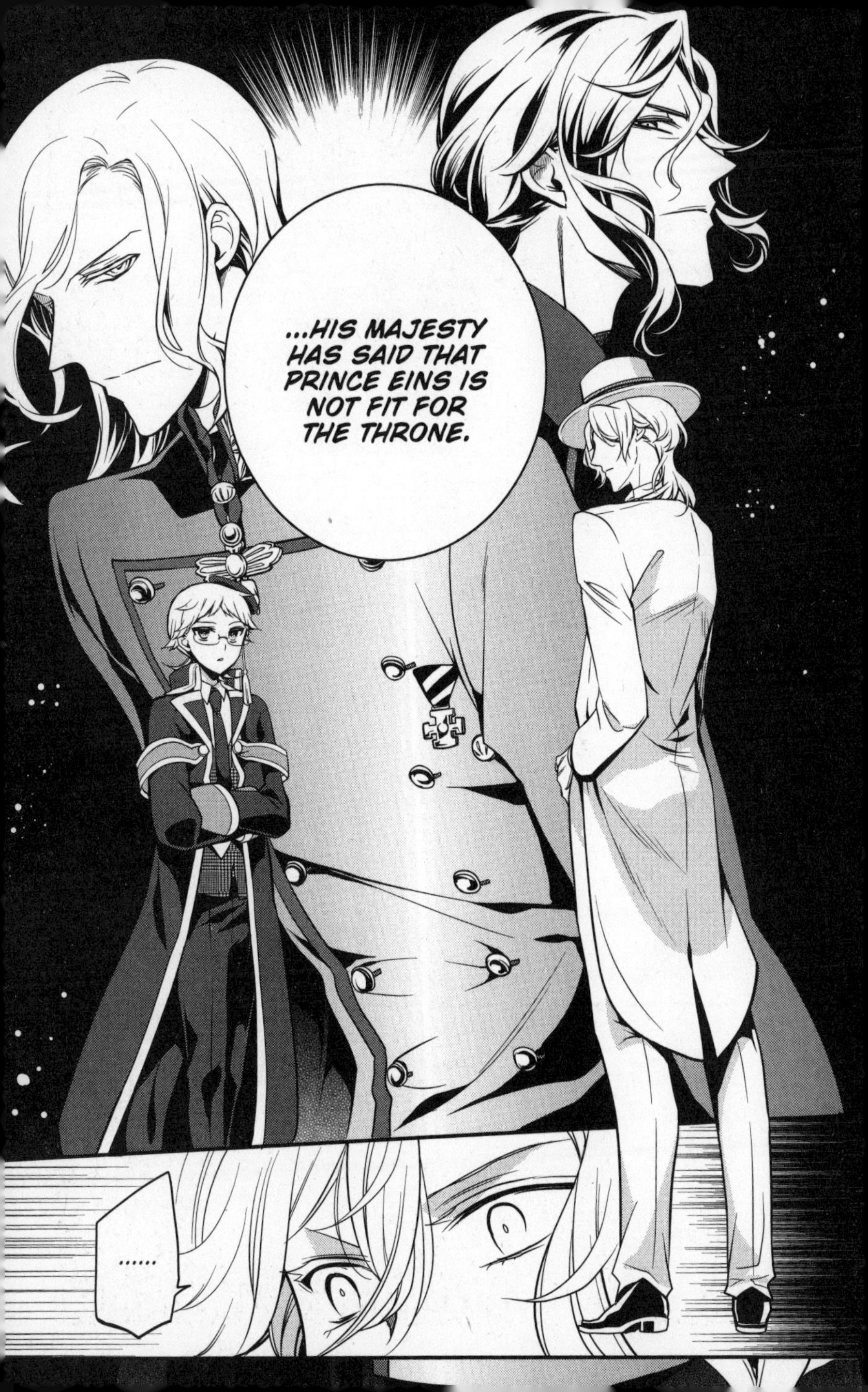
...HIS MAJESTY HAS SAID THAT PRINCE EINS IS NOT FIT FOR THE THRONE.
......

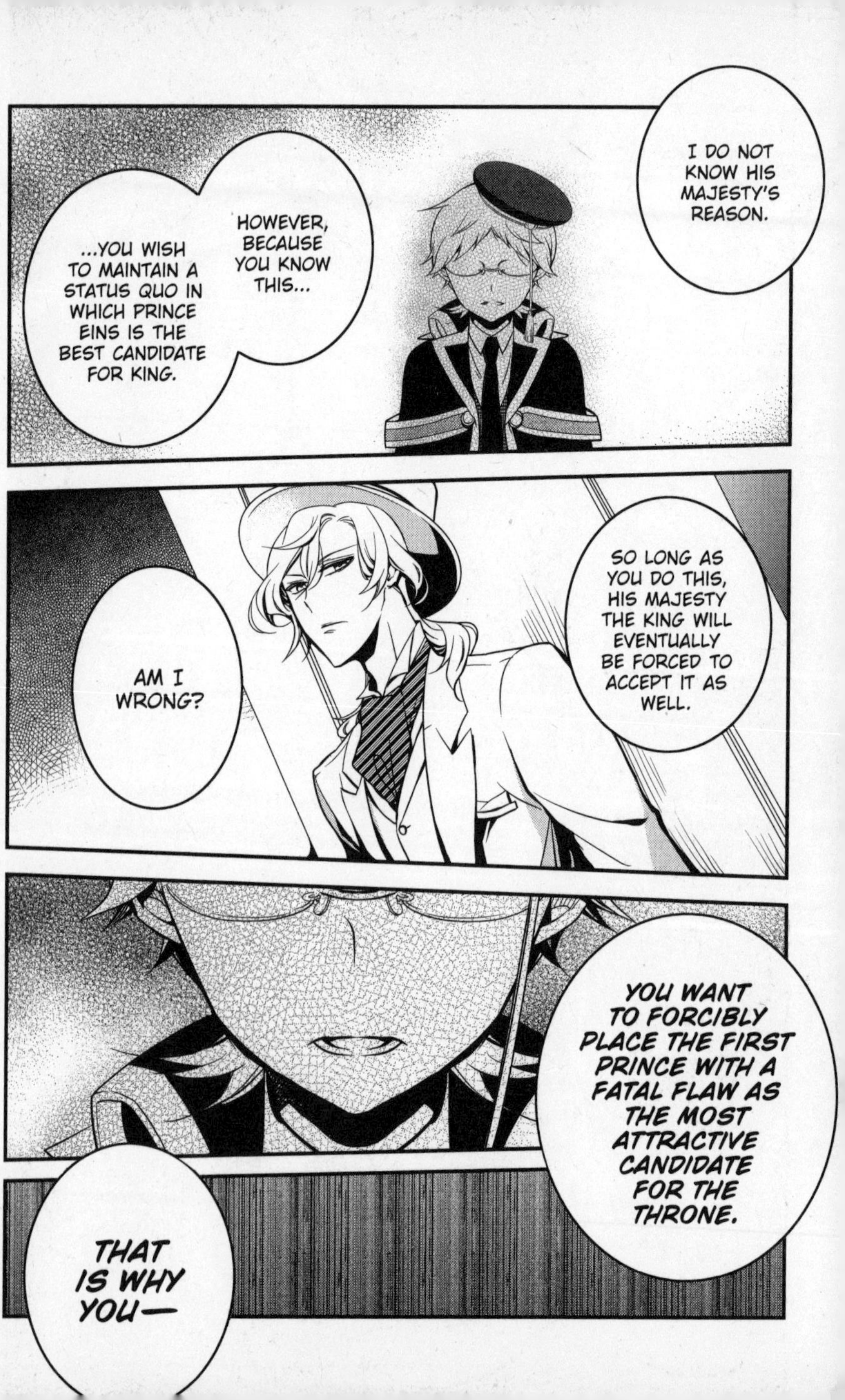
I DO NOT KNOW HIS MAJESTY'S REASON.
HOWEVER, BECAUSE YOU KNOW THIS...
...YOU WISH TO MAINTAIN A STATUS QUO IN WHICH PRINCE EINS IS THE BEST CANDIDATE FOR KING.
SO LONG AS YOU DO THIS, HIS MAJESTY THE KING WILL EVENTUALLY BE FORCED TO ACCEPT IT AS WELL.
AM I WRONG?
YOU WANT TO FORCIBLY PLACE THE FIRST PRINCE WITH A FATAL FLAW AS THE MOST ATTRACTIVE CANDIDATE FOR THE THRONE.
THAT IS WHY YOU—

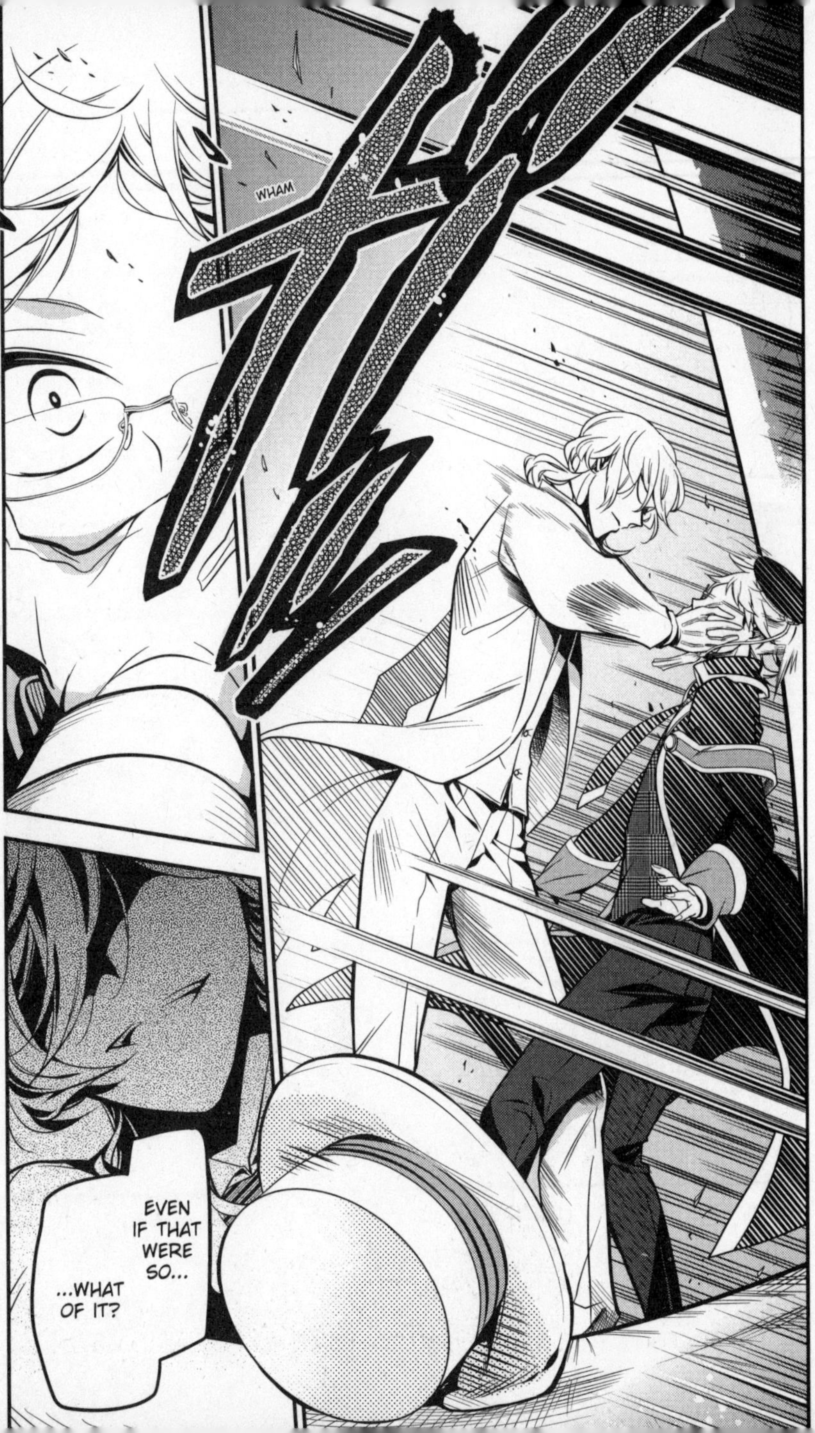
WHAM
EVEN IF THAT WERE SO...
...WHAT OF IT?

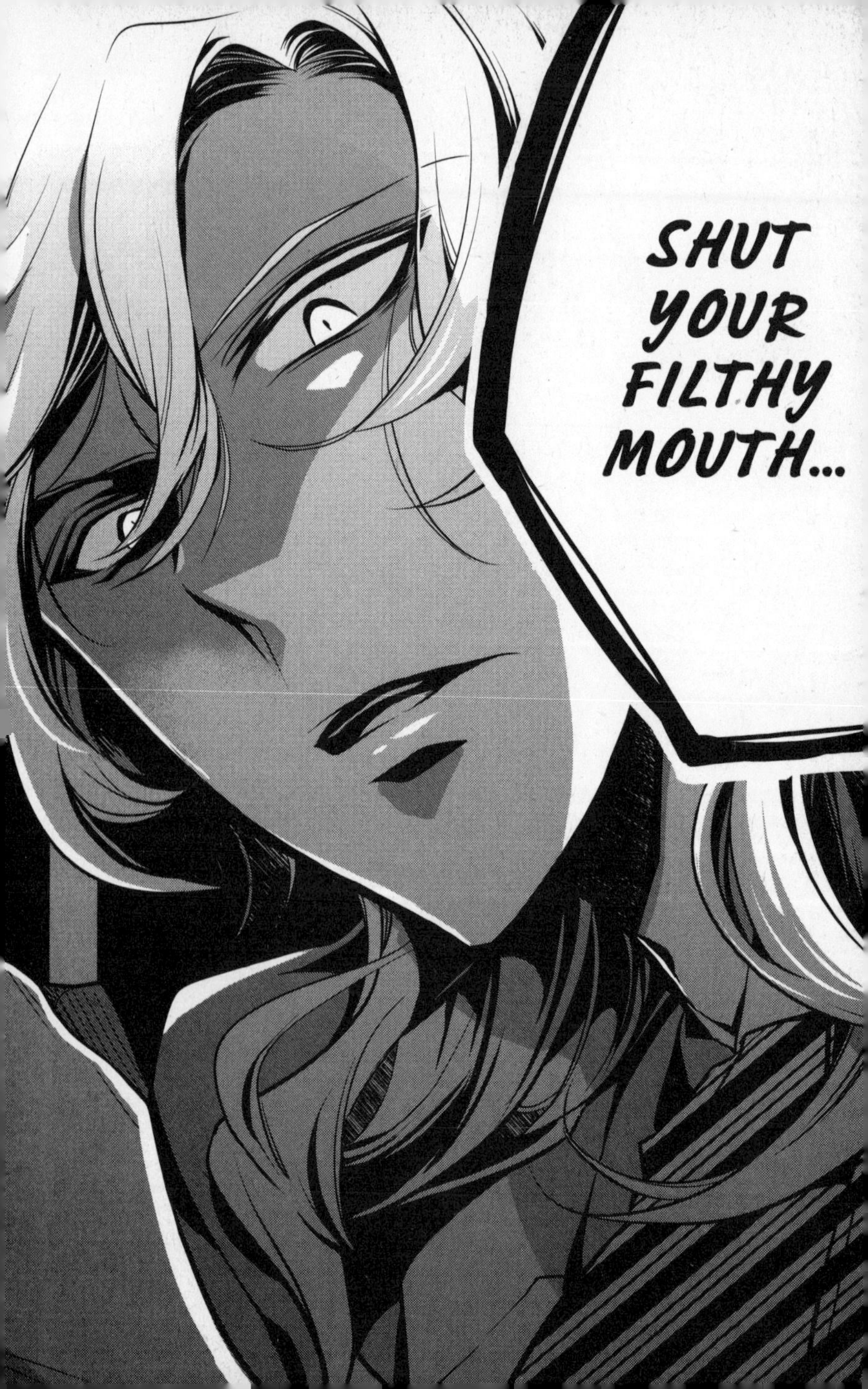
SHUT YOUR FILTHY MOUTH...

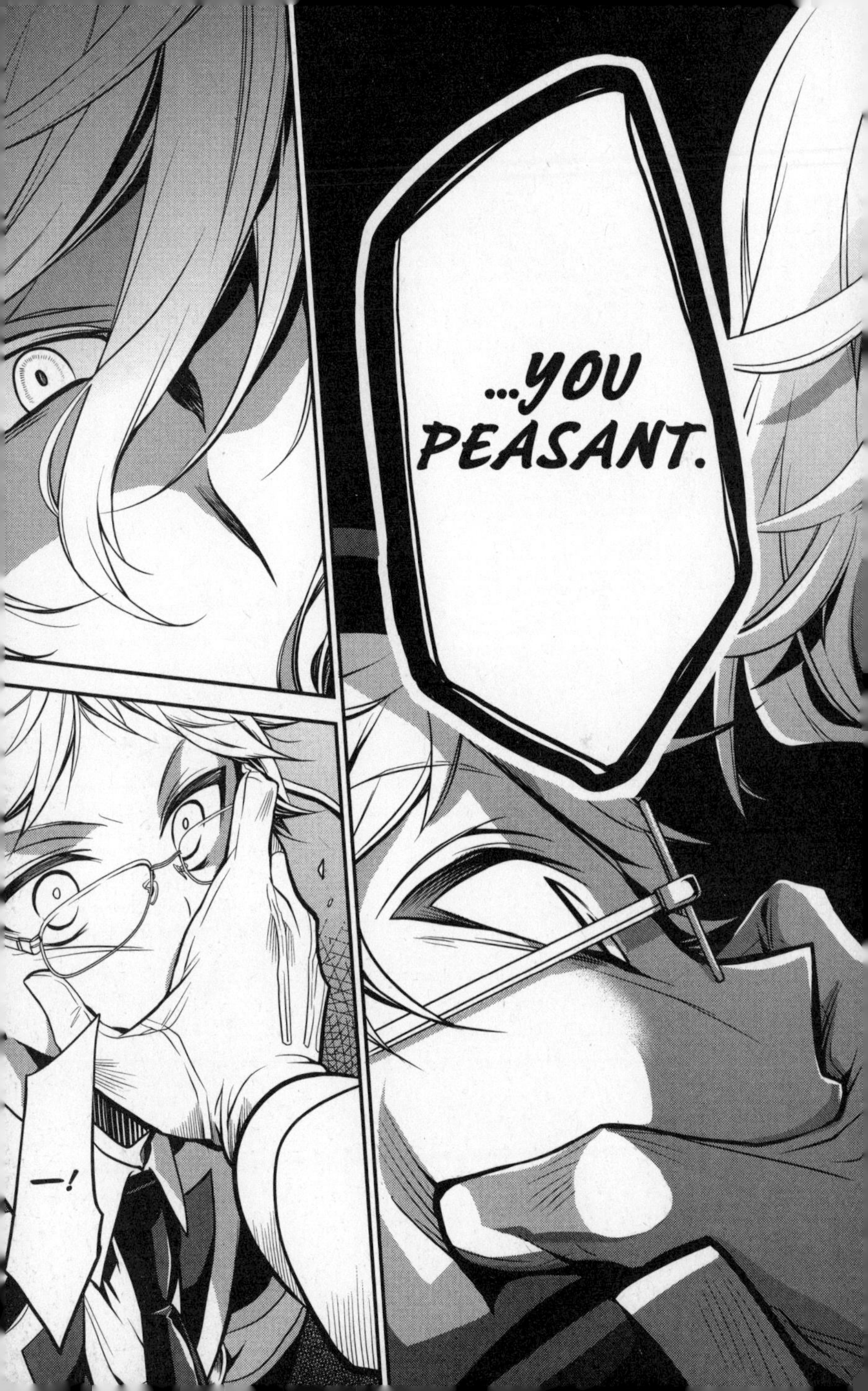
...YOU PEASANT.
—!

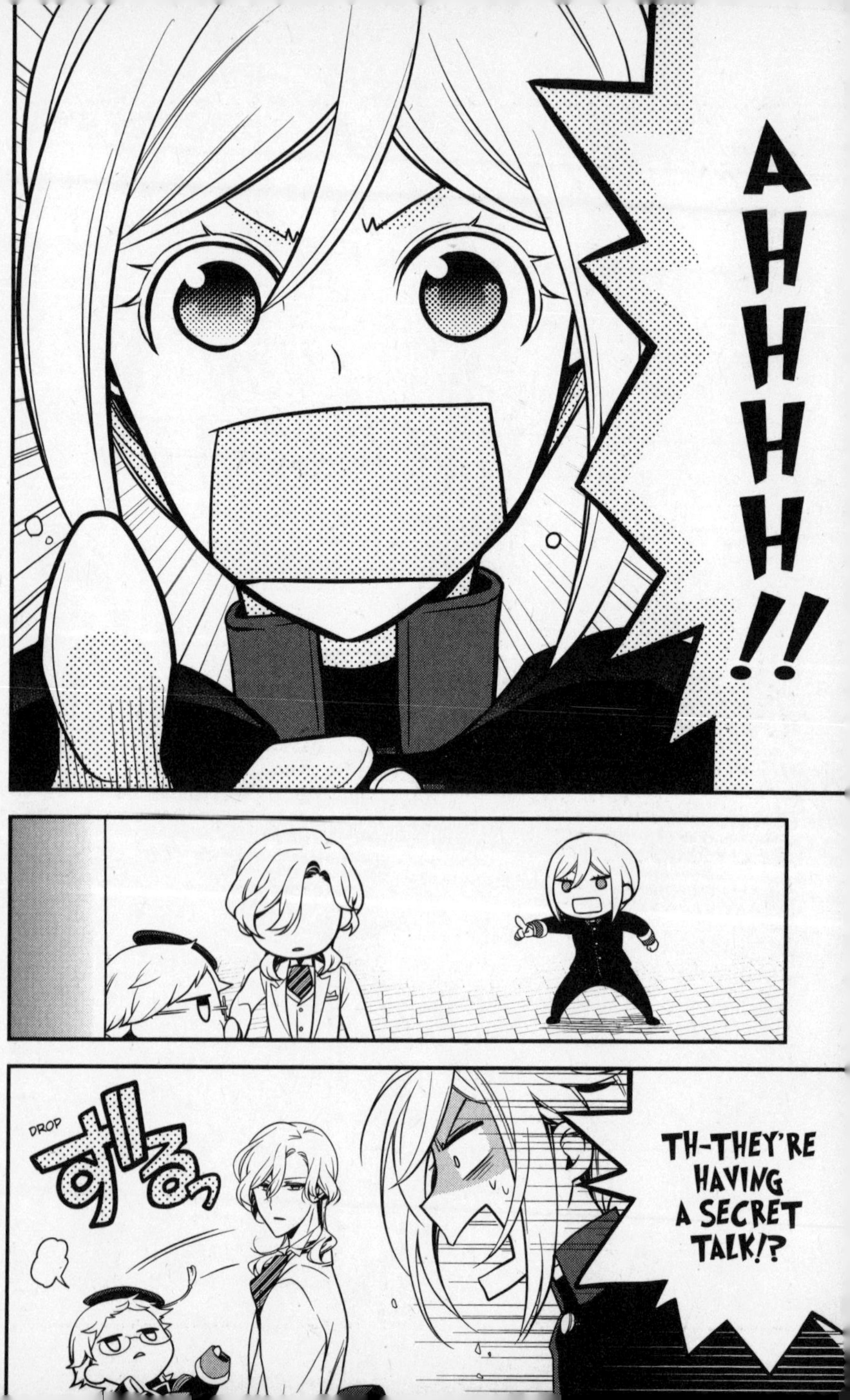
AHHHHH!!
DROP
する
TH-THEY'RE HAVING A SECRET TALK!?

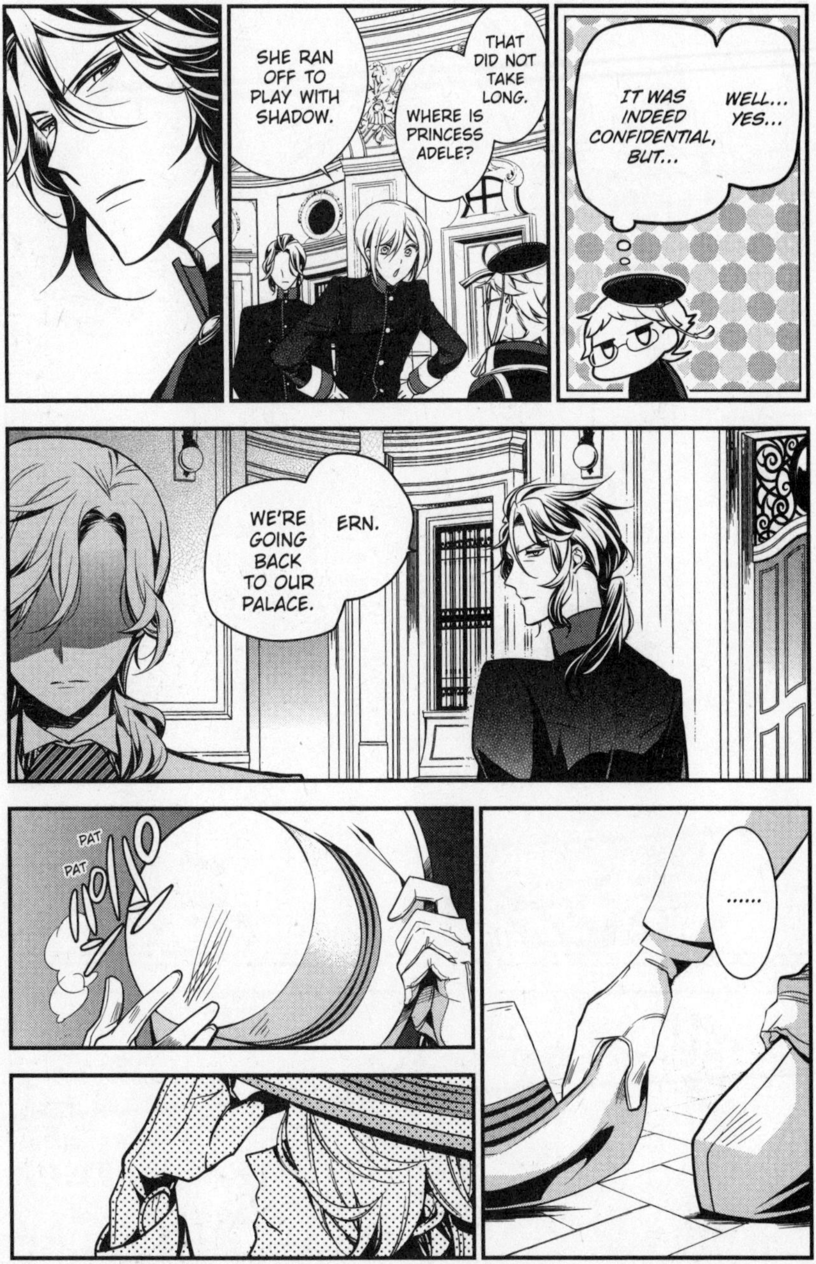
WELL... YES... IT WAS INDEED CONFIDENTIAL, BUT...
THAT DID NOT TAKE LONG.
WHERE IS PRINCESS ADELE?
SHE RAN OFF TO PLAY WITH SHADOW.
ERN. WE'RE GOING BACK TO OUR PALACE.
......
PAT PAT

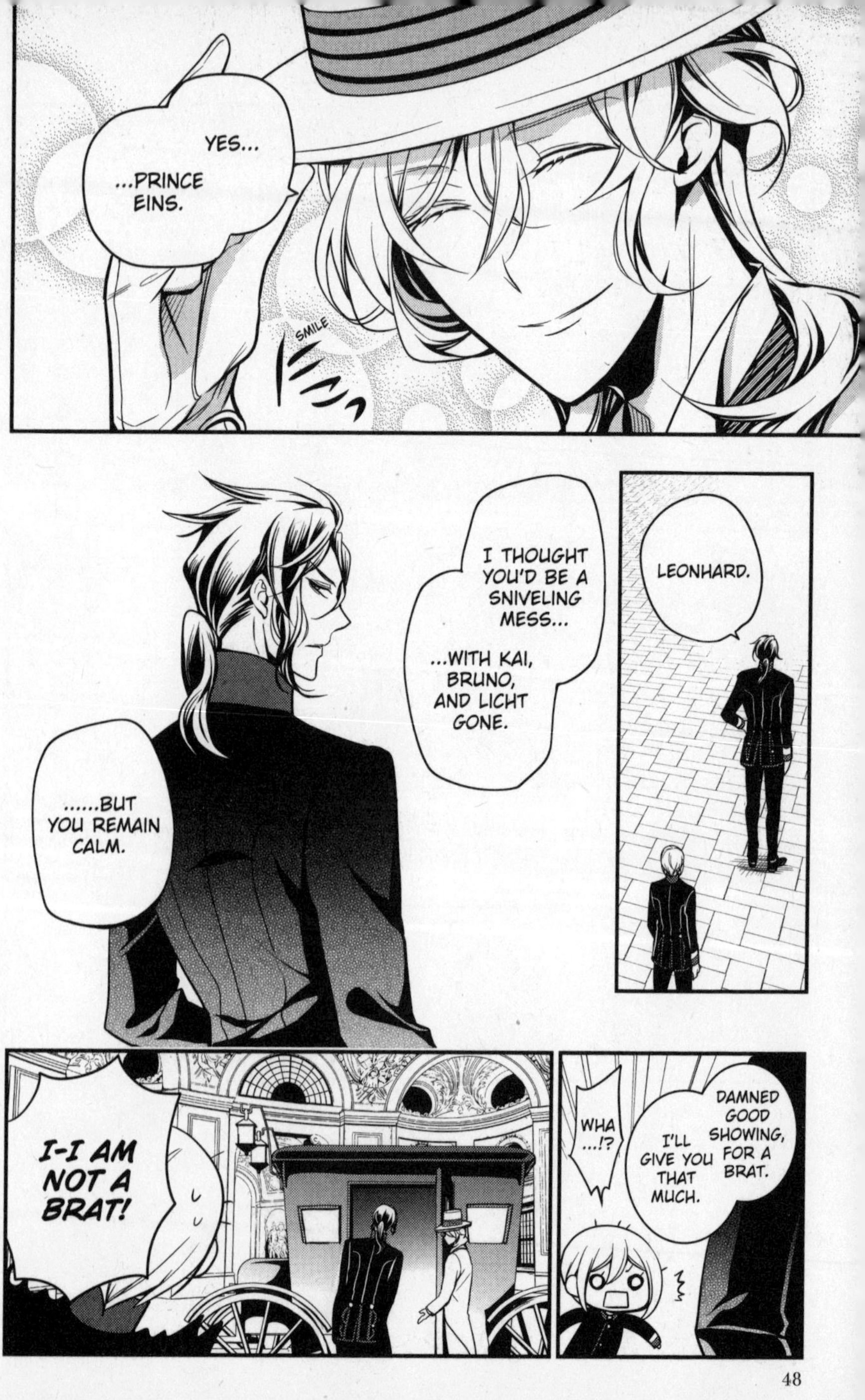
YES...
...PRINCE EINS.
SMILE
LEONHARD.
I THOUGHT YOU'D BE A SNIVELING MESS...
...WITH KAI, BRUNO, AND LICHT GONE.
......BUT YOU REMAIN CALM.
DAMNED GOOD SHOWING, FOR A BRAT.
I'LL GIVE YOU THAT MUCH.
WHA ...!?
I-I AM NOT A BRAT!

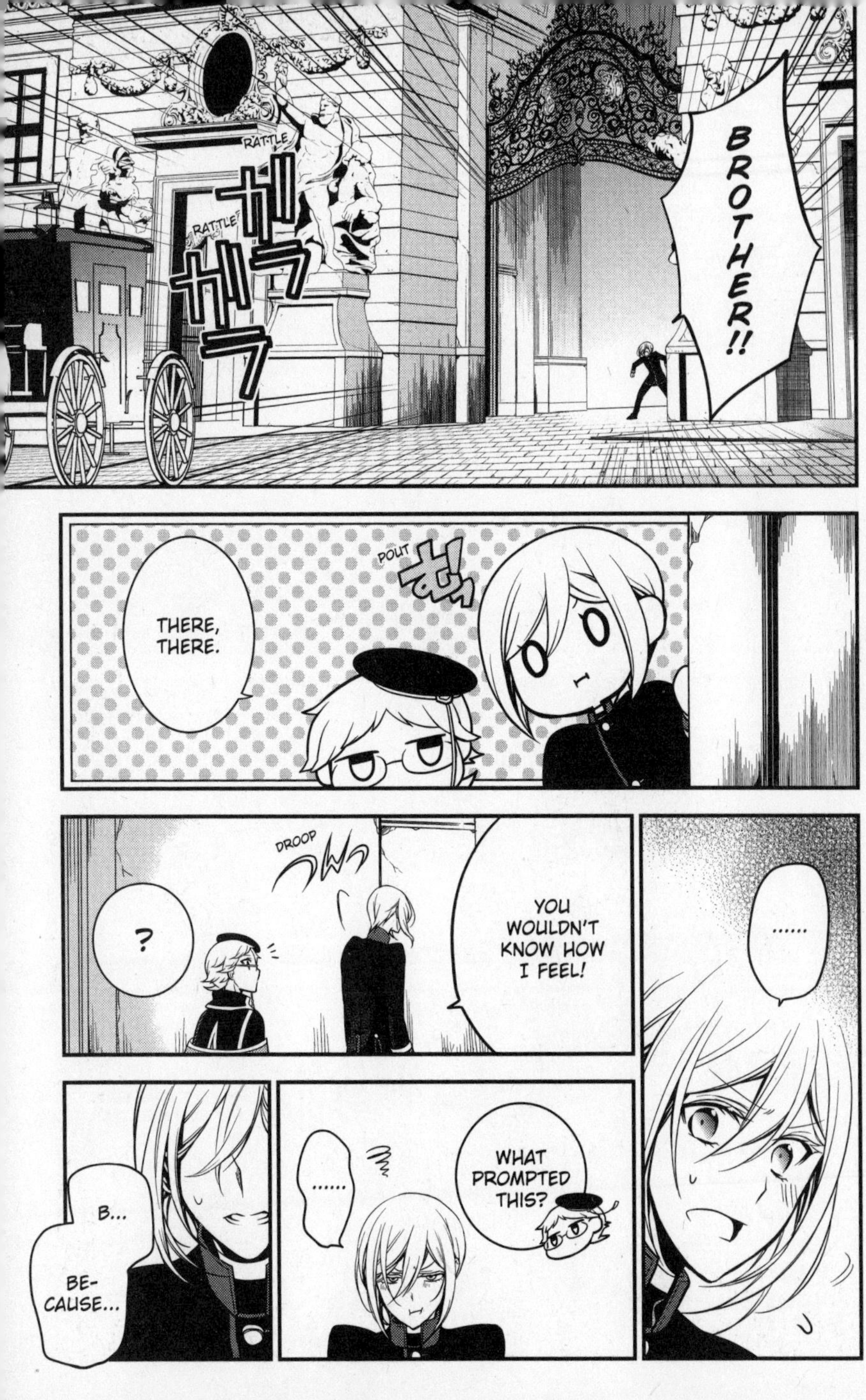
BROTHER!!
RATTLE
RATTLE
POUT
THERE, THERE.
......
YOU WOULDN'T KNOW HOW I FEEL!
DROOP
?
WHAT PROMPTED THIS?
......
B...
BE-CAUSE...

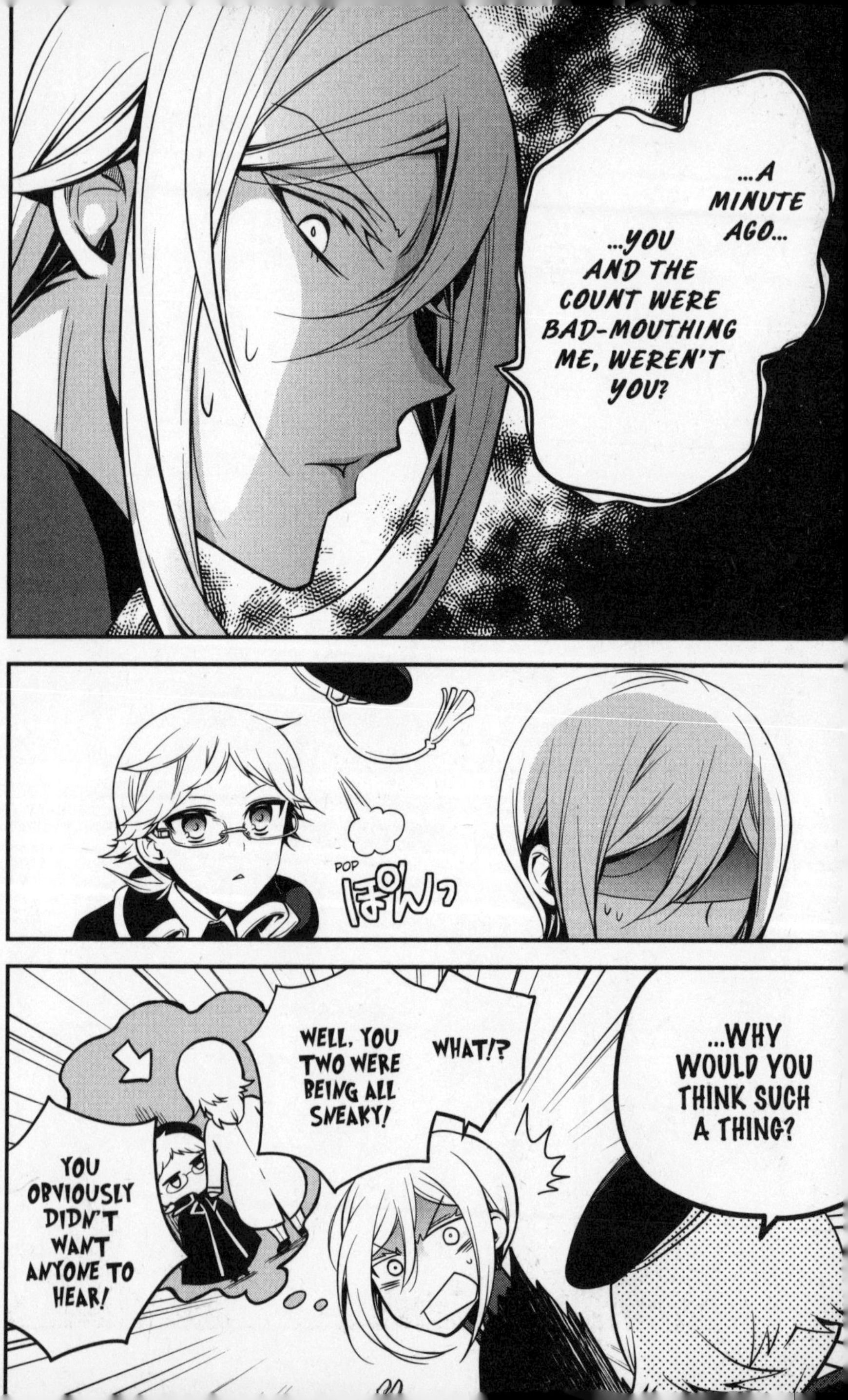
...A MINUTE AGO...
...YOU AND THE COUNT WERE BAD-MOUTHING ME, WEREN'T YOU?
POP
ぽんっ
...WHY WOULD YOU THINK SUCH A THING?
WHAT!?
WELL, YOU TWO WERE BEING ALL SNEAKY!
YOU OBVIOUSLY DIDN'T WANT ANYONE TO HEAR!

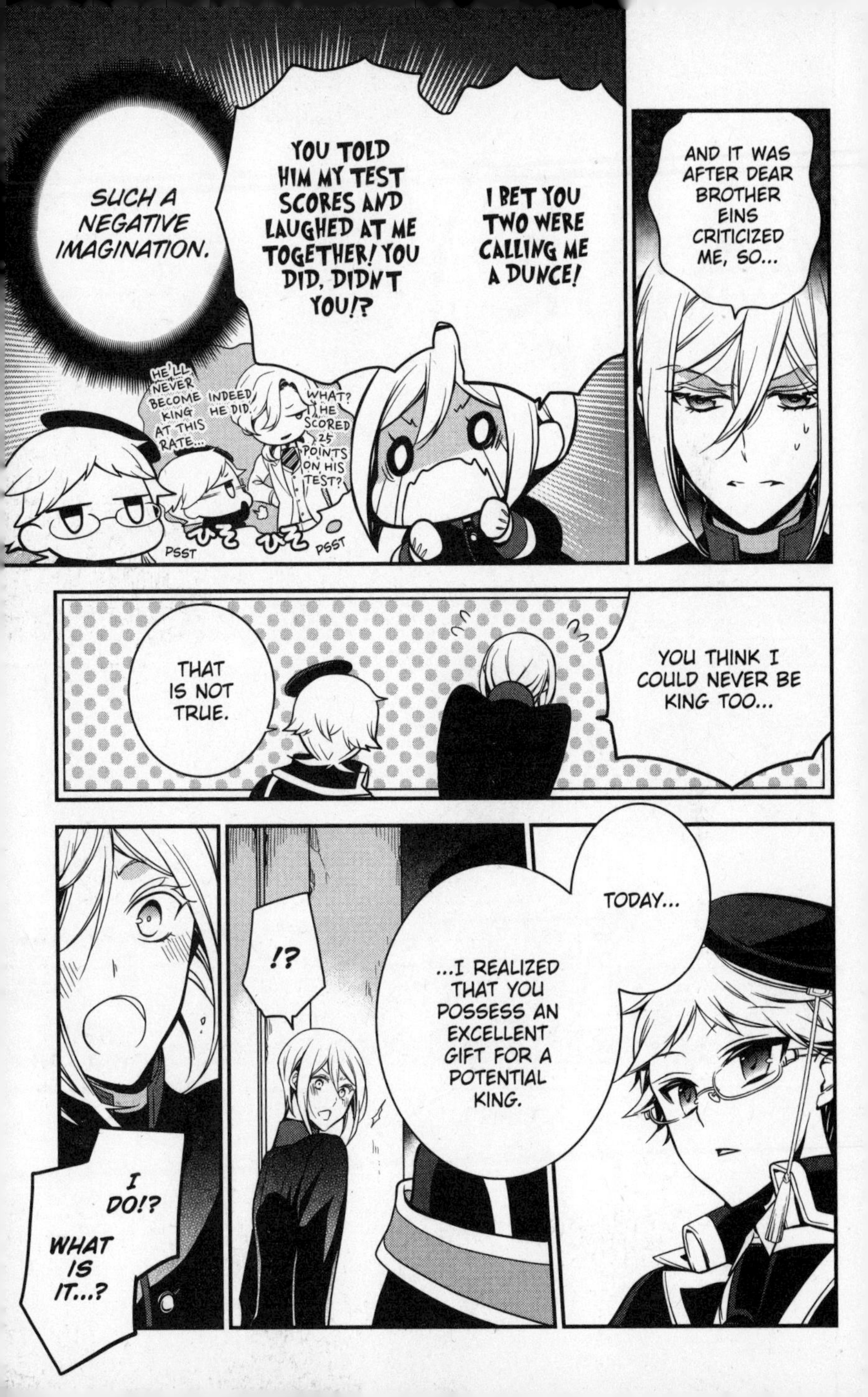
AND IT WAS AFTER DEAR BROTHER EINS CRITICIZED ME, SO...
I BET YOU TWO WERE CALLING ME A DUNCE!
YOU TOLD HIM MY TEST SCORES AND LAUGHED AT ME TOGETHER! YOU DID, DIDN'T YOU!?
WHAT? HE SCORED 25 POINTS ON HIS TEST?
PSST
INDEED HE DID.
HE'LL NEVER BECOME KING AT THIS RATE...
ひそ ひそ
PSST
SUCH A NEGATIVE IMAGINATION.
YOU THINK I COULD NEVER BE KING TOO...
THAT IS NOT TRUE.
TODAY...
...I REALIZED THAT YOU POSSESS AN EXCELLENT GIFT FOR A POTENTIAL KING.
!?
I DO!?
WHAT IS IT...?

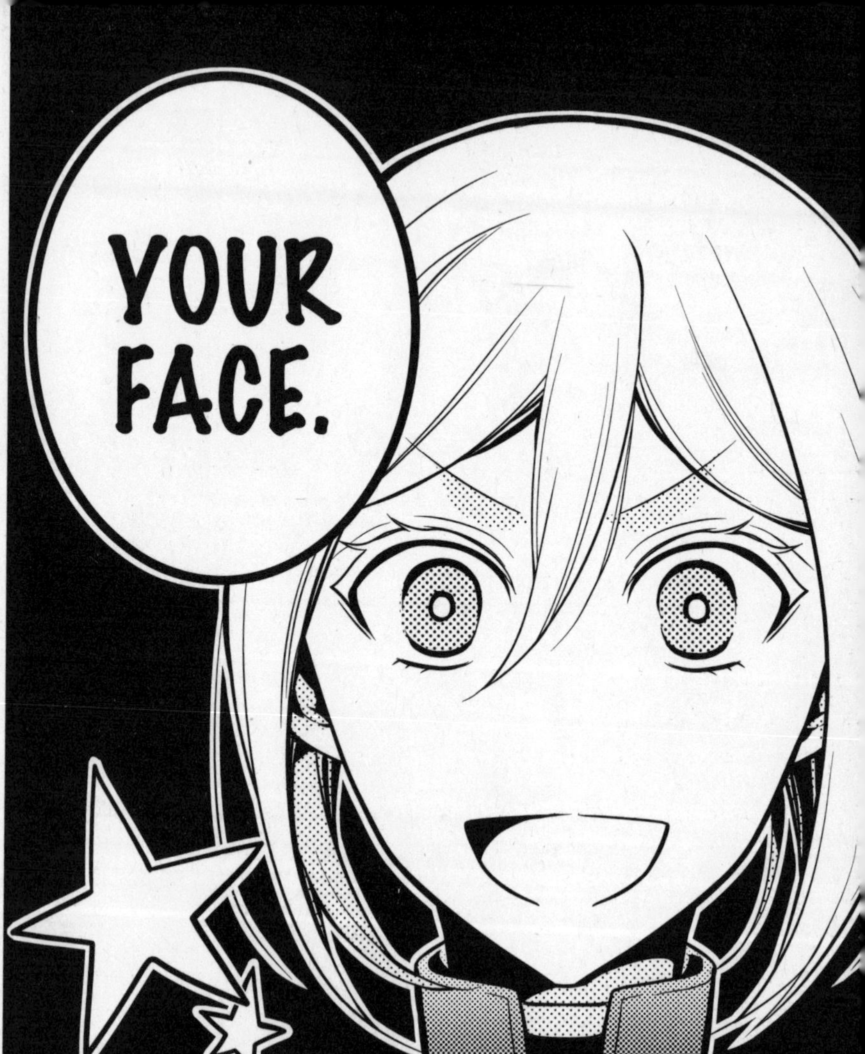
YOUR FACE.
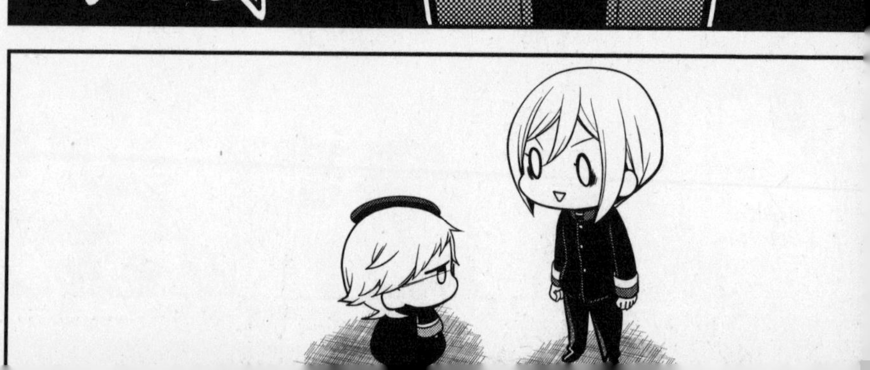

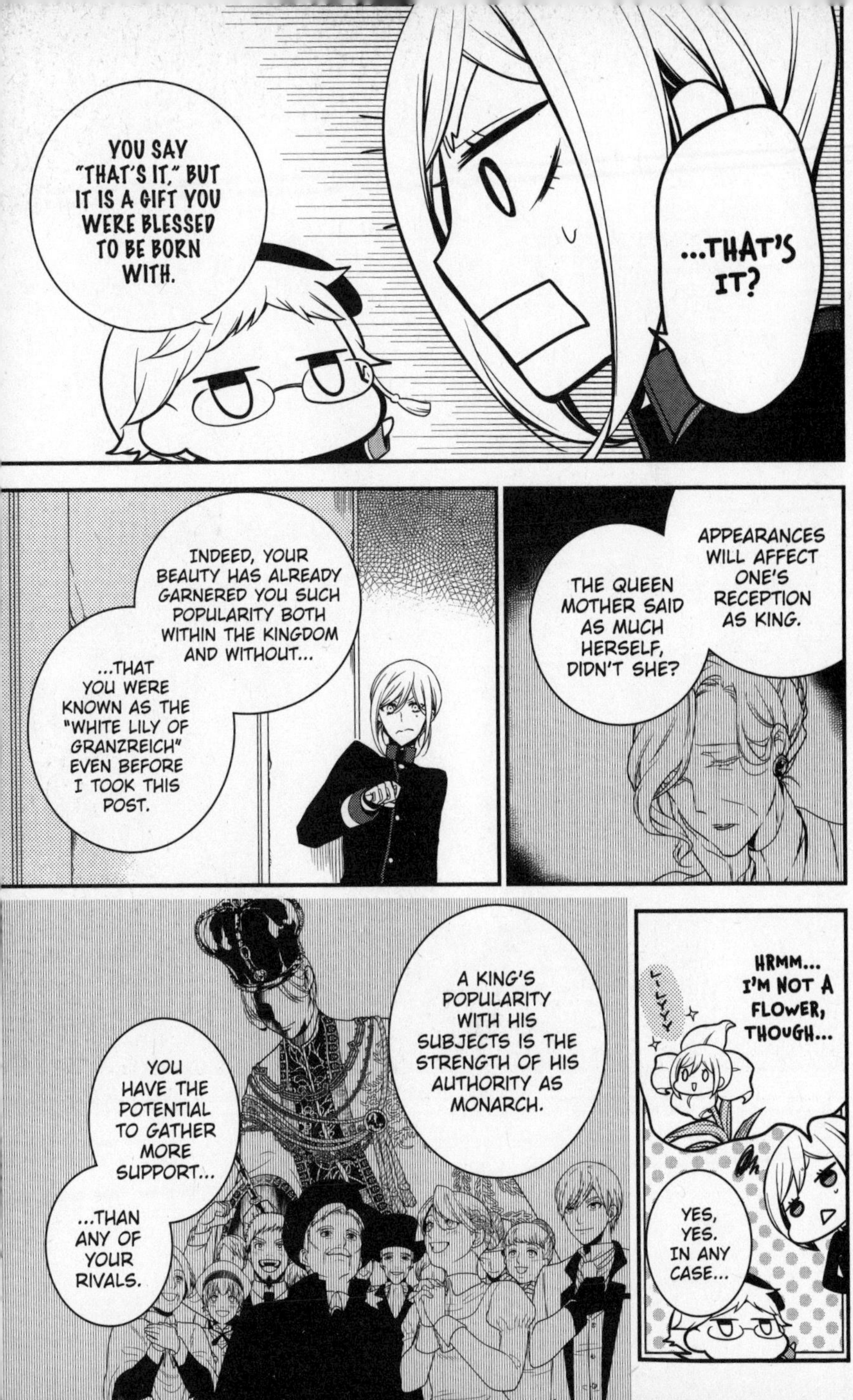
...THAT'S IT?
YOU SAY "THAT'S IT," BUT IT IS A GIFT YOU WERE BLESSED TO BE BORN WITH.
APPEARANCES WILL AFFECT ONE'S RECEPTION AS KING.
THE QUEEN MOTHER SAID AS MUCH HERSELF, DIDN'T SHE?
INDEED, YOUR BEAUTY HAS ALREADY GARNERED YOU SUCH POPULARITY BOTH WITHIN THE KINGDOM AND WITHOUT...
...THAT YOU WERE KNOWN AS THE "WHITE LILY OF GRANZREICH" EVEN BEFORE I TOOK THIS POST.
HRMM... I'M NOT A FLOWER, THOUGH...
YES, YES. IN ANY CASE...
A KING'S POPULARITY WITH HIS SUBJECTS IS THE STRENGTH OF HIS AUTHORITY AS MONARCH.
YOU HAVE THE POTENTIAL TO GATHER MORE SUPPORT...
...THAN ANY OF YOUR RIVALS.

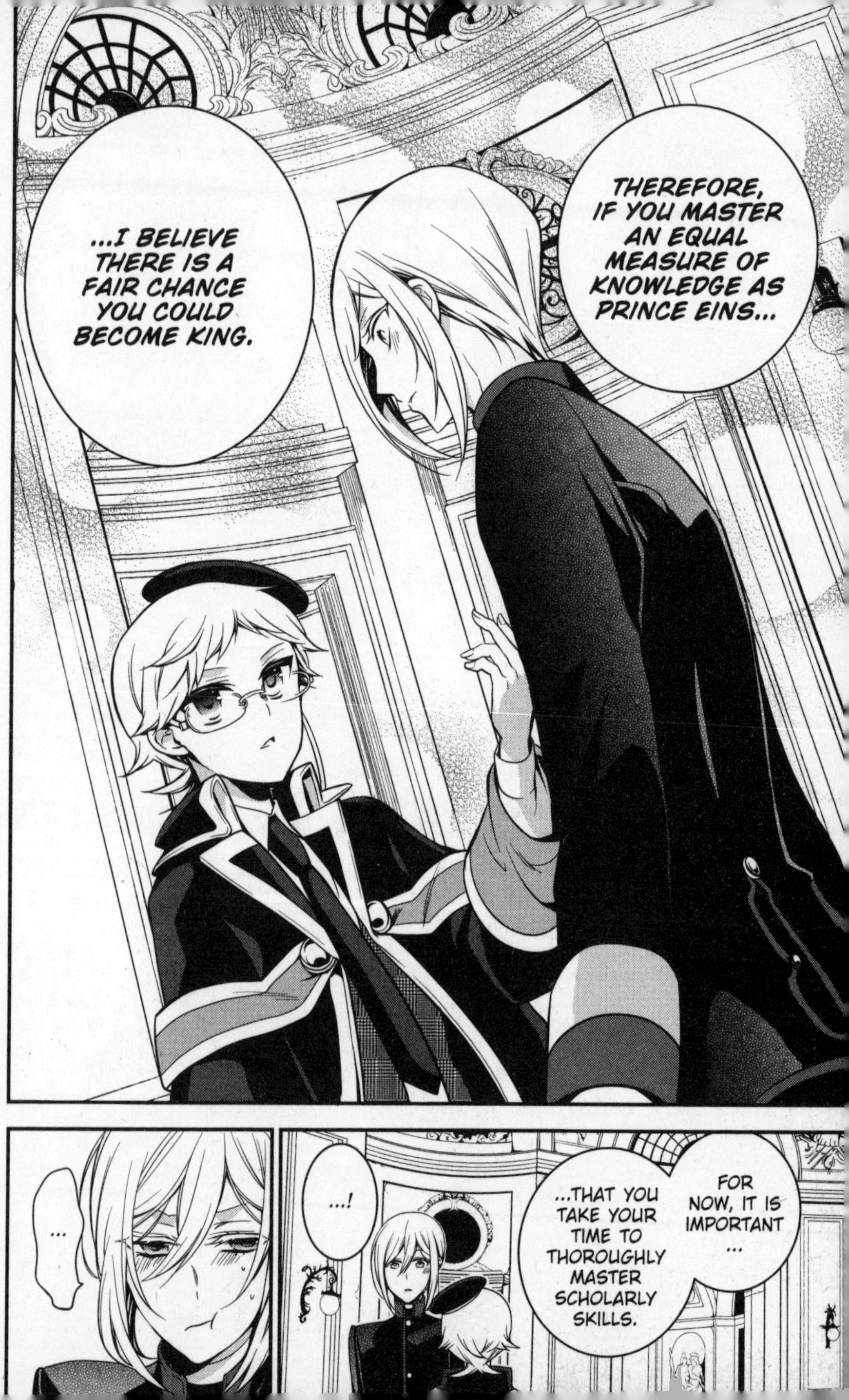
THEREFORE, IF YOU MASTER AN EQUAL MEASURE OF KNOWLEDGE AS PRINCE EINS...
...I BELIEVE THERE IS A FAIR CHANCE YOU COULD BECOME KING.
FOR NOW, IT IS IMPORTANT ...
...THAT YOU TAKE YOUR TIME TO THOROUGHLY MASTER SCHOLARLY SKILLS.
...!
...

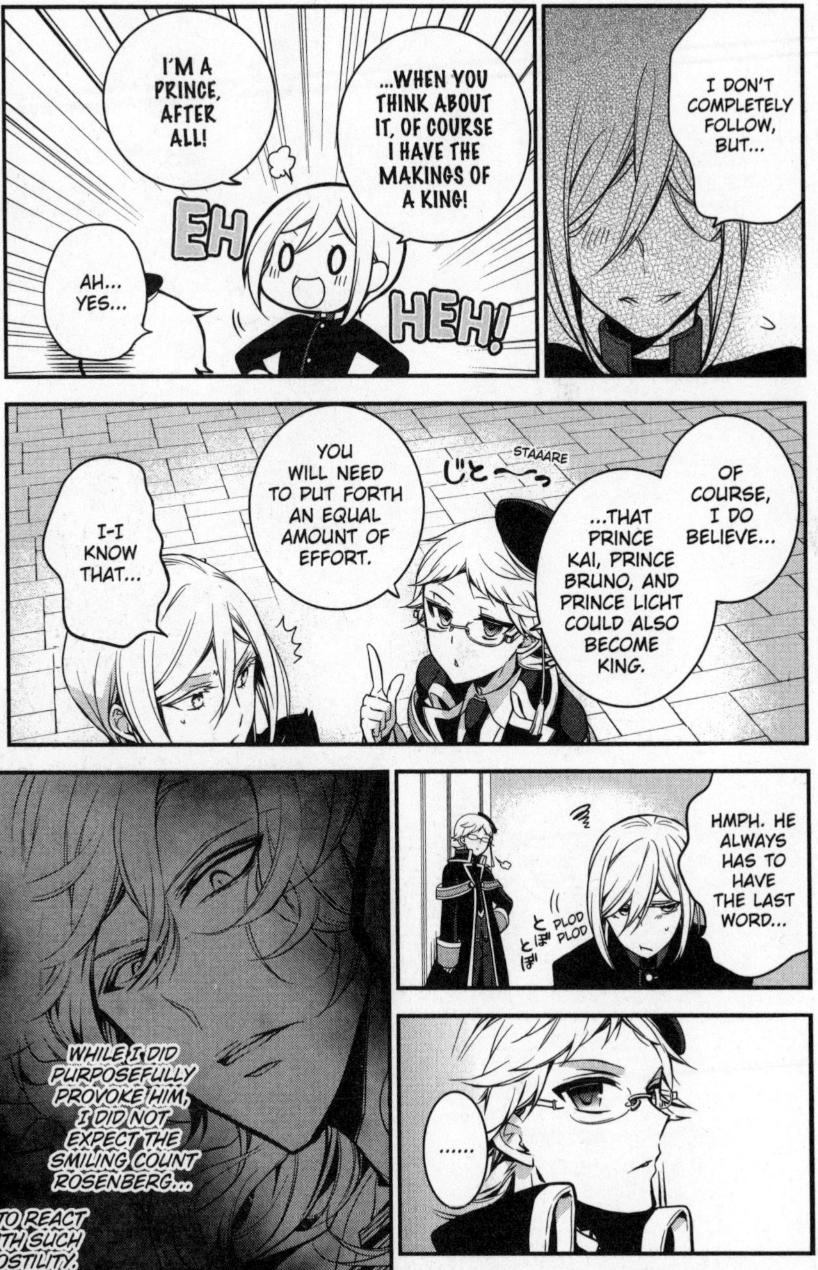
I DON'T COMPLETELY FOLLOW, BUT...
...WHEN YOU THINK ABOUT IT, OF COURSE I HAVE THE MAKINGS OF A KING!
I'M A PRINCE, AFTER ALL!
EH HEH!
AH... YES...
OF COURSE, I DO BELIEVE...
...THAT PRINCE KAI, PRINCE BRUNO, AND PRINCE LICHT COULD ALSO BECOME KING.
じと〜っ
STAAARE
YOU WILL NEED TO PUT FORTH AN EQUAL AMOUNT OF EFFORT.
I-I KNOW THAT...
HMPH. HE ALWAYS HAS TO HAVE THE LAST WORD...
とぼとぼ
PLOD PLOD
......
WHILE I DID PURPOSEFULLY PROVOKE HIM, I DID NOT EXPECT THE SMILING COUNT ROSENBERG...
...TO REACT WITH SUCH HOSTILITY.

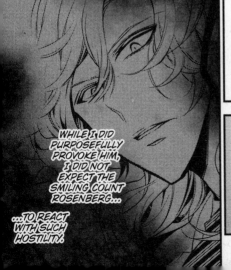

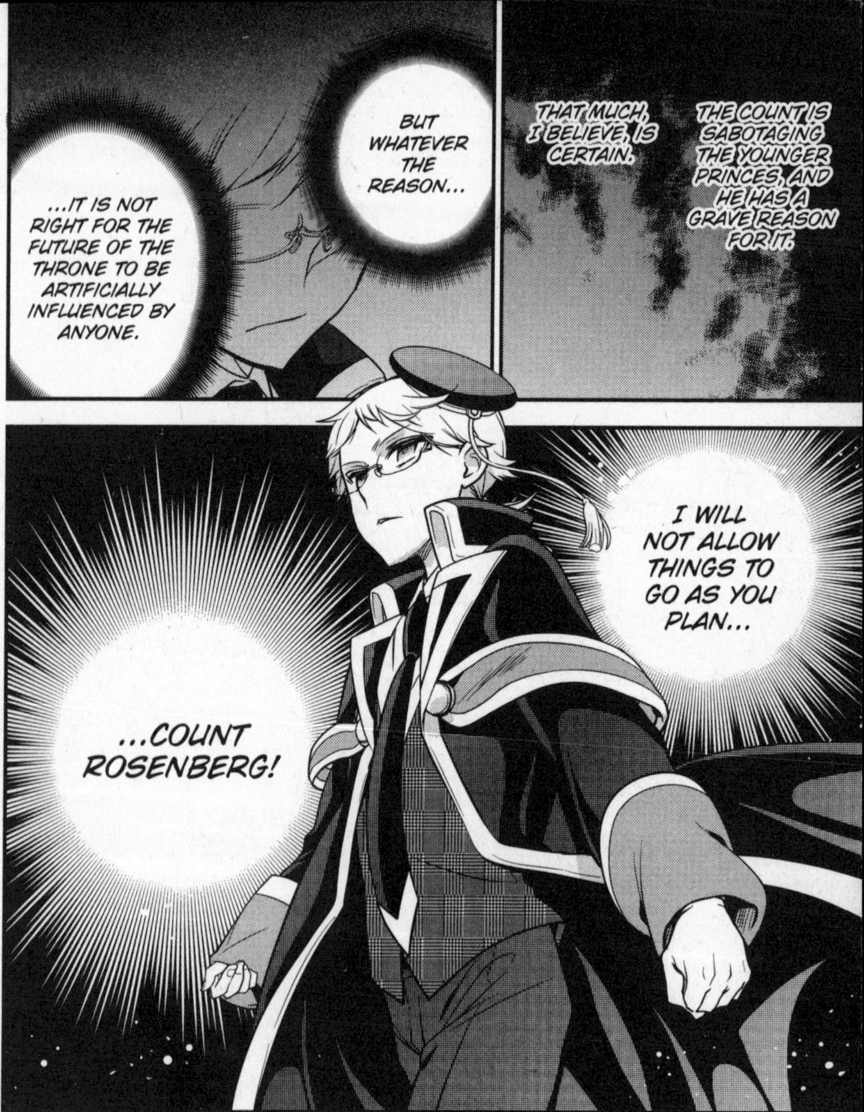
THE COUNT IS SABOTAGING THE YOUNGER PRINCES, AND HE HAS A GRAVE REASON FOR IT.
THAT MUCH, I BELIEVE, IS CERTAIN.
BUT WHATEVER THE REASON...
...IT IS NOT RIGHT FOR THE FUTURE OF THE THRONE TO BE ARTIFICIALLY INFLUENCED BY ANYONE.
I WILL NOT ALLOW THINGS TO GO AS YOU PLAN...
...COUNT ROSENBERG!

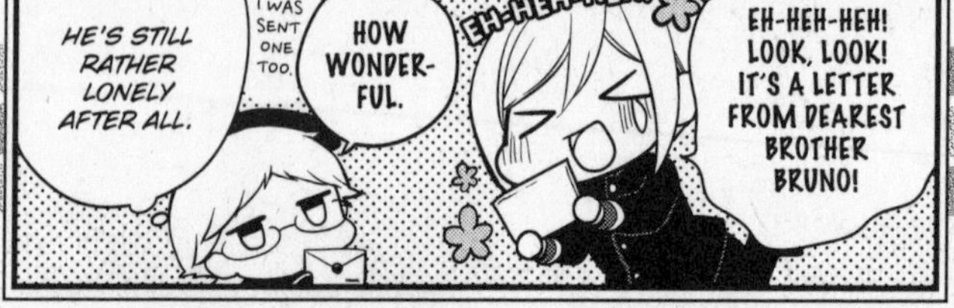
EH-HEH-HEH! LOOK, LOOK! IT'S A LETTER FROM DEAREST BROTHER BRUNO!
EH-HEH-HEH!
HOW WONDER-FUL.
I WAS SENT ONE TOO.
HE'S STILL RATHER LONELY AFTER ALL.

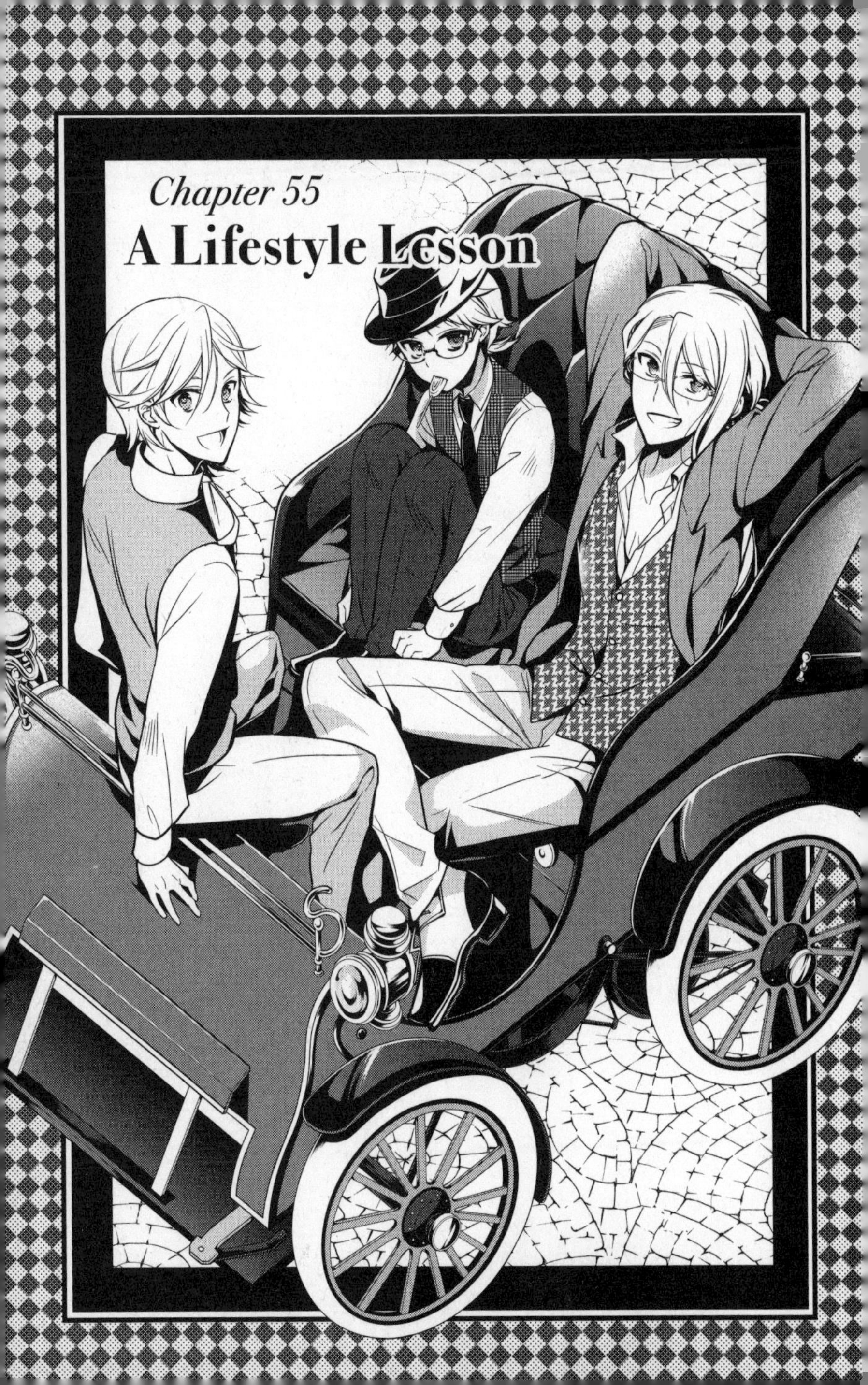
Chapter 55
A Lifestyle Lesson

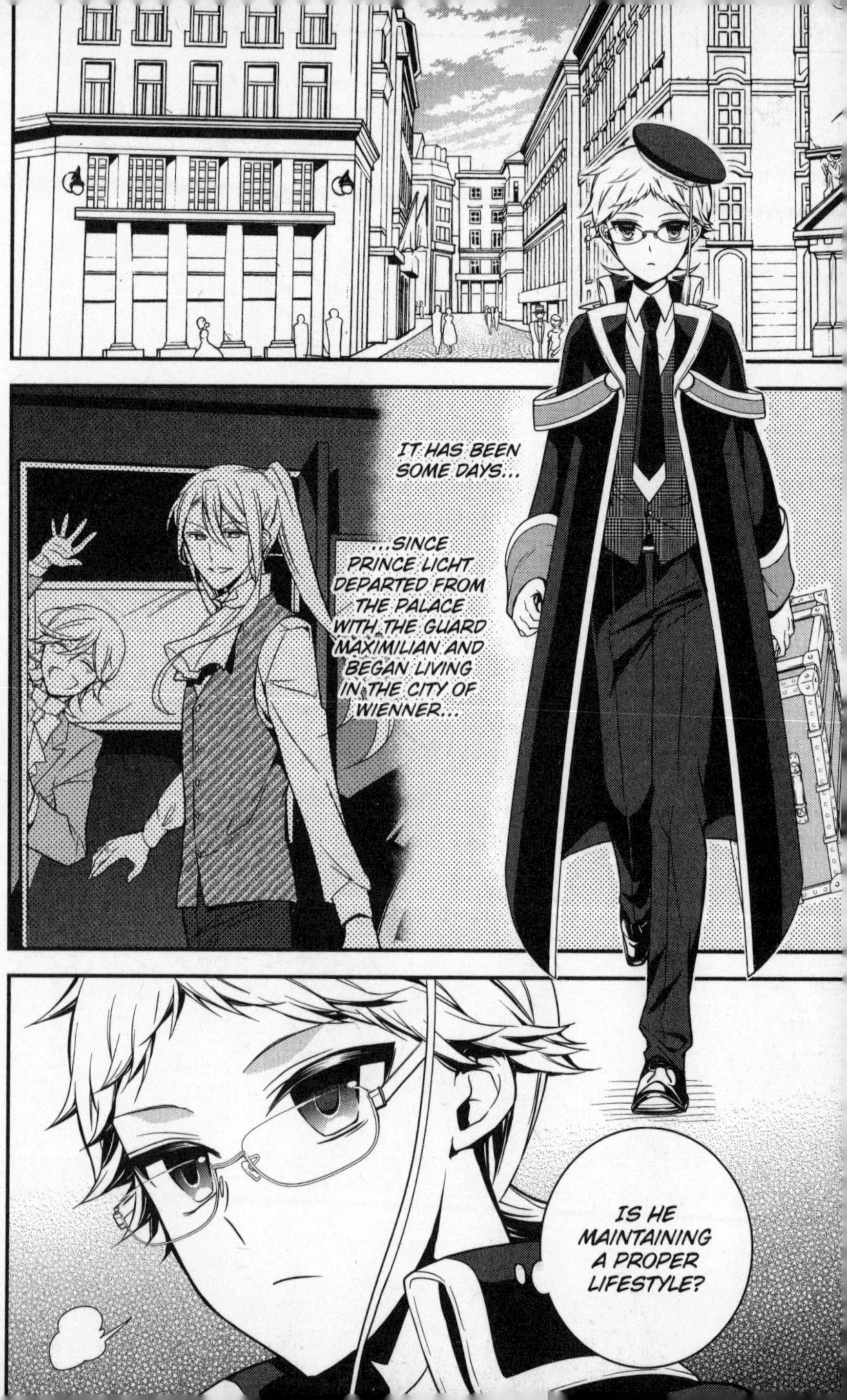
IT HAS BEEN SOME DAYS...
...SINCE PRINCE LICHT DEPARTED FROM THE PALACE WITH THE GUARD MAXIMILIAN AND BEGAN LIVING IN THE CITY OF WIENNER...
IS HE MAINTAINING A PROPER LIFESTYLE?

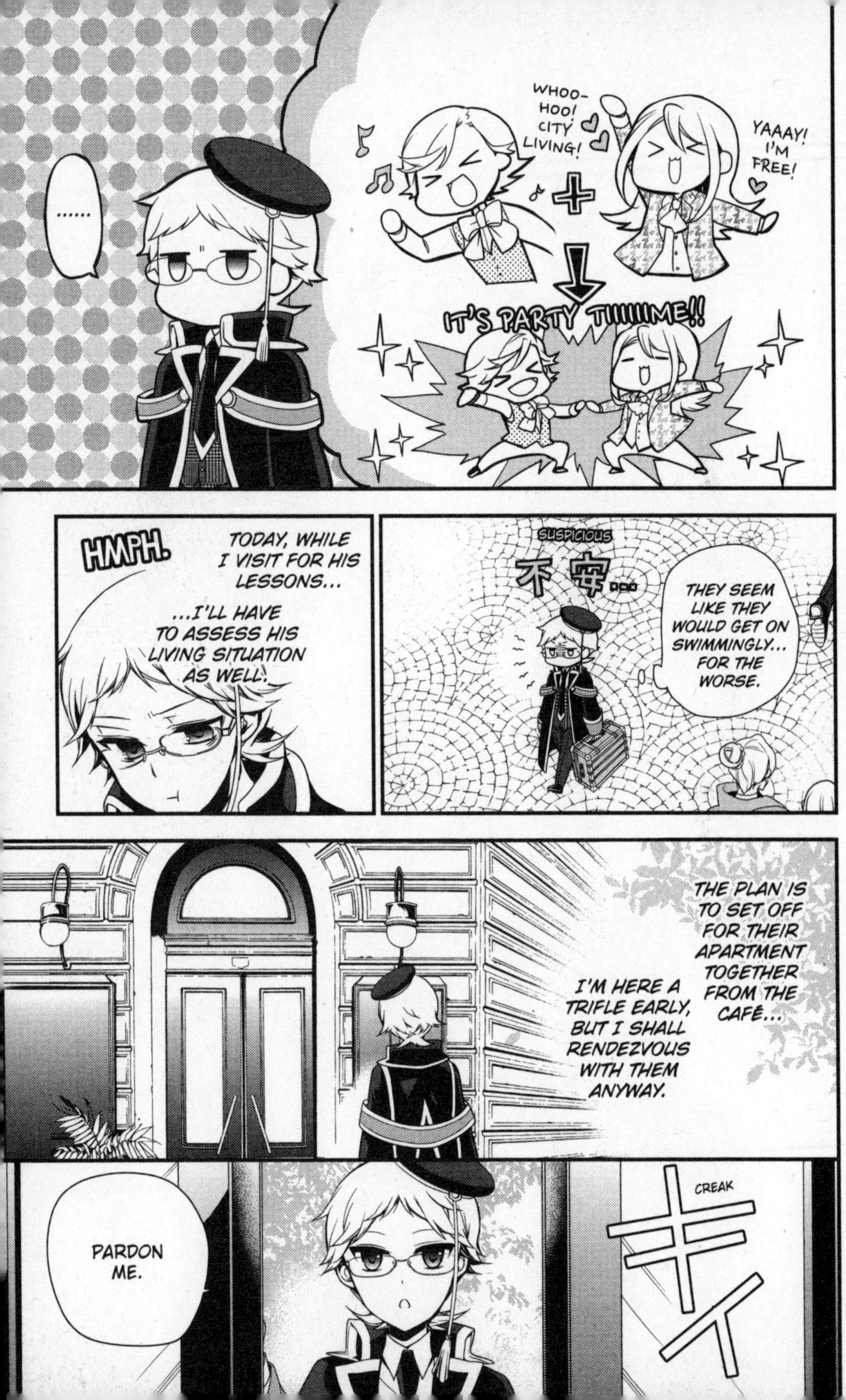
YAAAY! I'M FREE!
WHOO-HOO! CITY LIVING!
IT'S PARTY TIIIIIIME!!
......
SUSPICIOUS
不安...
THEY SEEM LIKE THEY WOULD GET ON SWIMMINGLY... FOR THE WORSE.
HMPH.
TODAY, WHILE I VISIT FOR HIS LESSONS...
...I'LL HAVE TO ASSESS HIS LIVING SITUATION AS WELL.
THE PLAN IS TO SET OFF FOR THEIR APARTMENT TOGETHER FROM THE CAFÉ...
I'M HERE A TRIFLE EARLY, BUT I SHALL RENDEZVOUS WITH THEM ANYWAY.
CREAK
PARDON ME.

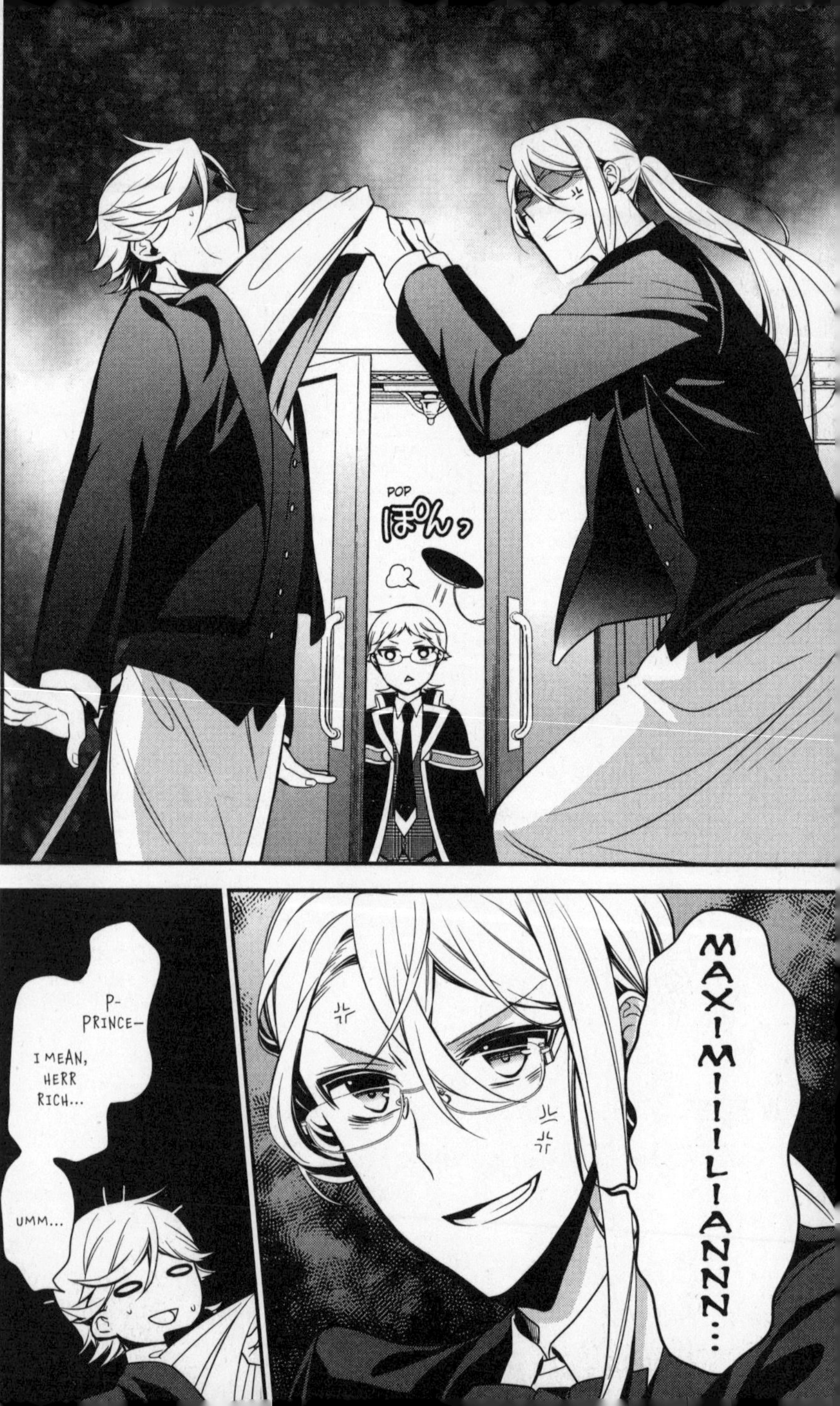
POP
ぽんっ
MAXIMIIIILIANNN...
P-PRINCE—
I MEAN, HERR RICH...
UMM...

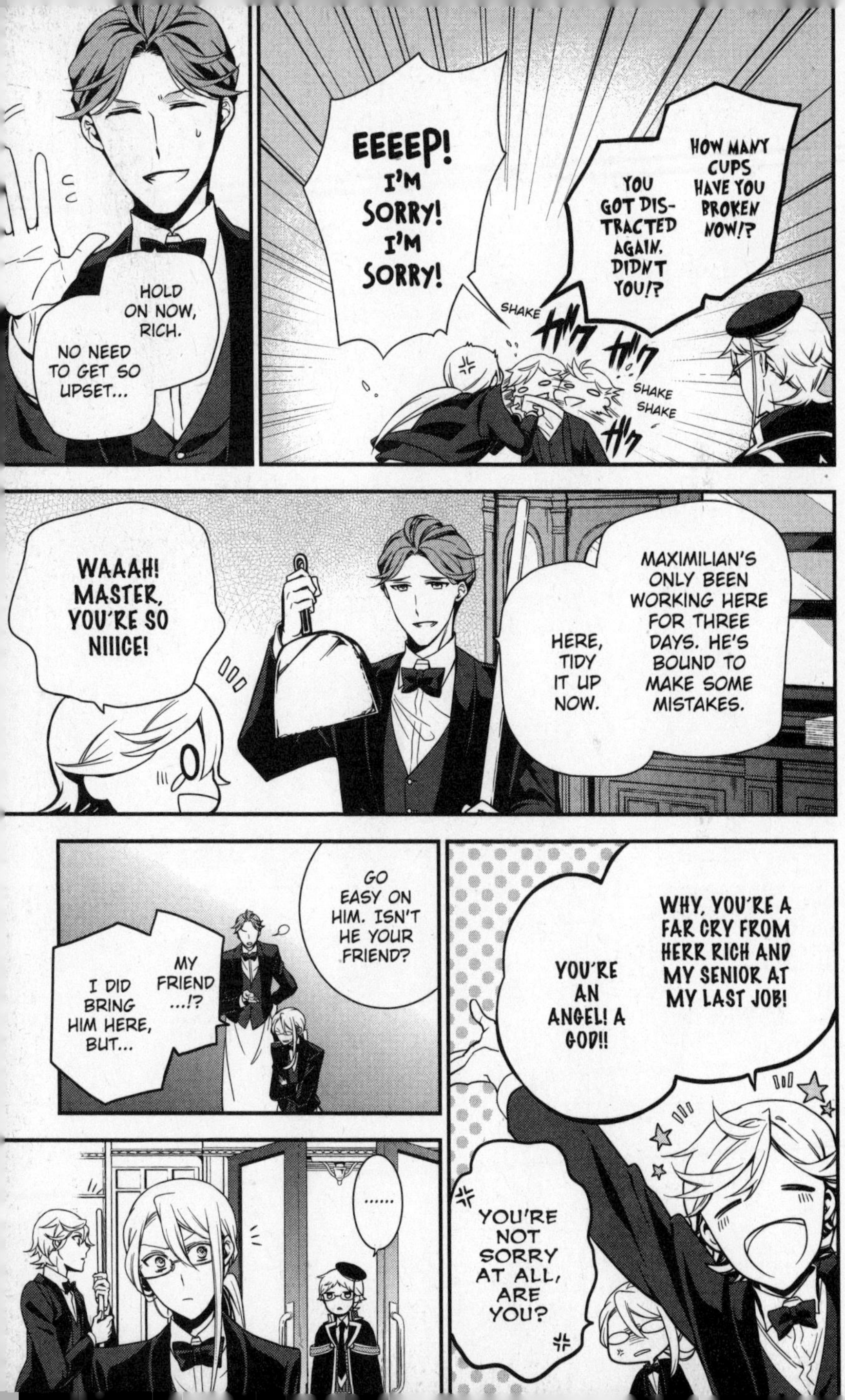
HOW MANY CUPS HAVE YOU BROKEN NOW!?
YOU GOT DIS-TRACTED AGAIN, DIDN'T YOU!?
EEEEP! I'M SORRY! I'M SORRY!
SHAKE
SHAKE SHAKE
HOLD ON NOW, RICH.
NO NEED TO GET SO UPSET...
MAXIMILIAN'S ONLY BEEN WORKING HERE FOR THREE DAYS. HE'S BOUND TO MAKE SOME MISTAKES.
HERE, TIDY IT UP NOW.
WAAAH! MASTER, YOU'RE SO NIIICE!
WHY, YOU'RE A FAR CRY FROM HERR RICH AND MY SENIOR AT MY LAST JOB!
YOU'RE AN ANGEL! A GOD!!
YOU'RE NOT SORRY AT ALL, ARE YOU?
GO EASY ON HIM. ISN'T HE YOUR FRIEND?
MY FRIEND ...!?
I DID BRING HIM HERE, BUT...
......

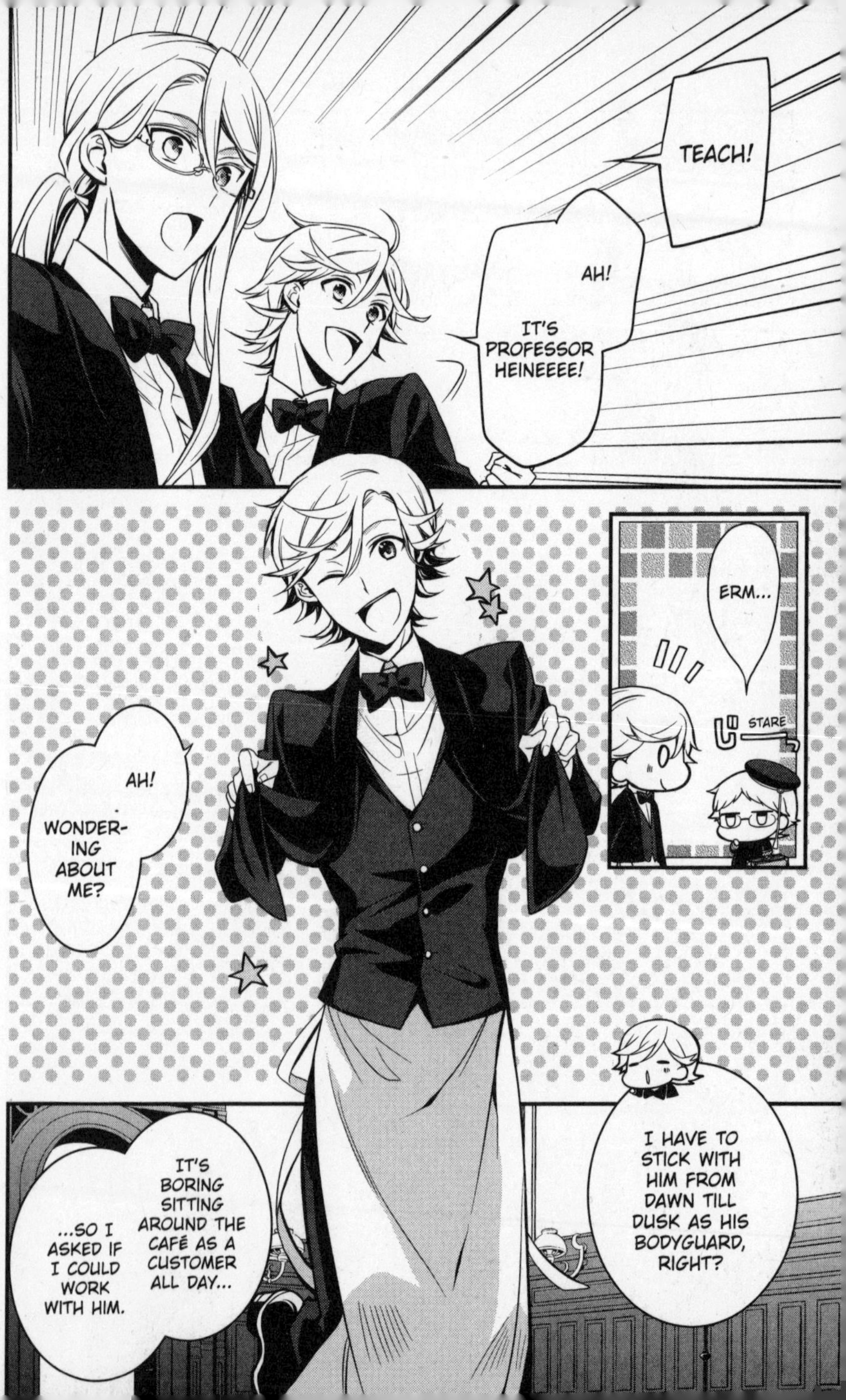

TEACH!
AH! IT'S PROFESSOR HEINEEEE!
ERM...
STARE
AH! WONDERING ABOUT ME?
I HAVE TO STICK WITH HIM FROM DAWN TILL DUSK AS HIS BODYGUARD, RIGHT?
IT'S BORING SITTING AROUND THE CAFÉ AS A CUSTOMER ALL DAY...
...SO I ASKED IF I COULD WORK WITH HIM.

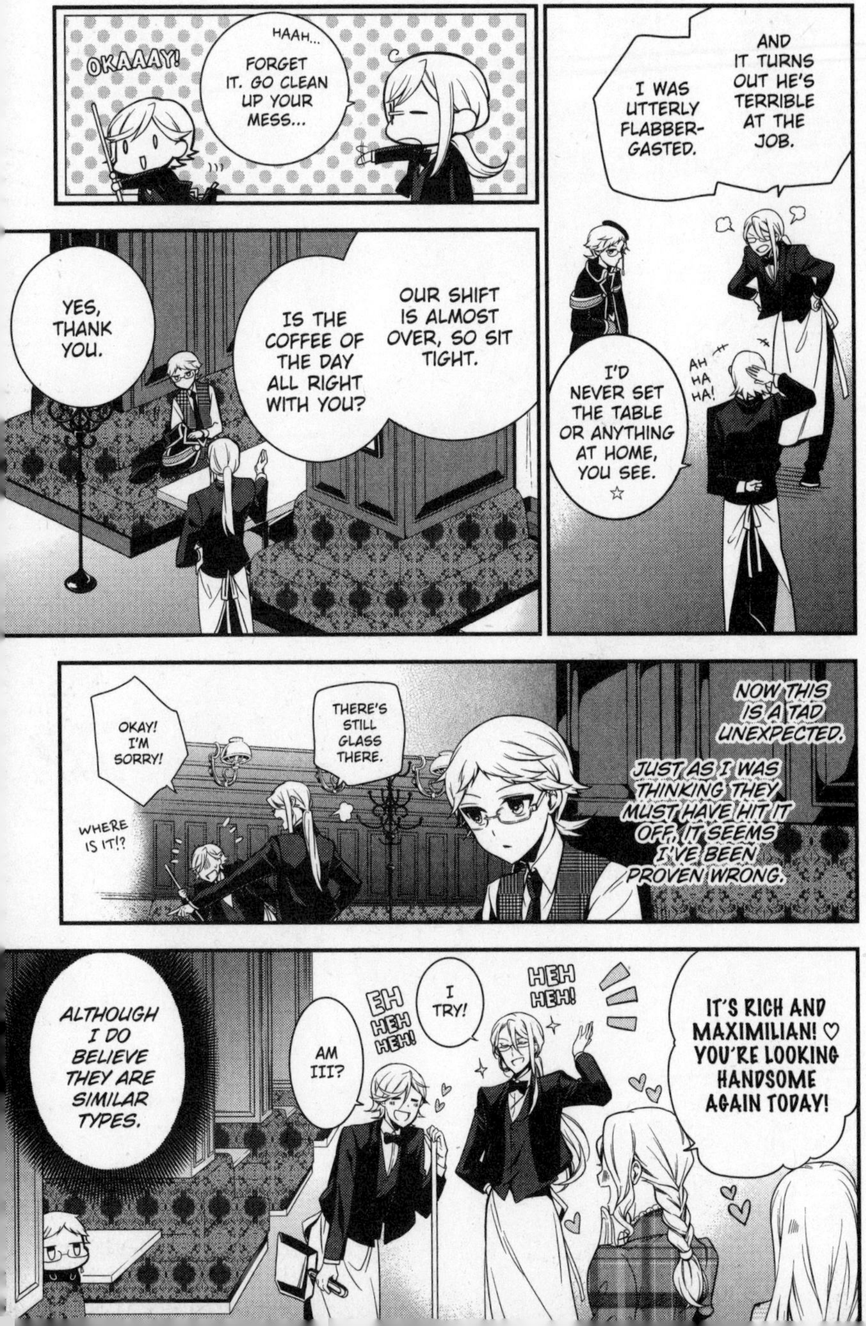
I WAS UTTERLY FLABBERGASTED.
AND IT TURNS OUT HE'S TERRIBLE AT THE JOB.
AH HA HA!
I'D NEVER SET THE TABLE OR ANYTHING AT HOME, YOU SEE. ☆
HAAH... FORGET IT. GO CLEAN UP YOUR MESS...
OKAAAY!
OUR SHIFT IS ALMOST OVER, SO SIT TIGHT.
IS THE COFFEE OF THE DAY ALL RIGHT WITH YOU?
YES, THANK YOU.
NOW THIS IS A TAD UNEXPECTED.
JUST AS I WAS THINKING THEY MUST HAVE HIT IT OFF, IT SEEMS I'VE BEEN PROVEN WRONG.
THERE'S STILL GLASS THERE.
OKAY! I'M SORRY!
WHERE IS IT!?
IT'S RICH AND MAXIMILIAN! ♡ YOU'RE LOOKING HANDSOME AGAIN TODAY!
HEH HEH!
I TRY!
EH HEH HEH!
AM III?
ALTHOUGH I DO BELIEVE THEY ARE SIMILAR TYPES.

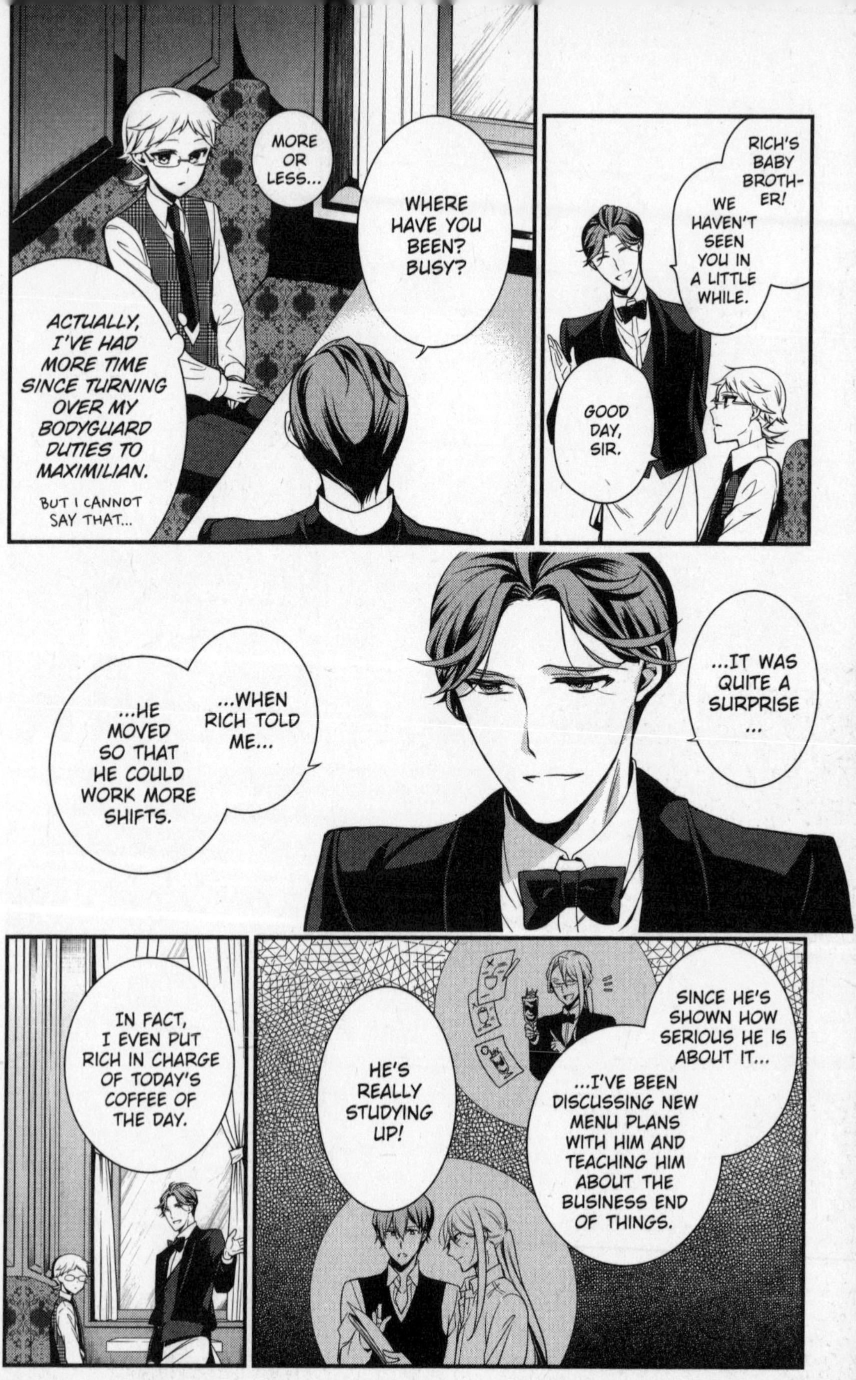
RICH'S BABY BROTHER! WE HAVEN'T SEEN YOU IN A LITTLE WHILE.
GOOD DAY, SIR.
WHERE HAVE YOU BEEN? BUSY?
MORE OR LESS...
ACTUALLY, I'VE HAD MORE TIME SINCE TURNING OVER MY BODYGUARD DUTIES TO MAXIMILIAN.
BUT I CANNOT SAY THAT...
...IT WAS QUITE A SURPRISE...
...WHEN RICH TOLD ME...
...HE MOVED SO THAT HE COULD WORK MORE SHIFTS.
SINCE HE'S SHOWN HOW SERIOUS HE IS ABOUT IT...
...I'VE BEEN DISCUSSING NEW MENU PLANS WITH HIM AND TEACHING HIM ABOUT THE BUSINESS END OF THINGS.
HE'S REALLY STUDYING UP!
IN FACT, I EVEN PUT RICH IN CHARGE OF TODAY'S COFFEE OF THE DAY.

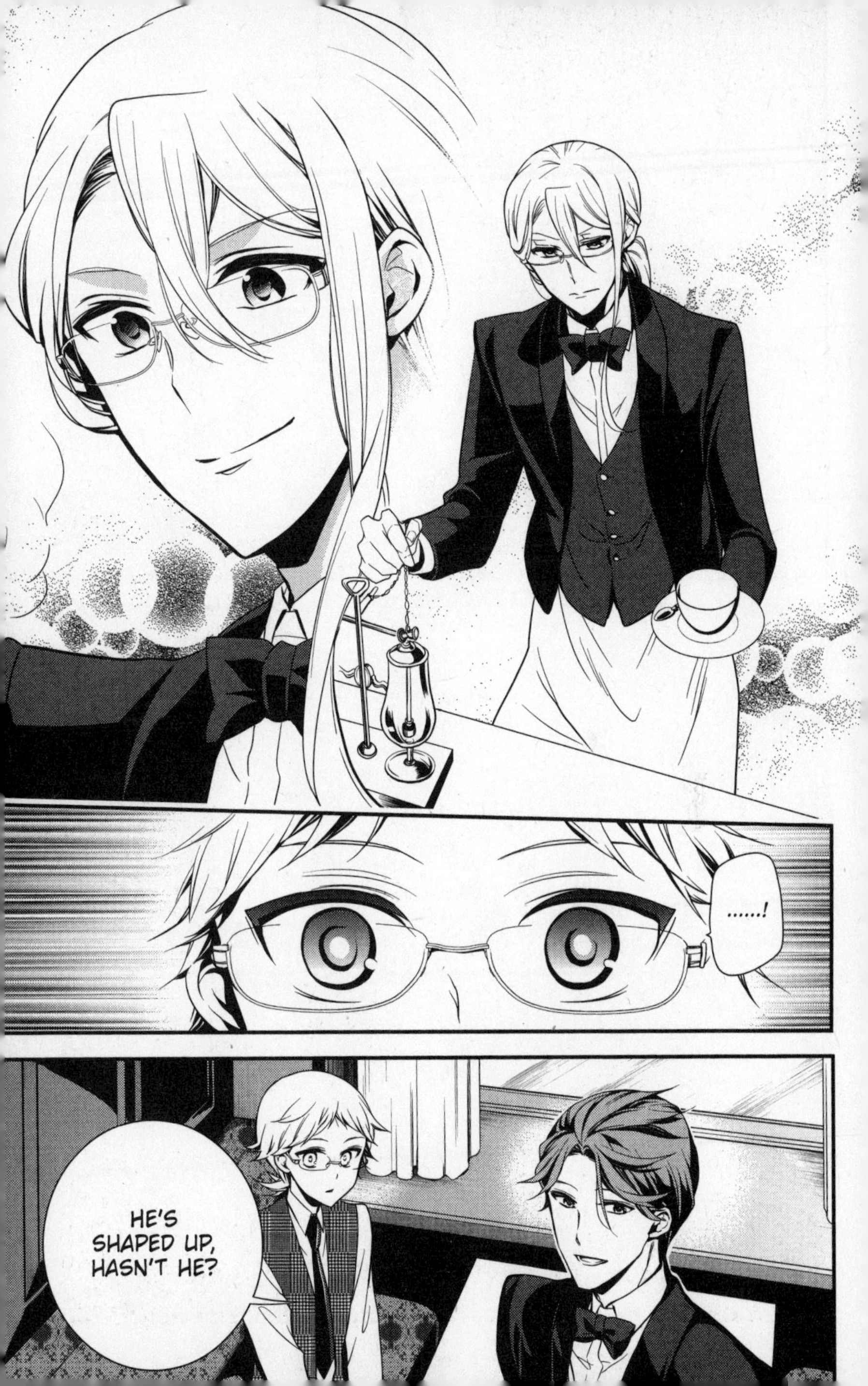
......!
HE'S SHAPED UP, HASN'T HE?

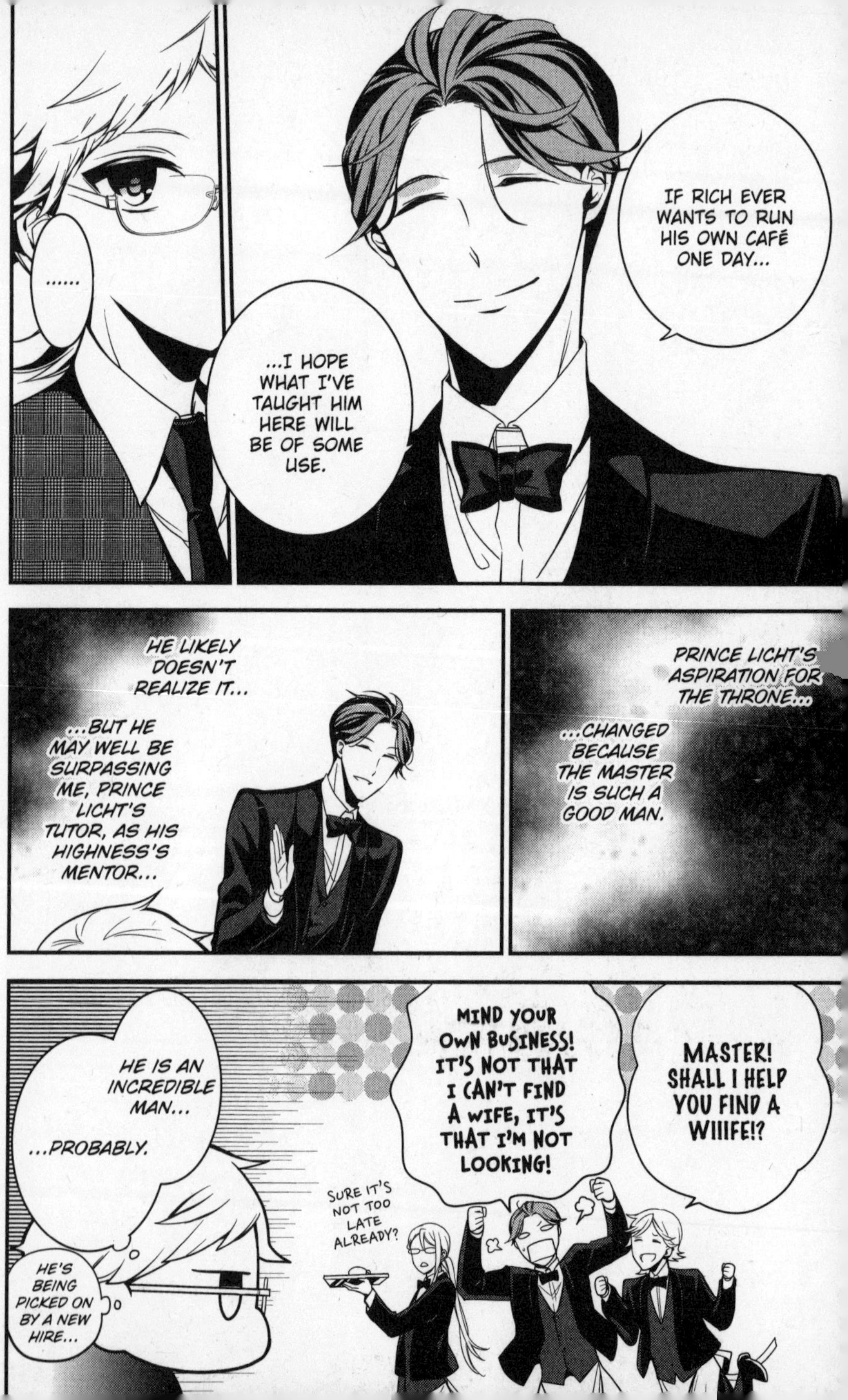
IF RICH EVER WANTS TO RUN HIS OWN CAFÉ ONE DAY...
...I HOPE WHAT I'VE TAUGHT HIM HERE WILL BE OF SOME USE.
......
PRINCE LICHT'S ASPIRATION FOR THE THRONE...
...CHANGED BECAUSE THE MASTER IS SUCH A GOOD MAN.
HE LIKELY DOESN'T REALIZE IT...
...BUT HE MAY WELL BE SURPASSING ME, PRINCE LICHT'S TUTOR, AS HIS HIGHNESS'S MENTOR...
MASTER! SHALL I HELP YOU FIND A WIIIFE!?
MIND YOUR OWN BUSINESS! IT'S NOT THAT I CAN'T FIND A WIFE, IT'S THAT I'M NOT LOOKING!
SURE IT'S NOT TOO LATE ALREADY?
HE IS AN INCREDIBLE MAN...
...PROBABLY.
HE'S BEING PICKED ON BY A NEW HIRE...

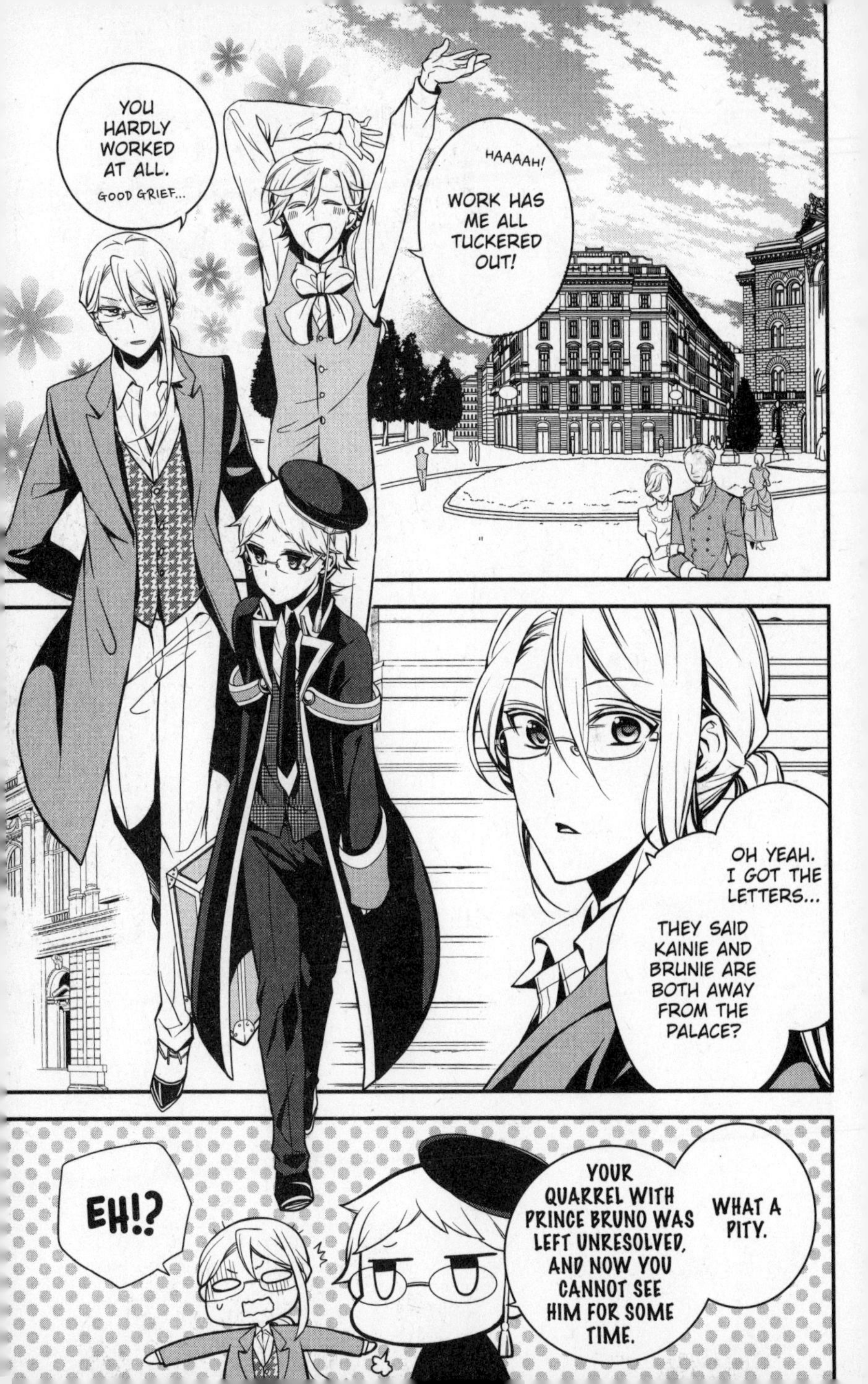
HAAAAH!
WORK HAS ME ALL TUCKERED OUT!
YOU HARDLY WORKED AT ALL.
GOOD GRIEF...
OH YEAH. I GOT THE LETTERS...
THEY SAID KAINIE AND BRUNIE ARE BOTH AWAY FROM THE PALACE?
WHAT A PITY.
YOUR QUARREL WITH PRINCE BRUNO WAS LEFT UNRESOLVED, AND NOW YOU CANNOT SEE HIM FOR SOME TIME.
EH!?

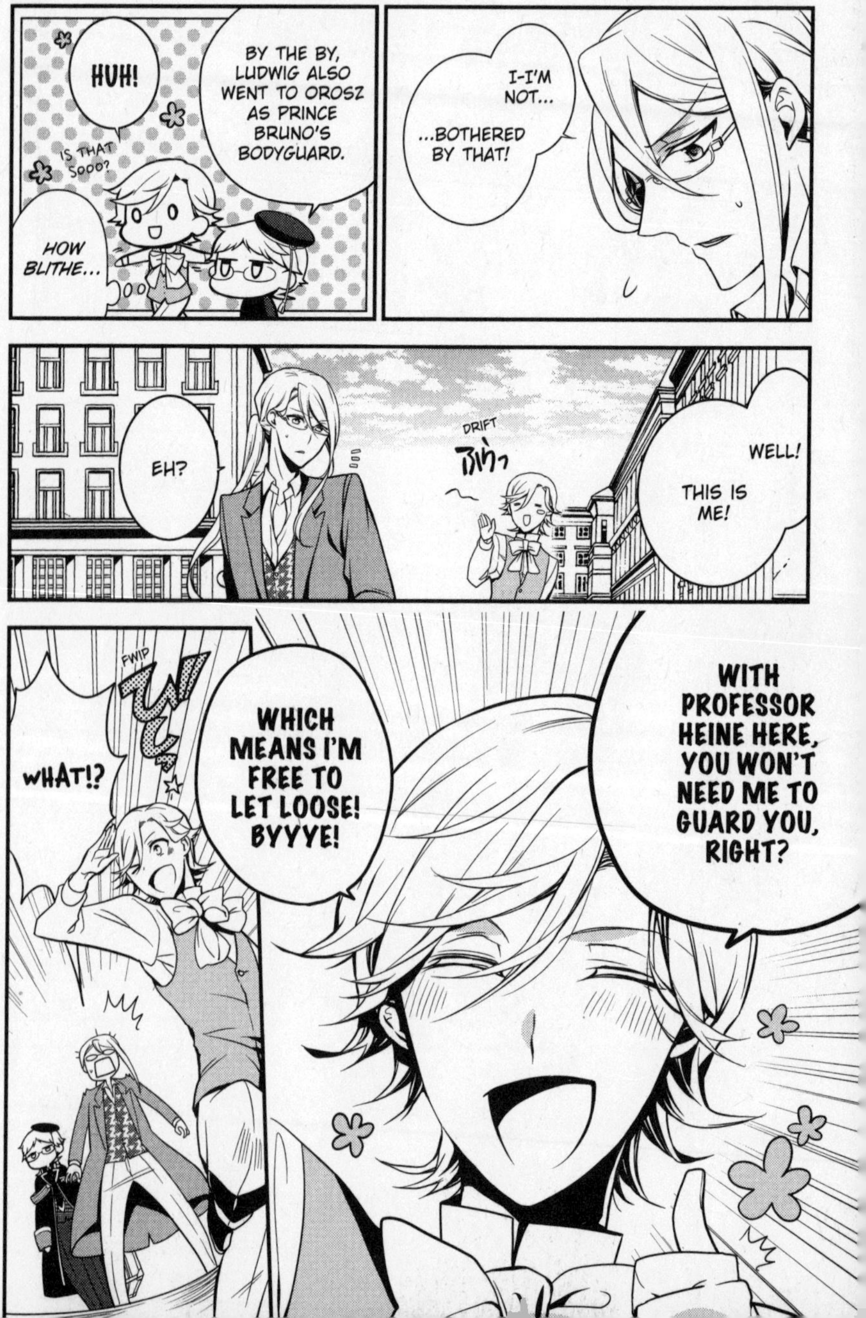
I-I'M NOT...
...BOTHERED BY THAT!
BY THE BY, LUDWIG ALSO WENT TO OROSZ AS PRINCE BRUNO'S BODYGUARD.
HUH!
IS THAT SOOO?
HOW BLITHE...
WELL! THIS IS ME!
DRIFT
EH?
WITH PROFESSOR HEINE HERE, YOU WON'T NEED ME TO GUARD YOU, RIGHT?
WHICH MEANS I'M FREE TO LET LOOSE! BYYYE!
FWIP
WHAT!?

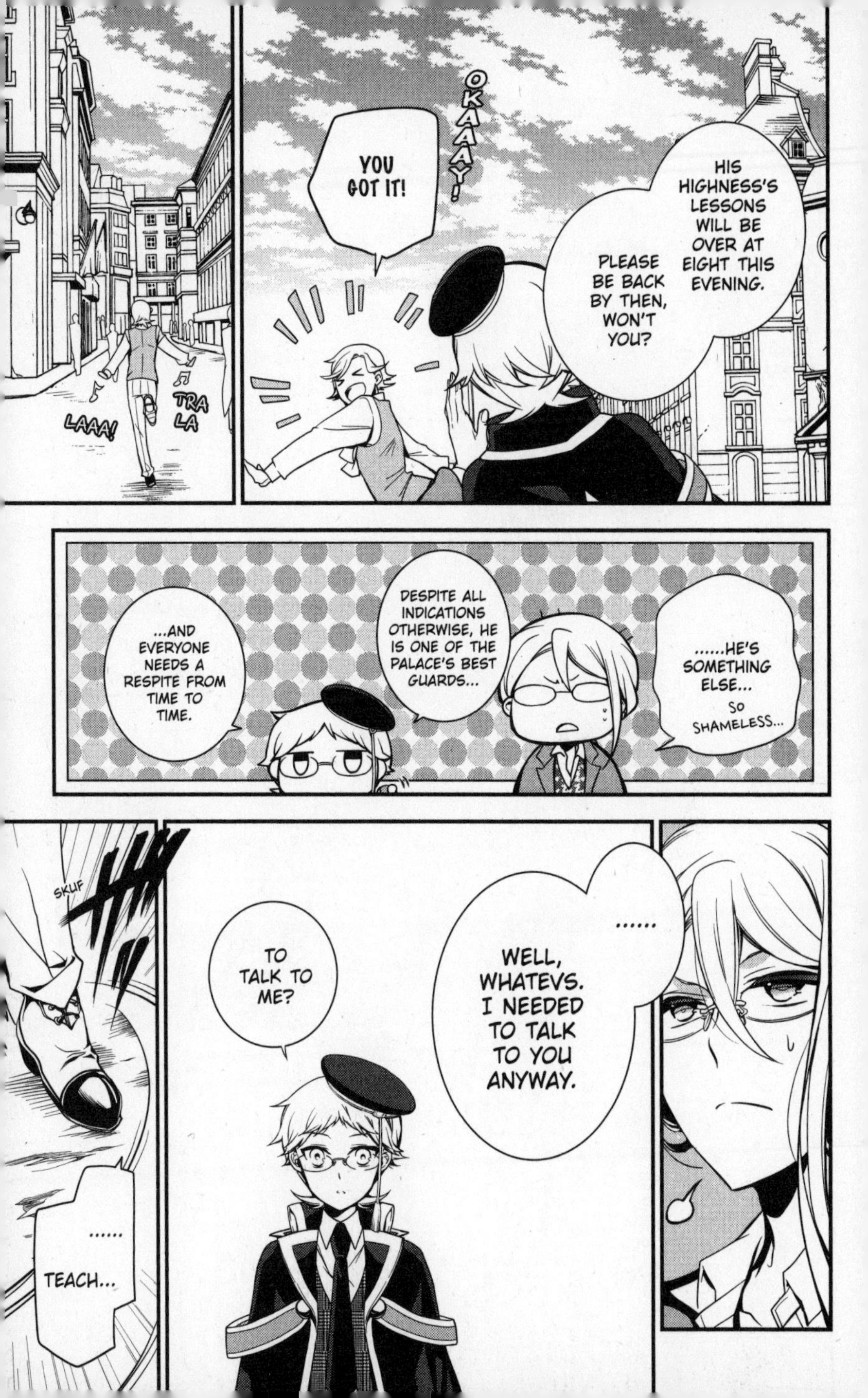
HIS HIGHNESS'S LESSONS WILL BE OVER AT EIGHT THIS EVENING.
PLEASE BE BACK BY THEN, WON'T YOU?
OKAAAY!
YOU GOT IT!
TRA LA
LAAA!
......HE'S SOMETHING ELSE...
SO SHAMELESS...
DESPITE ALL INDICATIONS OTHERWISE, HE IS ONE OF THE PALACE'S BEST GUARDS...
...AND EVERYONE NEEDS A RESPITE FROM TIME TO TIME.
......
WELL, WHATEVS. I NEEDED TO TALK TO YOU ANYWAY.
TO TALK TO ME?
SKUF
...... TEACH...

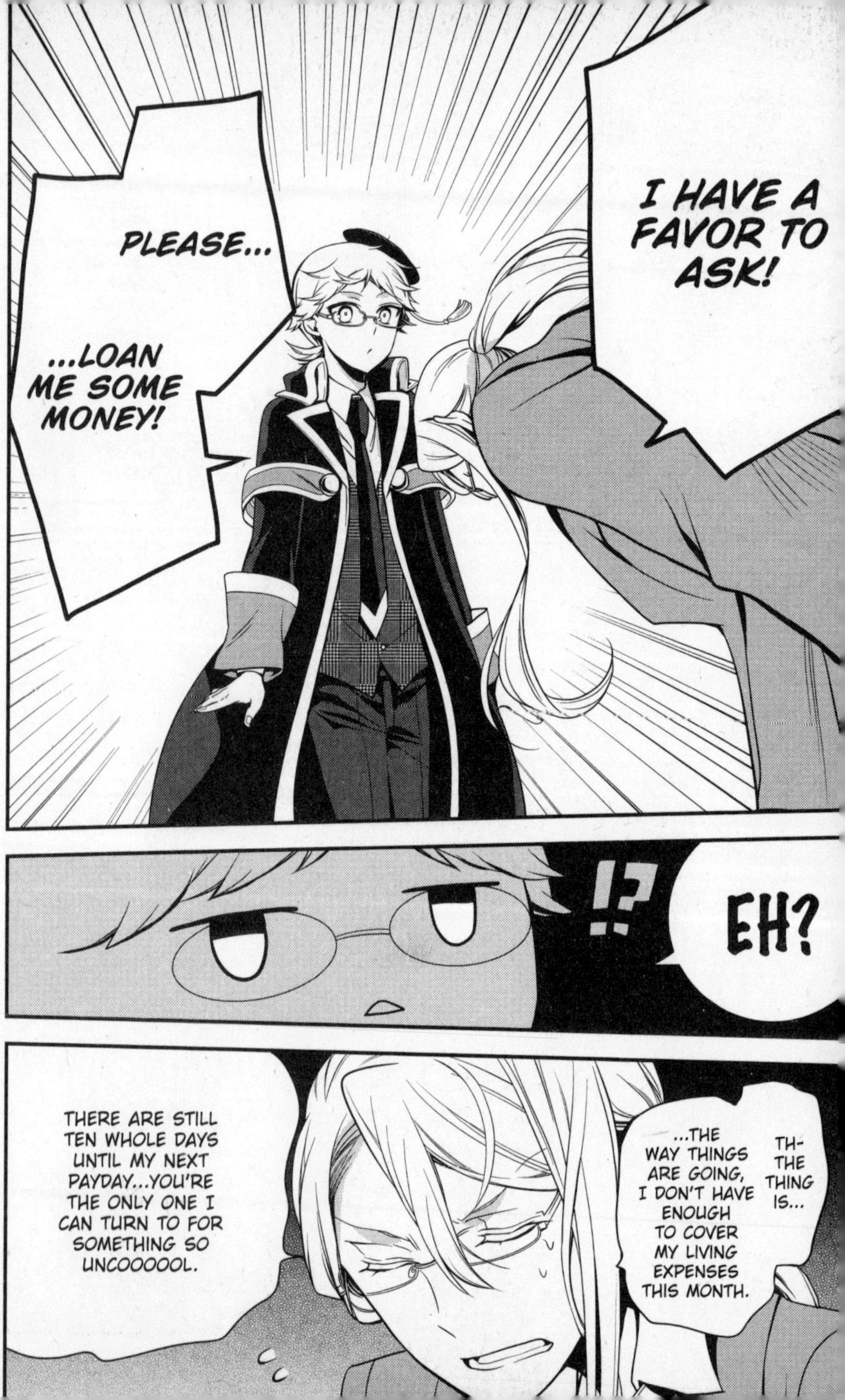
I HAVE A FAVOR TO ASK!
PLEASE...
...LOAN ME SOME MONEY!
EH?
!?
TH- THE THING IS...
...THE WAY THINGS ARE GOING, I DON'T HAVE ENOUGH TO COVER MY LIVING EXPENSES THIS MONTH.
THERE ARE STILL TEN WHOLE DAYS UNTIL MY NEXT PAYDAY...YOU'RE THE ONLY ONE I CAN TURN TO FOR SOMETHING SO UNCOOOOOL.

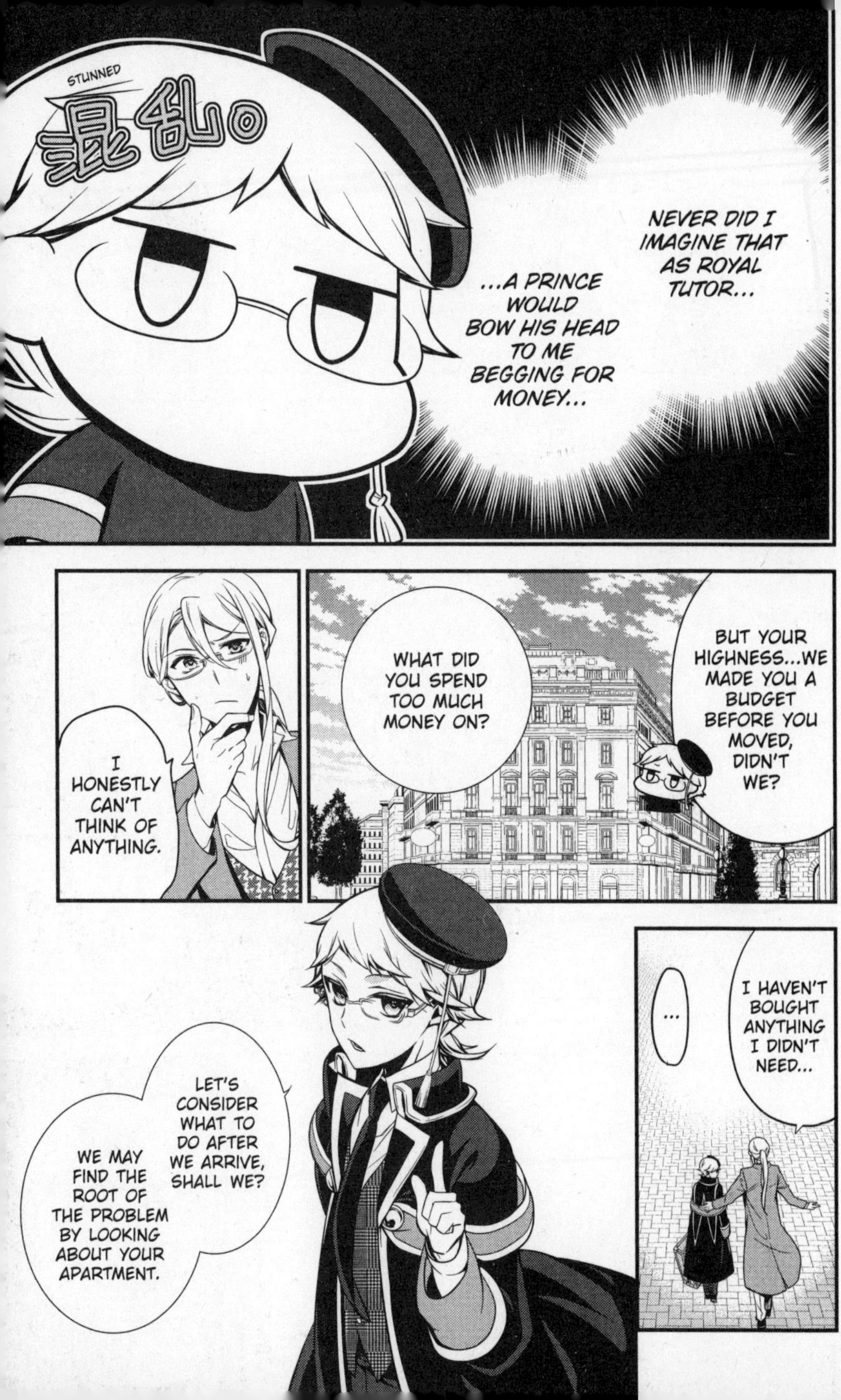
STUNNED
混乱。
NEVER DID I IMAGINE THAT AS ROYAL TUTOR...
...A PRINCE WOULD BOW HIS HEAD TO ME BEGGING FOR MONEY...
BUT YOUR HIGHNESS...WE MADE YOU A BUDGET BEFORE YOU MOVED, DIDN'T WE?
WHAT DID YOU SPEND TOO MUCH MONEY ON?
I HONESTLY CAN'T THINK OF ANYTHING.
I HAVEN'T BOUGHT ANYTHING I DIDN'T NEED...
...
LET'S CONSIDER WHAT TO DO AFTER WE ARRIVE, SHALL WE?
WE MAY FIND THE ROOT OF THE PROBLEM BY LOOKING ABOUT YOUR APARTMENT.

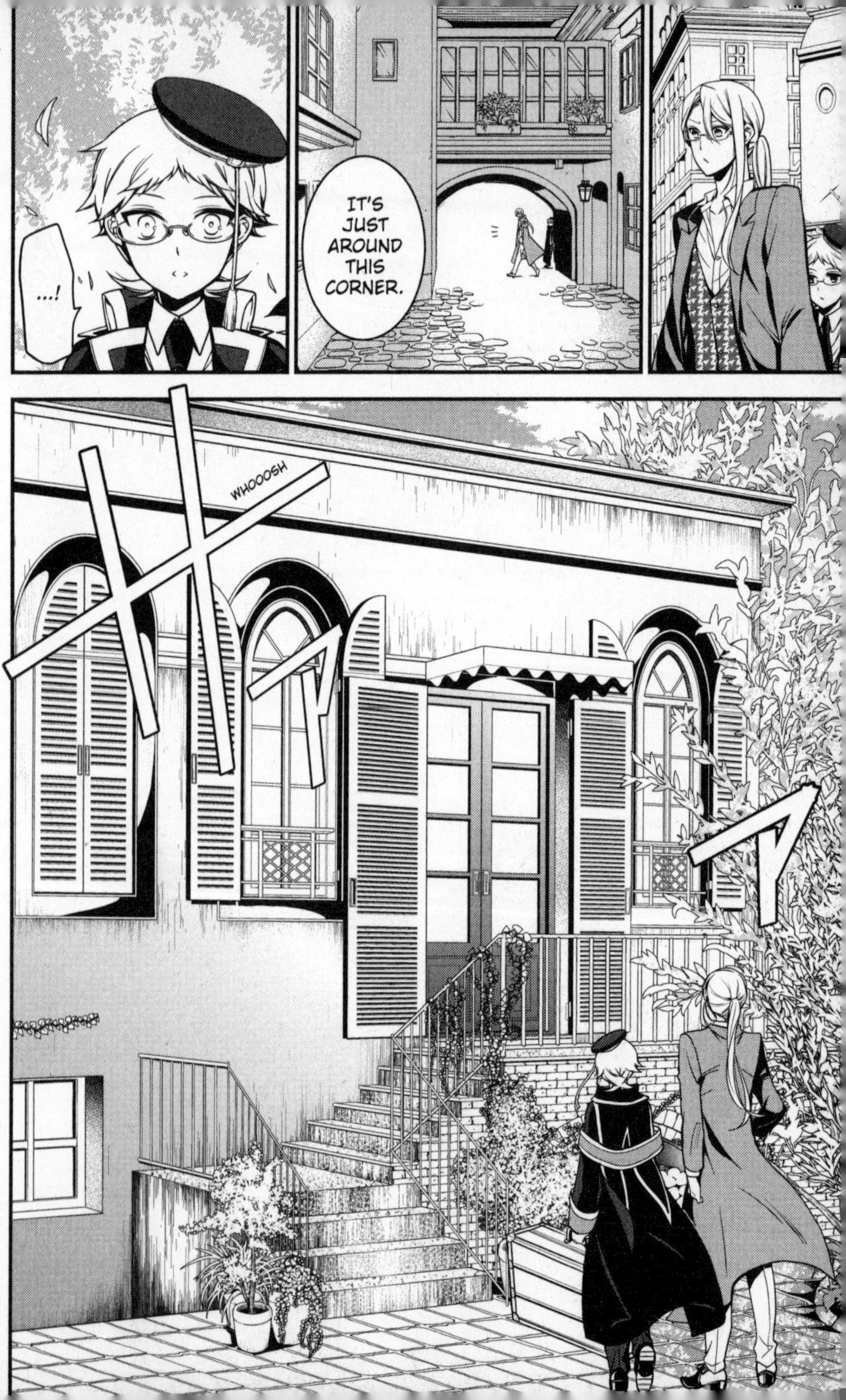
IT'S JUST AROUND THIS CORNER.
...!
WHOOOSH

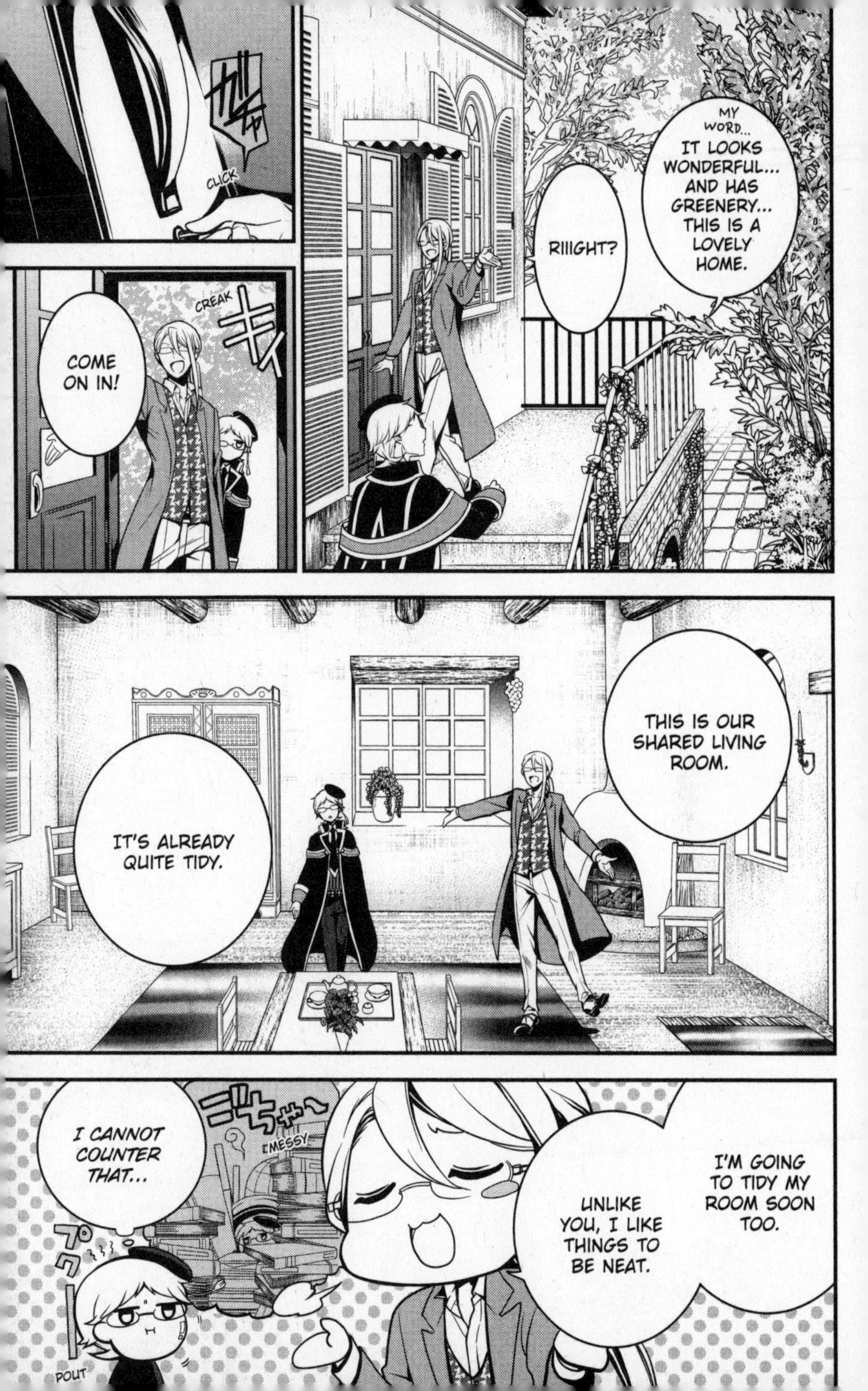
CLICK
CREAK
COME ON IN!
MY WORD... IT LOOKS WONDERFUL... AND HAS GREENERY... THIS IS A LOVELY HOME.
RIIIGHT?
THIS IS OUR SHARED LIVING ROOM.
IT'S ALREADY QUITE TIDY.
I'M GOING TO TIDY MY ROOM SOON TOO.
UNLIKE YOU, I LIKE THINGS TO BE NEAT.
MESSY
I CANNOT COUNTER THAT...
POUT

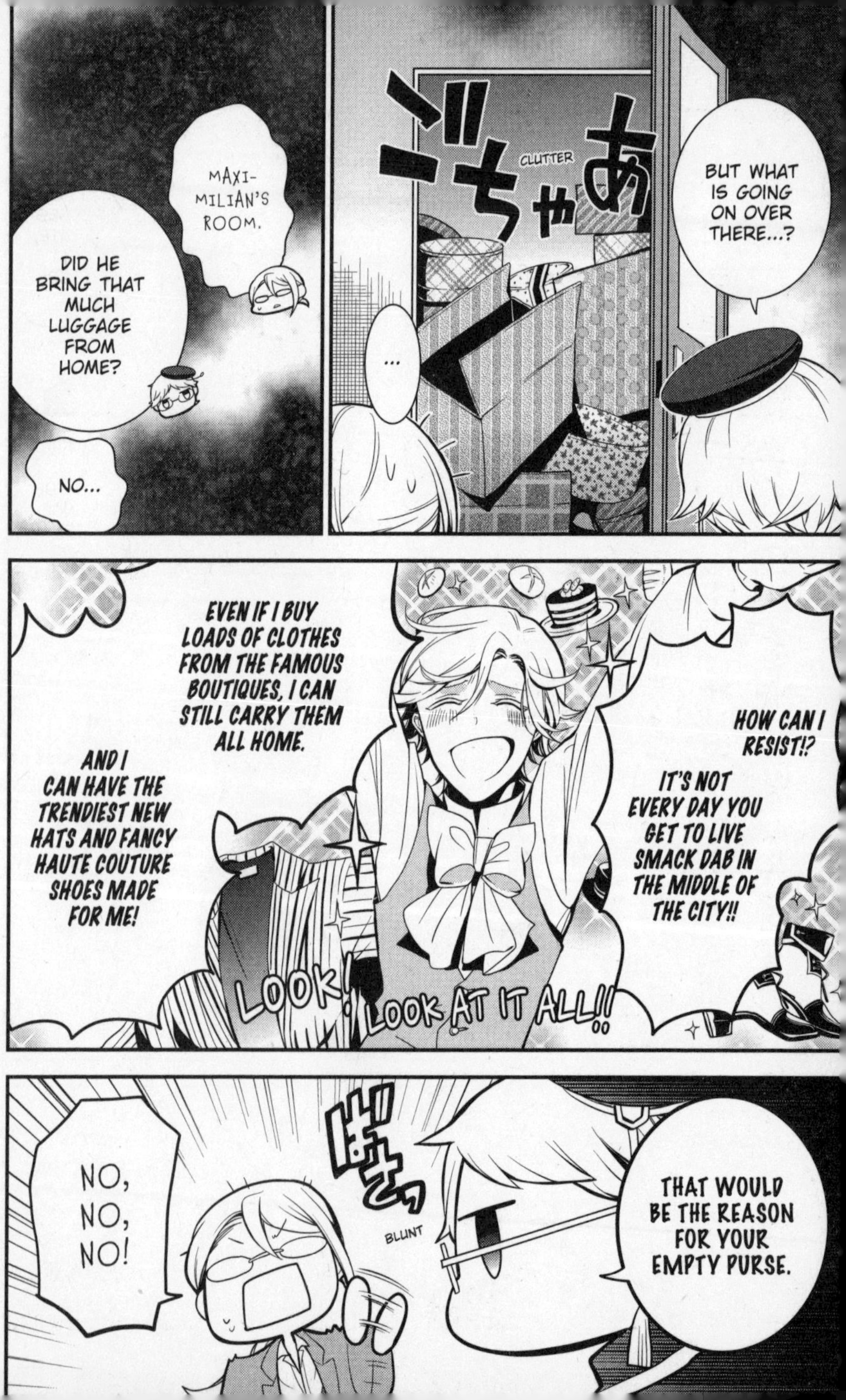
BUT WHAT IS GOING ON OVER THERE...?
ごちゃあ
CLUTTER
...
MAXI-MILIAN'S ROOM.
DID HE BRING THAT MUCH LUGGAGE FROM HOME?
NO...
HOW CAN I RESIST!?
IT'S NOT EVERY DAY YOU GET TO LIVE SMACK DAB IN THE MIDDLE OF THE CITY!!
EVEN IF I BUY LOADS OF CLOTHES FROM THE FAMOUS BOUTIQUES, I CAN STILL CARRY THEM ALL HOME.
AND I CAN HAVE THE TRENDIEST NEW HATS AND FANCY HAUTE COUTURE SHOES MADE FOR ME!
LOOK! LOOK AT IT ALL!!
THAT WOULD BE THE REASON FOR YOUR EMPTY PURSE.
ばさっ
BLUNT
NO, NO, NO!

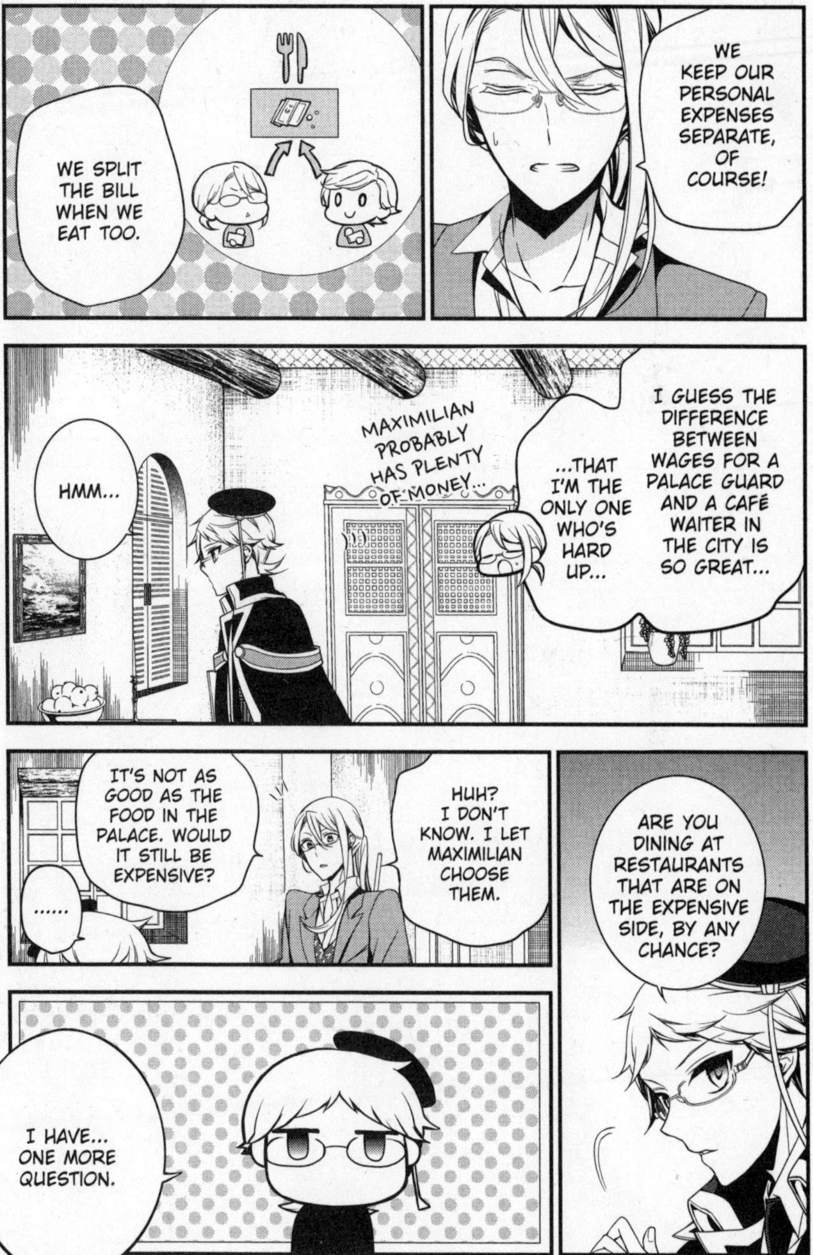
WE KEEP OUR PERSONAL EXPENSES SEPARATE, OF COURSE!
WE SPLIT THE BILL WHEN WE EAT TOO.
I GUESS THE DIFFERENCE BETWEEN WAGES FOR A PALACE GUARD AND A CAFÉ WAITER IN THE CITY IS SO GREAT...
...THAT I'M THE ONLY ONE WHO'S HARD UP...
MAXIMILIAN PROBABLY HAS PLENTY OF MONEY...
HMM...
ARE YOU DINING AT RESTAURANTS THAT ARE ON THE EXPENSIVE SIDE, BY ANY CHANCE?
HUH? I DON'T KNOW. I LET MAXIMILIAN CHOOSE THEM.
IT'S NOT AS GOOD AS THE FOOD IN THE PALACE. WOULD IT STILL BE EXPENSIVE?
......
I HAVE... ONE MORE QUESTION.

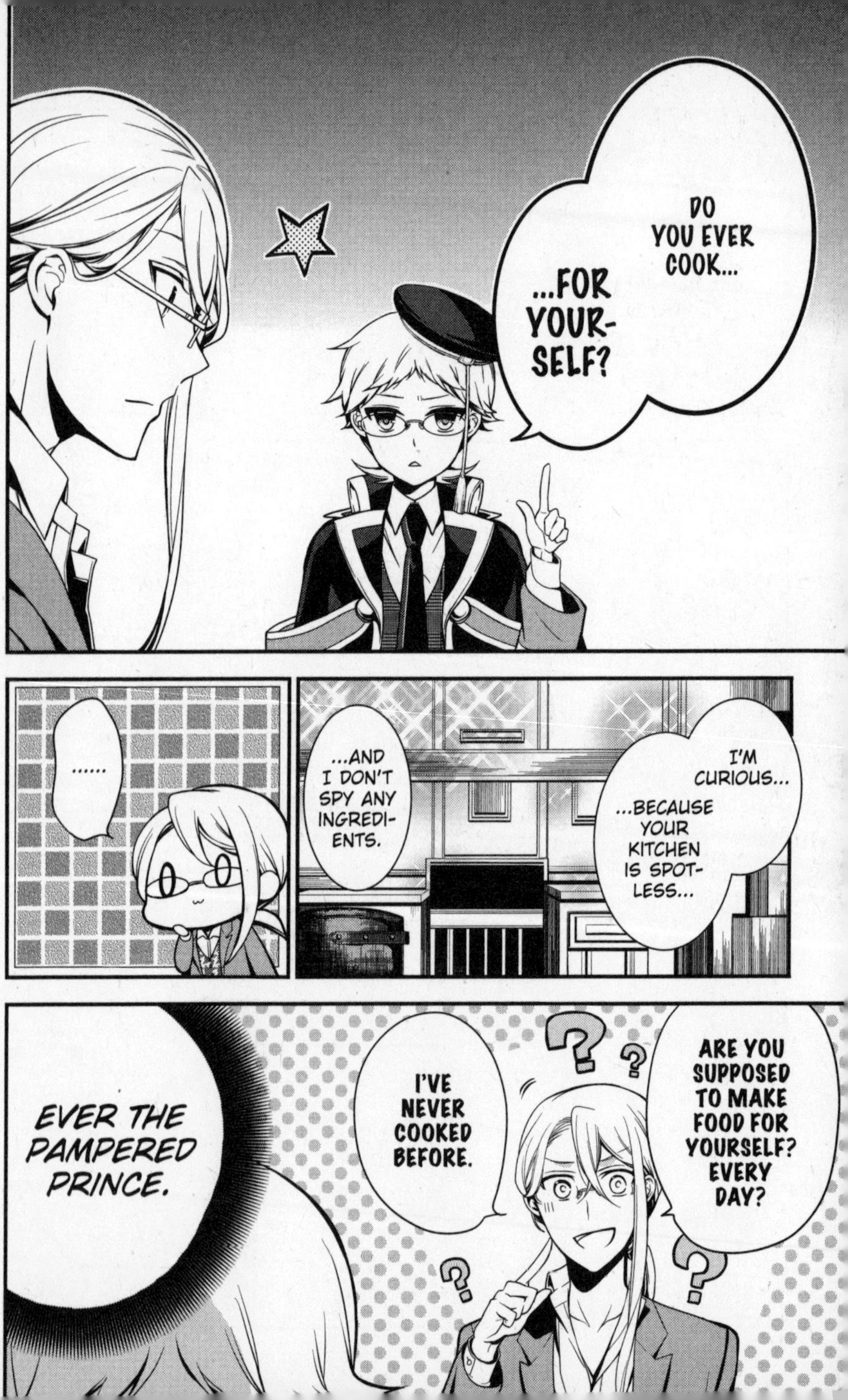
DO YOU EVER COOK... ...FOR YOURSELF?
I'M CURIOUS...
...BECAUSE YOUR KITCHEN IS SPOTLESS...
...AND I DON'T SPY ANY INGREDIENTS.
......
ARE YOU SUPPOSED TO MAKE FOOD FOR YOURSELF? EVERY DAY?
I'VE NEVER COOKED BEFORE.
EVER THE PAMPERED PRINCE.

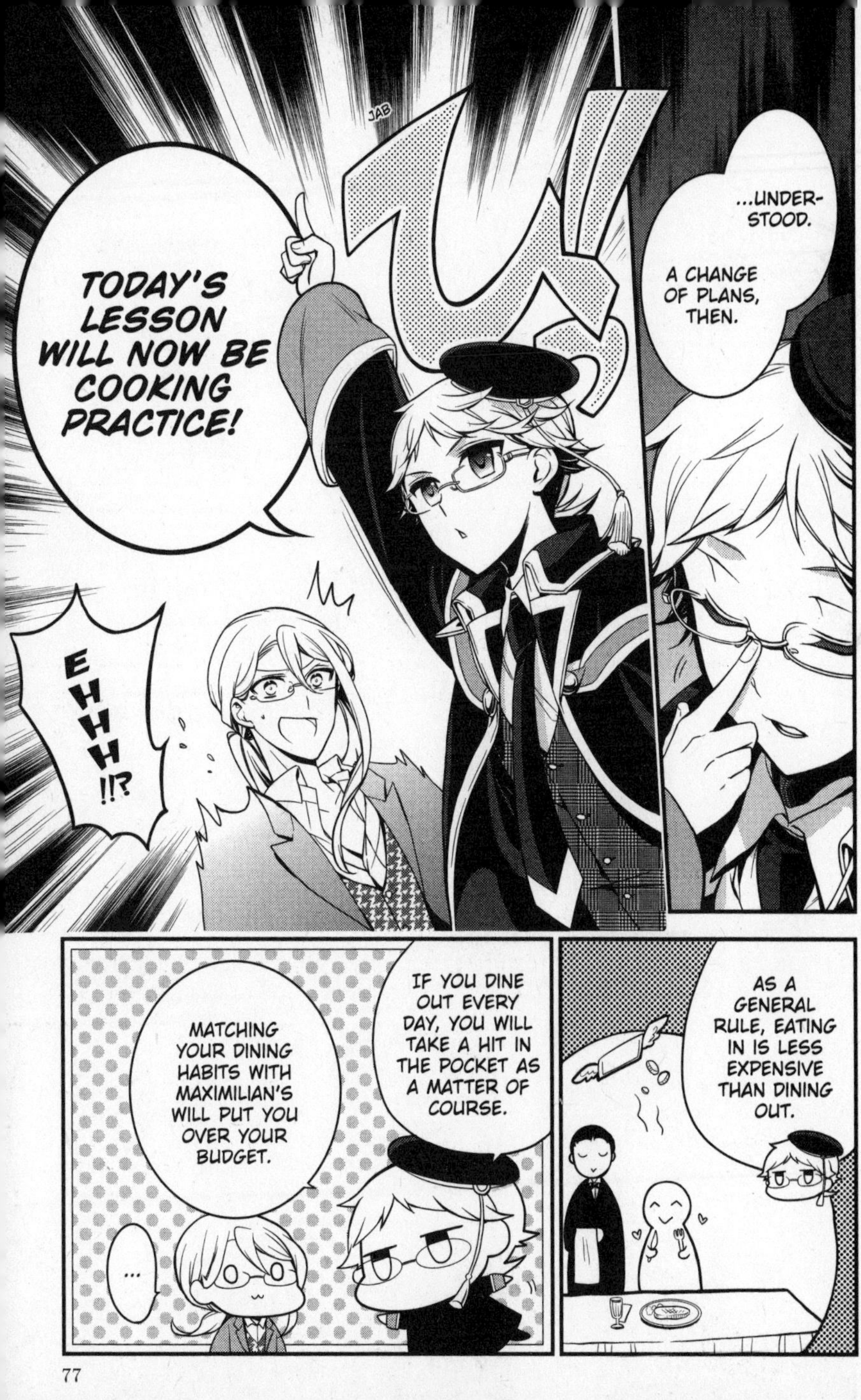
...UNDER-STOOD.
A CHANGE OF PLANS, THEN.
JAB
TODAY'S LESSON WILL NOW BE COOKING PRACTICE!
EHHH!!?
AS A GENERAL RULE, EATING IN IS LESS EXPENSIVE THAN DINING OUT.
IF YOU DINE OUT EVERY DAY, YOU WILL TAKE A HIT IN THE POCKET AS A MATTER OF COURSE.
MATCHING YOUR DINING HABITS WITH MAXIMILIAN'S WILL PUT YOU OVER YOUR BUDGET.
...

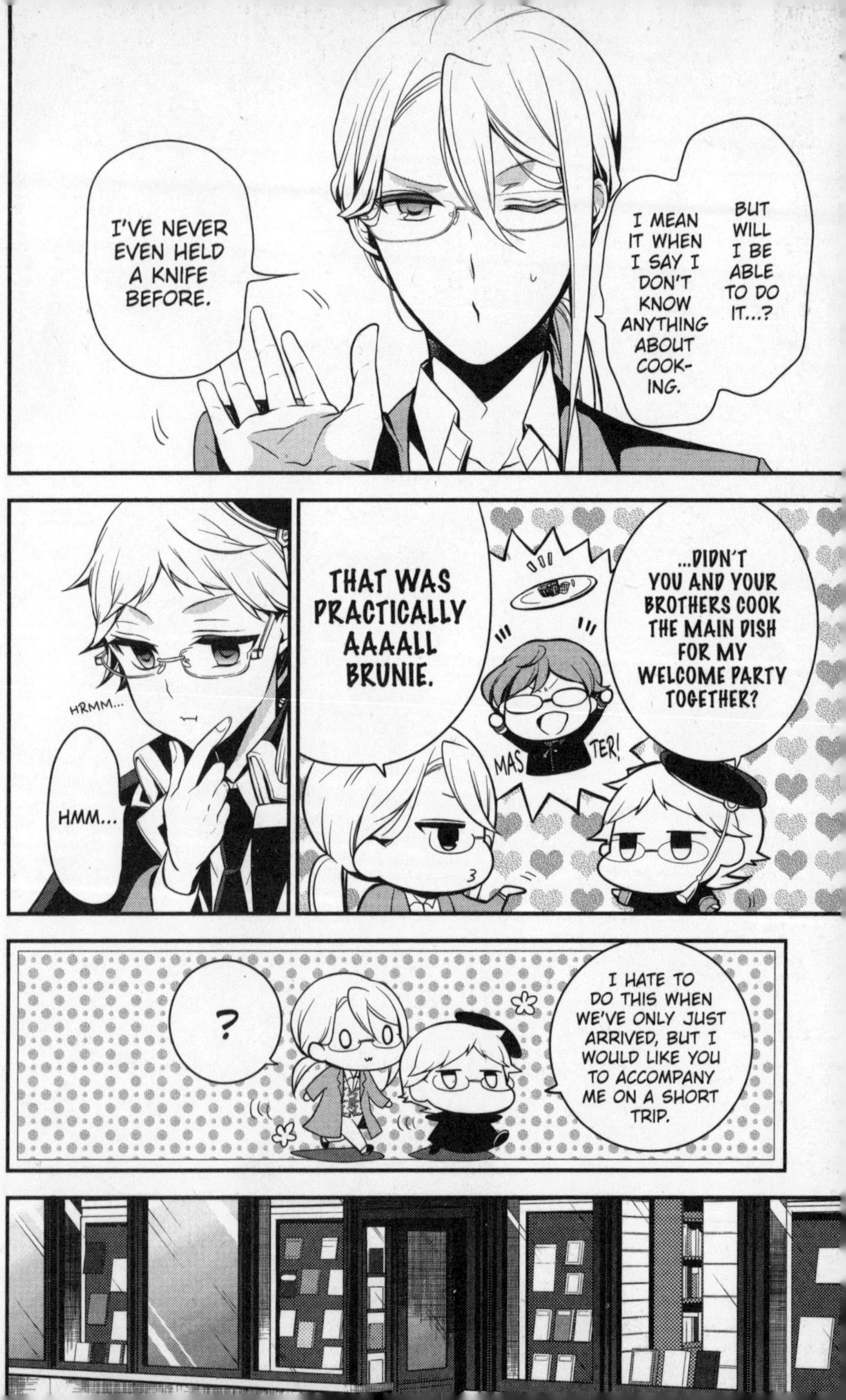
BUT WILL I BE ABLE TO DO IT...?
I MEAN IT WHEN I SAY I DON'T KNOW ANYTHING ABOUT COOK-ING.
I'VE NEVER EVEN HELD A KNIFE BEFORE.
...DIDN'T YOU AND YOUR BROTHERS COOK THE MAIN DISH FOR MY WELCOME PARTY TOGETHER?
MAS TER!
THAT WAS PRACTICALLY AAAALL BRUNIE.
HRMM...
HMM...
I HATE TO DO THIS WHEN WE'VE ONLY JUST ARRIVED, BUT I WOULD LIKE YOU TO ACCOMPANY ME ON A SHORT TRIP.
?

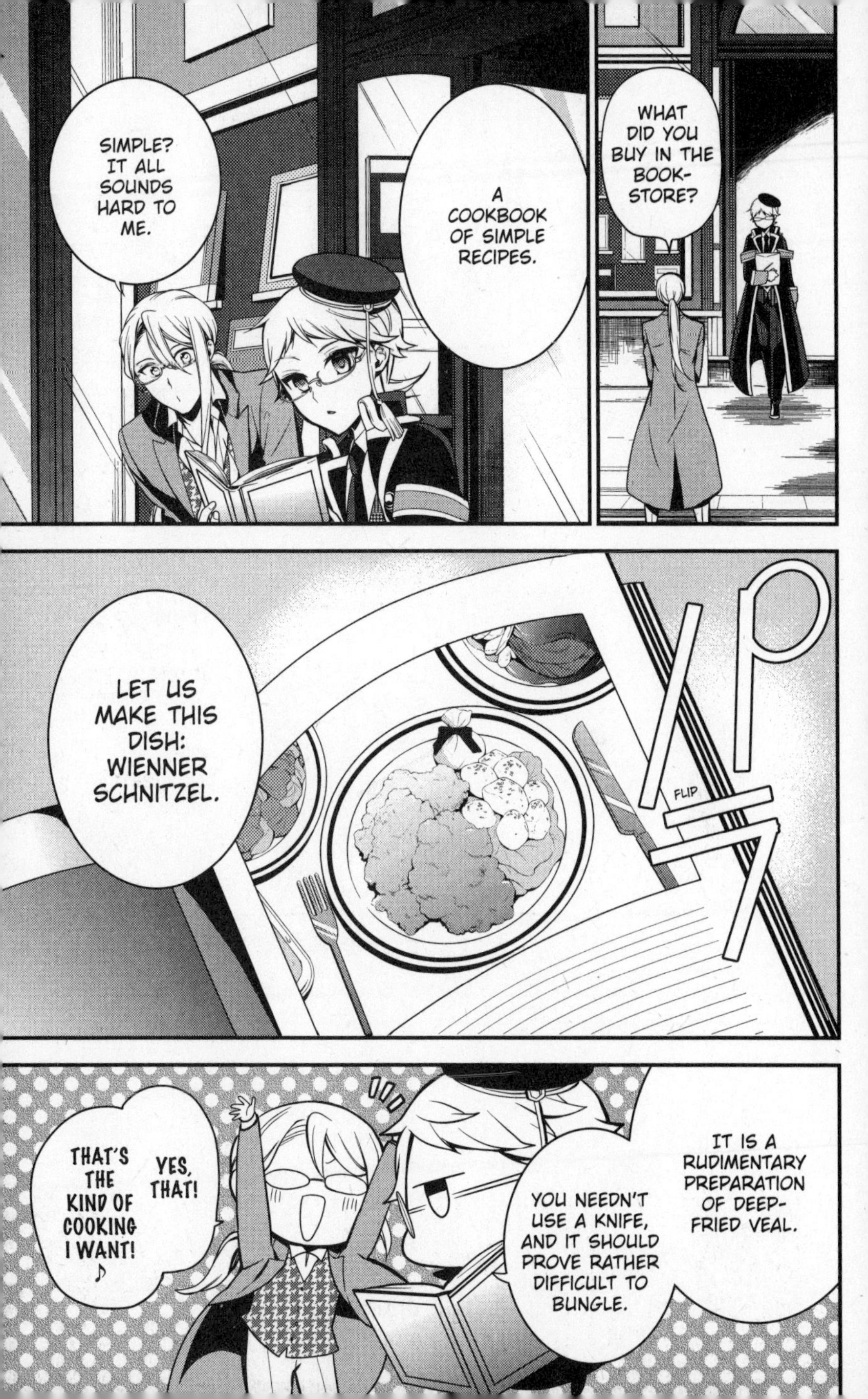
WHAT DID YOU BUY IN THE BOOK-STORE?
A COOKBOOK OF SIMPLE RECIPES.
SIMPLE? IT ALL SOUNDS HARD TO ME.
FLIP
LET US MAKE THIS DISH: WIENNER SCHNITZEL.
IT IS A RUDIMENTARY PREPARATION OF DEEP-FRIED VEAL.
YOU NEEDN'T USE A KNIFE, AND IT SHOULD PROVE RATHER DIFFICULT TO BUNGLE.
YES, THAT!
THAT'S THE KIND OF COOKING I WANT! ♪

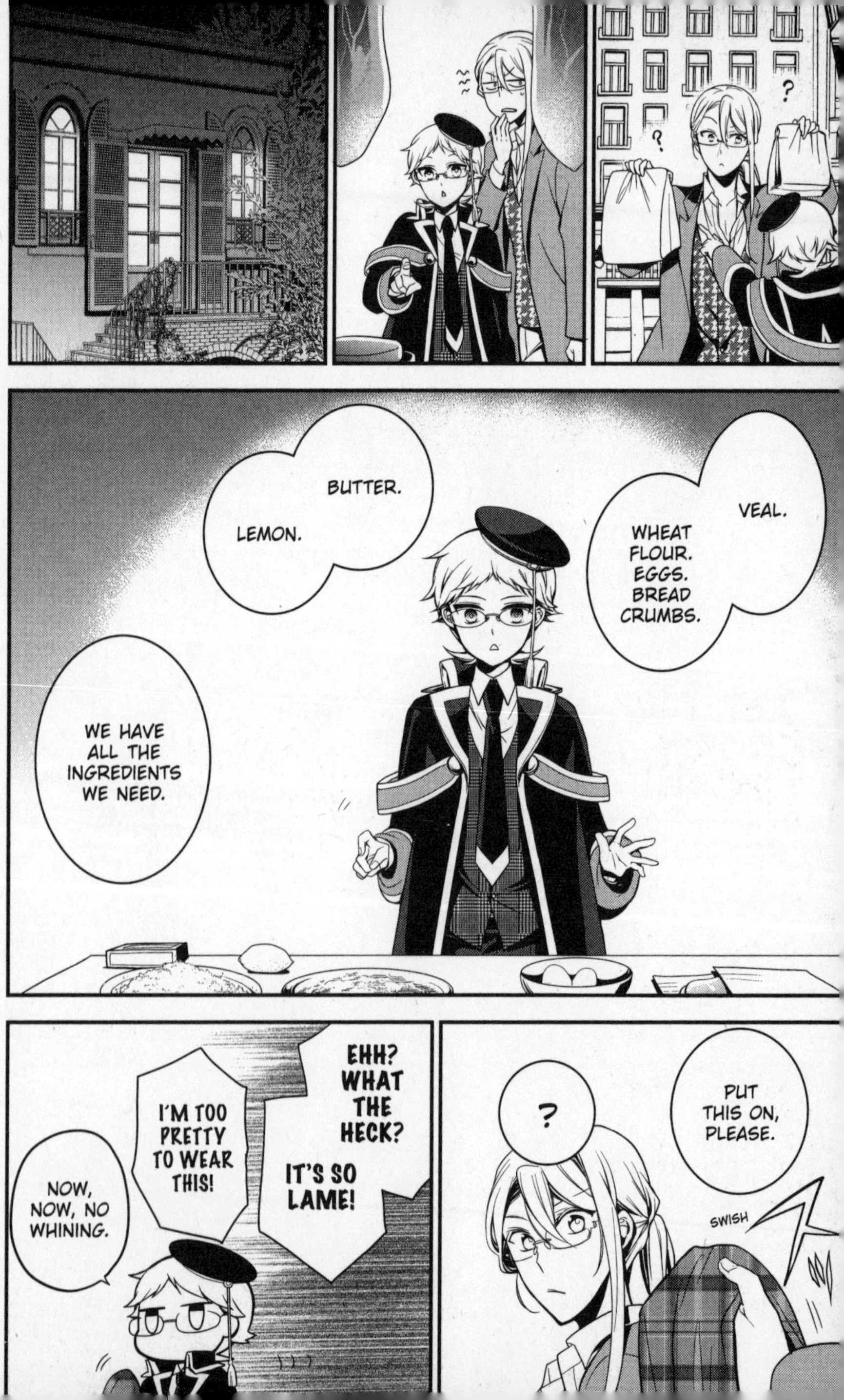
?
?
VEAL.
WHEAT FLOUR. EGGS. BREAD CRUMBS.
BUTTER.
LEMON.
WE HAVE ALL THE INGREDIENTS WE NEED.
PUT THIS ON, PLEASE.
?
SWISH
EHH? WHAT THE HECK?
IT'S SO LAME!
I'M TOO PRETTY TO WEAR THIS!
NOW, NOW, NO WHINING.

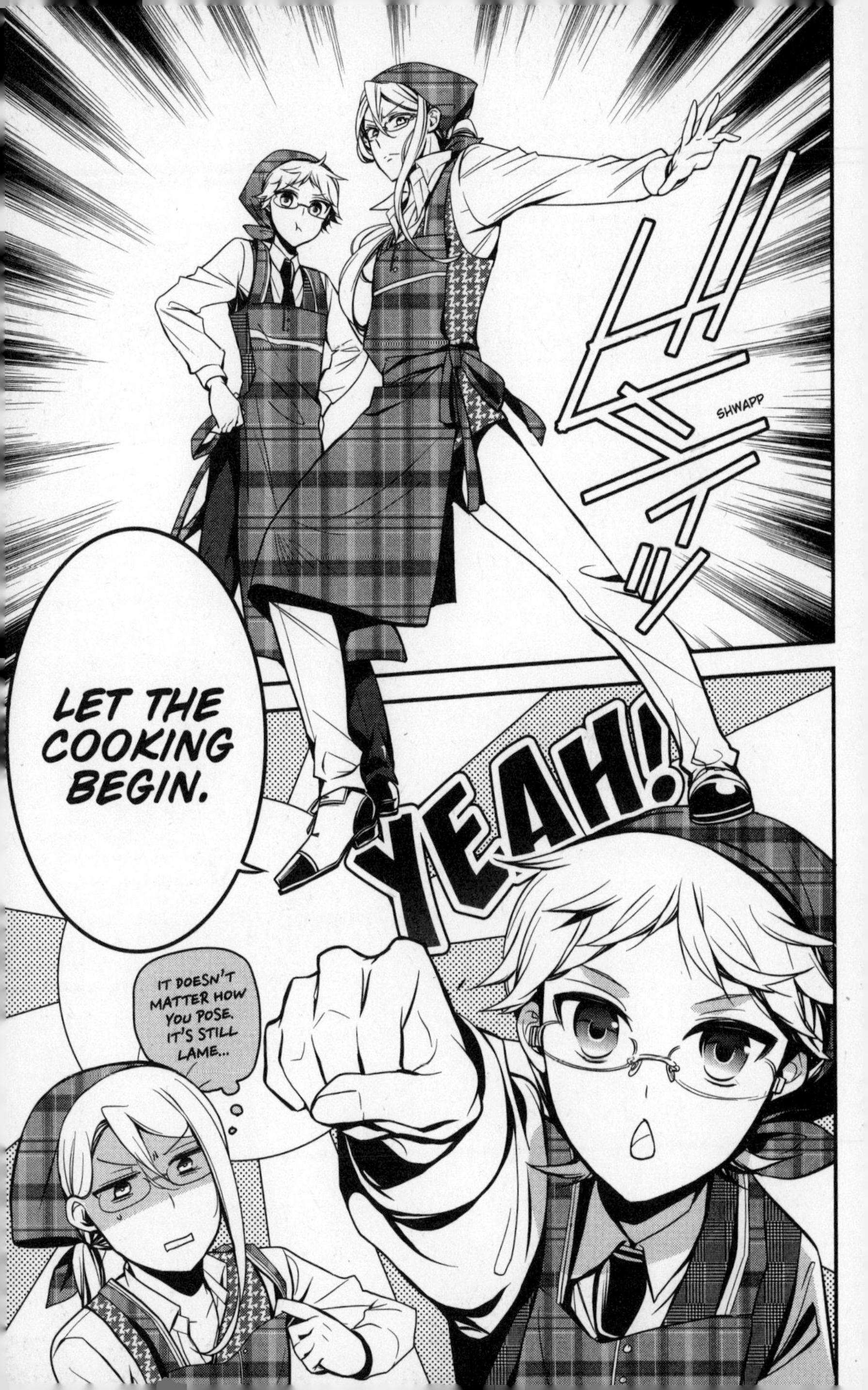
SHWAPP
LET THE COOKING BEGIN.
YEAH!
IT DOESN'T MATTER HOW YOU POSE. IT'S STILL LAME...

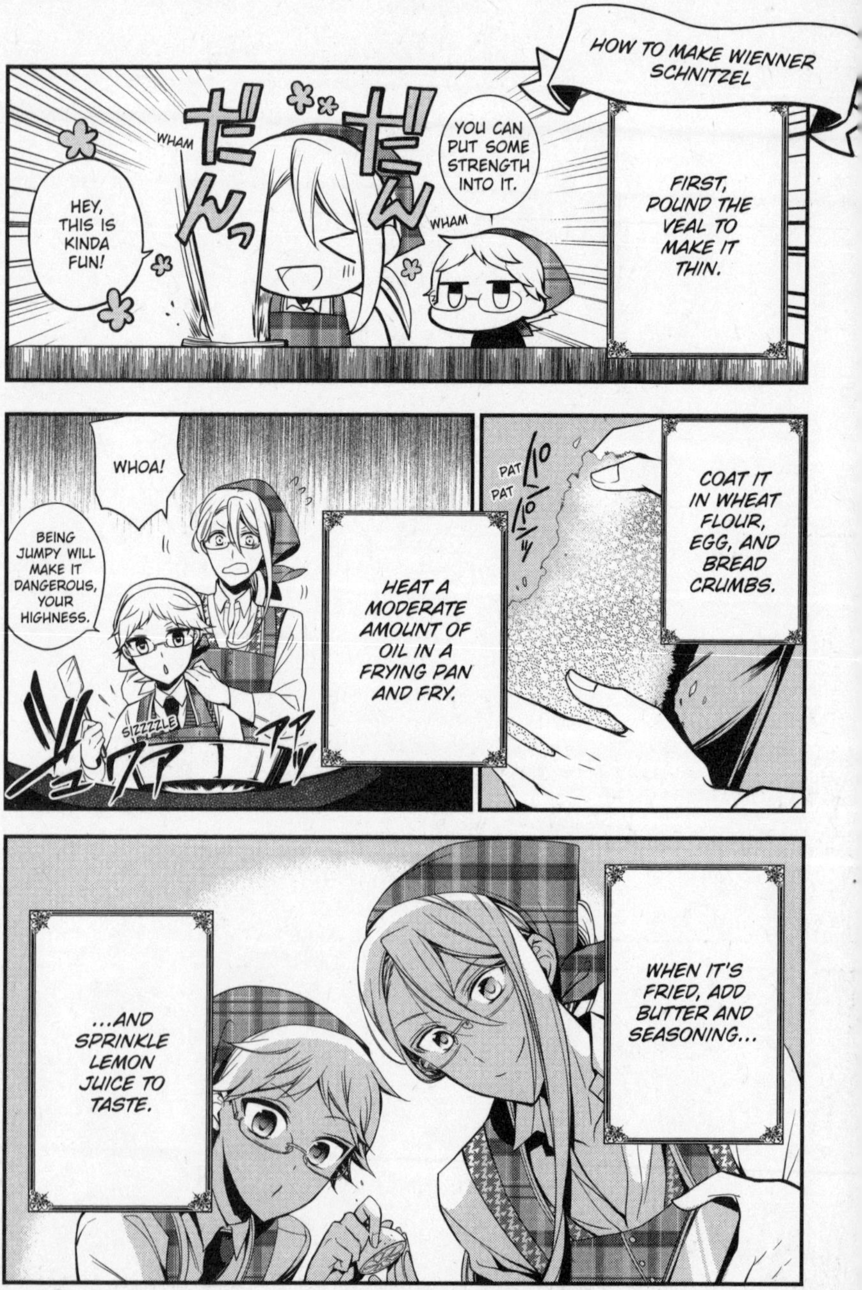
HOW TO MAKE WIENNER SCHNITZEL
FIRST, POUND THE VEAL TO MAKE IT THIN.
YOU CAN PUT SOME STRENGTH INTO IT.
WHAM
WHAM
HEY, THIS IS KINDA FUN!
COAT IT IN WHEAT FLOUR, EGG, AND BREAD CRUMBS.
PAT
PAT
HEAT A MODERATE AMOUNT OF OIL IN A FRYING PAN AND FRY.
WHOA!
BEING JUMPY WILL MAKE IT DANGEROUS, YOUR HIGHNESS.
SIZZZZLE
WHEN IT'S FRIED, ADD BUTTER AND SEASONING...
...AND SPRINKLE LEMON JUICE TO TASTE.

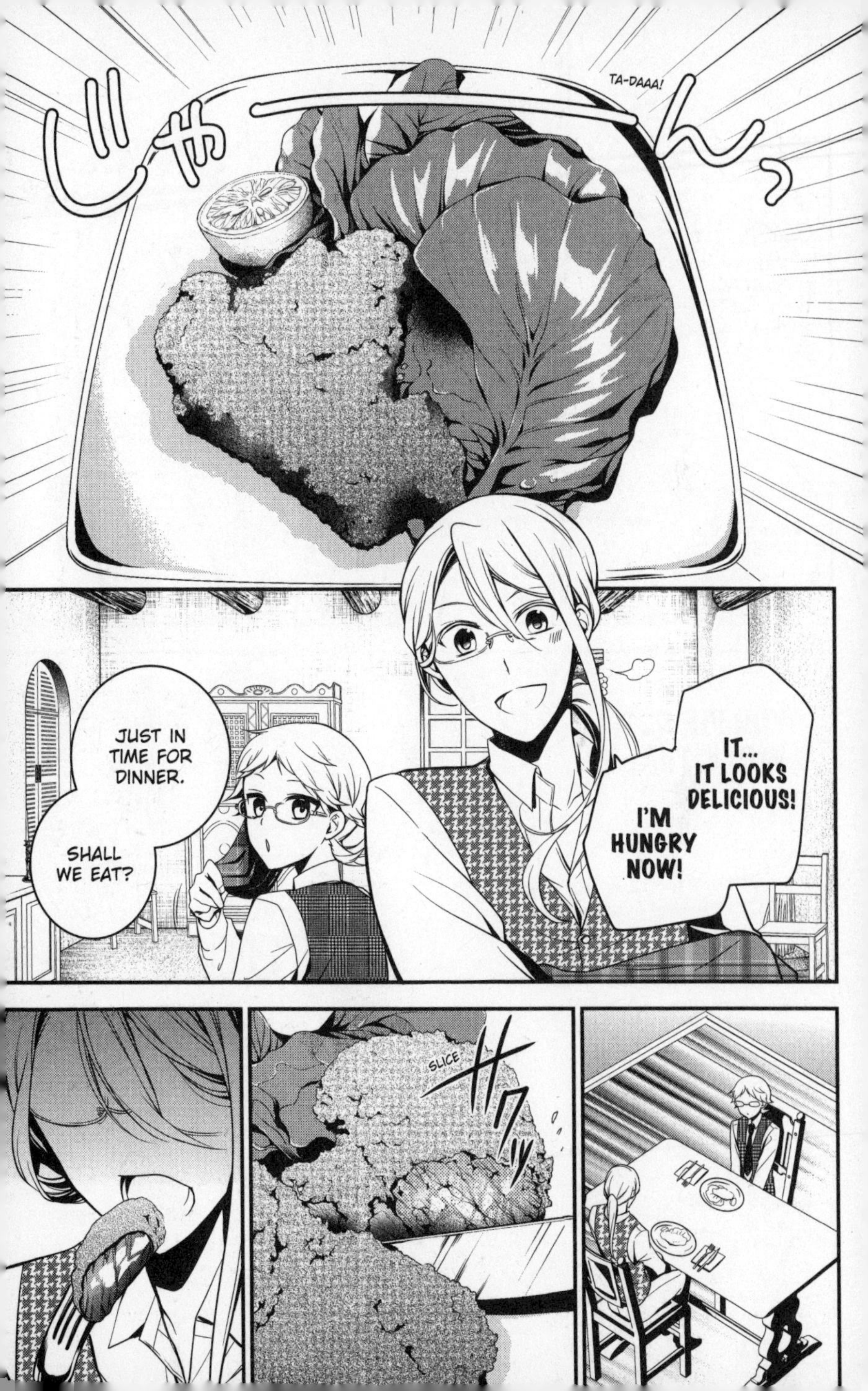
TA-DAAA!
IT... IT LOOKS DELICIOUS!
I'M HUNGRY NOW!
JUST IN TIME FOR DINNER.
SHALL WE EAT?
SLICE

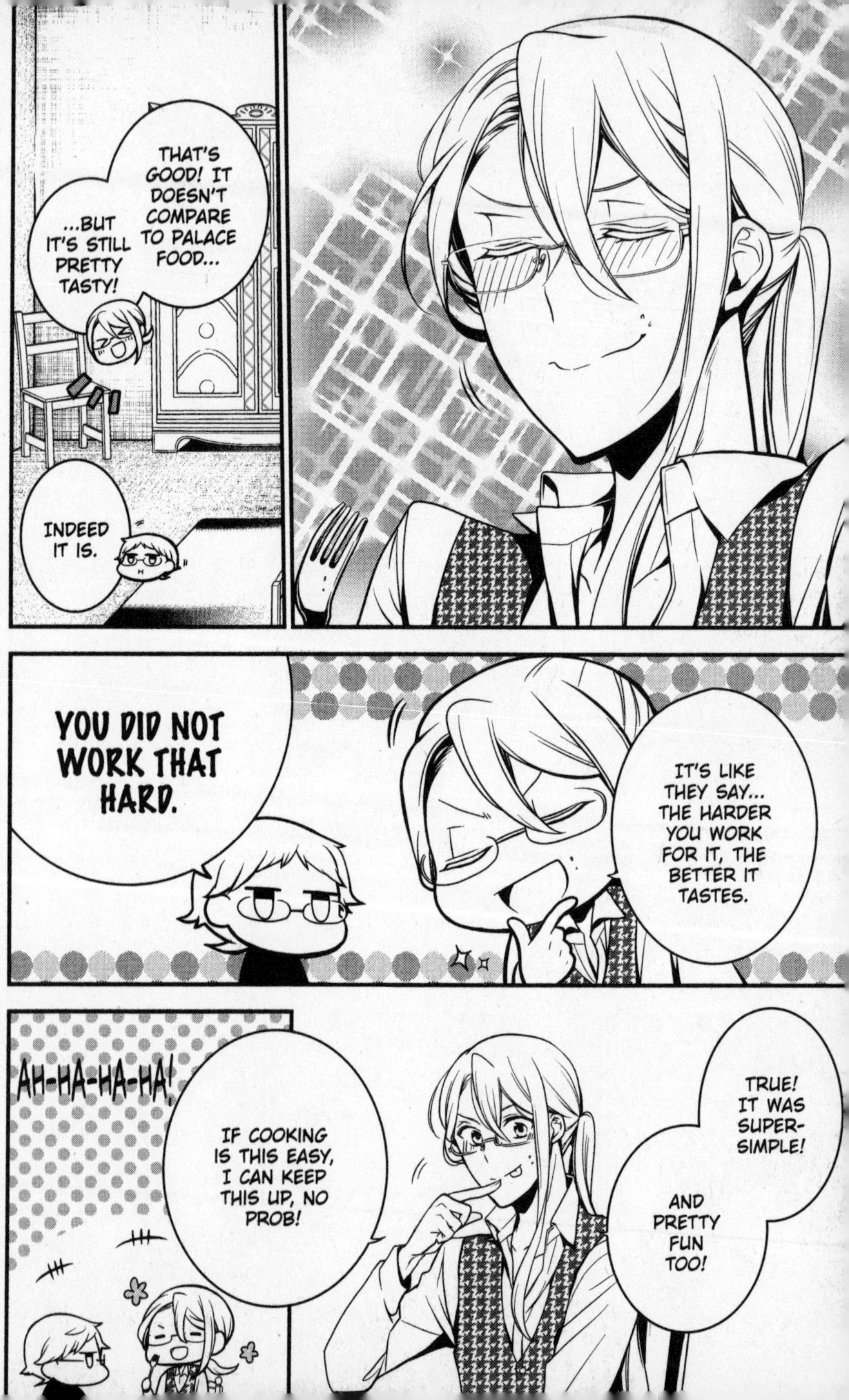
THAT'S GOOD! IT DOESN'T COMPARE TO PALACE FOOD...
...BUT IT'S STILL PRETTY TASTY!
INDEED IT IS.
IT'S LIKE THEY SAY... THE HARDER YOU WORK FOR IT, THE BETTER IT TASTES.
YOU DID NOT WORK THAT HARD.
TRUE! IT WAS SUPER-SIMPLE!
AND PRETTY FUN TOO!
IF COOKING IS THIS EASY, I CAN KEEP THIS UP, NO PROB!
AH-HA-HA-HA!

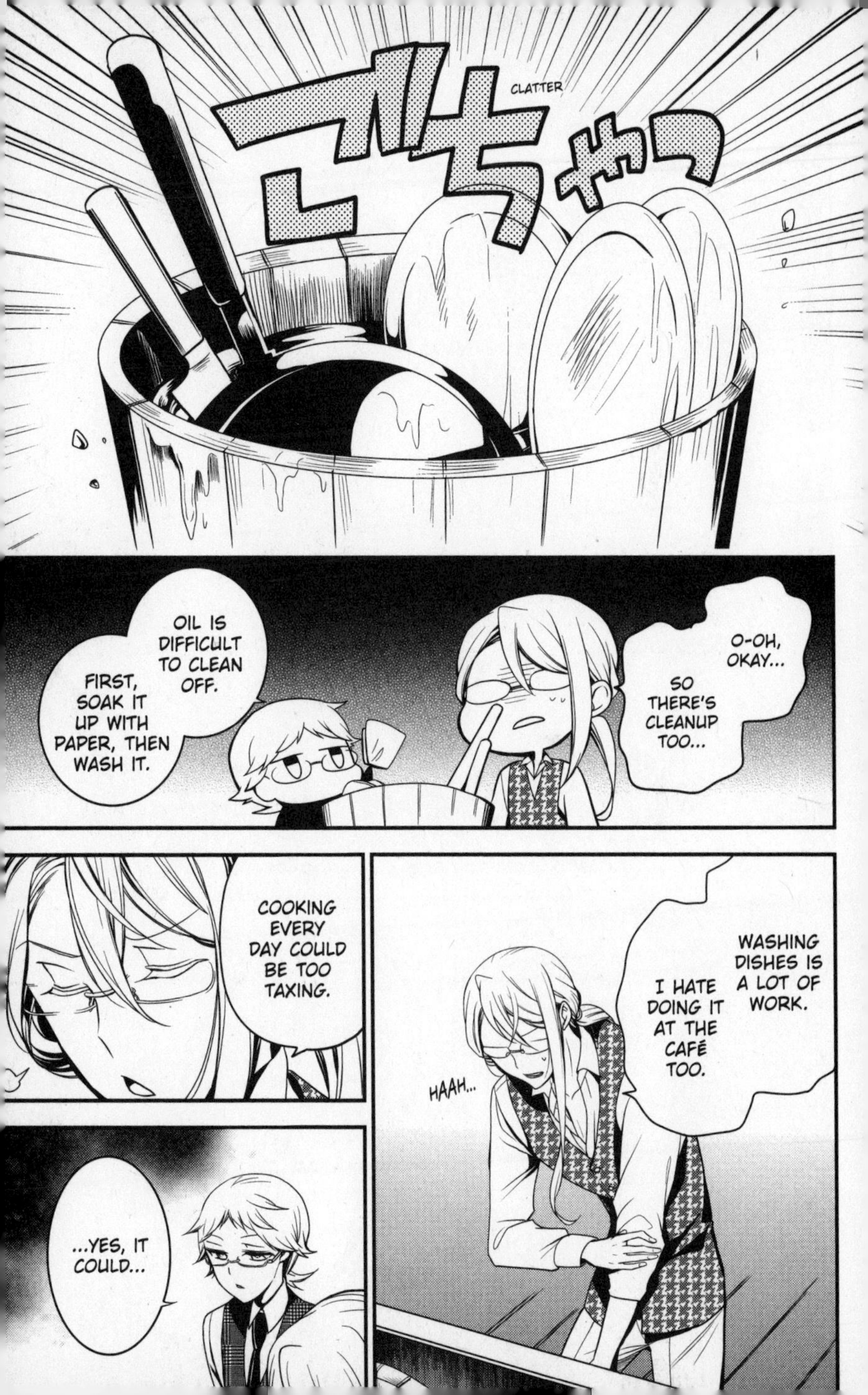
ゴチャッ
CLATTER
O-OH, OKAY...
SO THERE'S CLEANUP TOO...
OIL IS DIFFICULT TO CLEAN OFF.
FIRST, SOAK IT UP WITH PAPER, THEN WASH IT.
WASHING DISHES IS A LOT OF WORK.
I HATE DOING IT AT THE CAFÉ TOO.
HAAH...
COOKING EVERY DAY COULD BE TOO TAXING.
...YES, IT COULD...

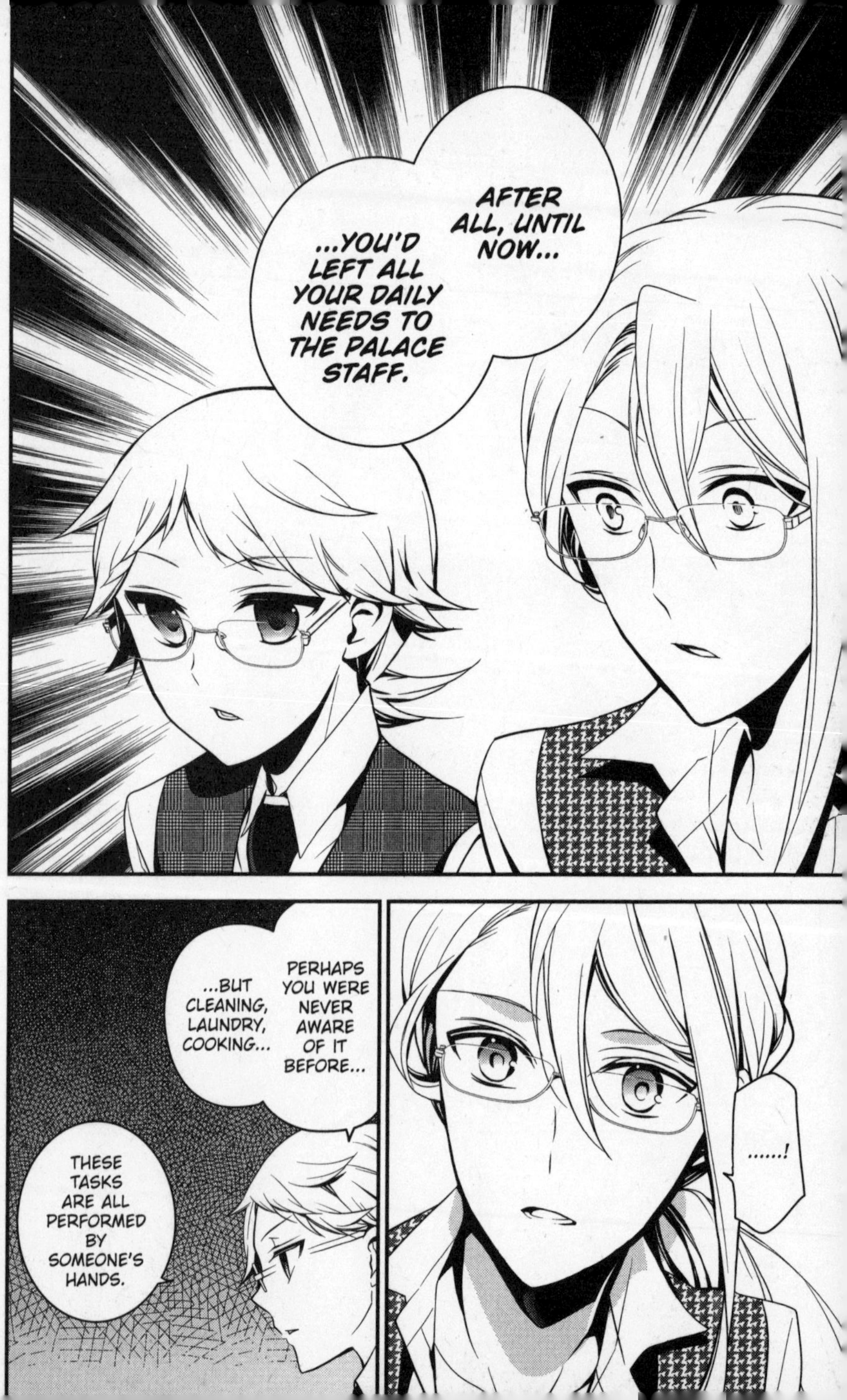
AFTER ALL, UNTIL NOW...
...YOU'D LEFT ALL YOUR DAILY NEEDS TO THE PALACE STAFF.
......!
PERHAPS YOU WERE NEVER AWARE OF IT BEFORE...
...BUT CLEANING, LAUNDRY, COOKING...
THESE TASKS ARE ALL PERFORMED BY SOMEONE'S HANDS.

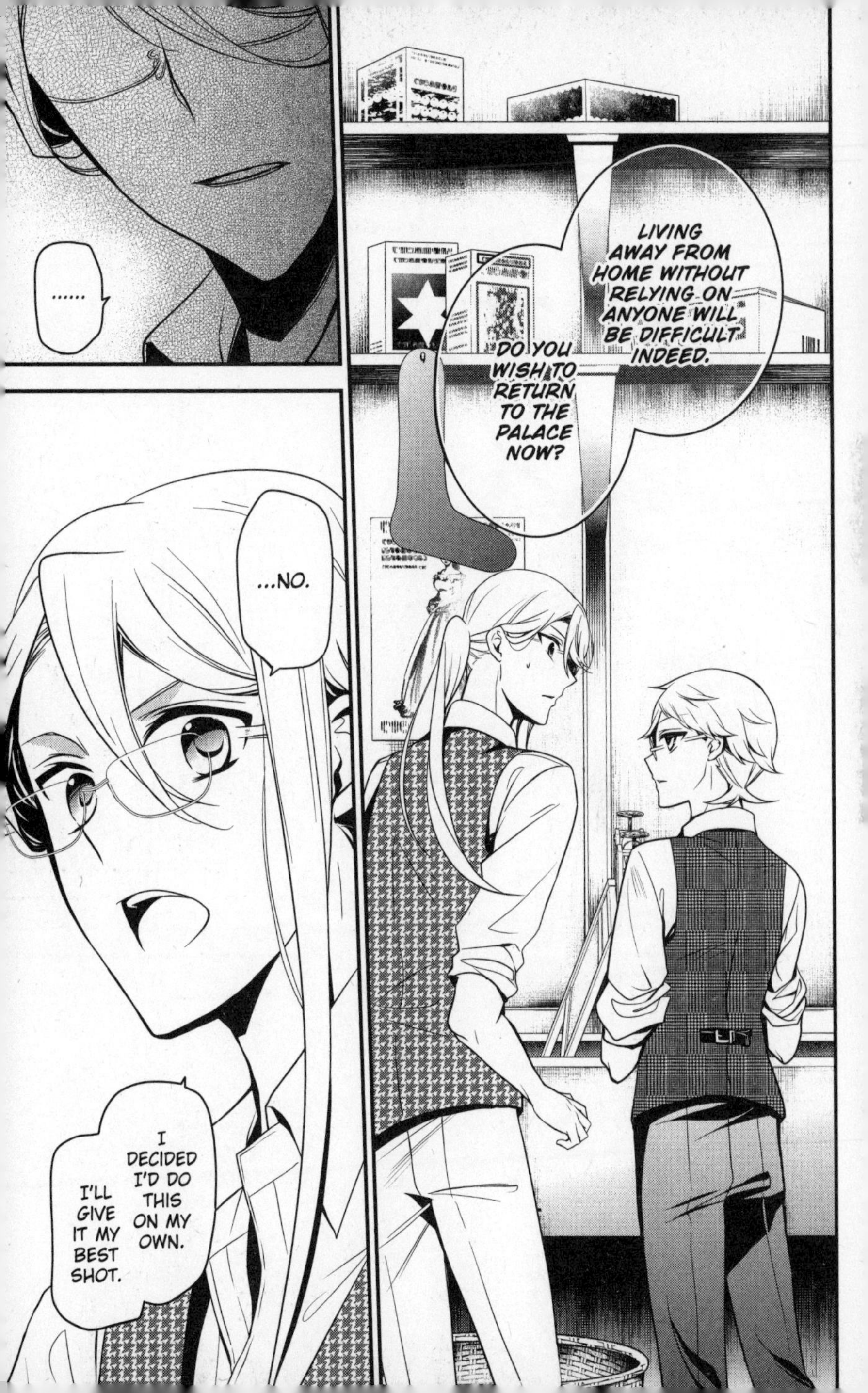
LIVING AWAY FROM HOME WITHOUT RELYING ON ANYONE WILL BE DIFFICULT INDEED.
DO YOU WISH TO RETURN TO THE PALACE NOW?
......
...NO.
I DECIDED I'D DO THIS ON MY OWN.
I'LL GIVE IT MY BEST SHOT.

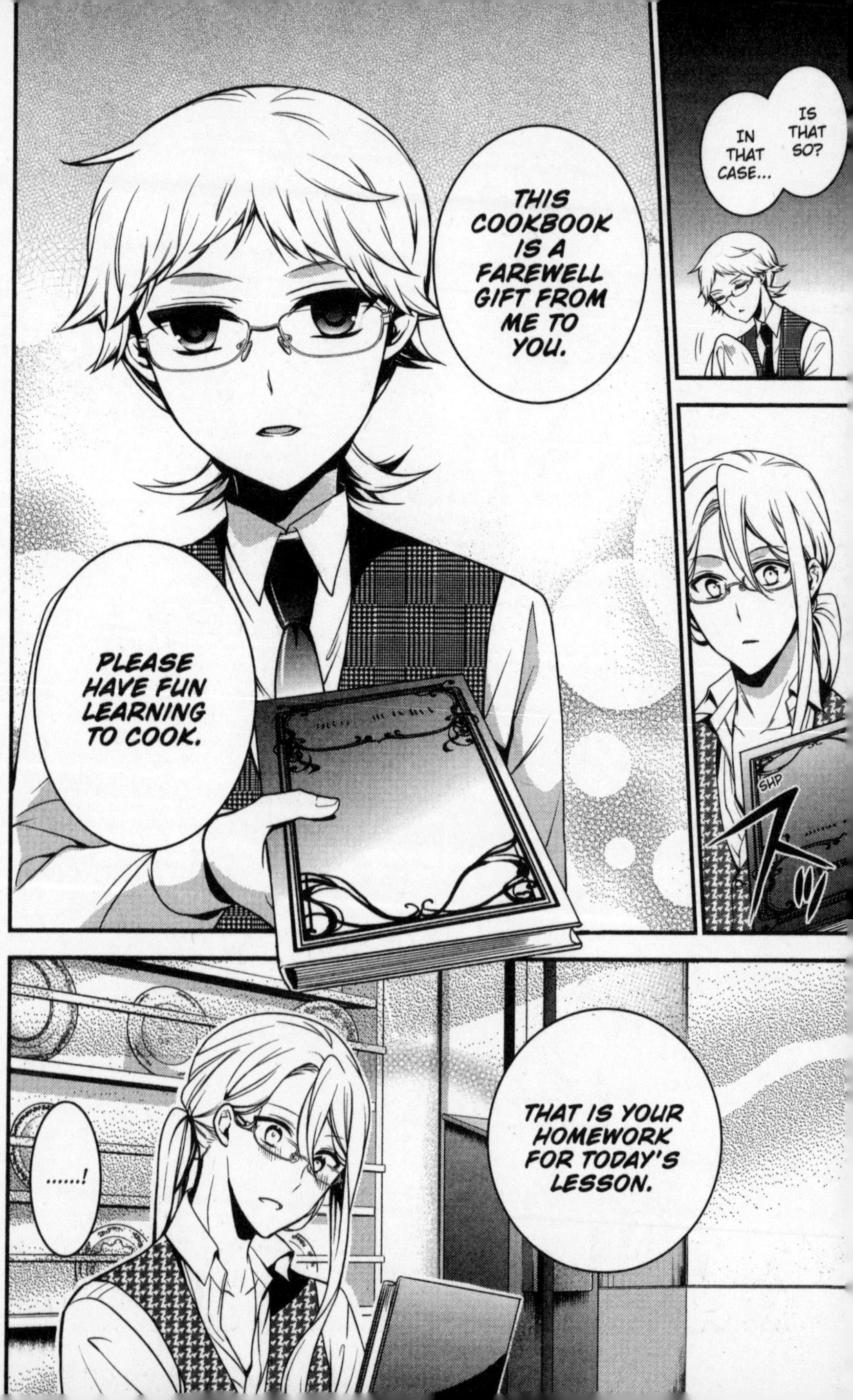
IS THAT SO?
IN THAT CASE...
SHP
THIS COOKBOOK IS A FAREWELL GIFT FROM ME TO YOU.
PLEASE HAVE FUN LEARNING TO COOK.
THAT IS YOUR HOMEWORK FOR TODAY'S LESSON.
......!

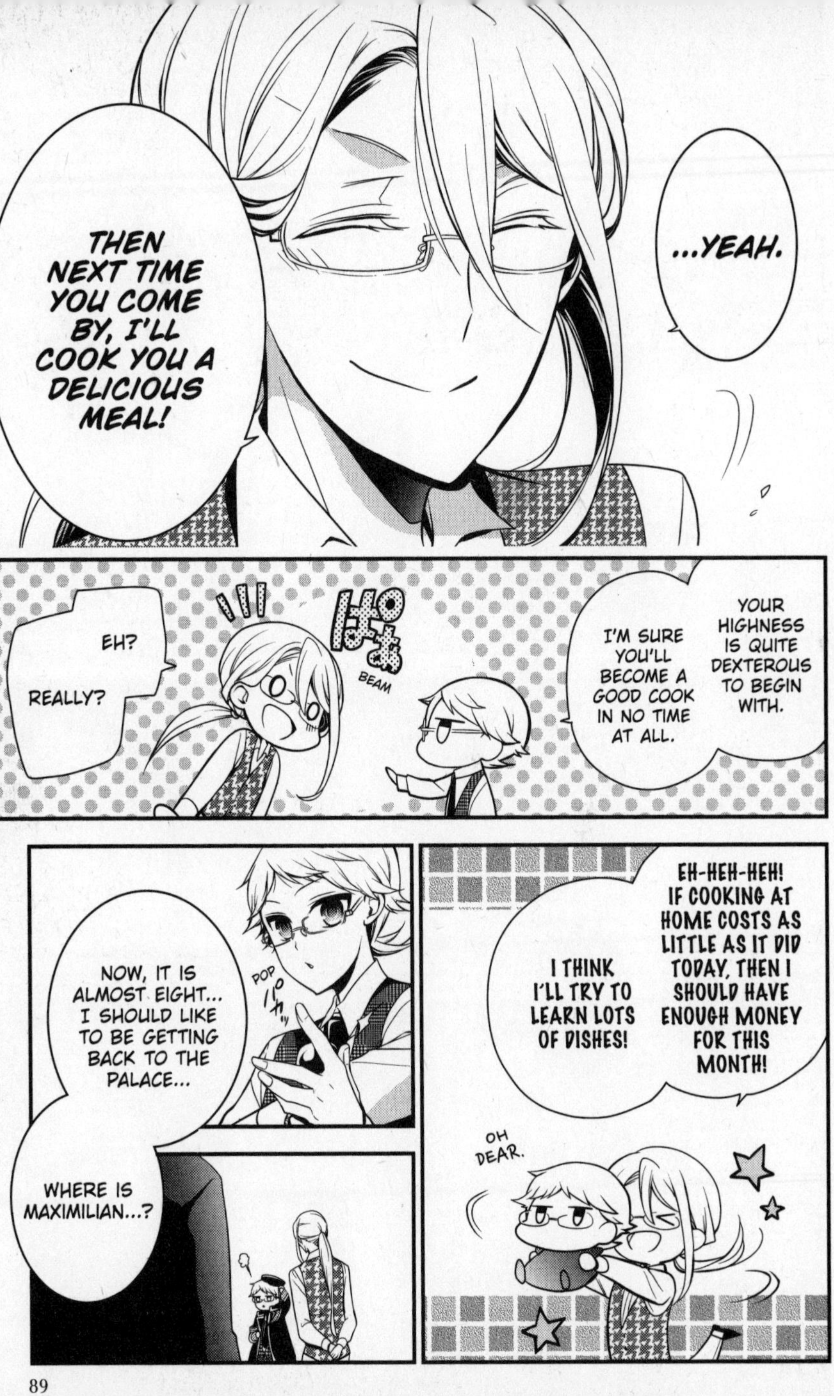
...YEAH.
THEN NEXT TIME YOU COME BY, I'LL COOK YOU A DELICIOUS MEAL!
YOUR HIGHNESS IS QUITE DEXTEROUS TO BEGIN WITH.
I'M SURE YOU'LL BECOME A GOOD COOK IN NO TIME AT ALL.
BEAM
EH?
REALLY?
EH-HEH-HEH! IF COOKING AT HOME COSTS AS LITTLE AS IT DID TODAY, THEN I SHOULD HAVE ENOUGH MONEY FOR THIS MONTH!
I THINK I'LL TRY TO LEARN LOTS OF DISHES!
OH DEAR.
NOW, IT IS ALMOST EIGHT... I SHOULD LIKE TO BE GETTING BACK TO THE PALACE...
POP
WHERE IS MAXIMILIAN...?

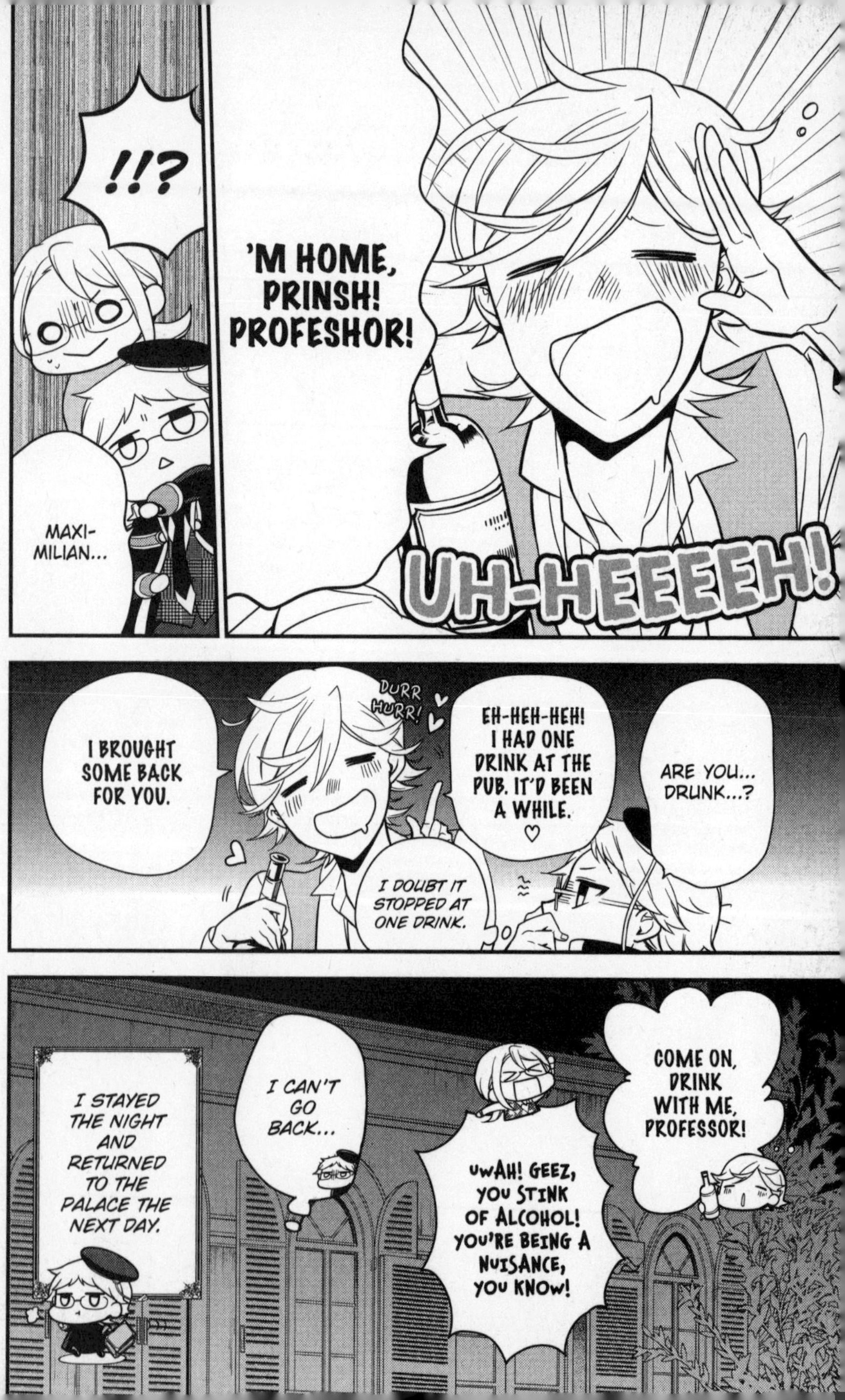

UH-HEEEEEH!
'M HOME, PRINSH! PROFESHOR!
!!?
MAXI-MILIAN...
ARE YOU... DRUNK...?
EH-HEH-HEH! I HAD ONE DRINK AT THE PUB. IT'D BEEN A WHILE. ♡
DURR HURR!
I BROUGHT SOME BACK FOR YOU.
I DOUBT IT STOPPED AT ONE DRINK.
COME ON, DRINK WITH ME, PROFESSOR!
UWAH! GEEZ, YOU STINK OF ALCOHOL! YOU'RE BEING A NUISANCE, YOU KNOW!
I CAN'T GO BACK...
I STAYED THE NIGHT AND RETURNED TO THE PALACE THE NEXT DAY.

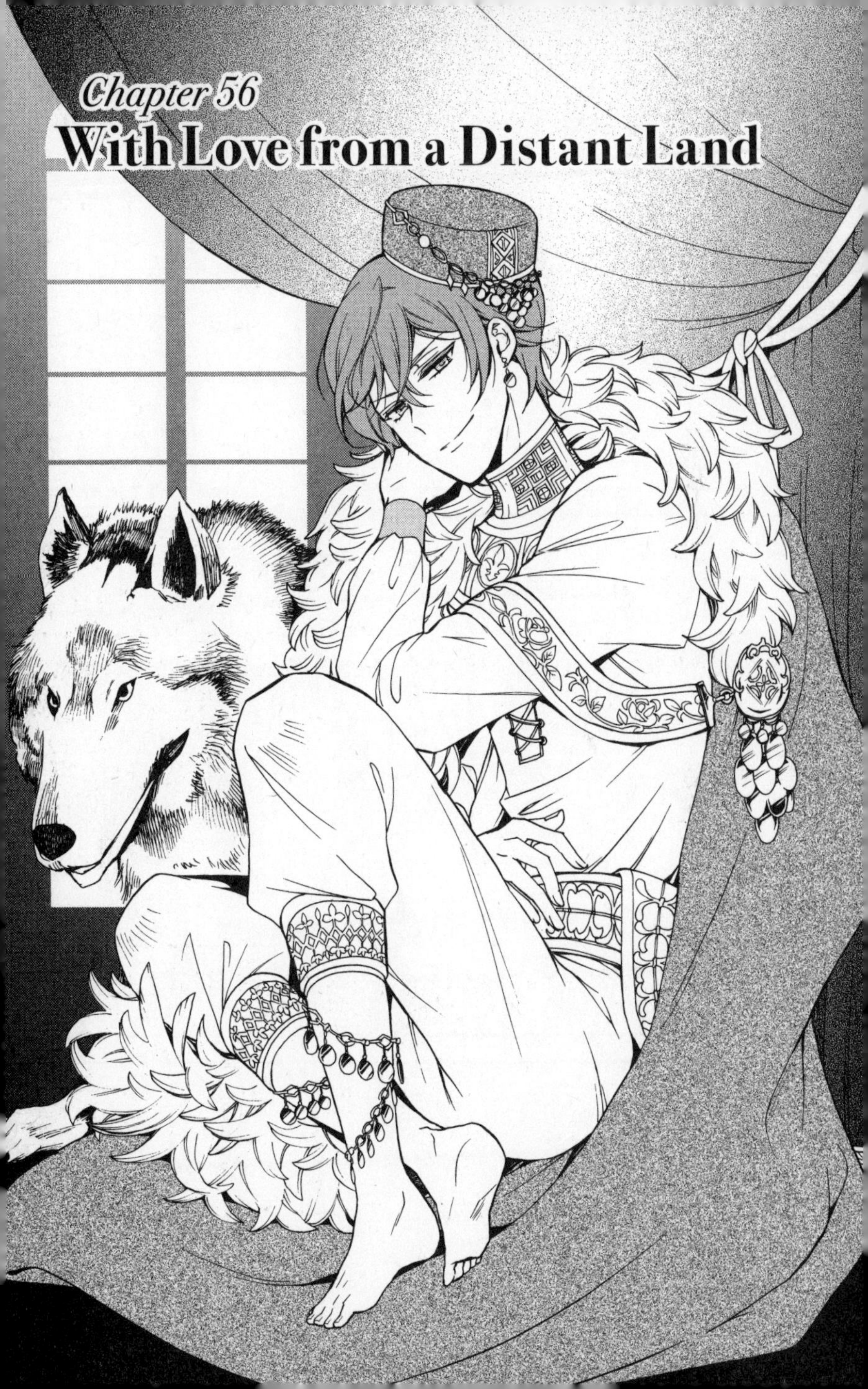
Chapter 56
With Love from a Distant Land

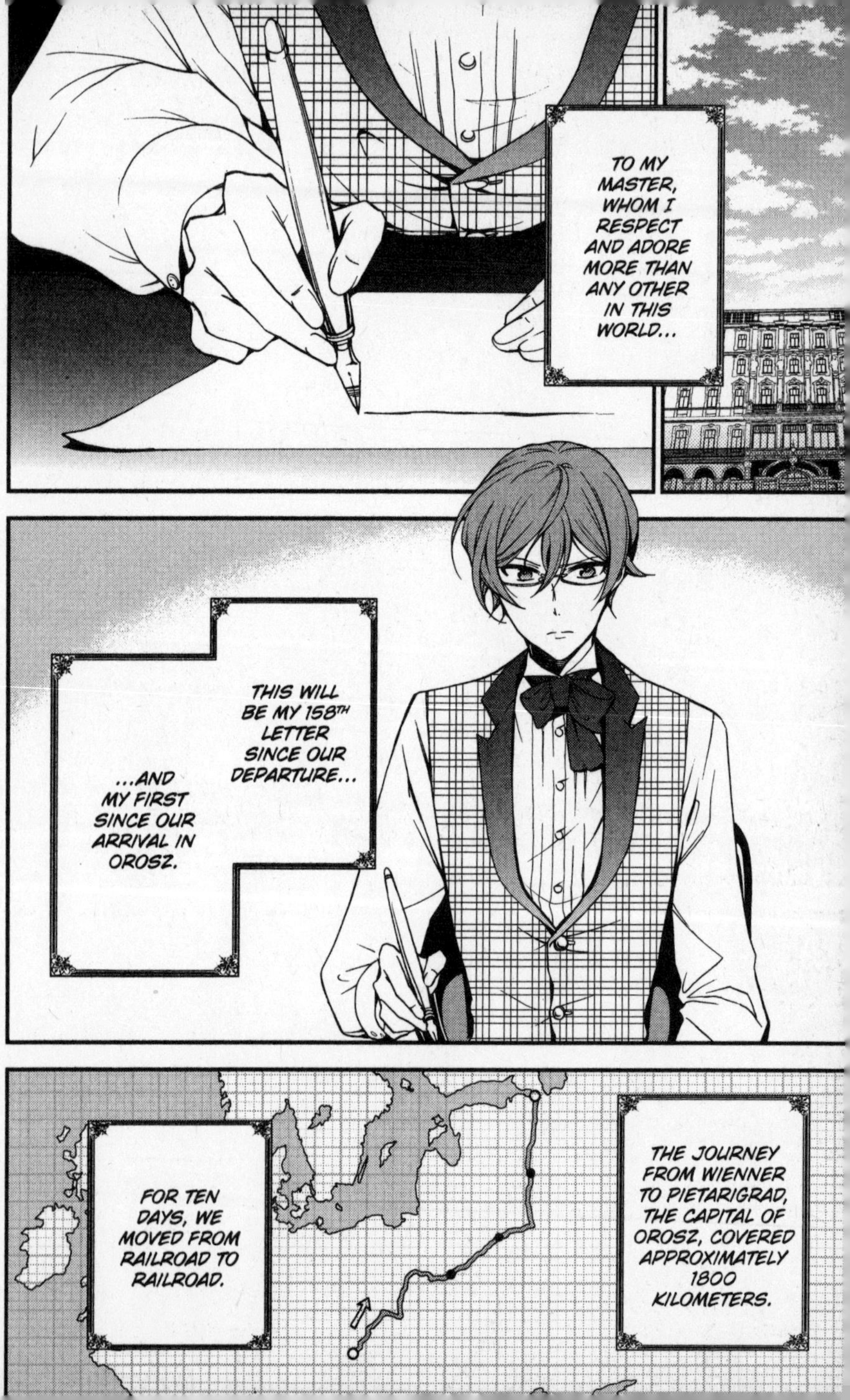
TO MY MASTER, WHOM I RESPECT AND ADORE MORE THAN ANY OTHER IN THIS WORLD...
THIS WILL BE MY 158TH LETTER SINCE OUR DEPARTURE...
...AND MY FIRST SINCE OUR ARRIVAL IN OROSZ.
THE JOURNEY FROM WIENNER TO PIETARIGRAD, THE CAPITAL OF OROSZ, COVERED APPROXIMATELY 1800 KILOMETERS.
FOR TEN DAYS, WE MOVED FROM RAILROAD TO RAILROAD.

ALTHOUGH WE TRAVELED IN A PRIVATE ROYAL TRAIN...

...I MUST CONFESS THAT, HAVING NEVER BEEN ON SUCH A LONG TRIP, IT LEFT ME...

WOOZY

く！ たぁ...

......

A-ARE YOU ALL RIGHT, YOUR HIGHNESS...!?

WE'VE PULLED INTO PIETARIGRAD'S CENTRAL STATION...

CAN YOU STAND...!?

Y... YES...

FORGIVE ME... I AM NOT NORMALLY THIS PRONE TO MOTION SICKNESS...

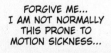

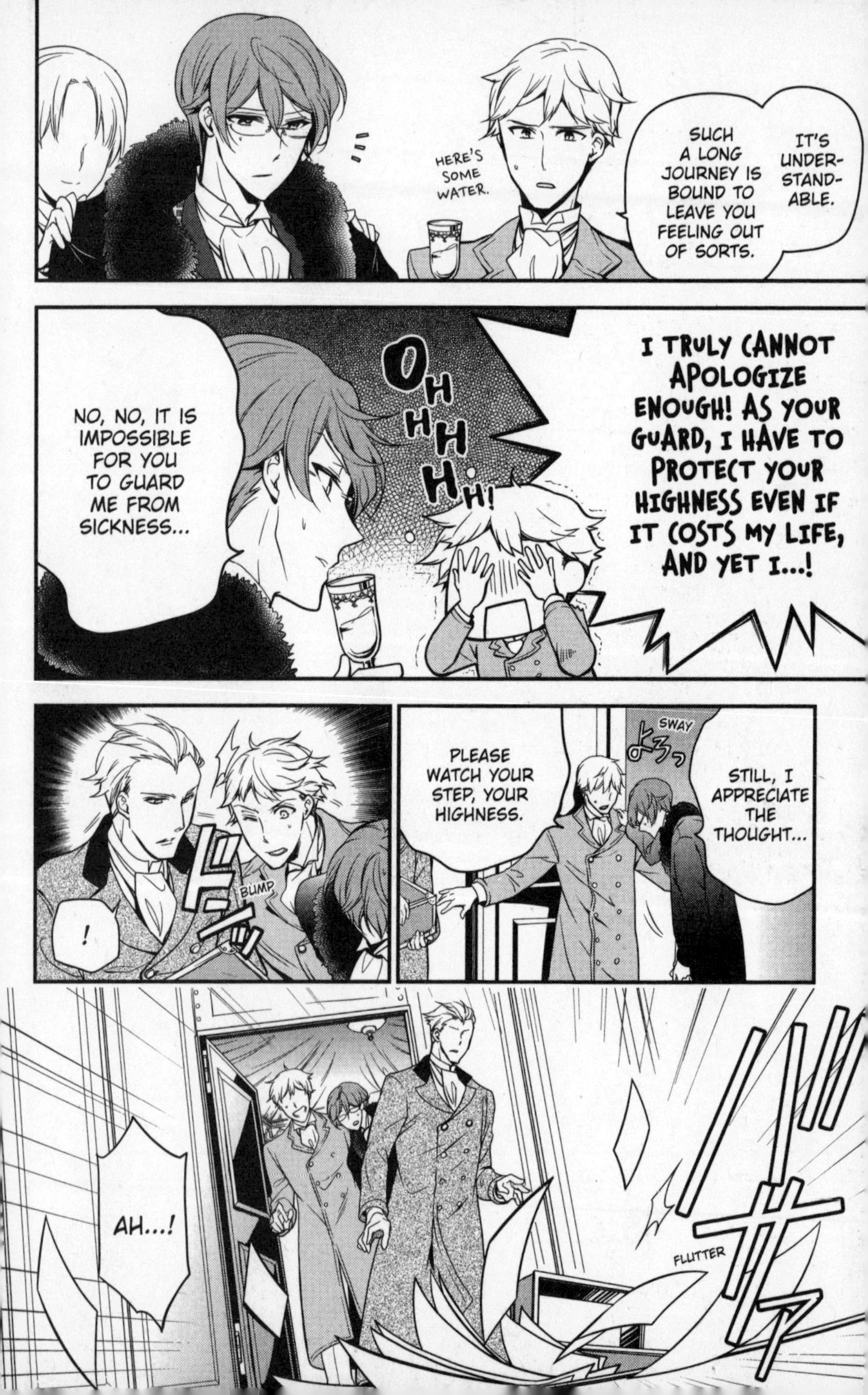
IT'S UNDERSTANDABLE.
SUCH A LONG JOURNEY IS BOUND TO LEAVE YOU FEELING OUT OF SORTS.
HERE'S SOME WATER.
I TRULY CANNOT APOLOGIZE ENOUGH! AS YOUR GUARD, I HAVE TO PROTECT YOUR HIGHNESS EVEN IF IT COSTS MY LIFE, AND YET I...!
OHHHHH!
NO, NO, IT IS IMPOSSIBLE FOR YOU TO GUARD ME FROM SICKNESS...
STILL, I APPRECIATE THE THOUGHT...
SWAY
PLEASE WATCH YOUR STEP, YOUR HIGHNESS.
BUMP
!
FLUTTER
AH...!

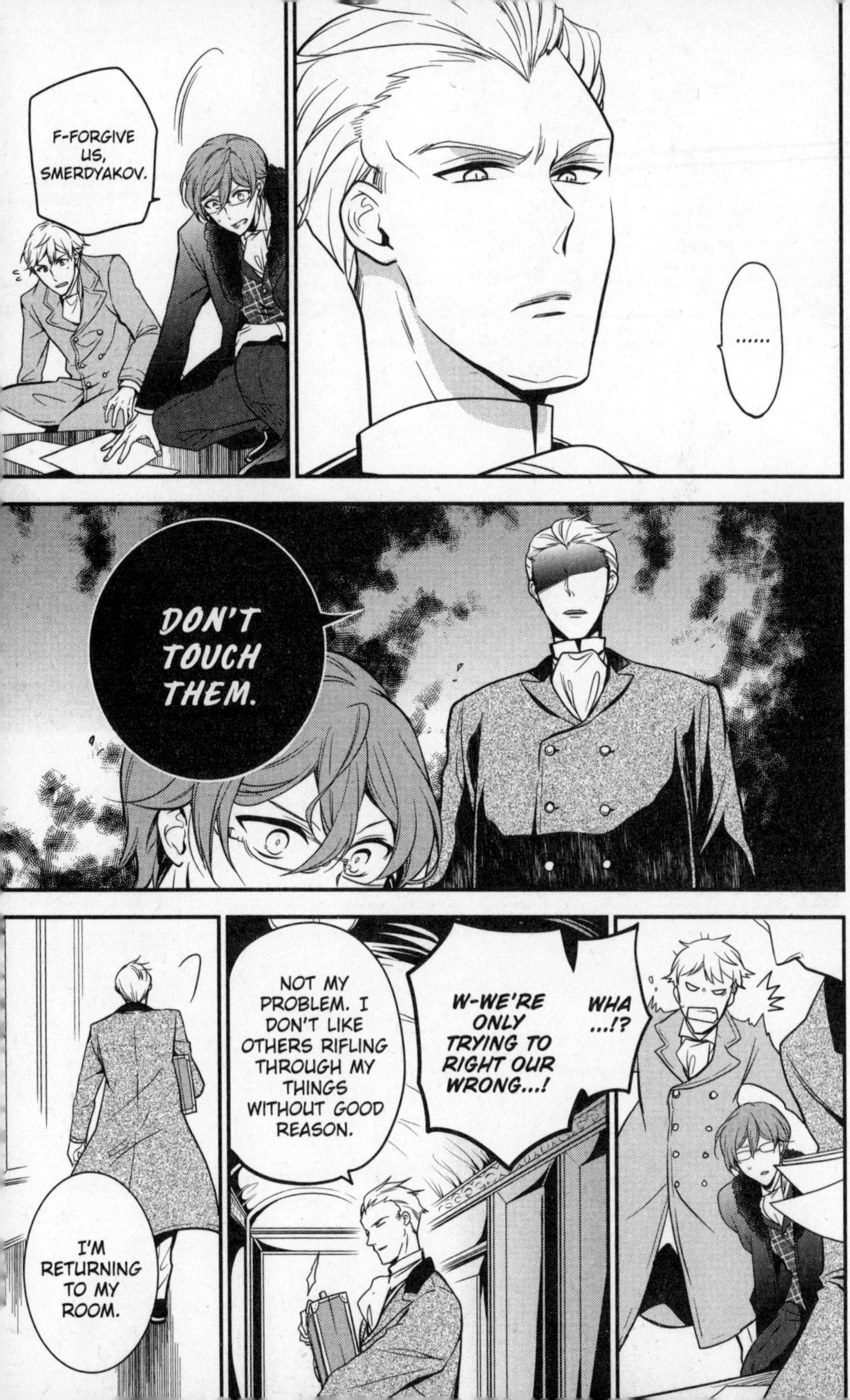
......
F-FORGIVE US, SMERDYAKOV.
DON'T TOUCH THEM.
WHA ...!?
W-WE'RE ONLY TRYING TO RIGHT OUR WRONG...!
NOT MY PROBLEM. I DON'T LIKE OTHERS RIFLING THROUGH MY THINGS WITHOUT GOOD REASON.
I'M RETURNING TO MY ROOM.

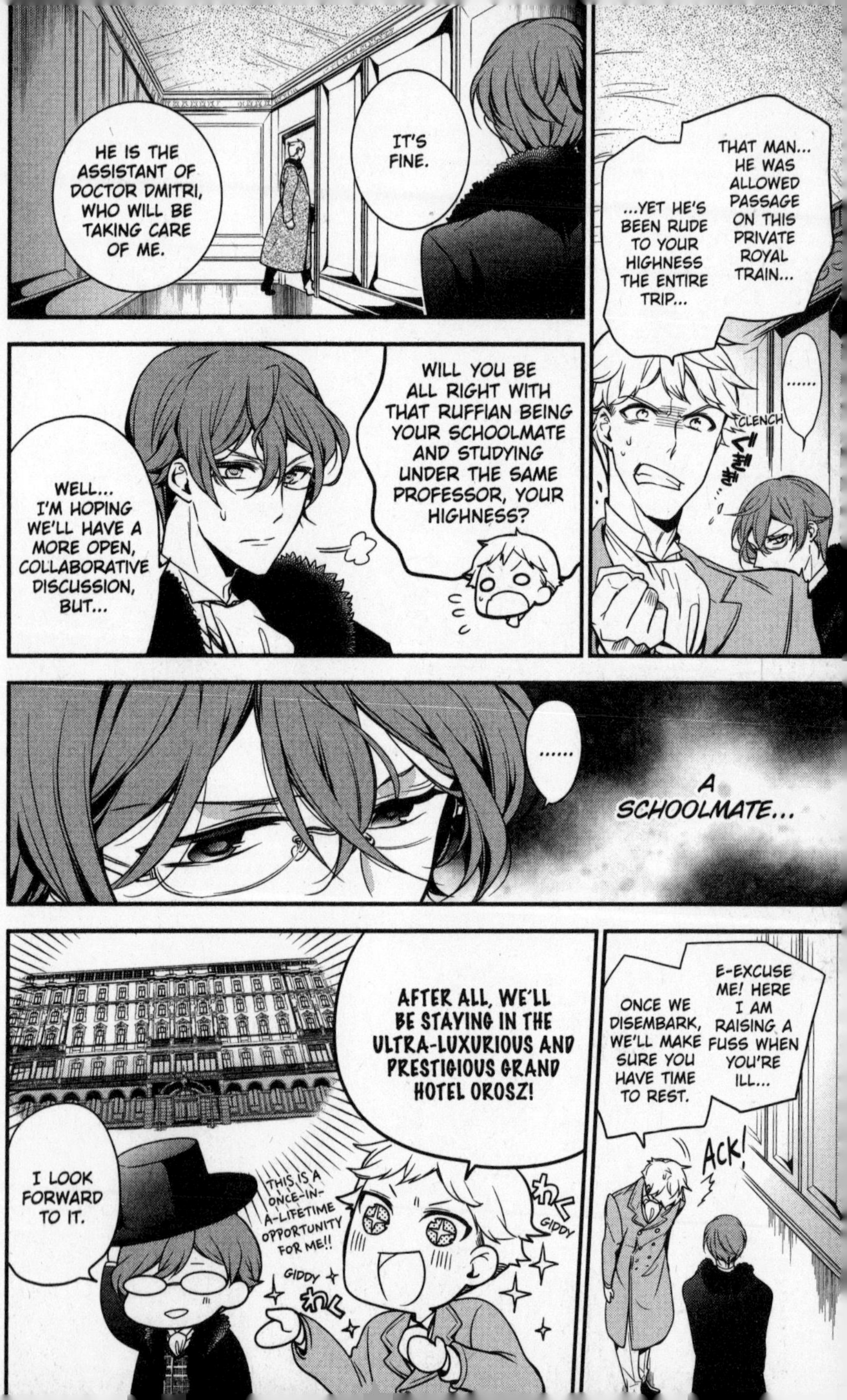
THAT MAN... HE WAS ALLOWED PASSAGE ON THIS PRIVATE ROYAL TRAIN...
...YET HE'S BEEN RUDE TO YOUR HIGHNESS THE ENTIRE TRIP...
......
CLENCH
IT'S FINE.
HE IS THE ASSISTANT OF DOCTOR DMITRI, WHO WILL BE TAKING CARE OF ME.
WILL YOU BE ALL RIGHT WITH THAT RUFFIAN BEING YOUR SCHOOLMATE AND STUDYING UNDER THE SAME PROFESSOR, YOUR HIGHNESS?
WELL... I'M HOPING WE'LL HAVE A MORE OPEN, COLLABORATIVE DISCUSSION, BUT...
......
A SCHOOLMATE...
E-EXCUSE ME! HERE I AM RAISING A FUSS WHEN YOU'RE ILL...
ONCE WE DISEMBARK, WE'LL MAKE SURE YOU HAVE TIME TO REST.
ACK!
AFTER ALL, WE'LL BE STAYING IN THE ULTRA-LUXURIOUS AND PRESTIGIOUS GRAND HOTEL OROSZ!
GIDDY
THIS IS A ONCE-IN-A-LIFETIME OPPORTUNITY FOR ME!!
GIDDY
I LOOK FORWARD TO IT.

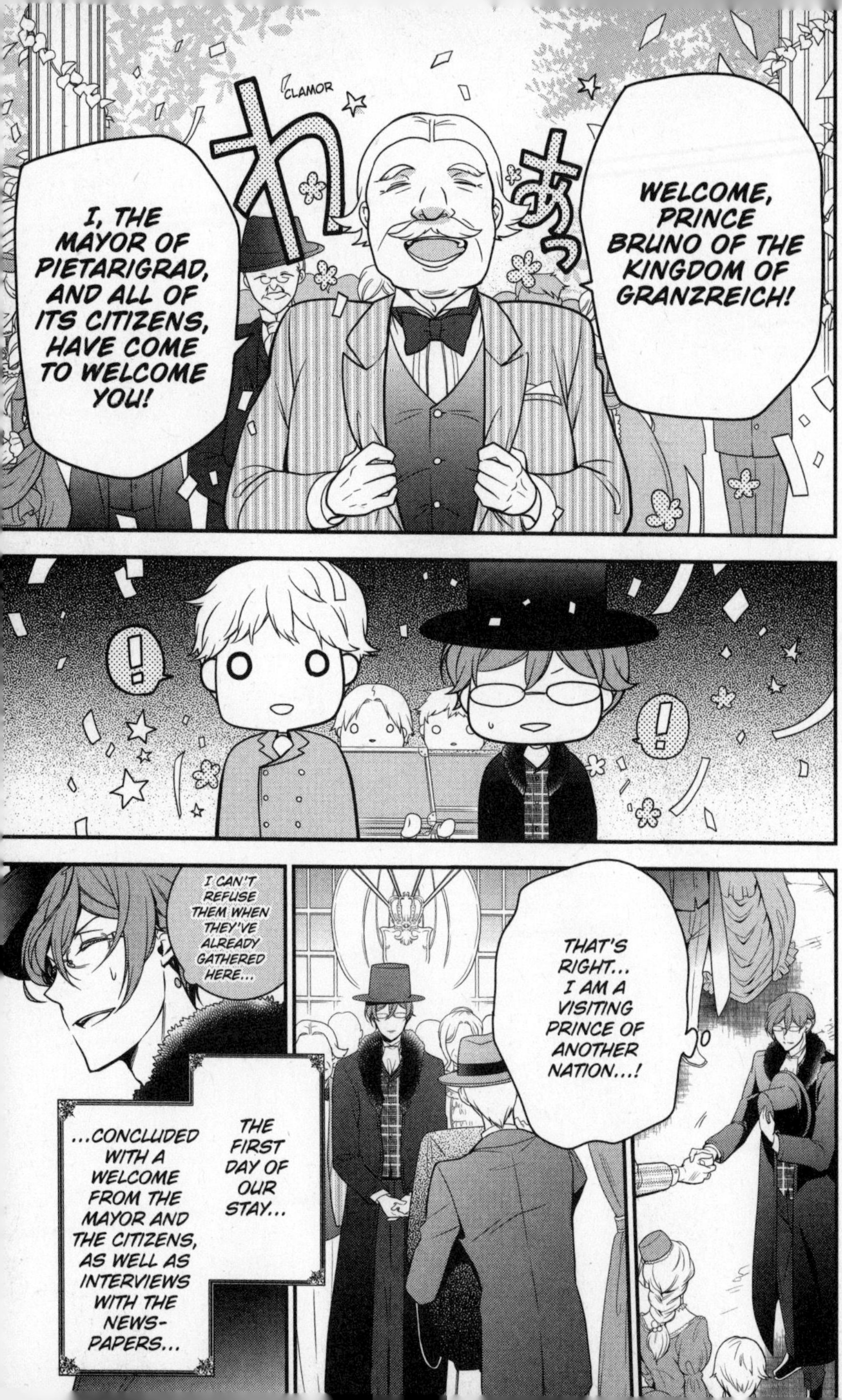
WELCOME, PRINCE BRUNO OF THE KINGDOM OF GRANZREICH!
わあっ
CLAMOR
I, THE MAYOR OF PIETARIGRAD, AND ALL OF ITS CITIZENS, HAVE COME TO WELCOME YOU!
!
!
THAT'S RIGHT... I AM A VISITING PRINCE OF ANOTHER NATION...!
I CAN'T REFUSE THEM WHEN THEY'VE ALREADY GATHERED HERE...
THE FIRST DAY OF OUR STAY...
...CONCLUDED WITH A WELCOME FROM THE MAYOR AND THE CITIZENS, AS WELL AS INTERVIEWS WITH THE NEWS-PAPERS...

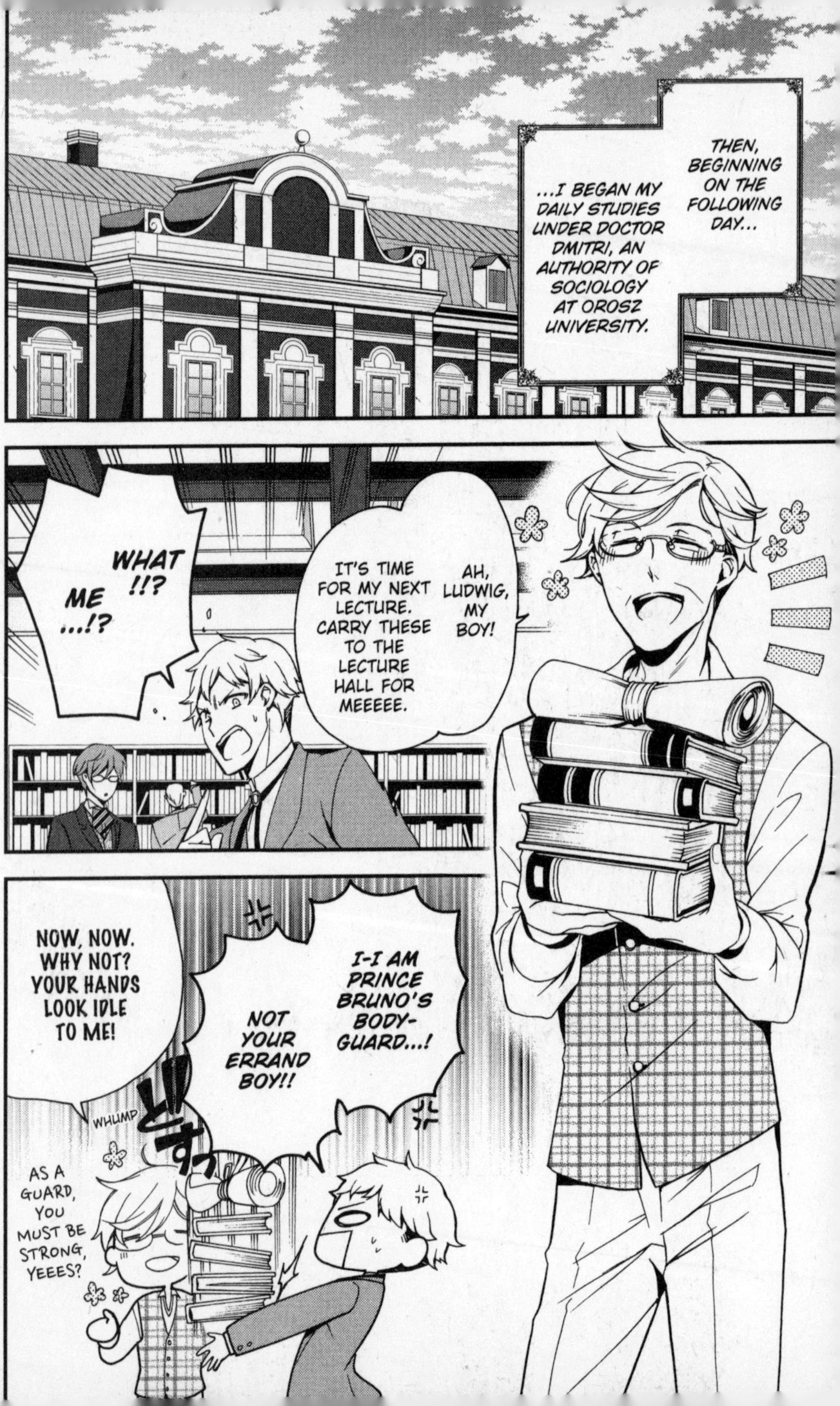

THEN, BEGINNING ON THE FOLLOWING DAY...
...I BEGAN MY DAILY STUDIES UNDER DOCTOR DMITRI, AN AUTHORITY OF SOCIOLOGY AT OROSZ UNIVERSITY.
AH, LUDWIG, MY BOY!
IT'S TIME FOR MY NEXT LECTURE. CARRY THESE TO THE LECTURE HALL FOR MEEEEE.
WHAT!!?
ME...!?
I-I AM PRINCE BRUNO'S BODY-GUARD...!
NOT YOUR ERRAND BOY!!
NOW, NOW. WHY NOT? YOUR HANDS LOOK IDLE TO ME!
WHUMP
AS A GUARD, YOU MUST BE STRONG, YEEES?

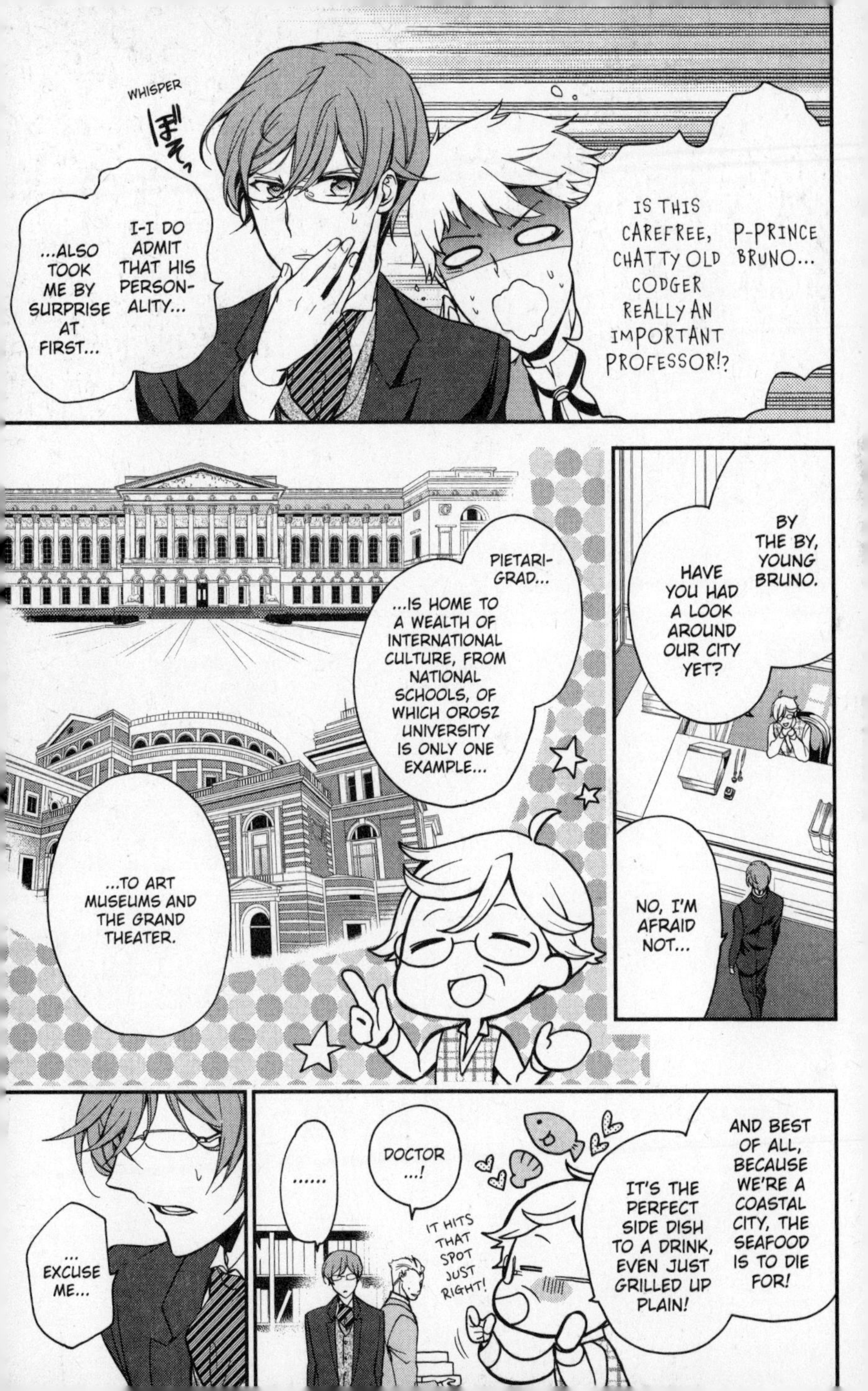
P-PRINCE BRUNO...
IS THIS CAREFREE, CHATTY OLD CODGER REALLY AN IMPORTANT PROFESSOR!?
WHISPER
ぼそっ
I-I DO ADMIT THAT HIS PERSONALITY...
...ALSO TOOK ME BY SURPRISE AT FIRST...
BY THE BY, YOUNG BRUNO.
HAVE YOU HAD A LOOK AROUND OUR CITY YET?
NO, I'M AFRAID NOT...
PIETARIGRAD...
...IS HOME TO A WEALTH OF INTERNATIONAL CULTURE, FROM NATIONAL SCHOOLS, OF WHICH OROSZ UNIVERSITY IS ONLY ONE EXAMPLE...
...TO ART MUSEUMS AND THE GRAND THEATER.
AND BEST OF ALL, BECAUSE WE'RE A COASTAL CITY, THE SEAFOOD IS TO DIE FOR!
IT'S THE PERFECT SIDE DISH TO A DRINK, EVEN JUST GRILLED UP PLAIN!
IT HITS THAT SPOT JUST RIGHT!
DOCTOR ...!
......
...EXCUSE ME...

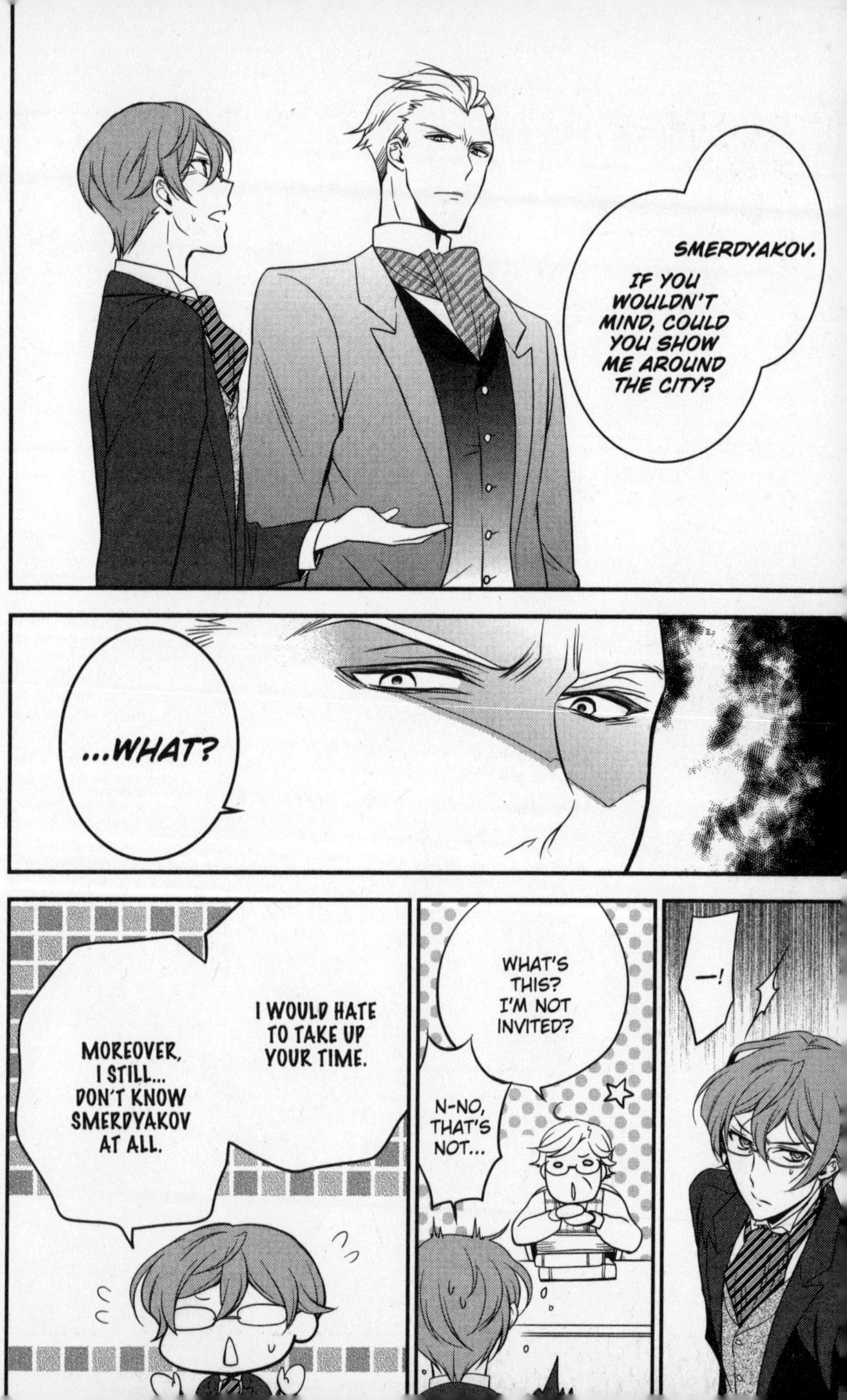
SMERDYAKOV.
IF YOU WOULDN'T MIND, COULD YOU SHOW ME AROUND THE CITY?
...WHAT?
—!
WHAT'S THIS? I'M NOT INVITED?
N-NO, THAT'S NOT...
I WOULD HATE TO TAKE UP YOUR TIME.
MOREOVER, I STILL... DON'T KNOW SMERDYAKOV AT ALL.

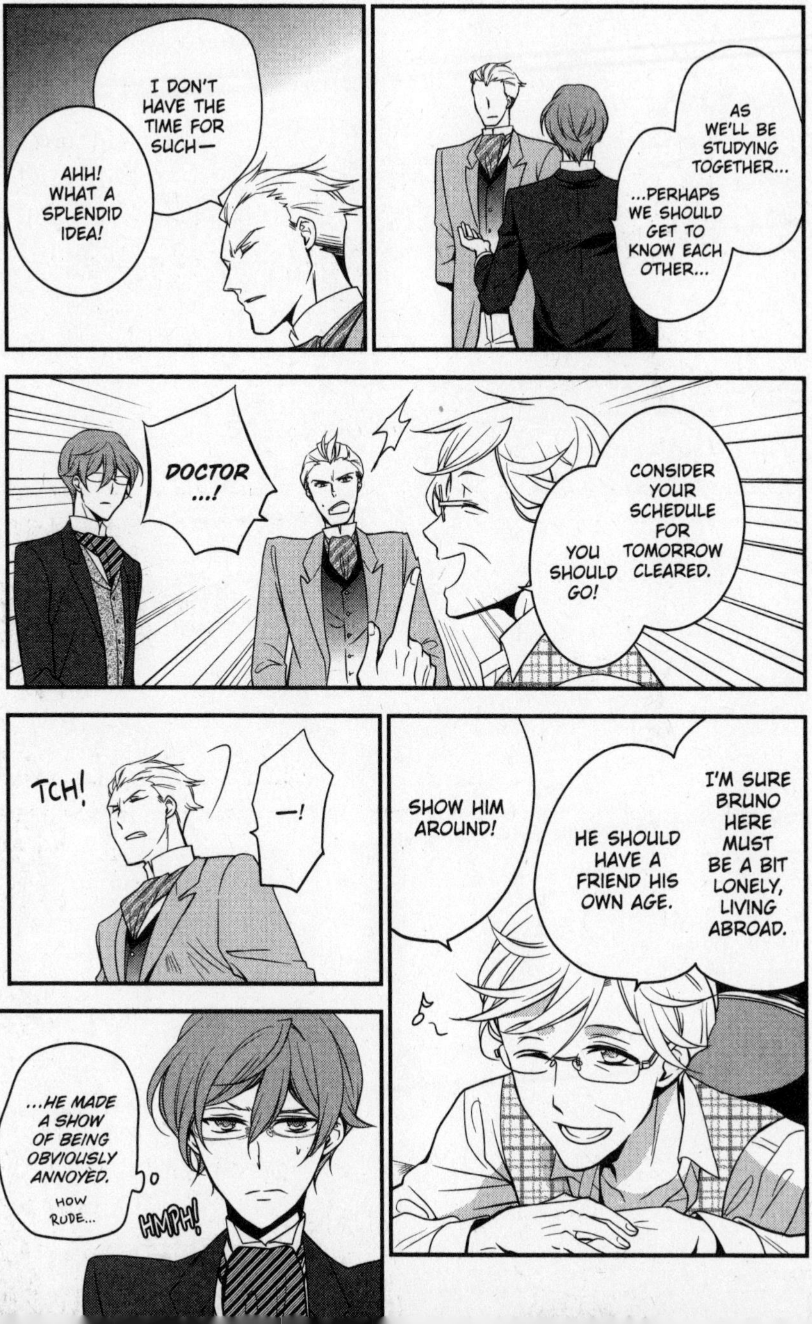
AS WE'LL BE STUDYING TOGETHER...
...PERHAPS WE SHOULD GET TO KNOW EACH OTHER...
I DON'T HAVE THE TIME FOR SUCH—
AHH! WHAT A SPLENDID IDEA!
CONSIDER YOUR SCHEDULE FOR TOMORROW CLEARED.
YOU SHOULD GO!
DOCTOR ...!
I'M SURE BRUNO HERE MUST BE A BIT LONELY, LIVING ABROAD.
HE SHOULD HAVE A FRIEND HIS OWN AGE.
SHOW HIM AROUND!
—!
TCH!
...HE MADE A SHOW OF BEING OBVIOUSLY ANNOYED.
HOW RUDE...
HMPH!

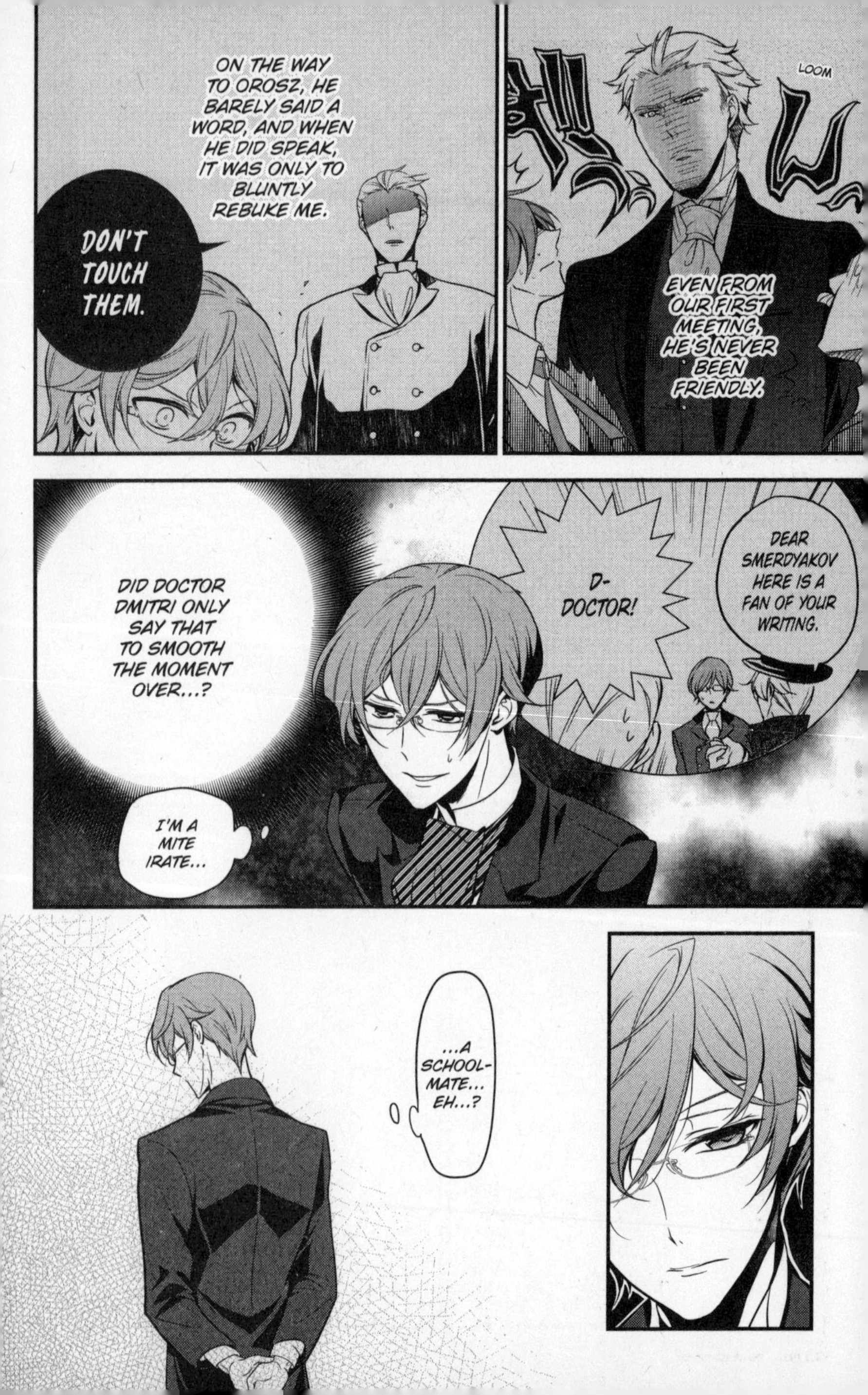
LOOM
EVEN FROM OUR FIRST MEETING, HE'S NEVER BEEN FRIENDLY.
ON THE WAY TO OROSZ, HE BARELY SAID A WORD, AND WHEN HE DID SPEAK, IT WAS ONLY TO BLUNTLY REBUKE ME.
DON'T TOUCH THEM.
DEAR SMERDYAKOV HERE IS A FAN OF YOUR WRITING.
D-DOCTOR!
DID DOCTOR DMITRI ONLY SAY THAT TO SMOOTH THE MOMENT OVER...?
I'M A MITE IRATE...
...A SCHOOL-MATE... EH...?

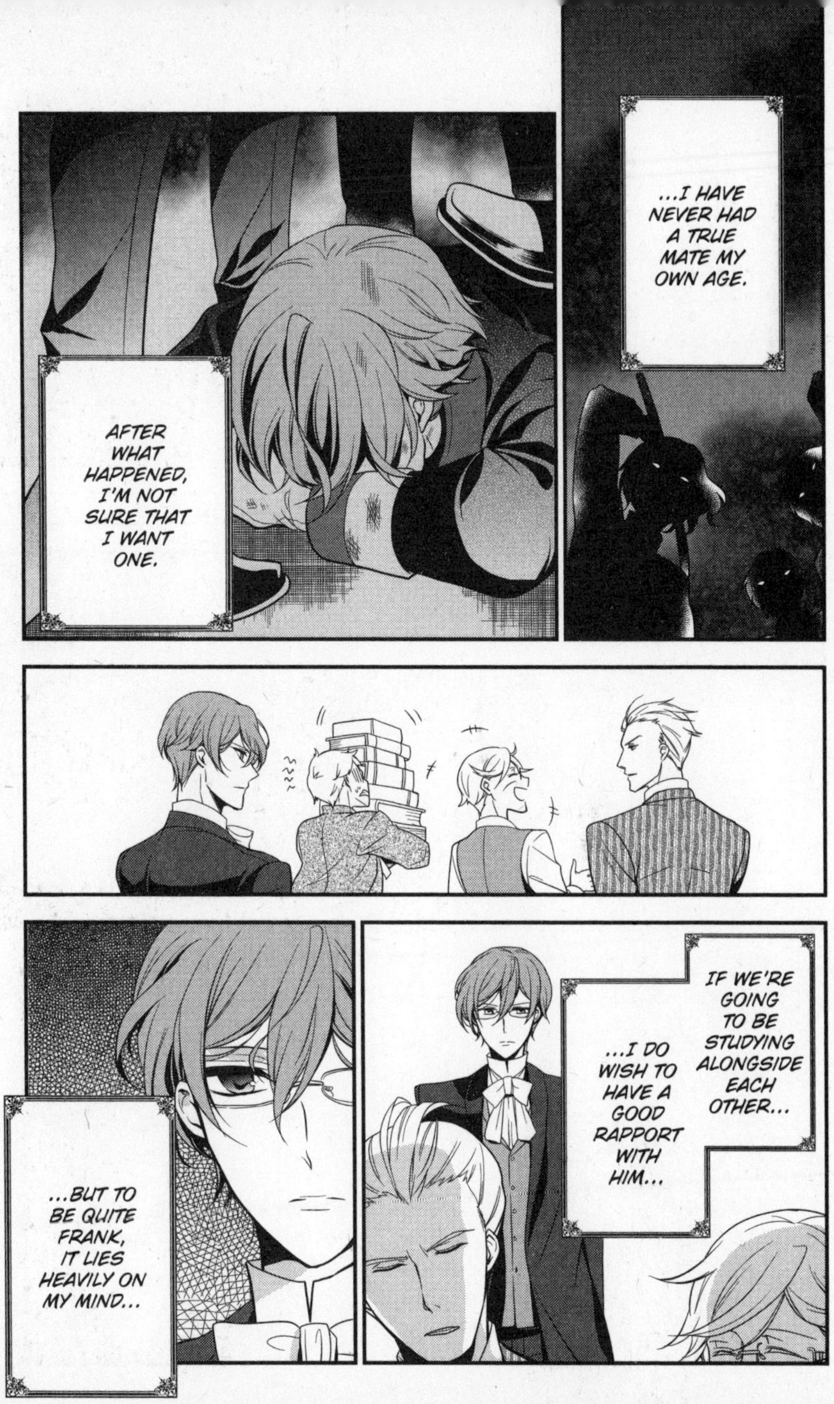
...I HAVE NEVER HAD A TRUE MATE MY OWN AGE.
AFTER WHAT HAPPENED, I'M NOT SURE THAT I WANT ONE.
IF WE'RE GOING TO BE STUDYING ALONGSIDE EACH OTHER...
...I DO WISH TO HAVE A GOOD RAPPORT WITH HIM...
...BUT TO BE QUITE FRANK, IT LIES HEAVILY ON MY MIND...

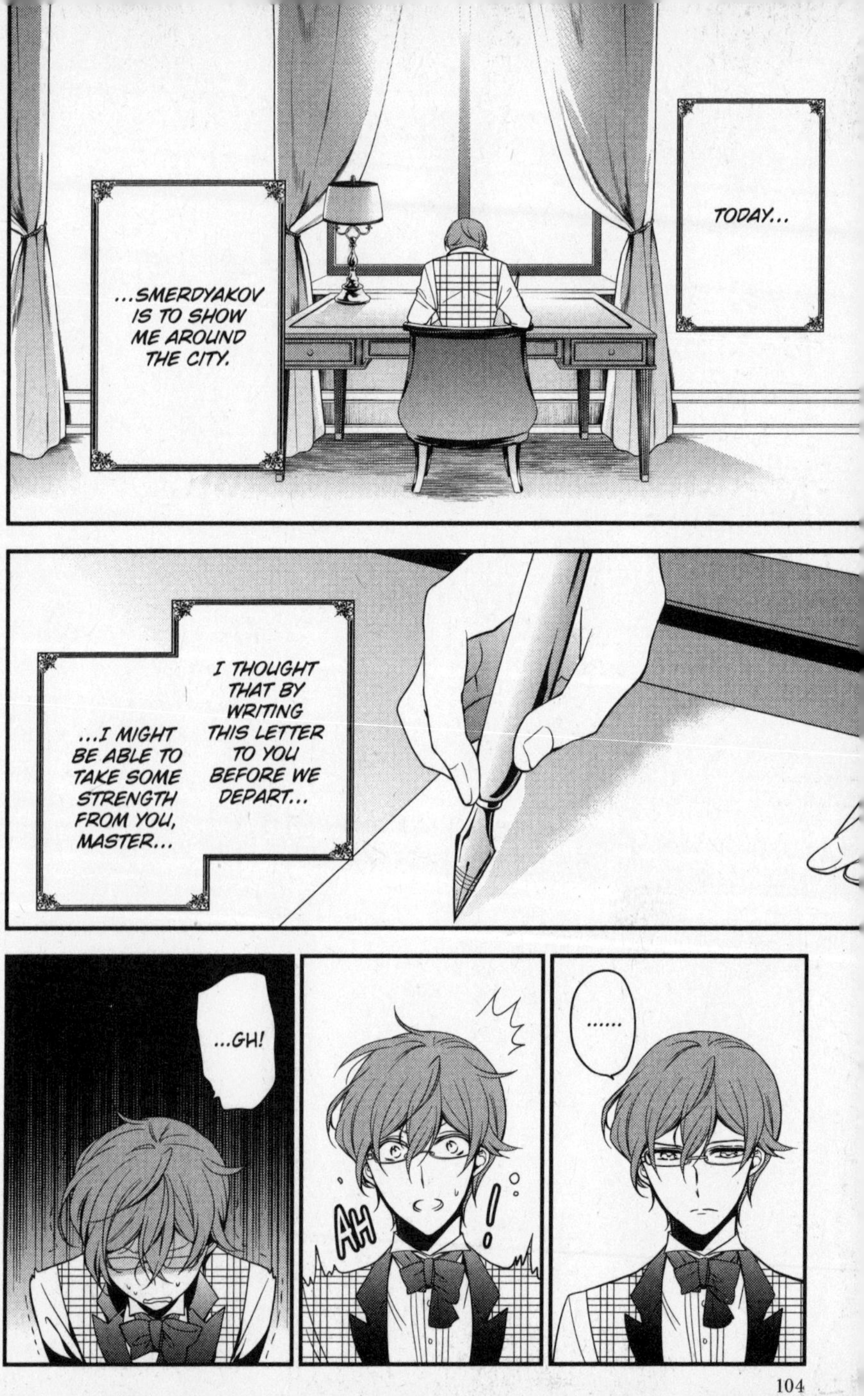
TODAY...
...SMERDYAKOV IS TO SHOW ME AROUND THE CITY.
I THOUGHT THAT BY WRITING THIS LETTER TO YOU BEFORE WE DEPART...
...I MIGHT BE ABLE TO TAKE SOME STRENGTH FROM YOU, MASTER...
......
AH
!
...GH!

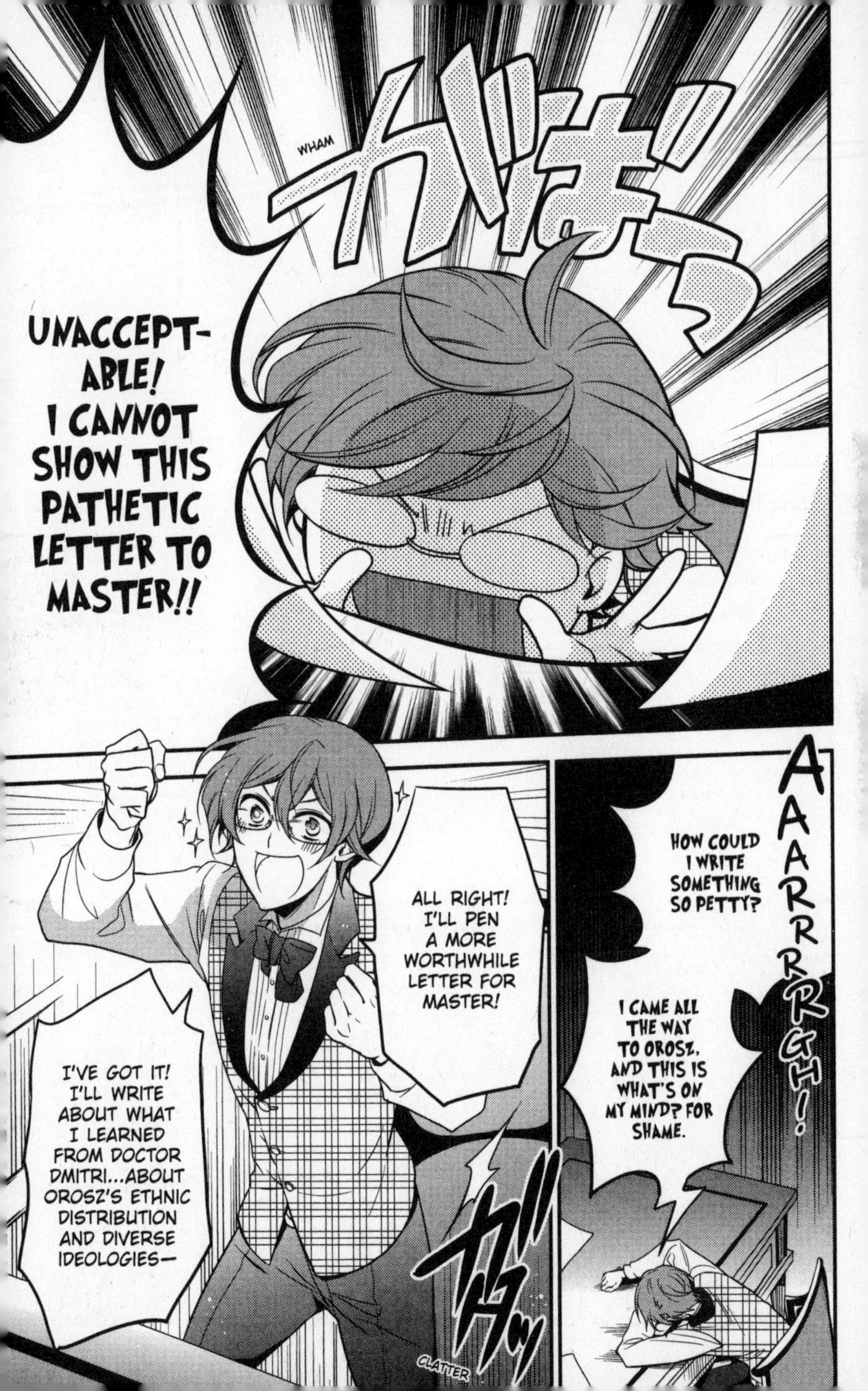
WHAM
UNACCEPT-ABLE! I CANNOT SHOW THIS PATHETIC LETTER TO MASTER!!
AAARRRRGH!
HOW COULD I WRITE SOMETHING SO PETTY?
I CAME ALL THE WAY TO OROSZ, AND THIS IS WHAT'S ON MY MIND? FOR SHAME.
ALL RIGHT! I'LL PEN A MORE WORTHWHILE LETTER FOR MASTER!
I'VE GOT IT! I'LL WRITE ABOUT WHAT I LEARNED FROM DOCTOR DMITRI...ABOUT OROSZ'S ETHNIC DISTRIBUTION AND DIVERSE IDEOLOGIES—
CLATTER

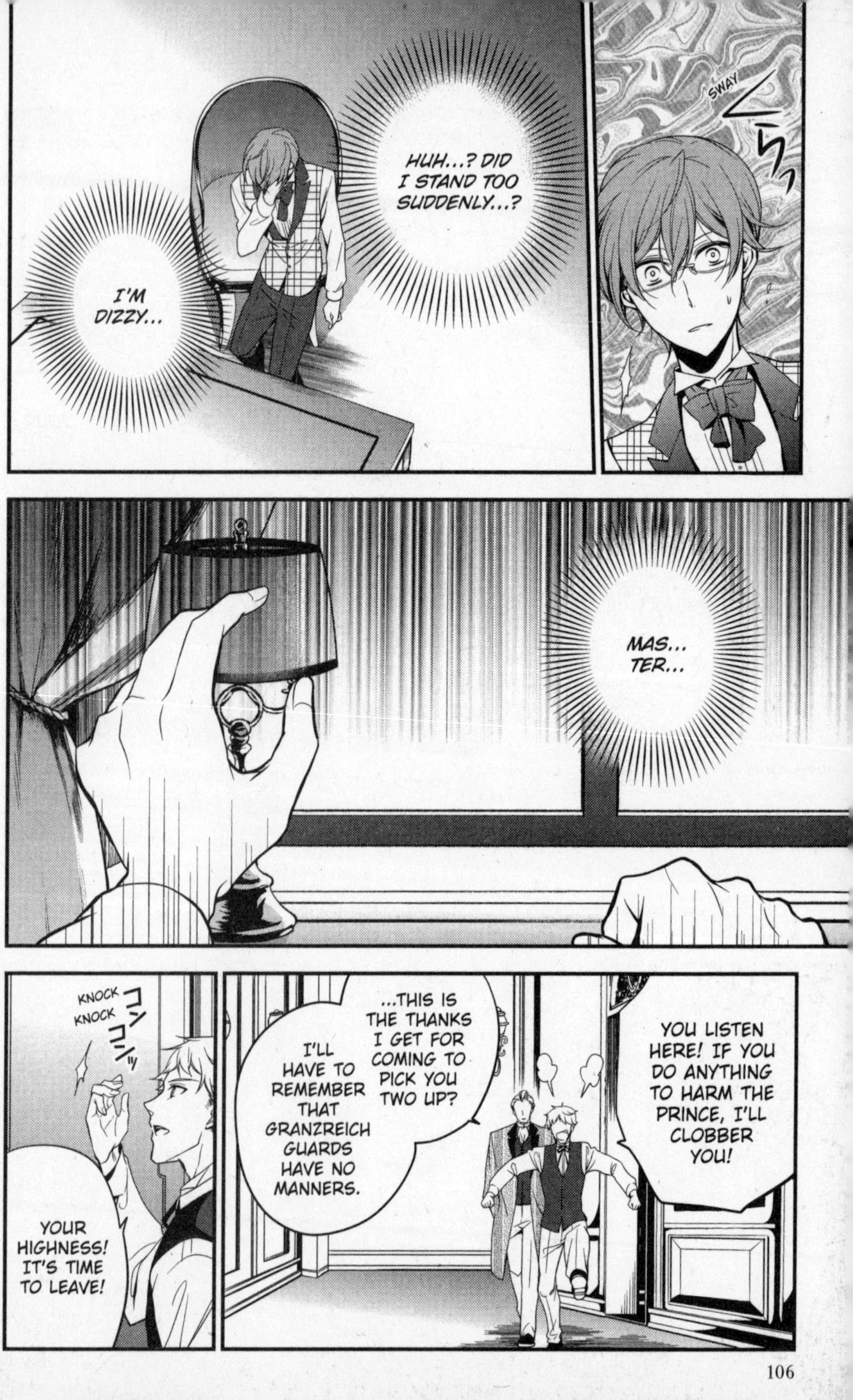
SWAY
HUH...? DID I STAND TOO SUDDENLY...?
I'M DIZZY...
MAS... TER...
YOU LISTEN HERE! IF YOU DO ANYTHING TO HARM THE PRINCE, I'LL CLOBBER YOU!
...THIS IS THE THANKS I GET FOR COMING TO PICK YOU TWO UP?
I'LL HAVE TO REMEMBER THAT GRANZREICH GUARDS HAVE NO MANNERS.
KNOCK KNOCK
YOUR HIGHNESS! IT'S TIME TO LEAVE!

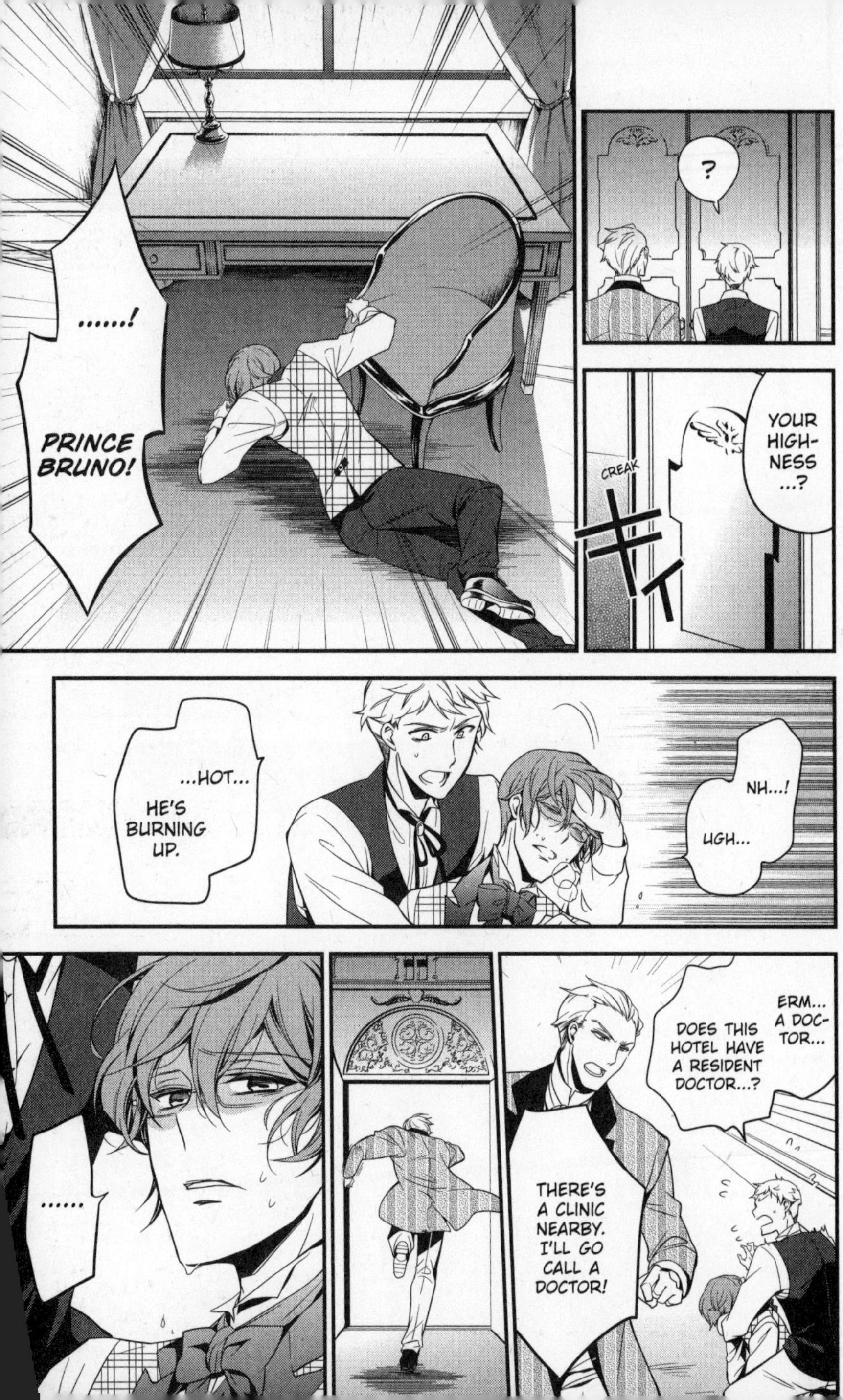
?
YOUR HIGH-NESS ...?
CREAK
......!
PRINCE BRUNO!
NH...!
UGH...
...HOT...
HE'S BURNING UP.
ERM... A DOC-TOR...
DOES THIS HOTEL HAVE A RESIDENT DOCTOR...?
THERE'S A CLINIC NEARBY. I'LL GO CALL A DOCTOR!
......

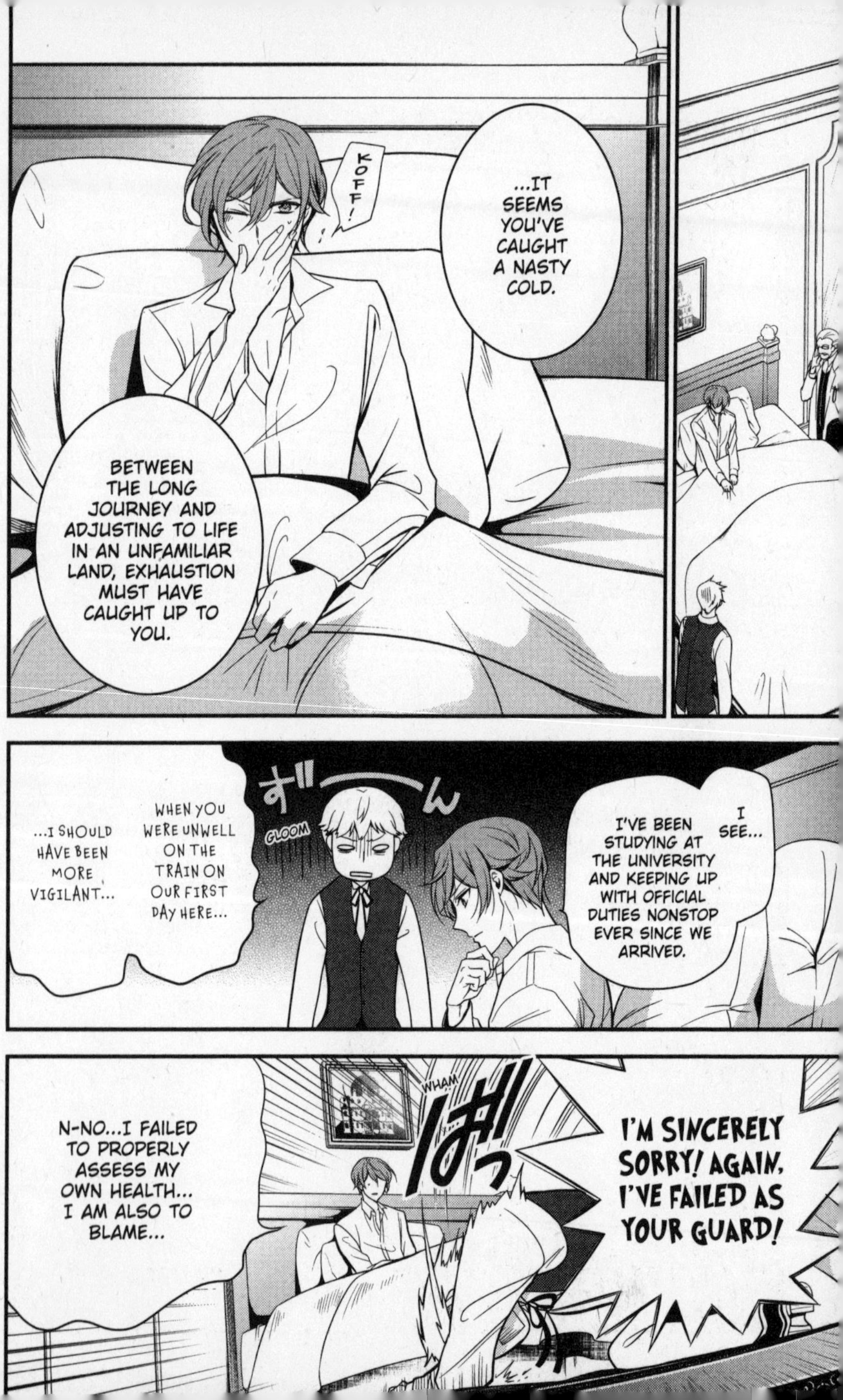
...IT SEEMS YOU'VE CAUGHT A NASTY COLD.
KOFF!
BETWEEN THE LONG JOURNEY AND ADJUSTING TO LIFE IN AN UNFAMILIAR LAND, EXHAUSTION MUST HAVE CAUGHT UP TO YOU.
I SEE...
I'VE BEEN STUDYING AT THE UNIVERSITY AND KEEPING UP WITH OFFICIAL DUTIES NONSTOP EVER SINCE WE ARRIVED.
ず──ん
GLOOM
WHEN YOU WERE UNWELL ON THE TRAIN ON OUR FIRST DAY HERE...
...I SHOULD HAVE BEEN MORE VIGILANT...
WHAM
ぱっ
I'M SINCERELY SORRY! AGAIN, I'VE FAILED AS YOUR GUARD!
N-NO...I FAILED TO PROPERLY ASSESS MY OWN HEALTH... I AM ALSO TO BLAME...

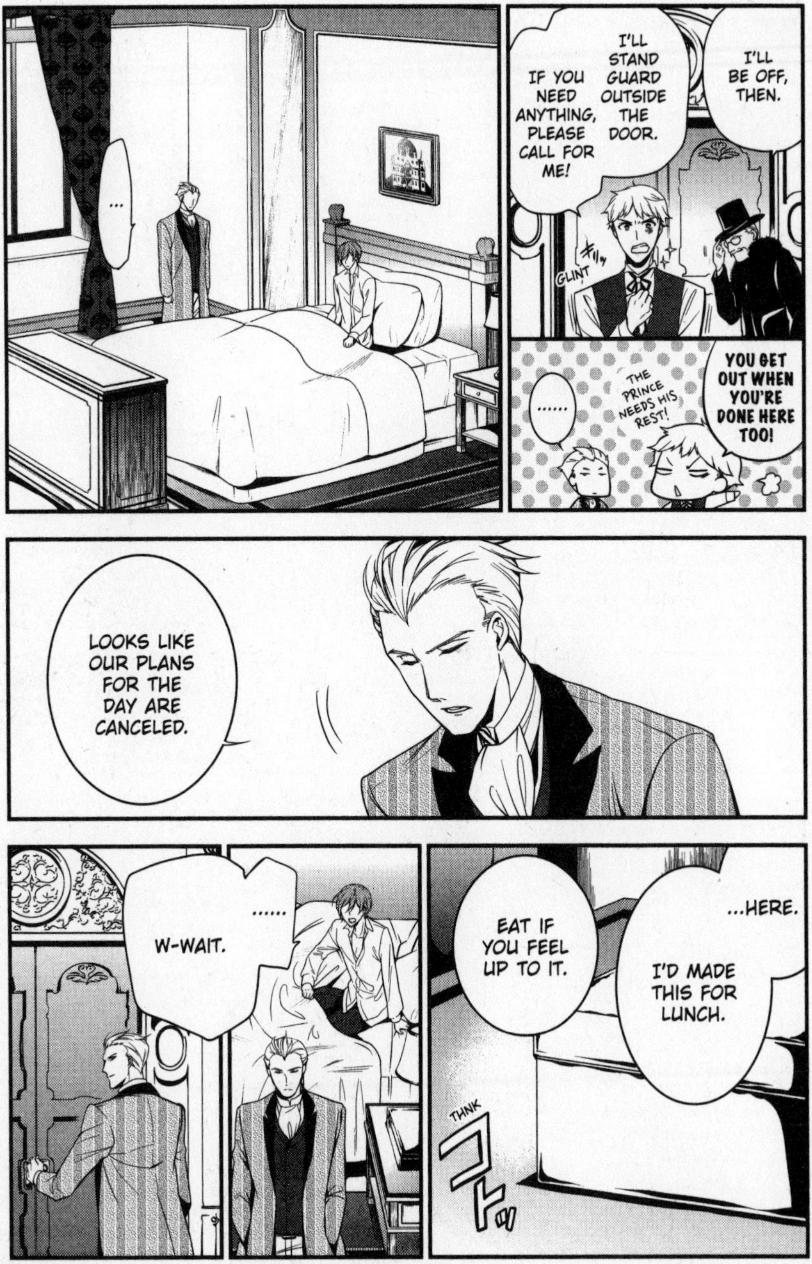
I'LL BE OFF, THEN.
I'LL STAND GUARD OUTSIDE THE DOOR.
IF YOU NEED ANYTHING, PLEASE CALL FOR ME!
GLINT
YOU GET OUT WHEN YOU'RE DONE HERE TOO!
THE PRINCE NEEDS HIS REST!
......
...
LOOKS LIKE OUR PLANS FOR THE DAY ARE CANCELED.
...HERE.
I'D MADE THIS FOR LUNCH.
EAT IF YOU FEEL UP TO IT.
THNK
......
W-WAIT.

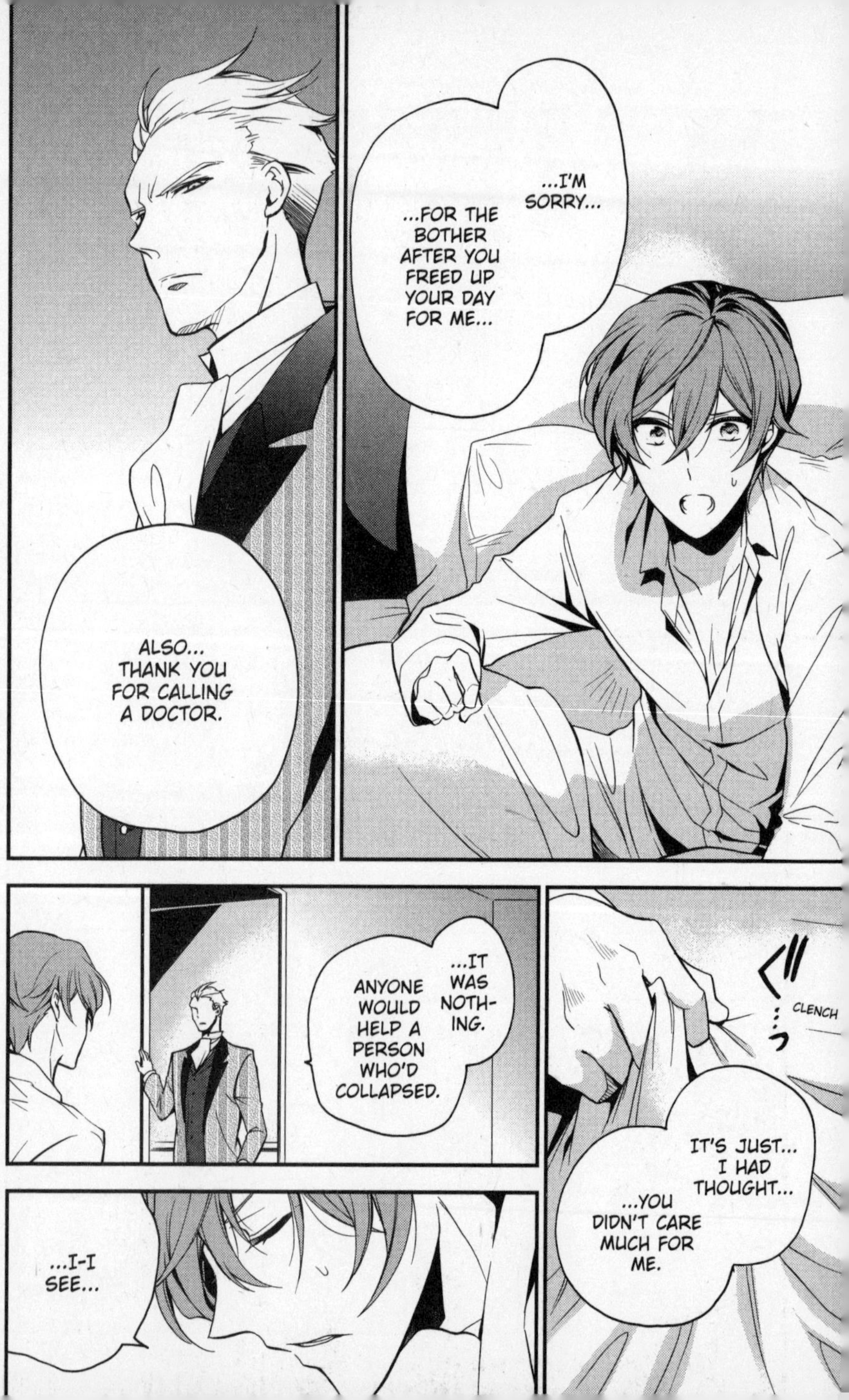
...I'M SORRY...
...FOR THE BOTHER AFTER YOU FREED UP YOUR DAY FOR ME...
ALSO... THANK YOU FOR CALLING A DOCTOR.
CLENCH
IT'S JUST... I HAD THOUGHT...
...YOU DIDN'T CARE MUCH FOR ME.
...IT WAS NOTH-ING.
ANYONE WOULD HELP A PERSON WHO'D COLLAPSED.
...I-I SEE...

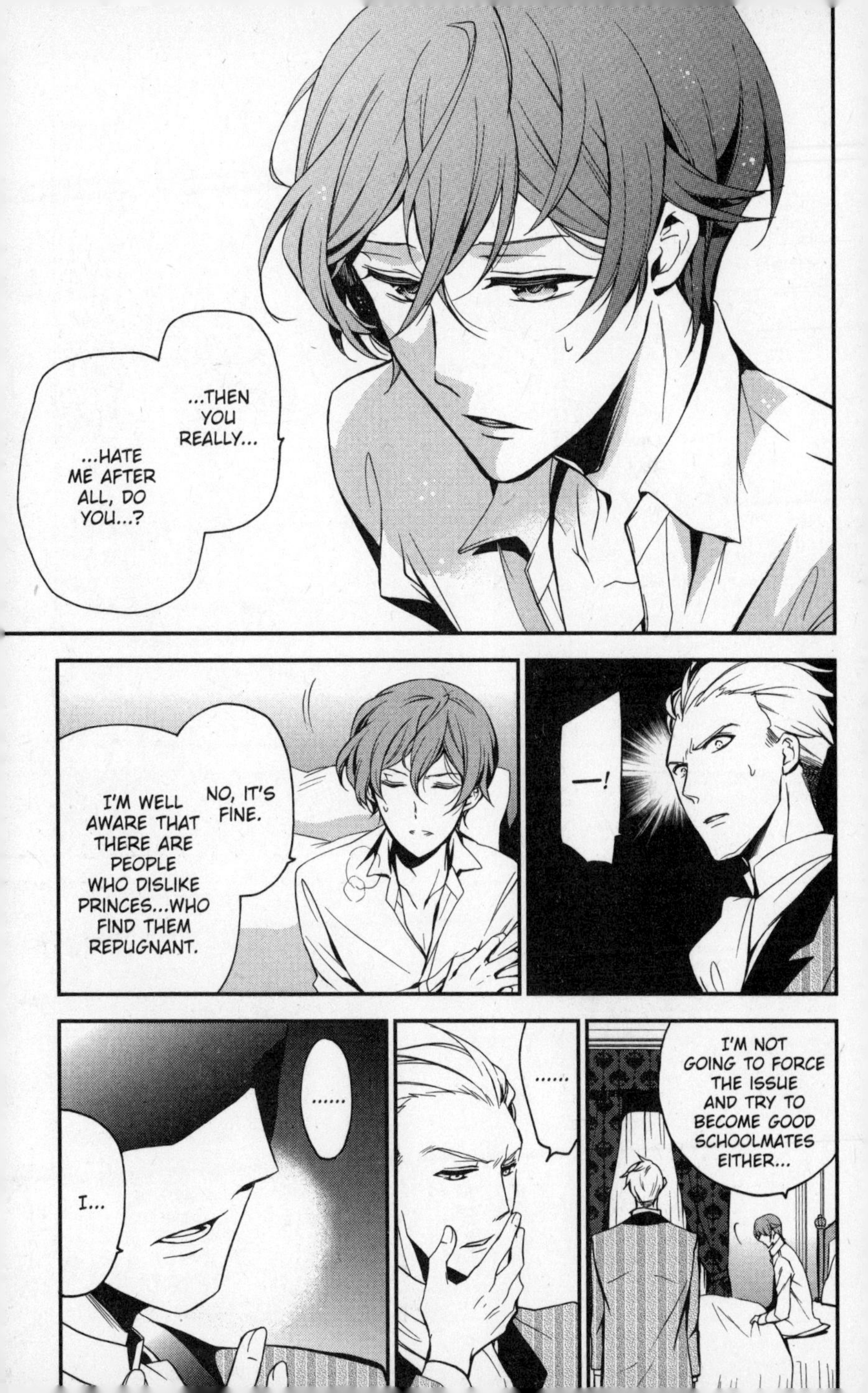
...THEN YOU REALLY...
...HATE ME AFTER ALL, DO YOU...?
—!
NO, IT'S FINE.
I'M WELL AWARE THAT THERE ARE PEOPLE WHO DISLIKE PRINCES...WHO FIND THEM REPUGNANT.
I'M NOT GOING TO FORCE THE ISSUE AND TRY TO BECOME GOOD SCHOOLMATES EITHER...
......
......
I...

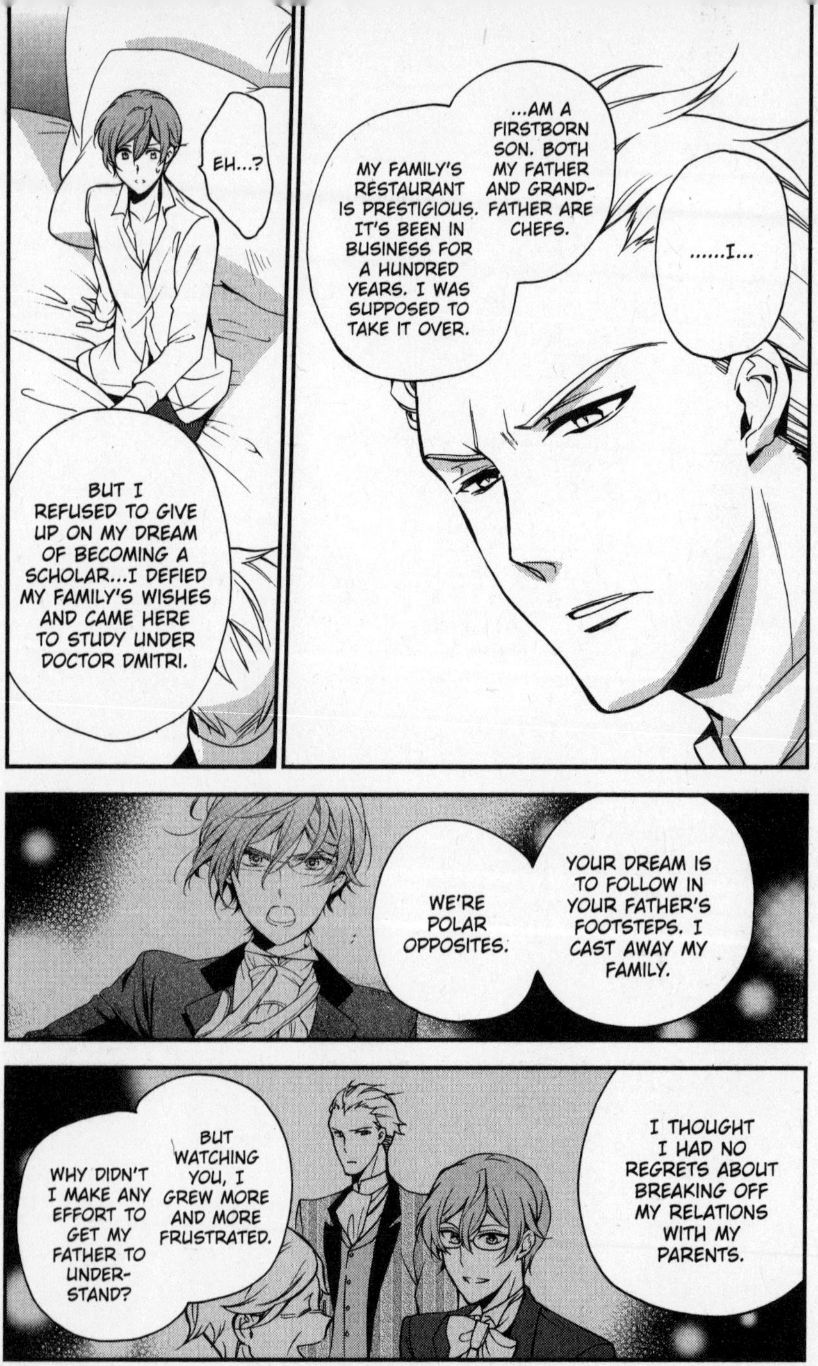
......I...
...AM A FIRSTBORN SON. BOTH MY FATHER AND GRAND-FATHER ARE CHEFS.
MY FAMILY'S RESTAURANT IS PRESTIGIOUS. IT'S BEEN IN BUSINESS FOR A HUNDRED YEARS. I WAS SUPPOSED TO TAKE IT OVER.
EH...?
BUT I REFUSED TO GIVE UP ON MY DREAM OF BECOMING A SCHOLAR...I DEFIED MY FAMILY'S WISHES AND CAME HERE TO STUDY UNDER DOCTOR DMITRI.
YOUR DREAM IS TO FOLLOW IN YOUR FATHER'S FOOTSTEPS. I CAST AWAY MY FAMILY.
WE'RE POLAR OPPOSITES.
I THOUGHT I HAD NO REGRETS ABOUT BREAKING OFF MY RELATIONS WITH MY PARENTS.
BUT WATCHING YOU, I GREW MORE AND MORE FRUSTRATED.
WHY DIDN'T I MAKE ANY EFFORT TO GET MY FATHER TO UNDER-STAND?

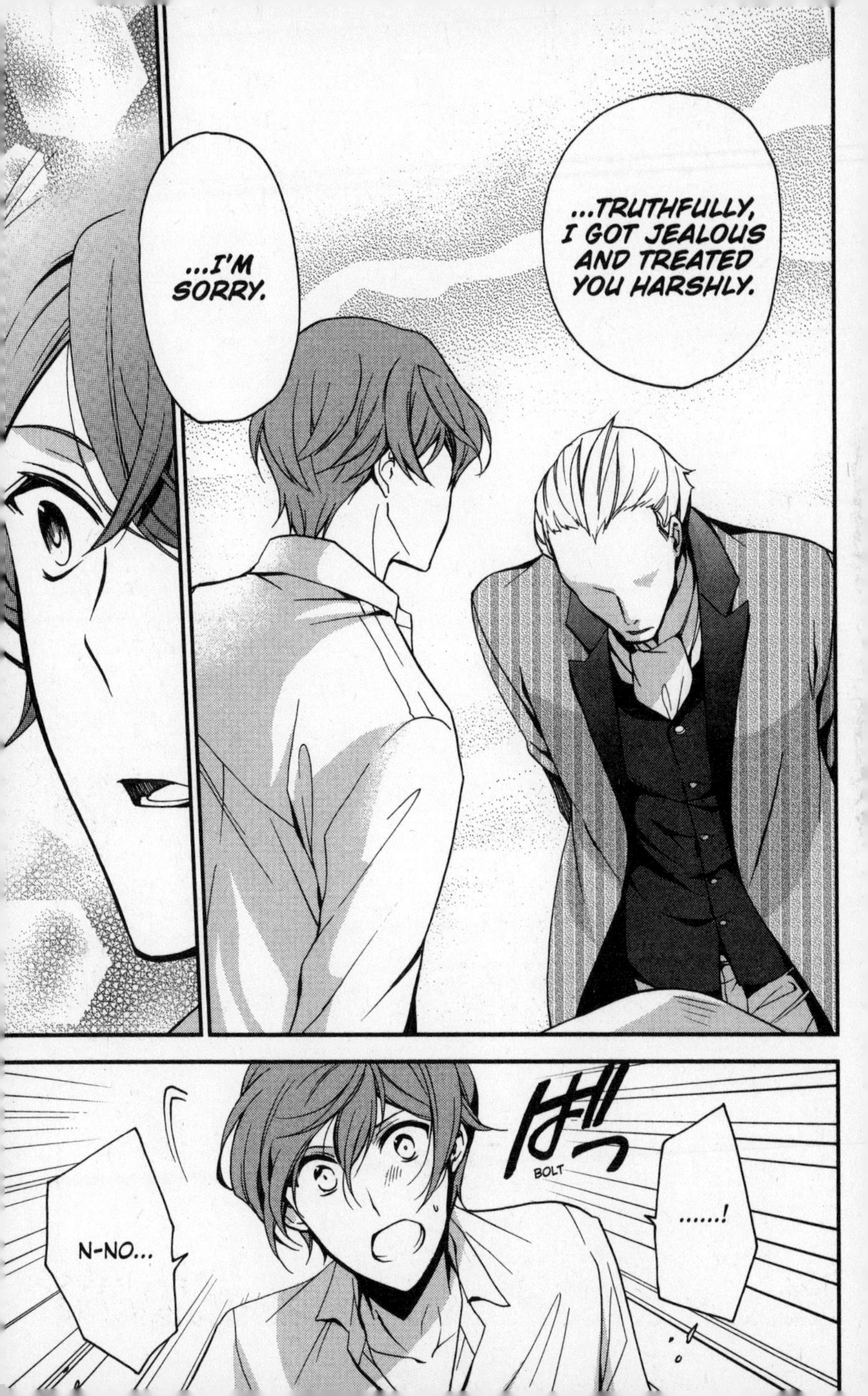
...TRUTHFULLY, I GOT JEALOUS AND TREATED YOU HARSHLY.
...I'M SORRY.
......!
BOLT
N-NO...

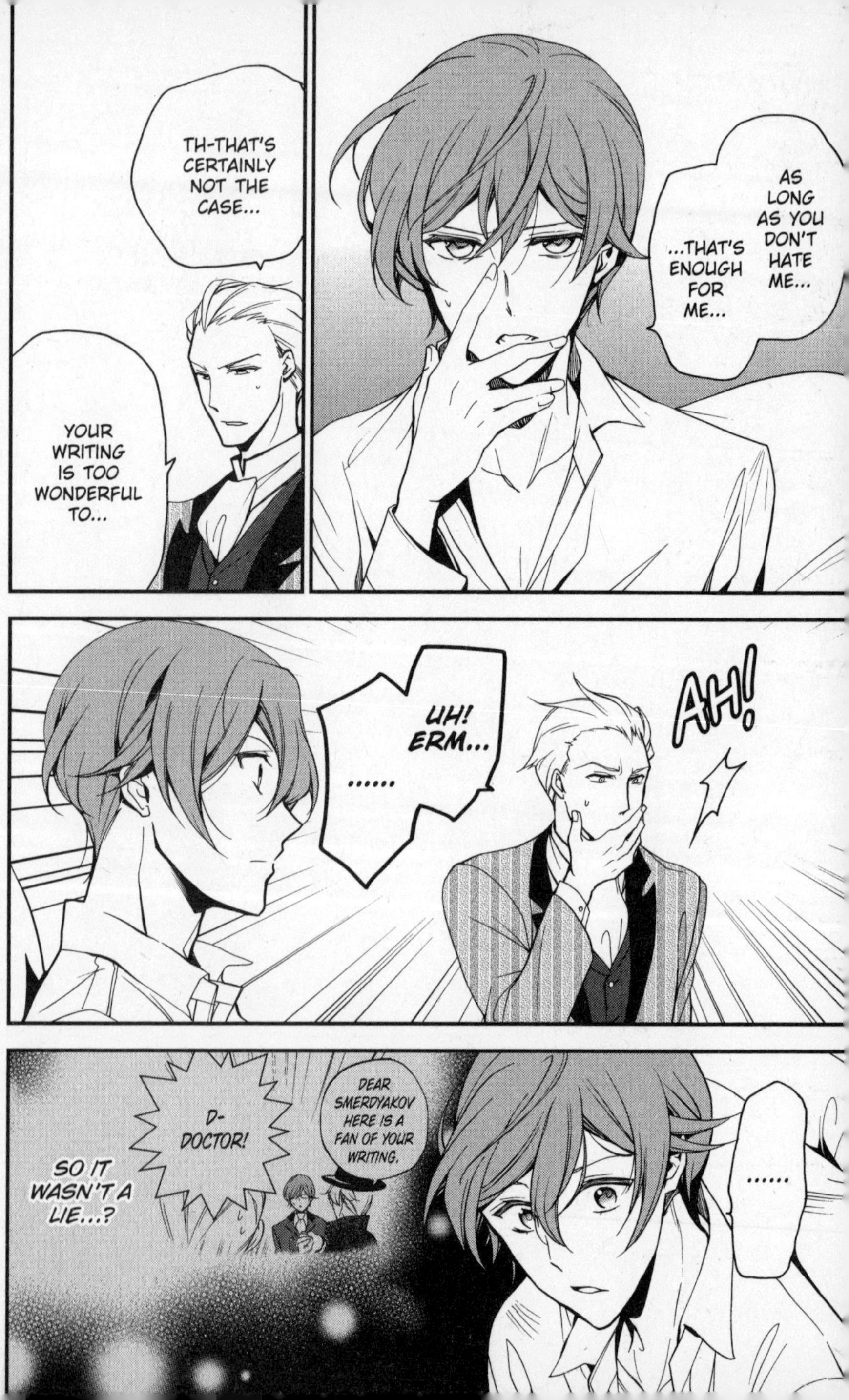
AS LONG AS YOU DON'T HATE ME...
...THAT'S ENOUGH FOR ME...
TH-THAT'S CERTAINLY NOT THE CASE...
YOUR WRITING IS TOO WONDERFUL TO...
AH!
UH! ERM...
......
......
DEAR SMERDYAKOV HERE IS A FAN OF YOUR WRITING.
D-DOCTOR!
SO IT WASN'T A LIE...?

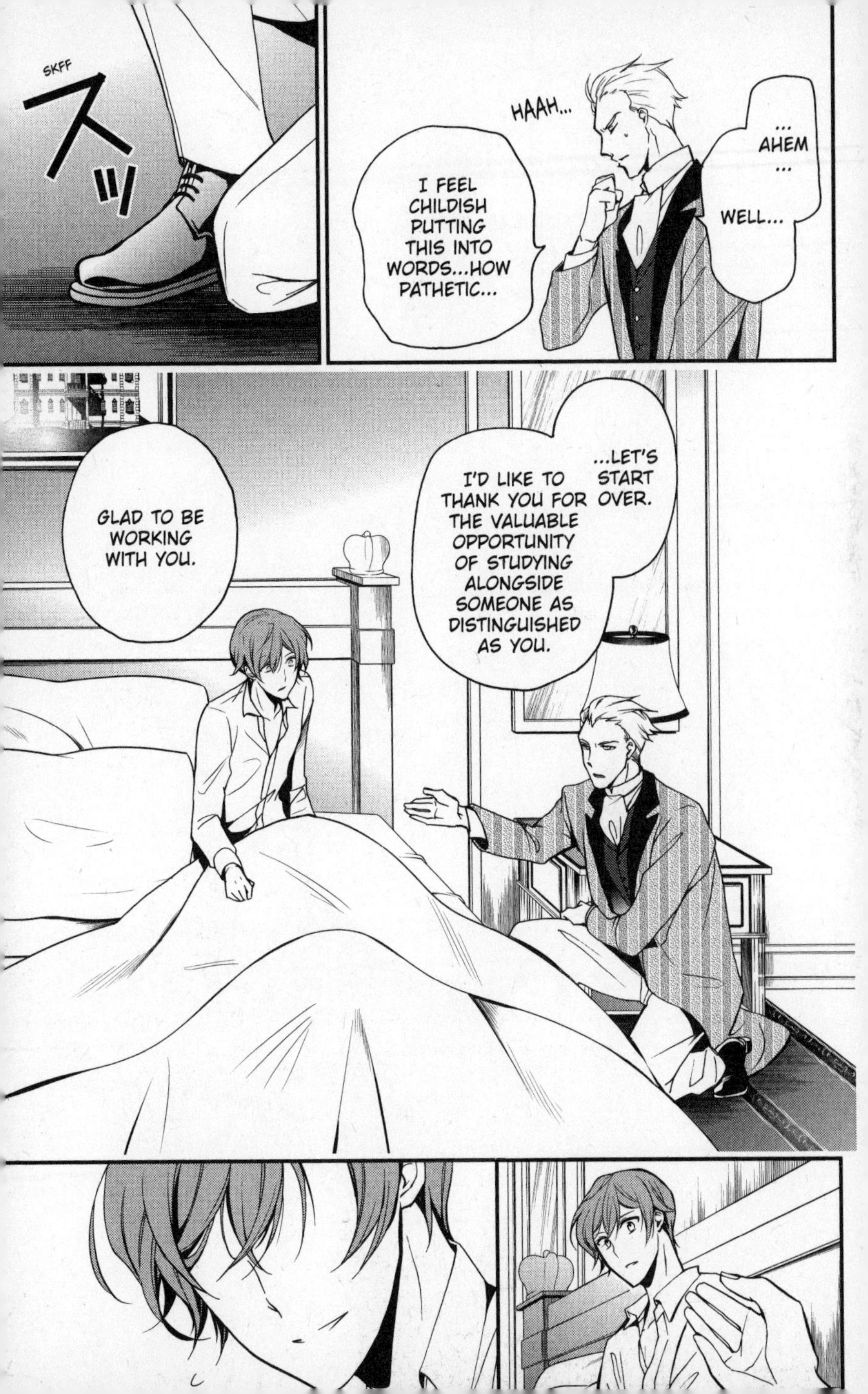
HAAH...
... AHEM ...
WELL...
I FEEL CHILDISH PUTTING THIS INTO WORDS...HOW PATHETIC...
SKFF
...LET'S START OVER.
I'D LIKE TO THANK YOU FOR THE VALUABLE OPPORTUNITY OF STUDYING ALONGSIDE SOMEONE AS DISTINGUISHED AS YOU.
GLAD TO BE WORKING WITH YOU.

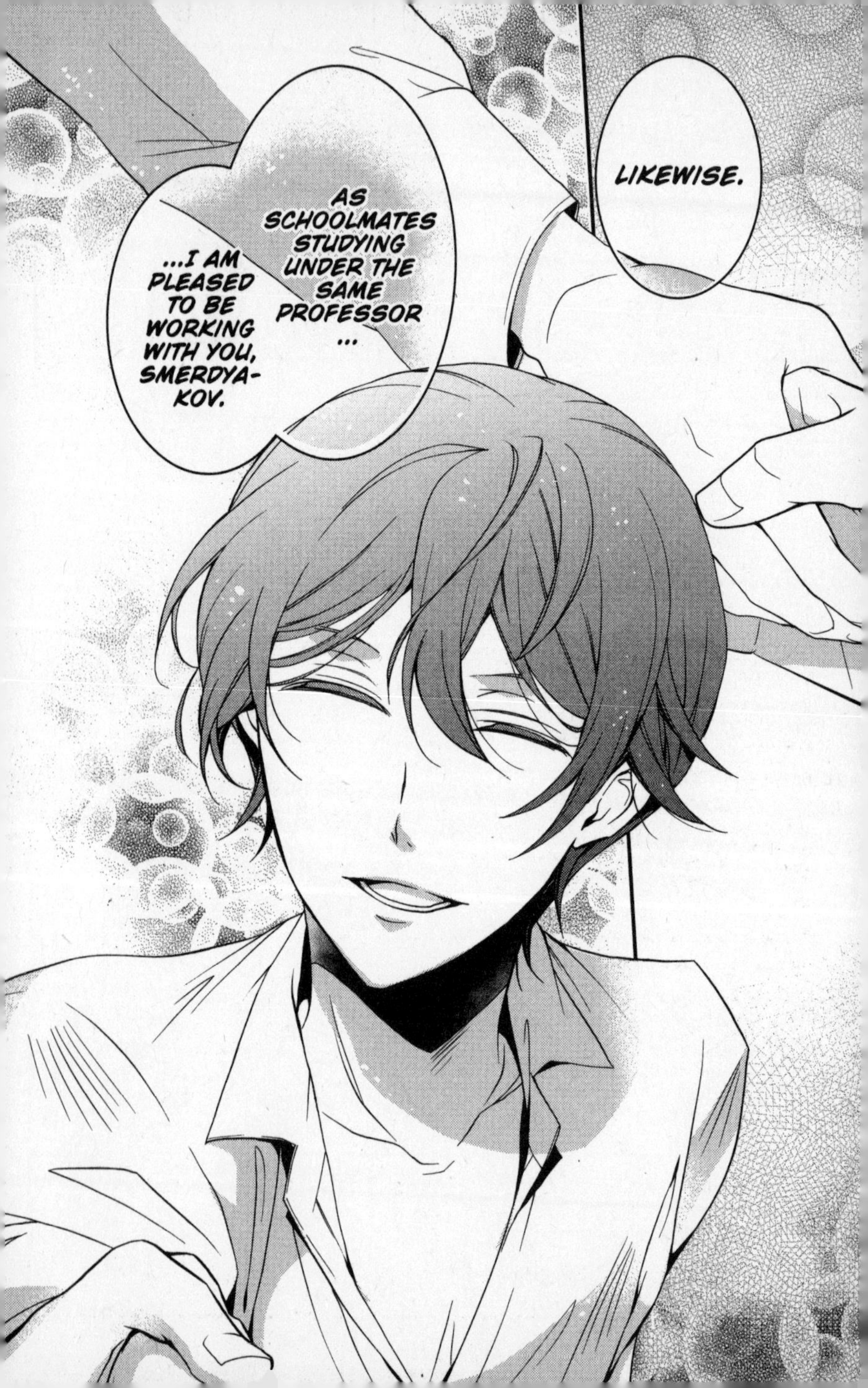
LIKEWISE.
AS SCHOOLMATES STUDYING UNDER THE SAME PROFESSOR...
...I AM PLEASED TO BE WORKING WITH YOU, SMERDYAKOV.

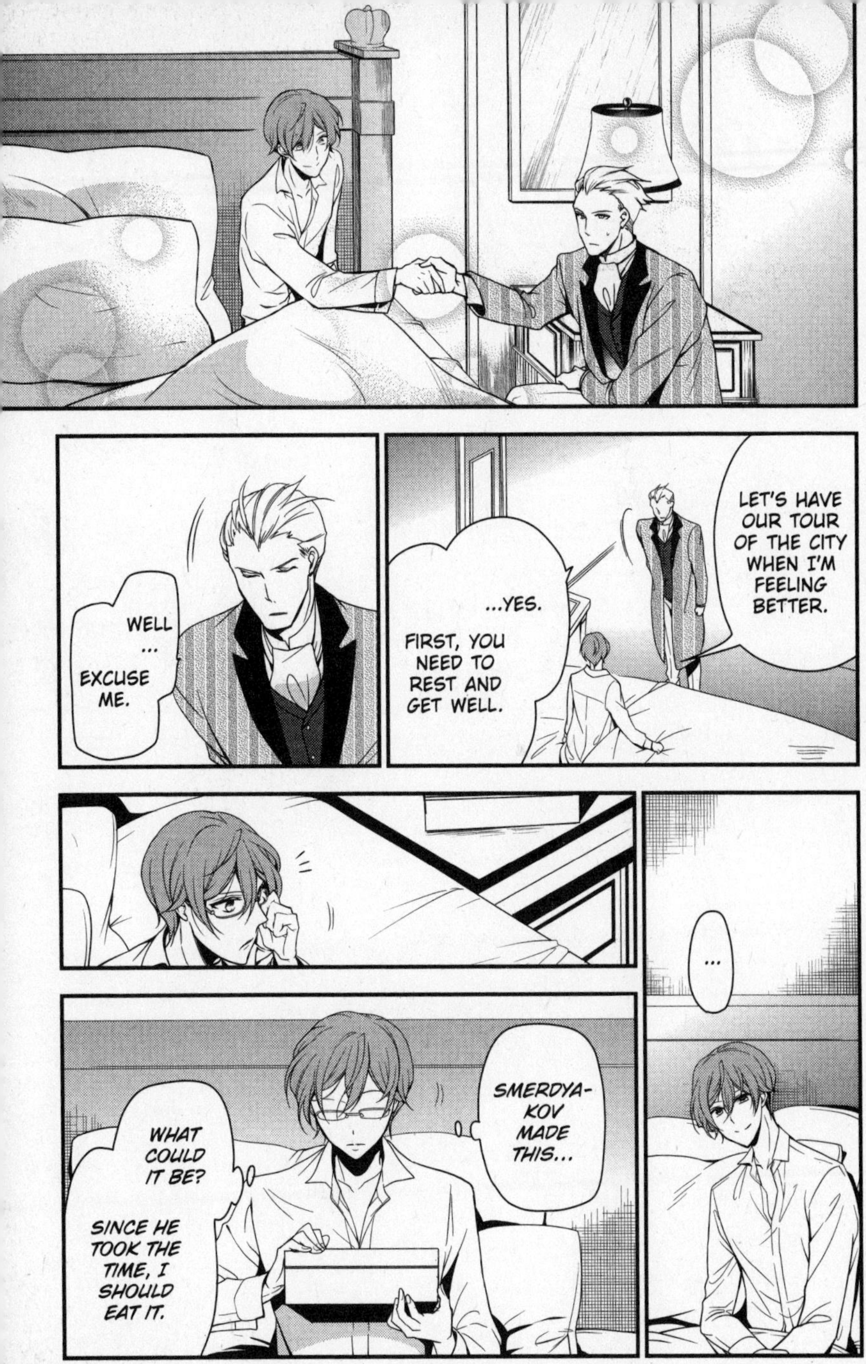
LET'S HAVE OUR TOUR OF THE CITY WHEN I'M FEELING BETTER.
...YES.
FIRST, YOU NEED TO REST AND GET WELL.
WELL ... EXCUSE ME.
...
SMERDYA-KOV MADE THIS...
WHAT COULD IT BE?
SINCE HE TOOK THE TIME, I SHOULD EAT IT.

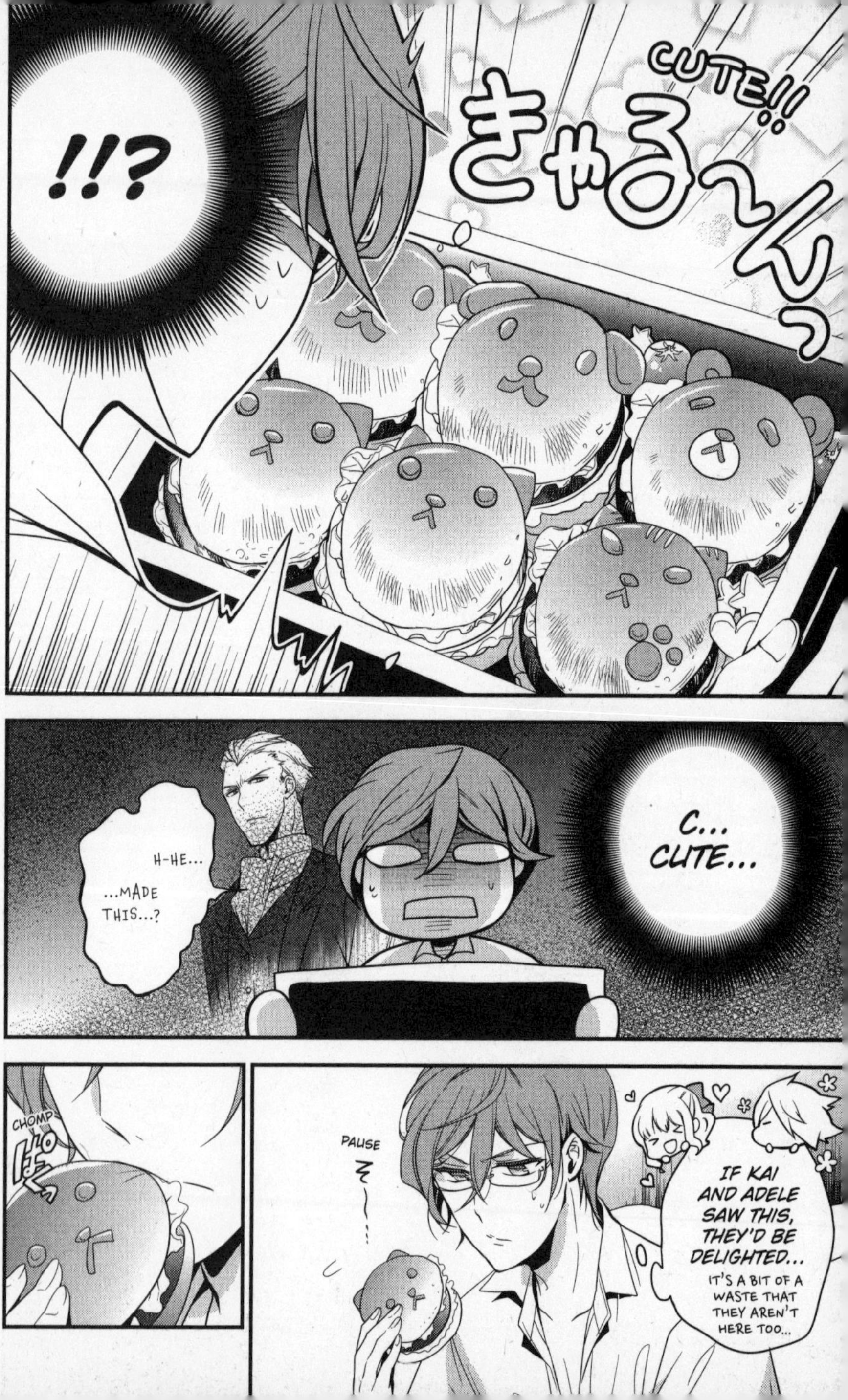
CUTE!!
きゅる〜んっ
!!?
C... CUTE...
H-HE...
...MADE THIS...?
PAUSE
IF KAI AND ADELE SAW THIS, THEY'D BE DELIGHTED...
IT'S A BIT OF A WASTE THAT THEY AREN'T HERE TOO...
CHOMP
ぱくっ

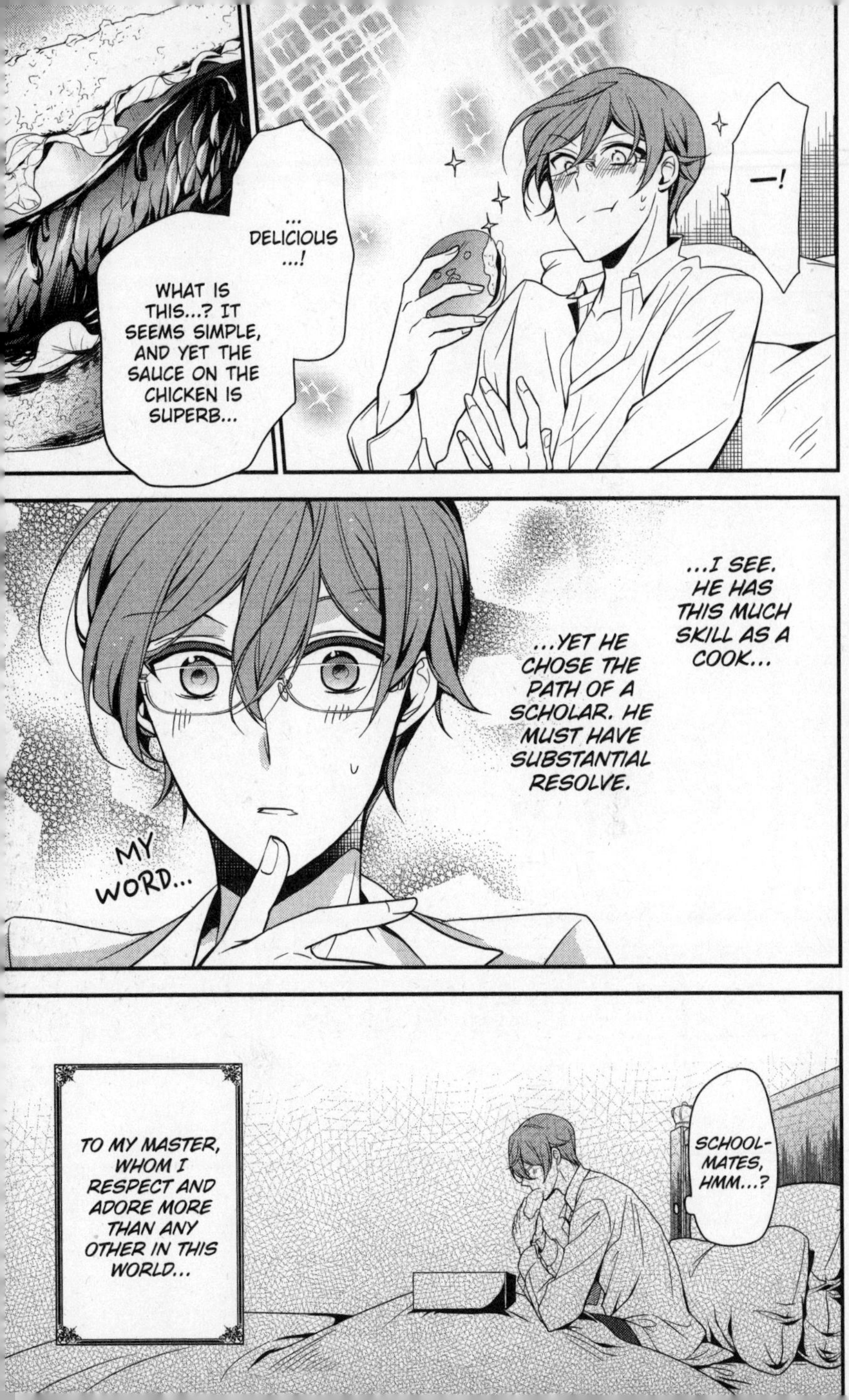
—!
... DELICIOUS ...!
WHAT IS THIS...? IT SEEMS SIMPLE, AND YET THE SAUCE ON THE CHICKEN IS SUPERB...
...I SEE. HE HAS THIS MUCH SKILL AS A COOK...
...YET HE CHOSE THE PATH OF A SCHOLAR. HE MUST HAVE SUBSTANTIAL RESOLVE.
MY WORD...
SCHOOL-MATES, HMM...?
TO MY MASTER, WHOM I RESPECT AND ADORE MORE THAN ANY OTHER IN THIS WORLD...

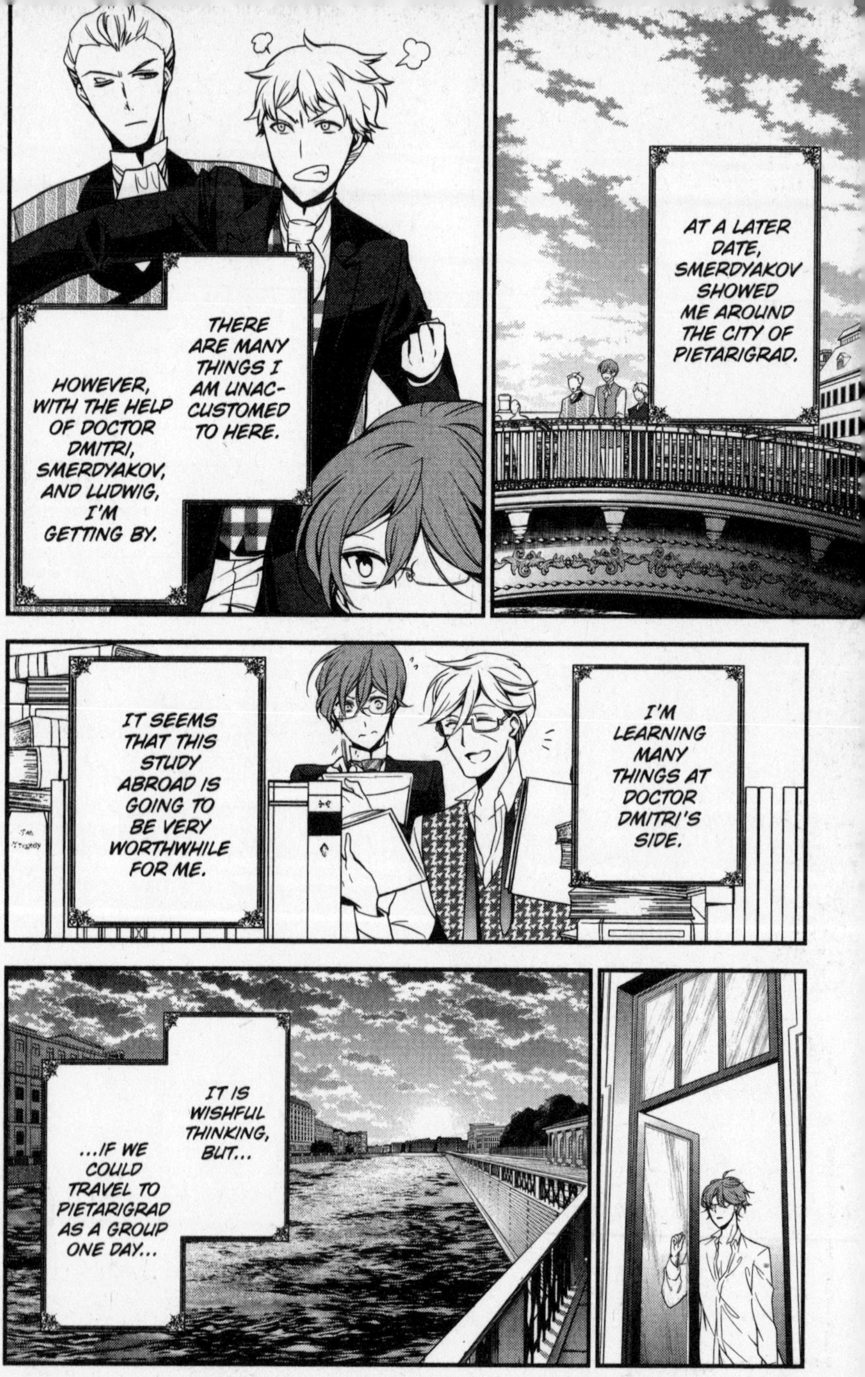
AT A LATER DATE, SMERDYAKOV SHOWED ME AROUND THE CITY OF PIETARIGRAD.
THERE ARE MANY THINGS I AM UNACCUSTOMED TO HERE.
HOWEVER, WITH THE HELP OF DOCTOR DMITRI, SMERDYAKOV, AND LUDWIG, I'M GETTING BY.
I'M LEARNING MANY THINGS AT DOCTOR DMITRI'S SIDE.
IT SEEMS THAT THIS STUDY ABROAD IS GOING TO BE VERY WORTHWHILE FOR ME.
IT IS WISHFUL THINKING, BUT...
...IF WE COULD TRAVEL TO PIETARIGRAD AS A GROUP ONE DAY...

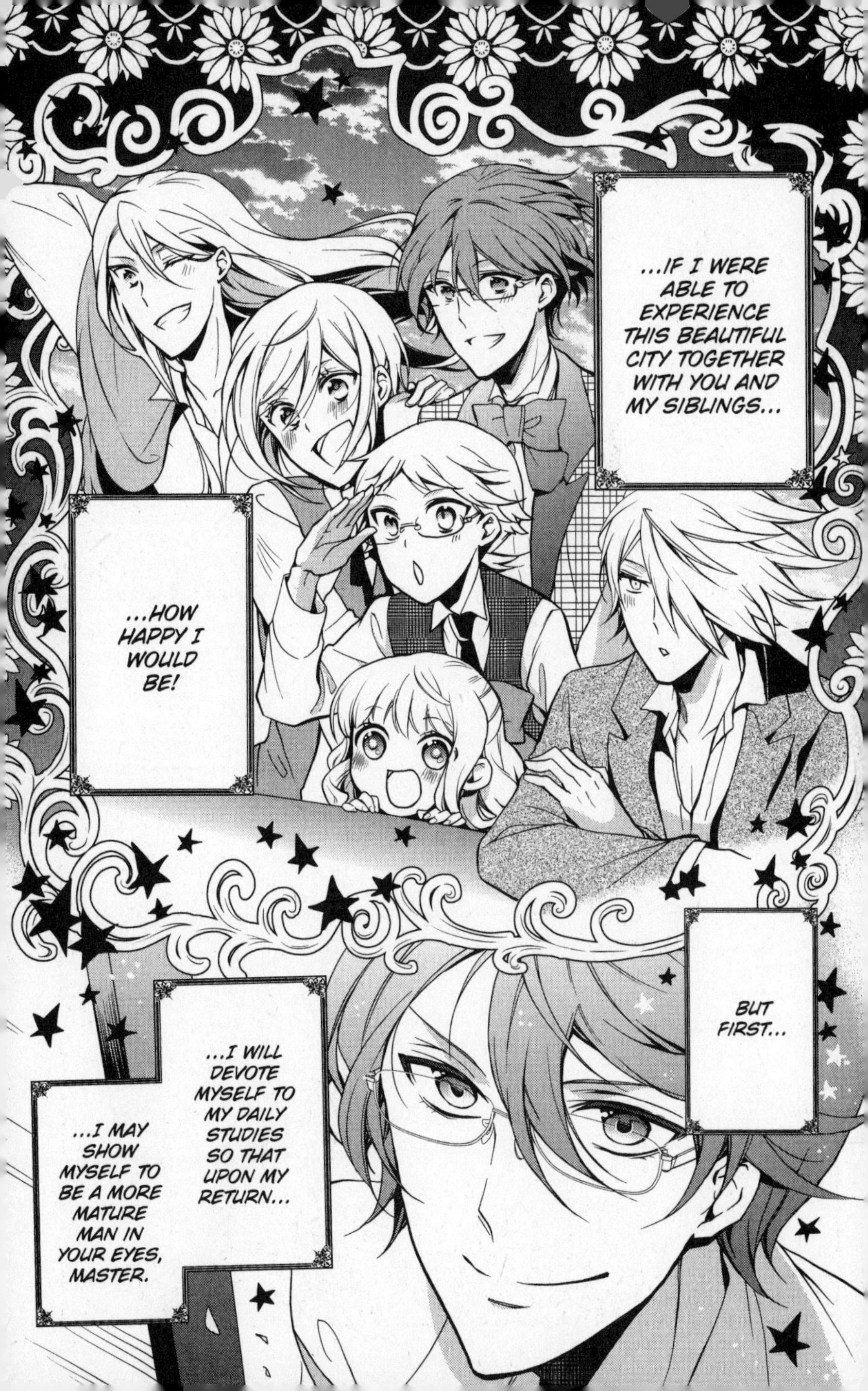
...IF I WERE ABLE TO EXPERIENCE THIS BEAUTIFUL CITY TOGETHER WITH YOU AND MY SIBLINGS...
...HOW HAPPY I WOULD BE!
BUT FIRST...
...I WILL DEVOTE MYSELF TO MY DAILY STUDIES SO THAT UPON MY RETURN...
...I MAY SHOW MYSELF TO BE A MORE MATURE MAN IN YOUR EYES, MASTER.

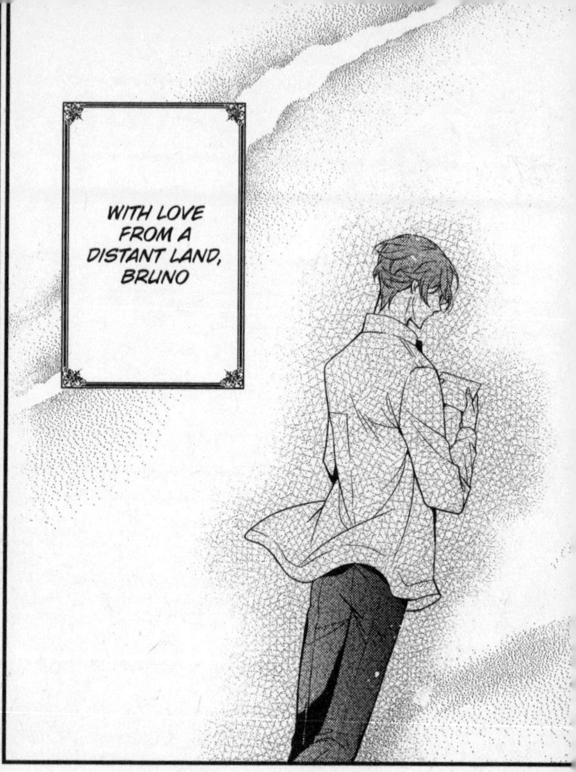
WITH LOVE
FROM A
DISTANT LAND,
BRUNO

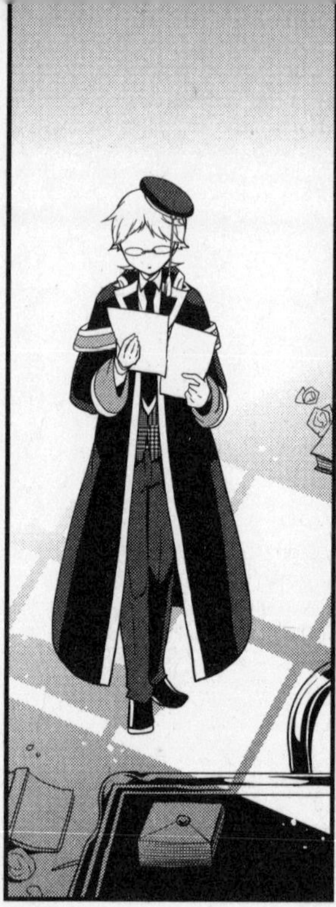

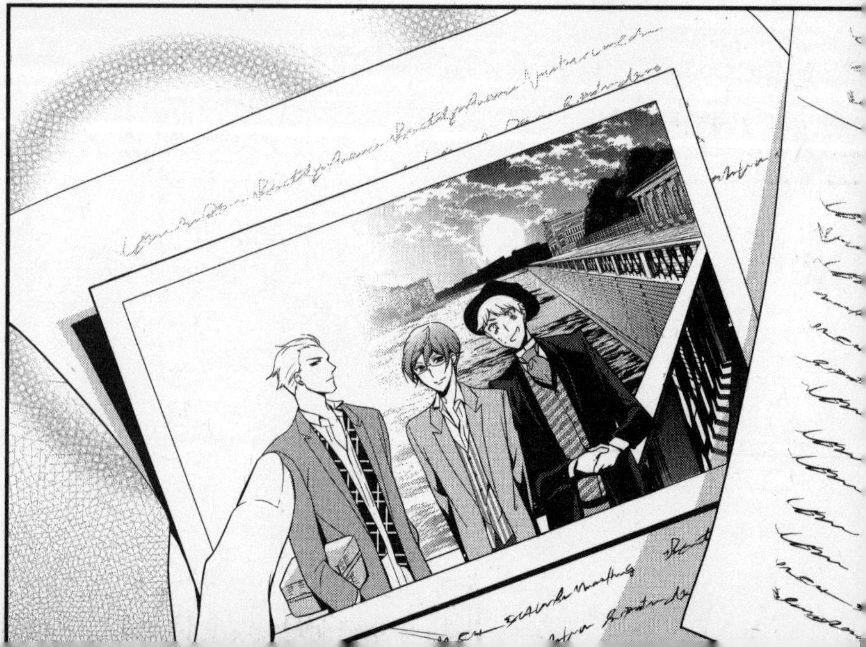

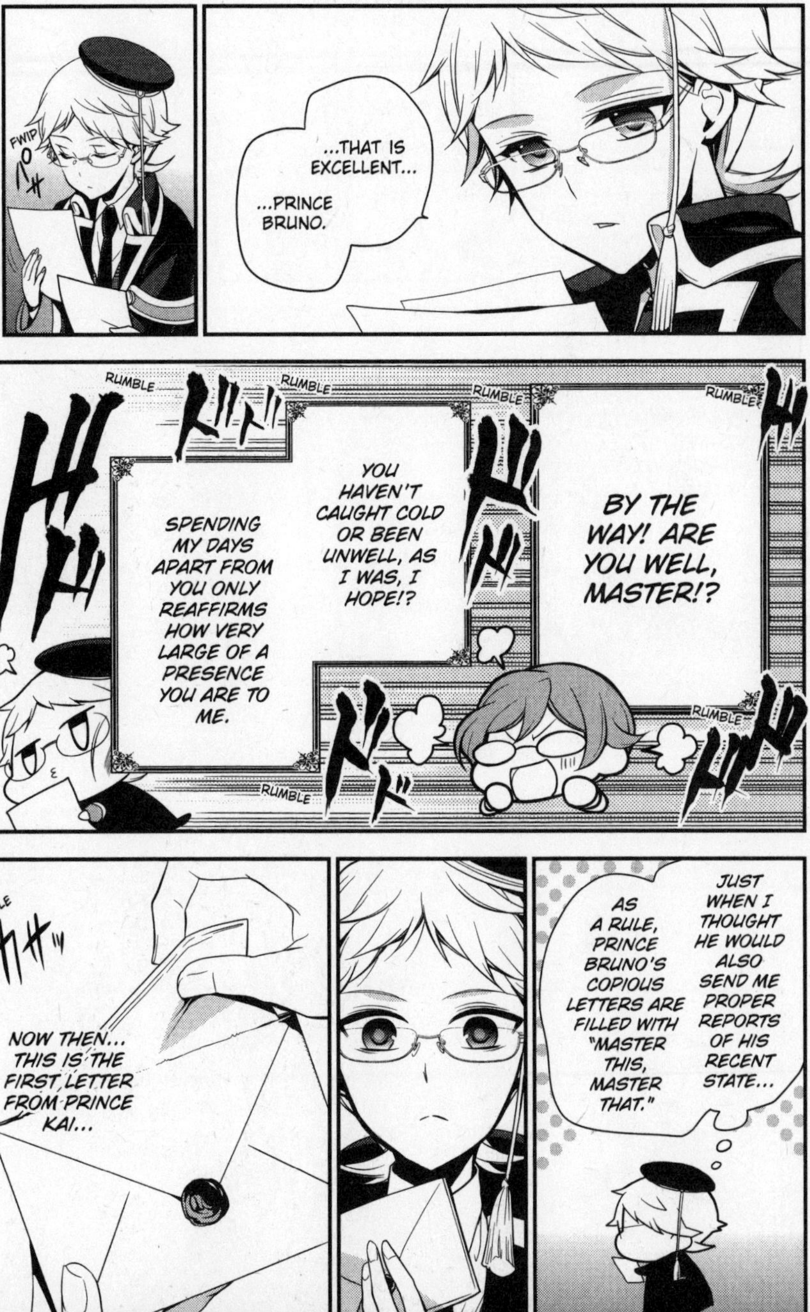
...THAT IS EXCELLENT...
...PRINCE BRUNO.
FWIP
RUMBLE
BY THE WAY! ARE YOU WELL, MASTER!?
RUMBLE
YOU HAVEN'T CAUGHT COLD OR BEEN UNWELL, AS I WAS, I HOPE!?
RUMBLE
SPENDING MY DAYS APART FROM YOU ONLY REAFFIRMS HOW VERY LARGE OF A PRESENCE YOU ARE TO ME.
RUMBLE
RUMBLE
RUMBLE
JUST WHEN I THOUGHT HE WOULD ALSO SEND ME PROPER REPORTS OF HIS RECENT STATE...
AS A RULE, PRINCE BRUNO'S COPIOUS LETTERS ARE FILLED WITH "MASTER THIS, MASTER THAT."
CRINKLE
NOW THEN... THIS IS THE FIRST LETTER FROM PRINCE KAI...

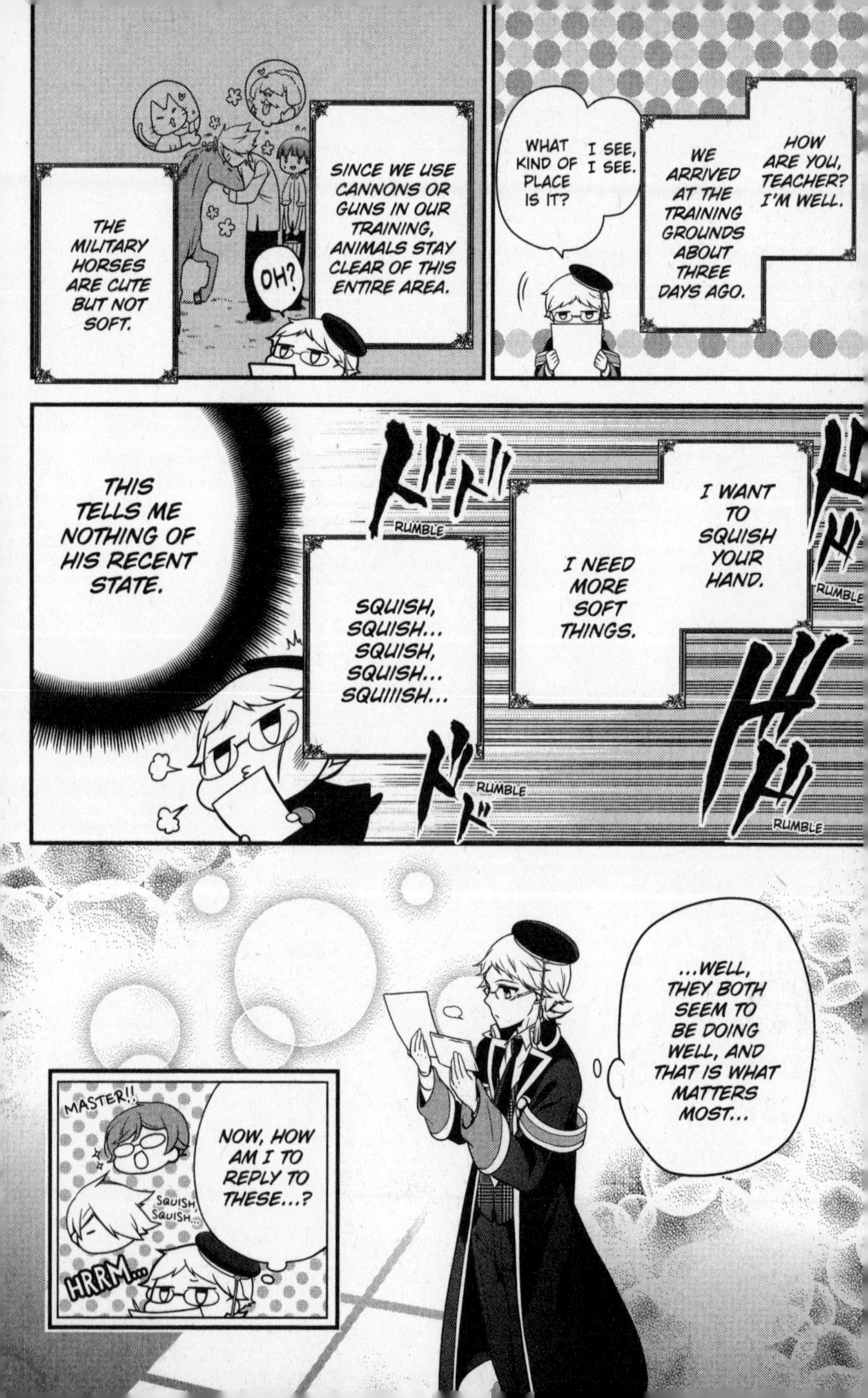
HOW ARE YOU, TEACHER? I'M WELL.
WE ARRIVED AT THE TRAINING GROUNDS ABOUT THREE DAYS AGO.
I SEE, I SEE.
WHAT KIND OF PLACE IS IT?
SINCE WE USE CANNONS OR GUNS IN OUR TRAINING, ANIMALS STAY CLEAR OF THIS ENTIRE AREA.
OH?
THE MILITARY HORSES ARE CUTE BUT NOT SOFT.
RUMBLE
I WANT TO SQUISH YOUR HAND.
I NEED MORE SOFT THINGS.
RUMBLE
SQUISH, SQUISH... SQUISH, SQUISH... SQUIIISH...
RUMBLE
RUMBLE
THIS TELLS ME NOTHING OF HIS RECENT STATE.
...WELL, THEY BOTH SEEM TO BE DOING WELL, AND THAT IS WHAT MATTERS MOST...
NOW, HOW AM I TO REPLY TO THESE...?
MASTER!!
SQUISH, SQUISH...
HRRM...

Chapter 57
Memories of Teachers

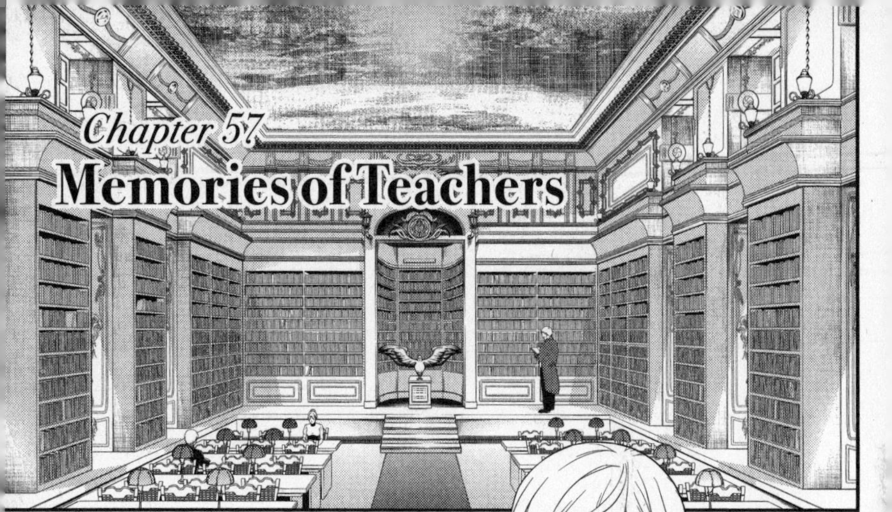

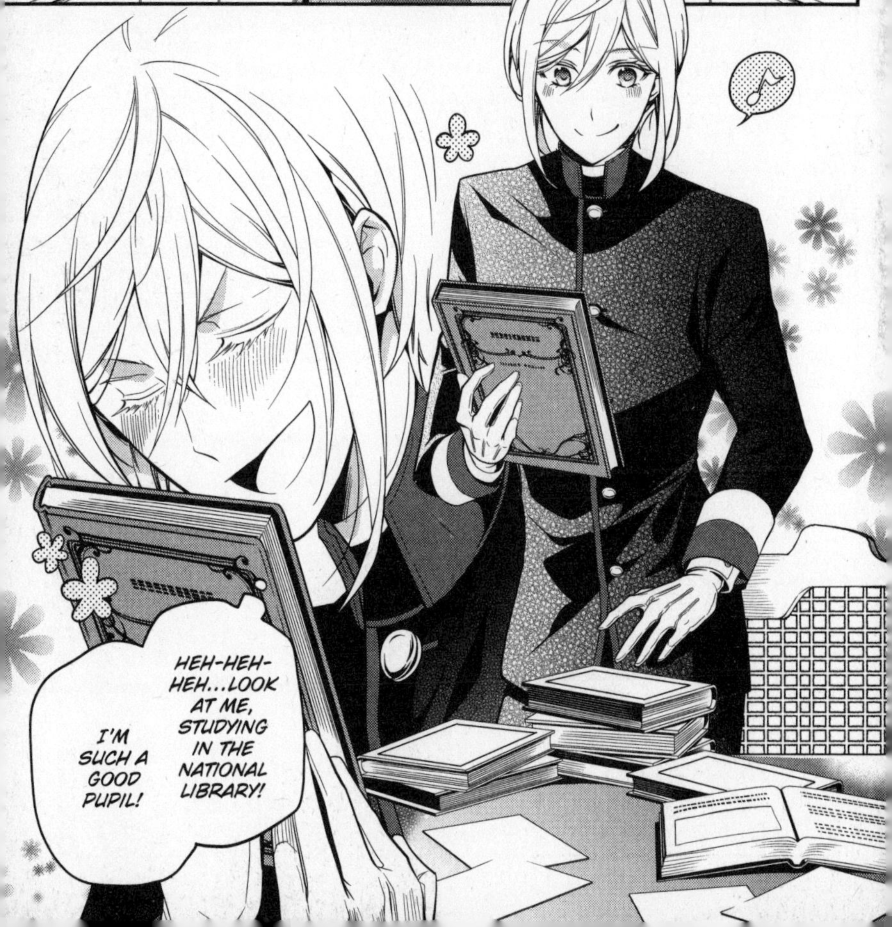
HEH-HEH-HEH...LOOK AT ME, STUDYING IN THE NATIONAL LIBRARY!
I'M SUCH A GOOD PUPIL!

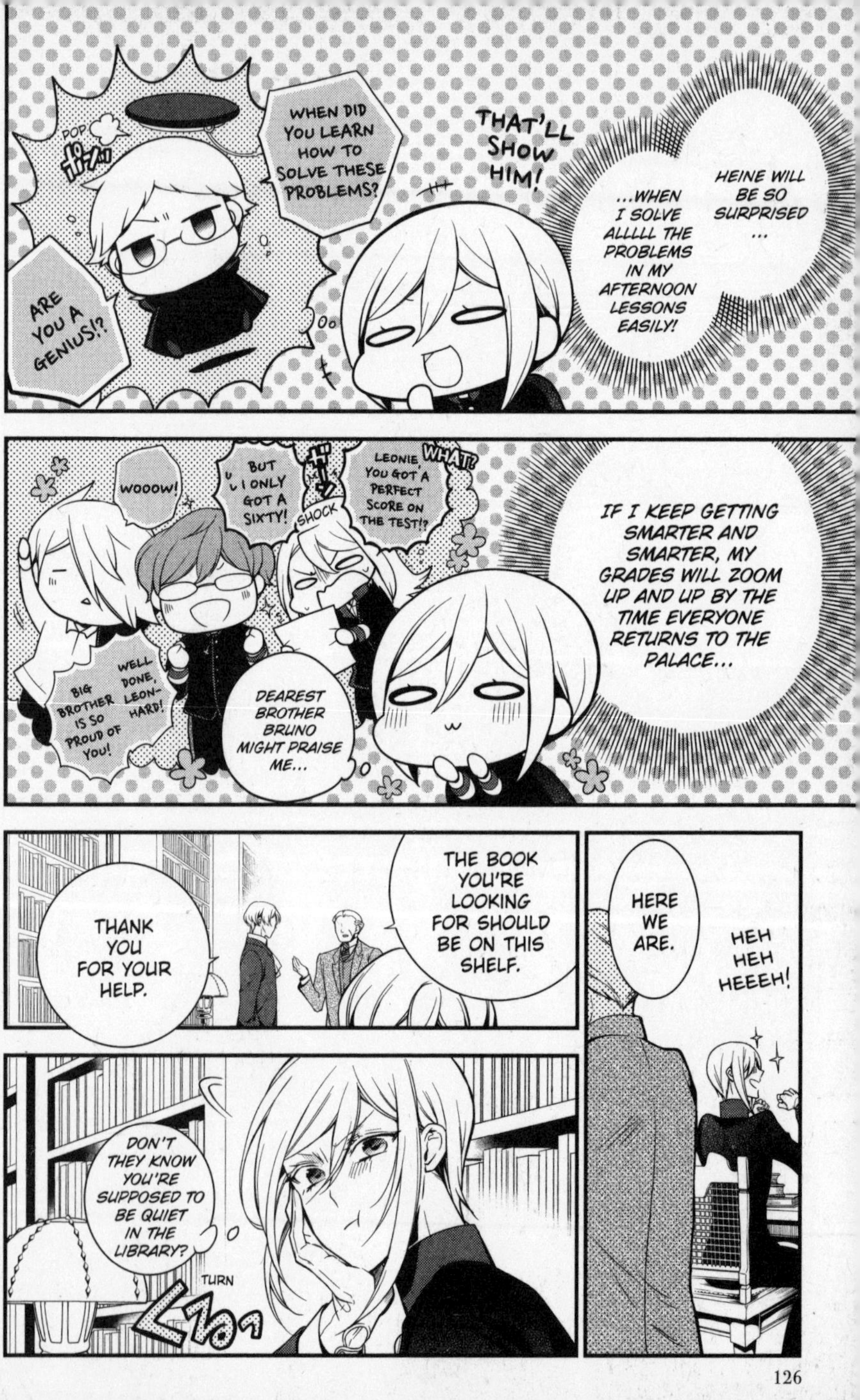
HEINE WILL BE SO SURPRISED...
...WHEN I SOLVE ALLLLL THE PROBLEMS IN MY AFTERNOON LESSONS EASILY!
THAT'LL SHOW HIM!
WHEN DID YOU LEARN HOW TO SOLVE THESE PROBLEMS?
POP
ARE YOU A GENIUS!?
IF I KEEP GETTING SMARTER AND SMARTER, MY GRADES WILL ZOOM UP AND UP BY THE TIME EVERYONE RETURNS TO THE PALACE...
WHAT!?
LEONIE, YOU GOT A PERFECT SCORE ON THE TEST!?
SHOCK
BUT I ONLY GOT A SIXTY!
WOOOW!
DEAREST BROTHER BRUNO MIGHT PRAISE ME...
WELL DONE, LEONHARD! BIG BROTHER IS SO PROUD OF YOU!
HERE WE ARE.
HEH HEH HEEEH!
THE BOOK YOU'RE LOOKING FOR SHOULD BE ON THIS SHELF.
THANK YOU FOR YOUR HELP.
DON'T THEY KNOW YOU'RE SUPPOSED TO BE QUIET IN THE LIBRARY?
TURN

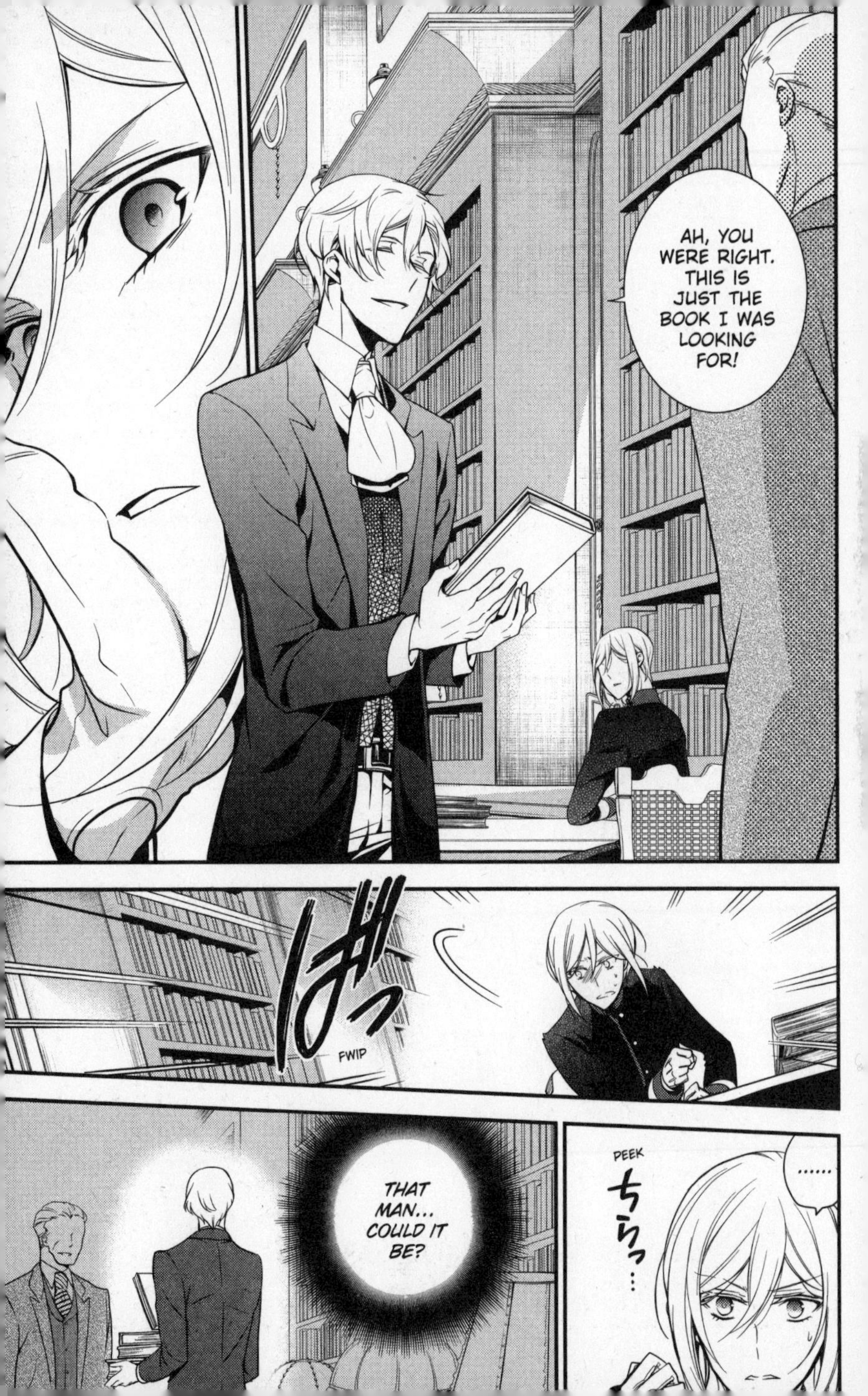
AH, YOU WERE RIGHT. THIS IS JUST THE BOOK I WAS LOOKING FOR!
ばっ
FWIP
THAT MAN... COULD IT BE?
......
ちらっ...
PEEK

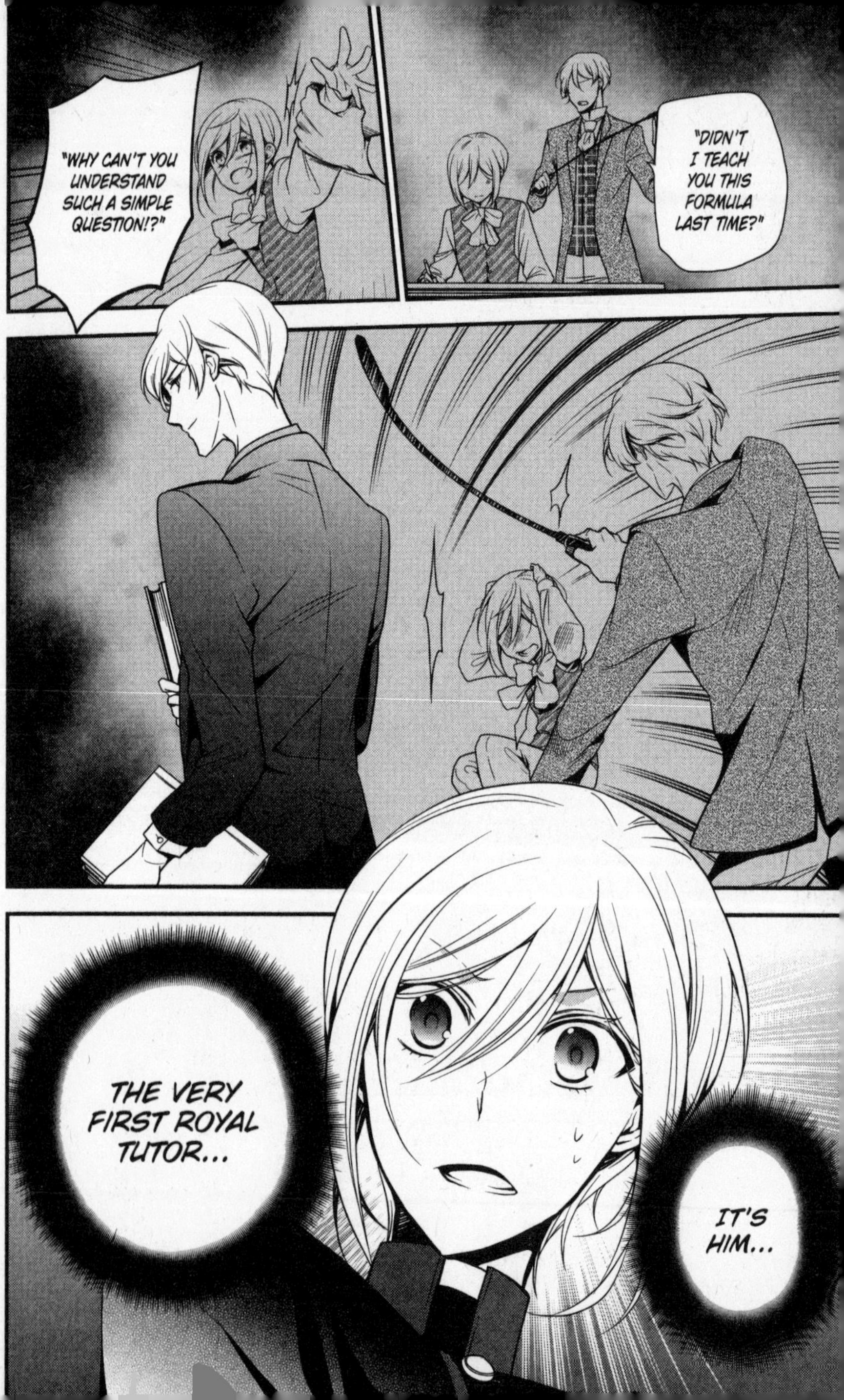
"DIDN'T I TEACH YOU THIS FORMULA LAST TIME?"
"WHY CAN'T YOU UNDERSTAND SUCH A SIMPLE QUESTION!?"
THE VERY FIRST ROYAL TUTOR...
IT'S HIM...

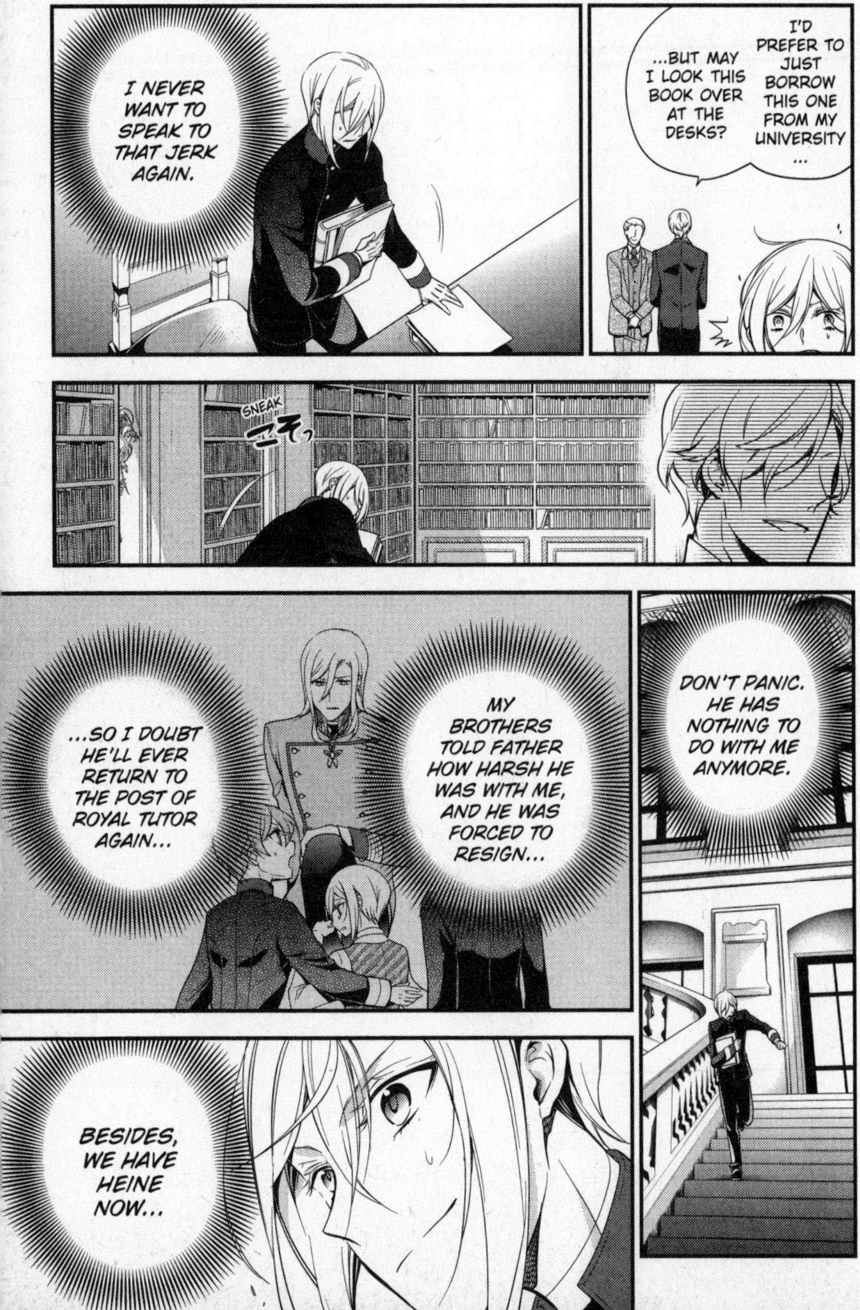
I'D PREFER TO JUST BORROW THIS ONE FROM MY UNIVERSITY...
...BUT MAY I LOOK THIS BOOK OVER AT THE DESKS?
I NEVER WANT TO SPEAK TO THAT JERK AGAIN.
SNEAK
DON'T PANIC. HE HAS NOTHING TO DO WITH ME ANYMORE.
MY BROTHERS TOLD FATHER HOW HARSH HE WAS WITH ME, AND HE WAS FORCED TO RESIGN...
...SO I DOUBT HE'LL EVER RETURN TO THE POST OF ROYAL TUTOR AGAIN...
BESIDES, WE HAVE HEINE NOW...

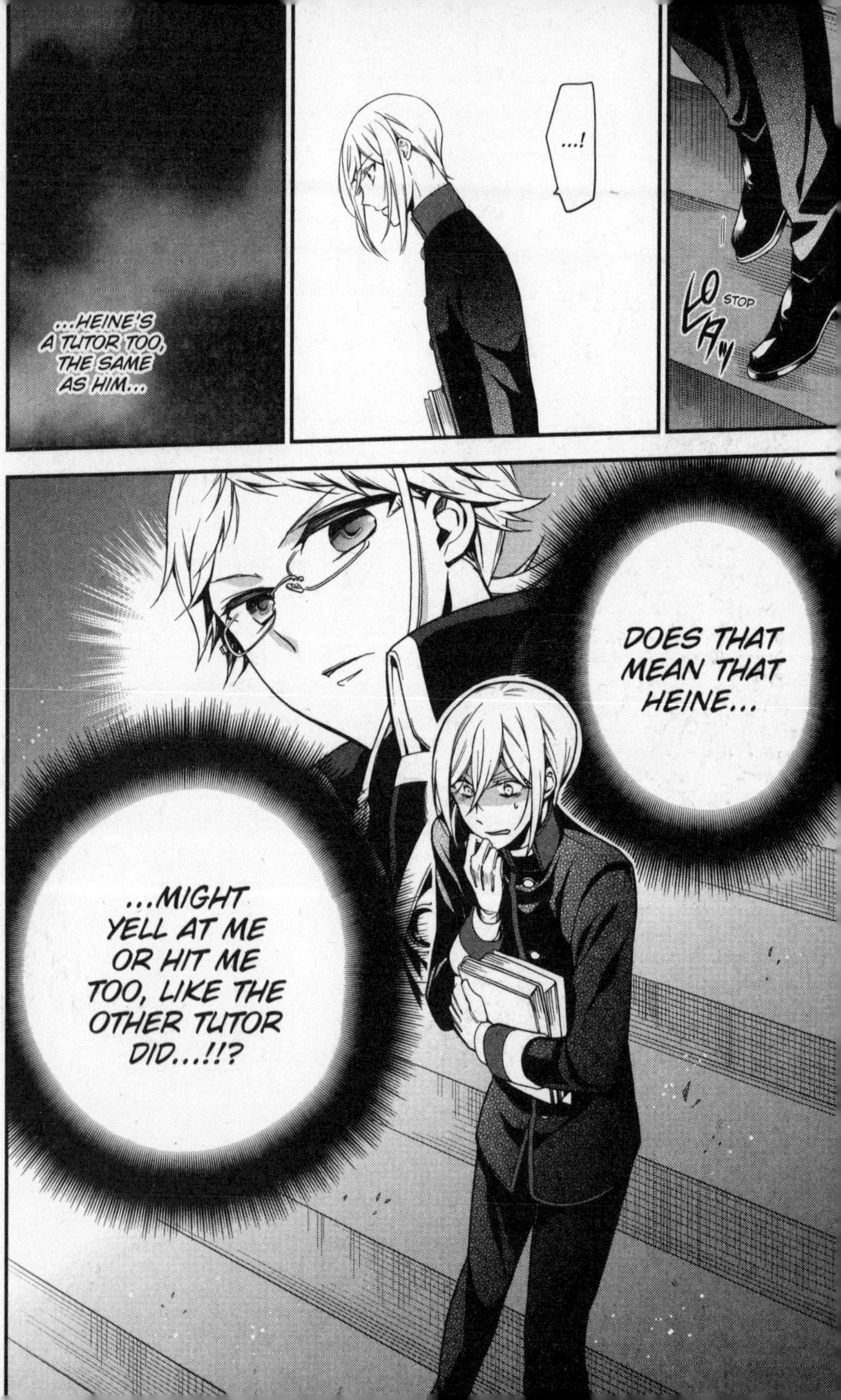
STOP
...!
...HEINE'S A TUTOR TOO, THE SAME AS HIM...
DOES THAT MEAN THAT HEINE...
...MIGHT YELL AT ME OR HIT ME TOO, LIKE THE OTHER TUTOR DID...!!?

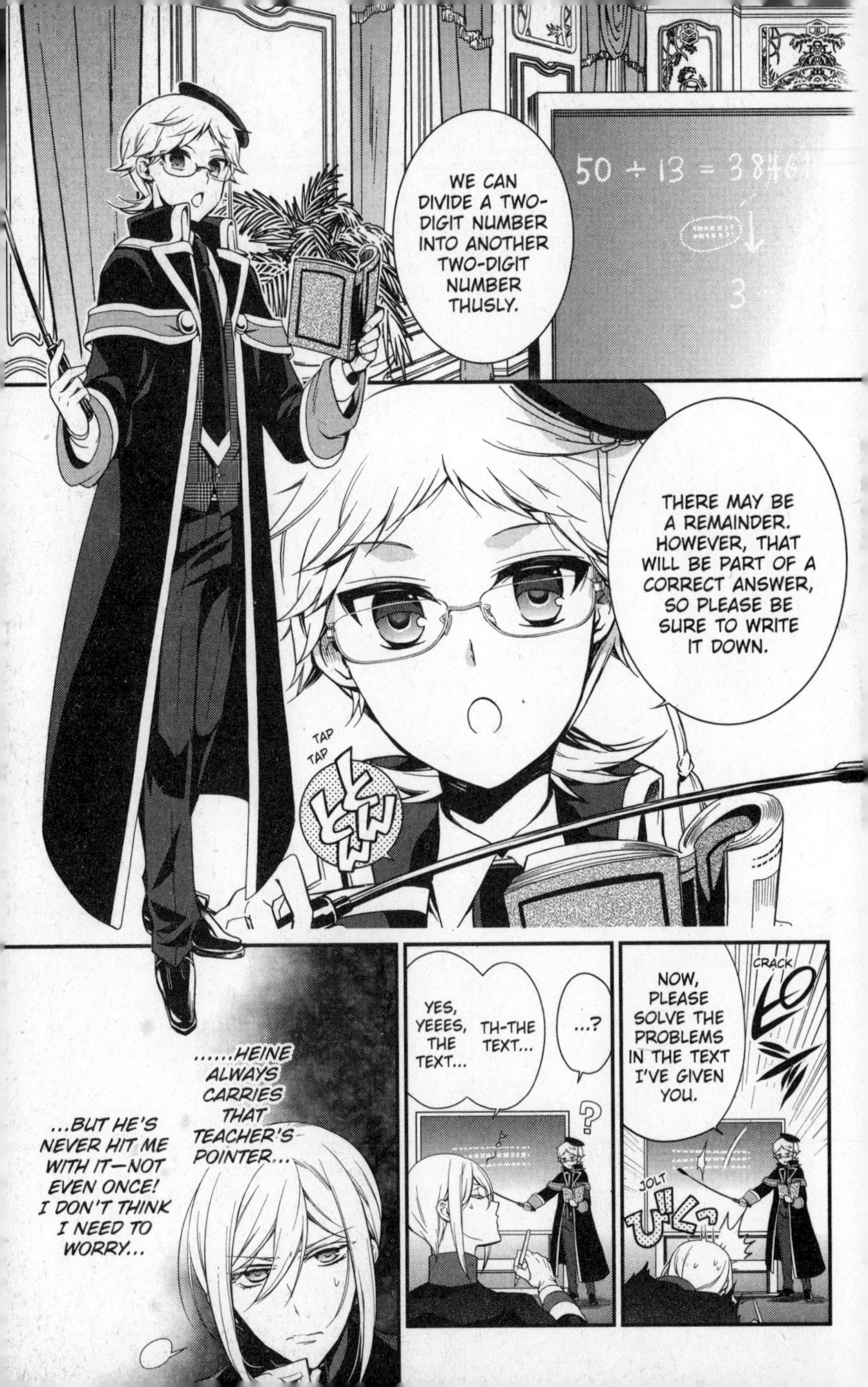
WE CAN DIVIDE A TWO-DIGIT NUMBER INTO ANOTHER TWO-DIGIT NUMBER THUSLY.
THERE MAY BE A REMAINDER. HOWEVER, THAT WILL BE PART OF A CORRECT ANSWER, SO PLEASE BE SURE TO WRITE IT DOWN.
TAP TAP
NOW, PLEASE SOLVE THE PROBLEMS IN THE TEXT I'VE GIVEN YOU.
CRACK
JOLT
...?
TH-THE TEXT...
YES, YEEES, THE TEXT...
......HEINE ALWAYS CARRIES THAT TEACHER'S POINTER...
...BUT HE'S NEVER HIT ME WITH IT—NOT EVEN ONCE! I DON'T THINK I NEED TO WORRY...

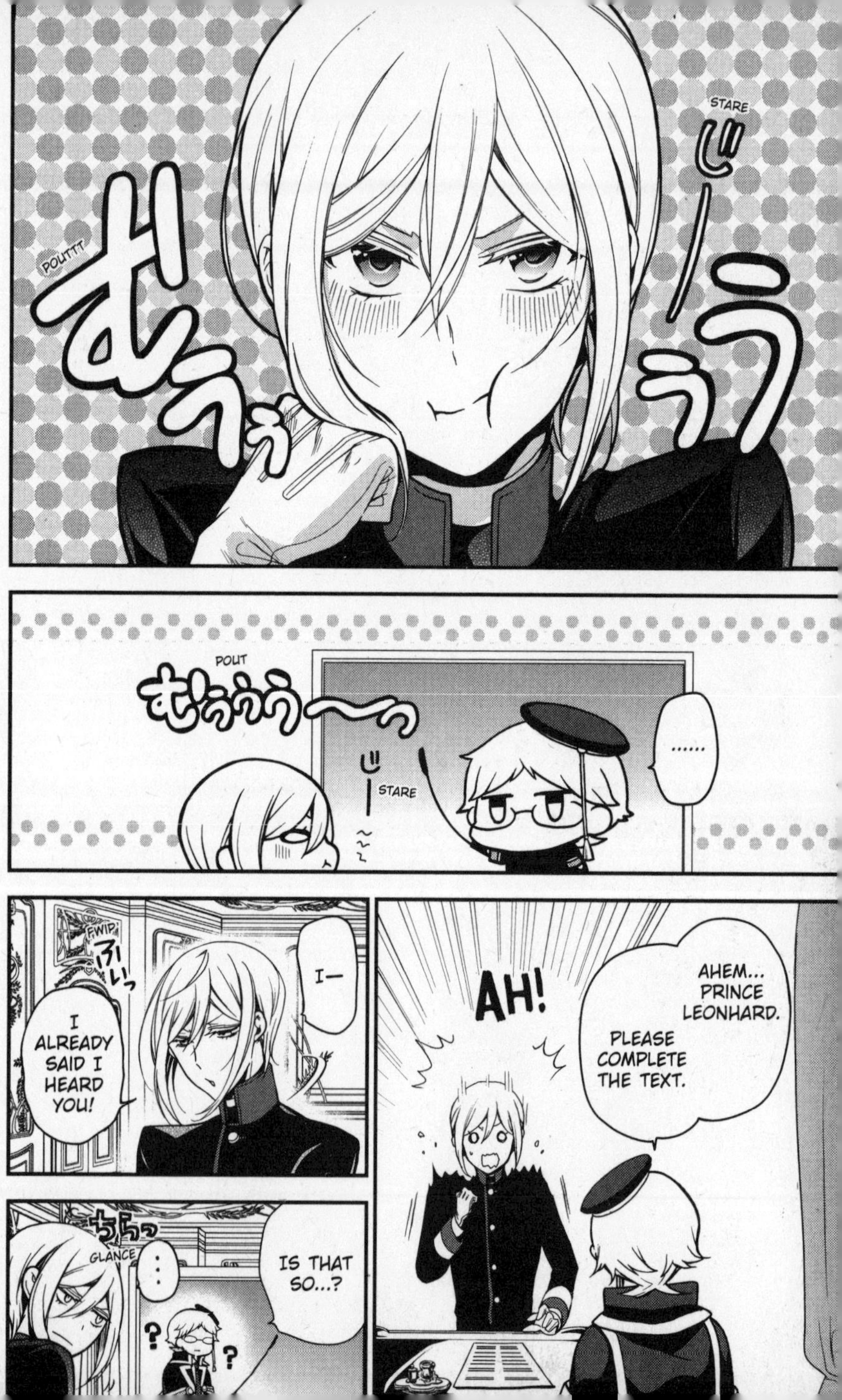
STARE
POUTTT
......
STARE
POUT
AHEM... PRINCE LEONHARD.
PLEASE COMPLETE THE TEXT.
AH!
I—
FWIP
I ALREADY SAID I HEARD YOU!
IS THAT SO...?
...
GLANCE

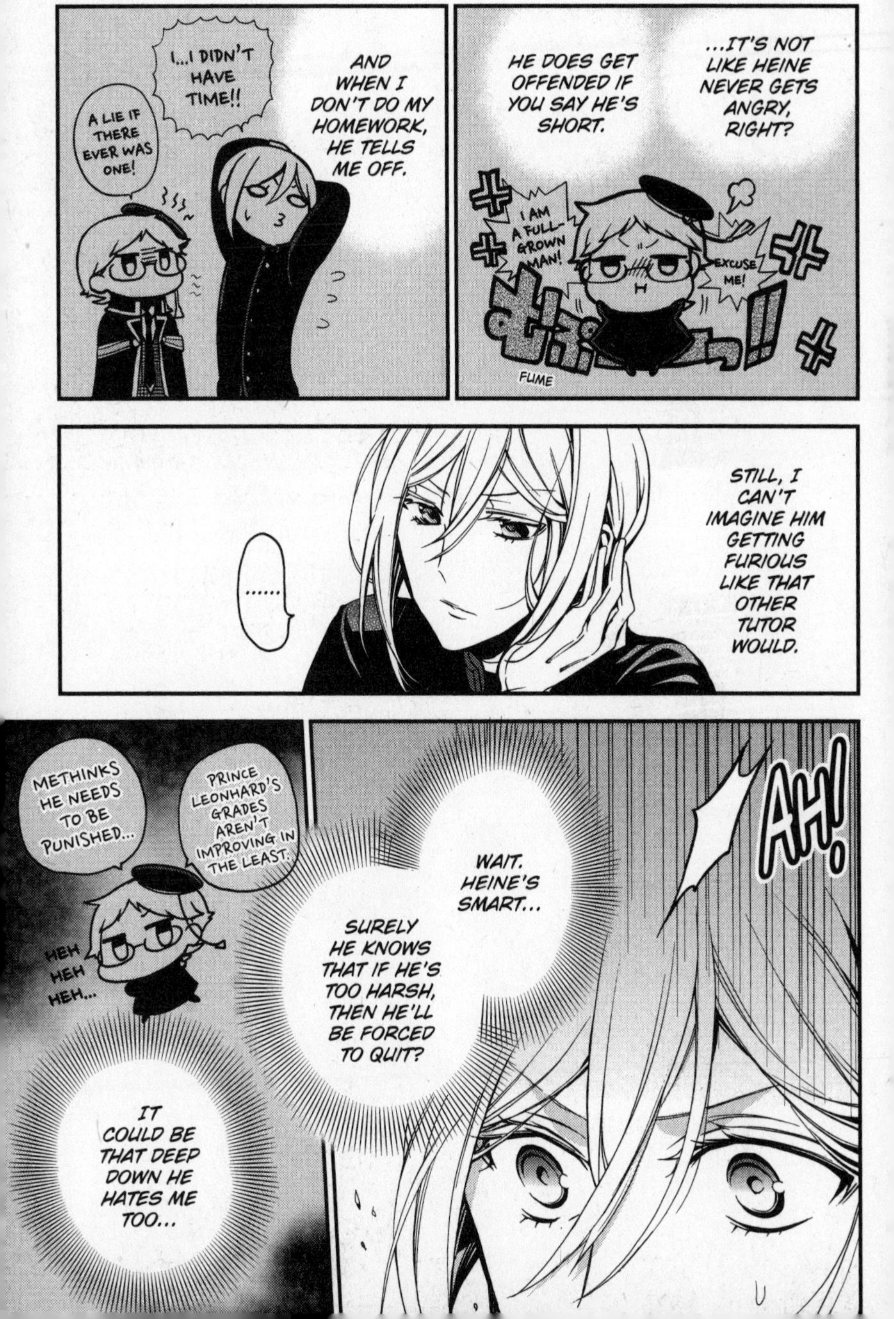
...IT'S NOT LIKE HEINE NEVER GETS ANGRY, RIGHT?
HE DOES GET OFFENDED IF YOU SAY HE'S SHORT.
EXCUSE ME!
I AM A FULL-GROWN MAN!
FUME
AND WHEN I DON'T DO MY HOMEWORK, HE TELLS ME OFF.
I...I DIDN'T HAVE TIME!!
A LIE IF THERE EVER WAS ONE!
STILL, I CAN'T IMAGINE HIM GETTING FURIOUS LIKE THAT OTHER TUTOR WOULD.
......
AH!
WAIT. HEINE'S SMART...
SURELY HE KNOWS THAT IF HE'S TOO HARSH, THEN HE'LL BE FORCED TO QUIT?
PRINCE LEONHARD'S GRADES AREN'T IMPROVING IN THE LEAST.
METHINKS HE NEEDS TO BE PUNISHED...
HEH HEH HEH...
IT COULD BE THAT DEEP DOWN HE HATES ME TOO...

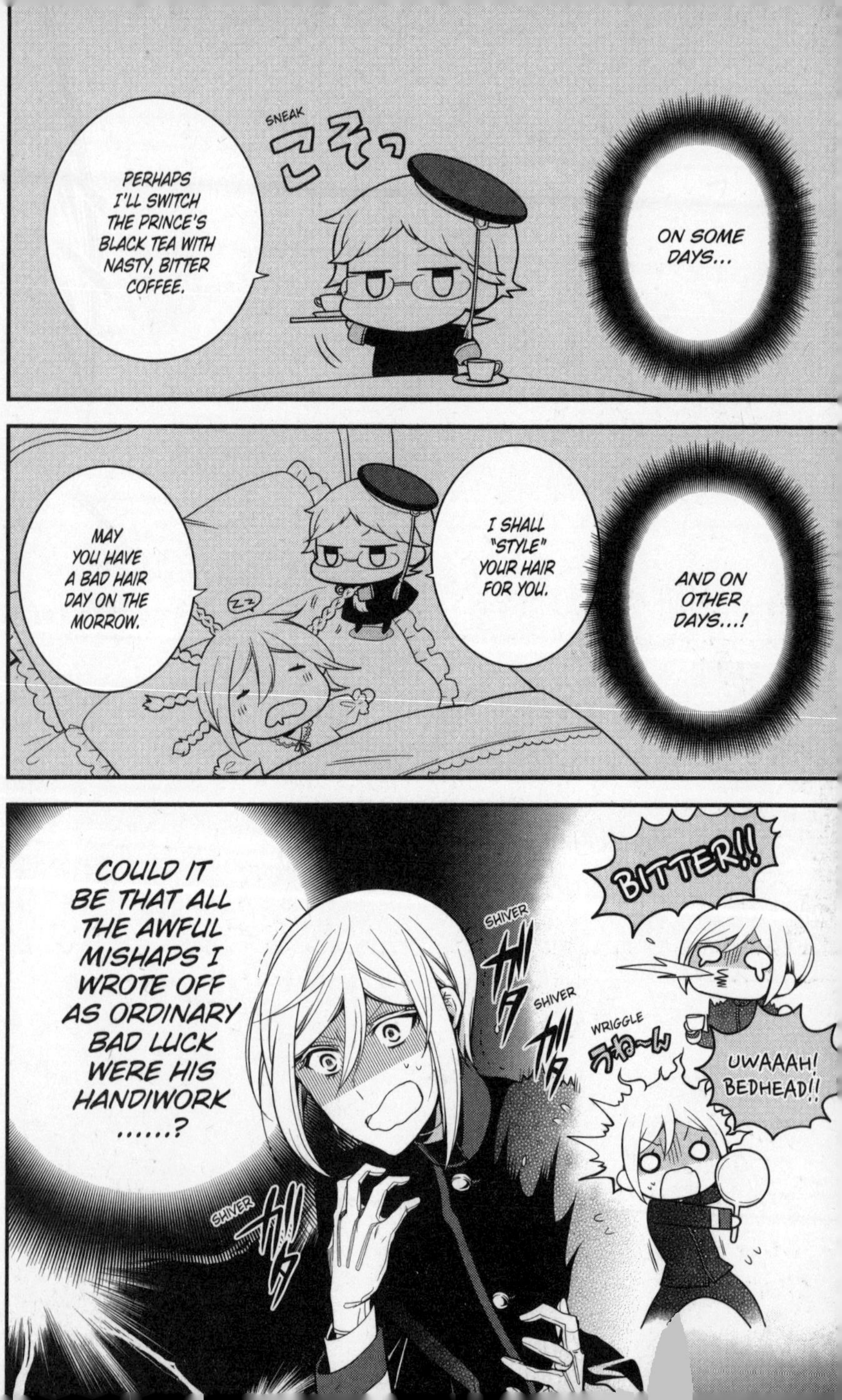
ON SOME DAYS...
SNEAK
PERHAPS I'LL SWITCH THE PRINCE'S BLACK TEA WITH NASTY, BITTER COFFEE.
AND ON OTHER DAYS...!
I SHALL "STYLE" YOUR HAIR FOR YOU.
MAY YOU HAVE A BAD HAIR DAY ON THE MORROW.
BITTER!!
UWAAAH! BEDHEAD!!
WRIGGLE
SHIVER
SHIVER
SHIVER
COULD IT BE THAT ALL THE AWFUL MISHAPS I WROTE OFF AS ORDINARY BAD LUCK WERE HIS HANDIWORK ......?

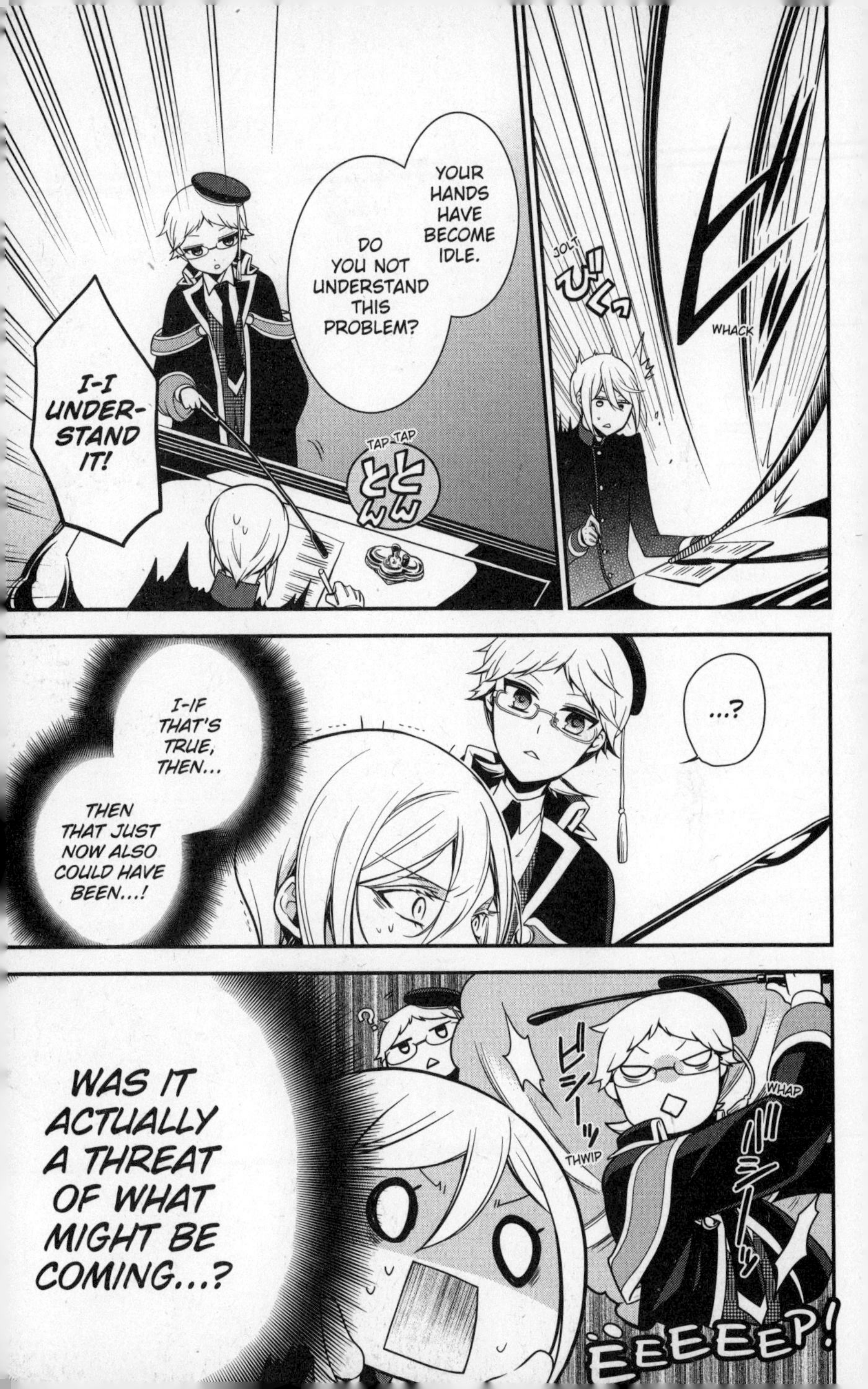
JOLT
WHACK
YOUR HANDS HAVE BECOME IDLE.
DO YOU NOT UNDERSTAND THIS PROBLEM?
TAP TAP
I-I UNDERSTAND IT!
...?
I-IF THAT'S TRUE, THEN...
THEN THAT JUST NOW ALSO COULD HAVE BEEN...!
WHAP
THWIP
EEEEEEP!
WAS IT ACTUALLY A THREAT OF WHAT MIGHT BE COMING...?

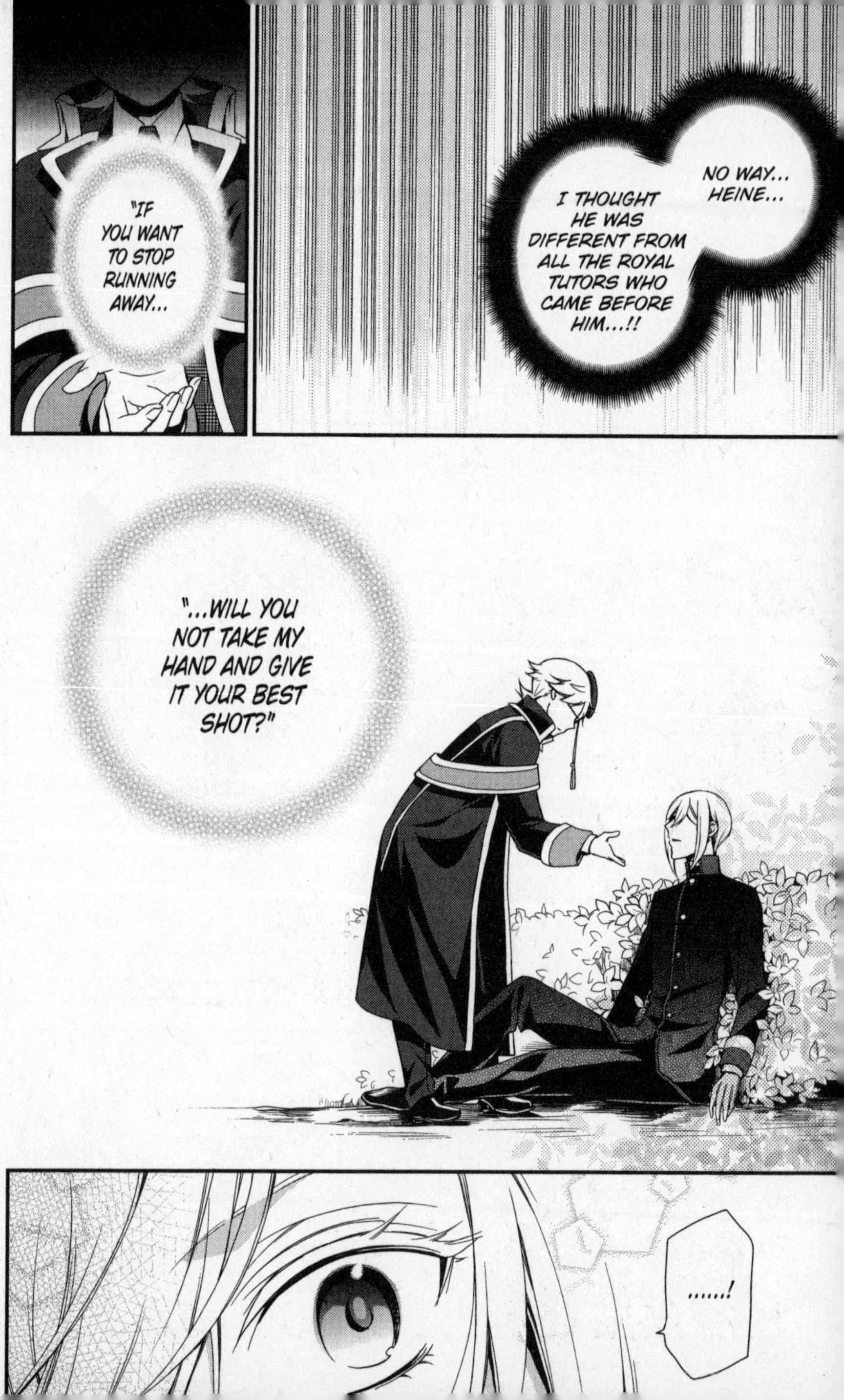
NO WAY... HEINE...
I THOUGHT HE WAS DIFFERENT FROM ALL THE ROYAL TUTORS WHO CAME BEFORE HIM...!!
"IF YOU WANT TO STOP RUNNING AWAY...
"...WILL YOU NOT TAKE MY HAND AND GIVE IT YOUR BEST SHOT?"
......!

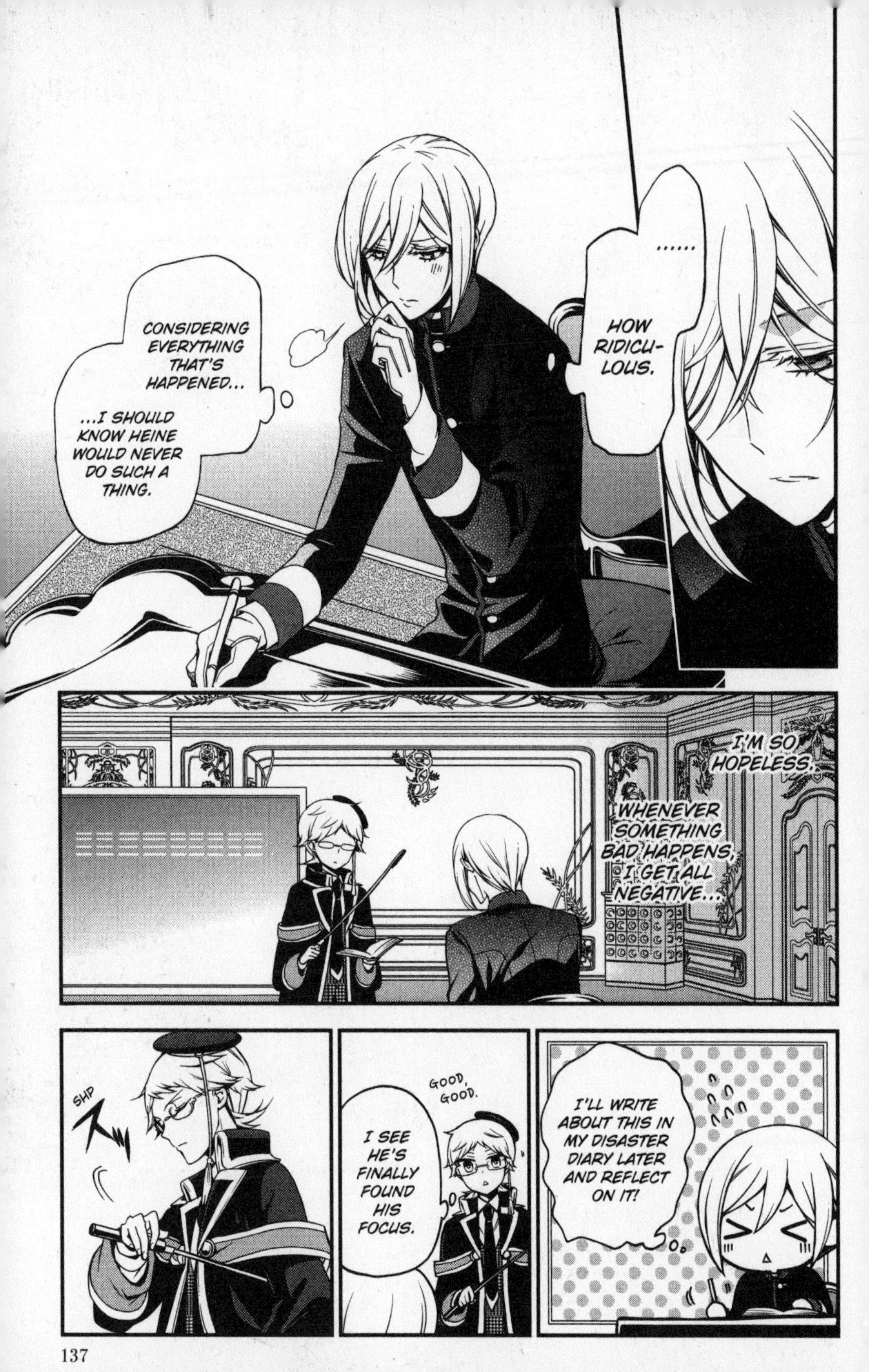
......
HOW RIDICULOUS.
CONSIDERING EVERYTHING THAT'S HAPPENED...
...I SHOULD KNOW HEINE WOULD NEVER DO SUCH A THING.
I'M SO HOPELESS.
WHENEVER SOMETHING BAD HAPPENS, I GET ALL NEGATIVE...
I'LL WRITE ABOUT THIS IN MY DISASTER DIARY LATER AND REFLECT ON IT!
GOOD, GOOD.
I SEE HE'S FINALLY FOUND HIS FOCUS.
SHP

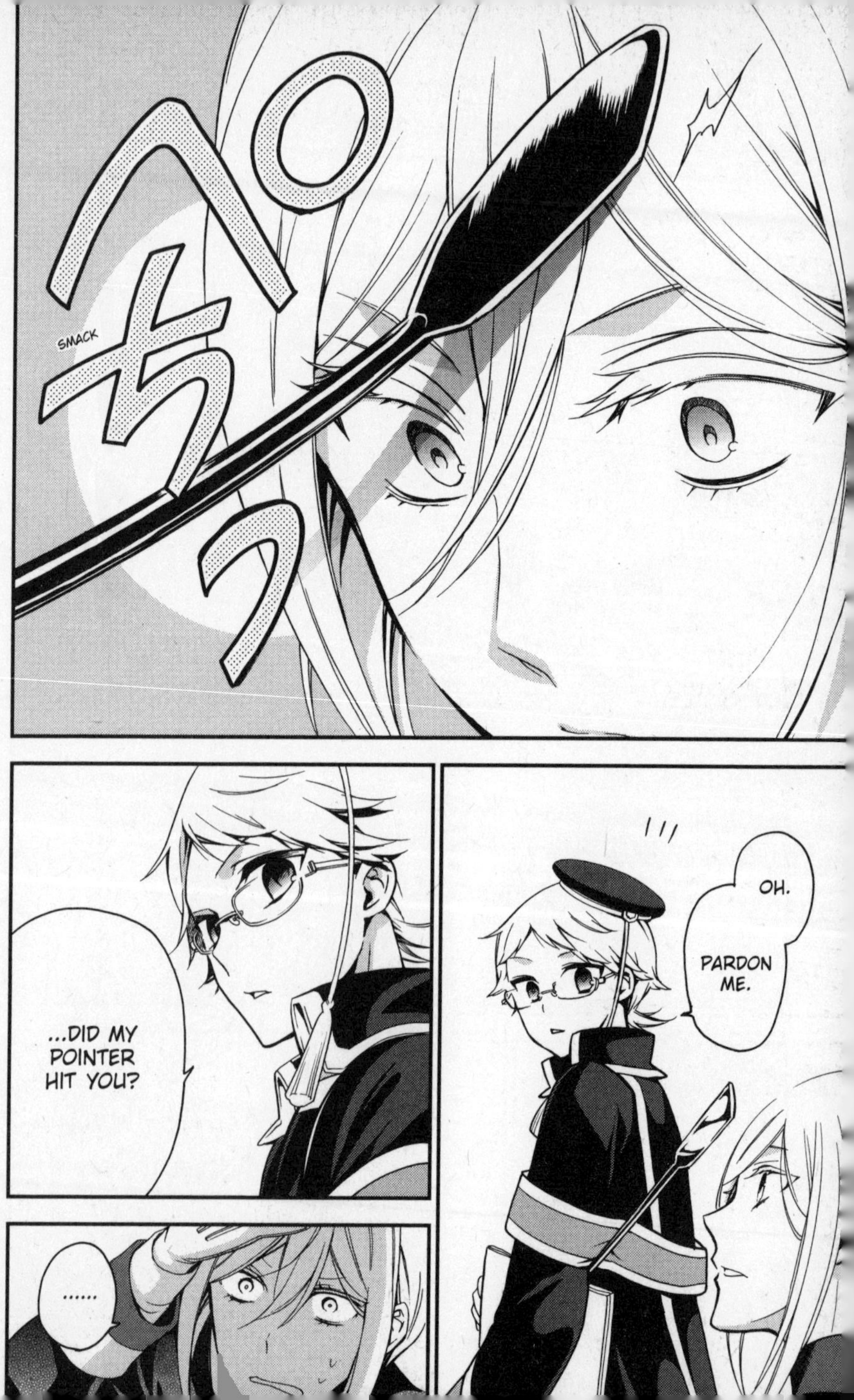
SMACK
OH. PARDON ME.
...DID MY POINTER HIT YOU?
......

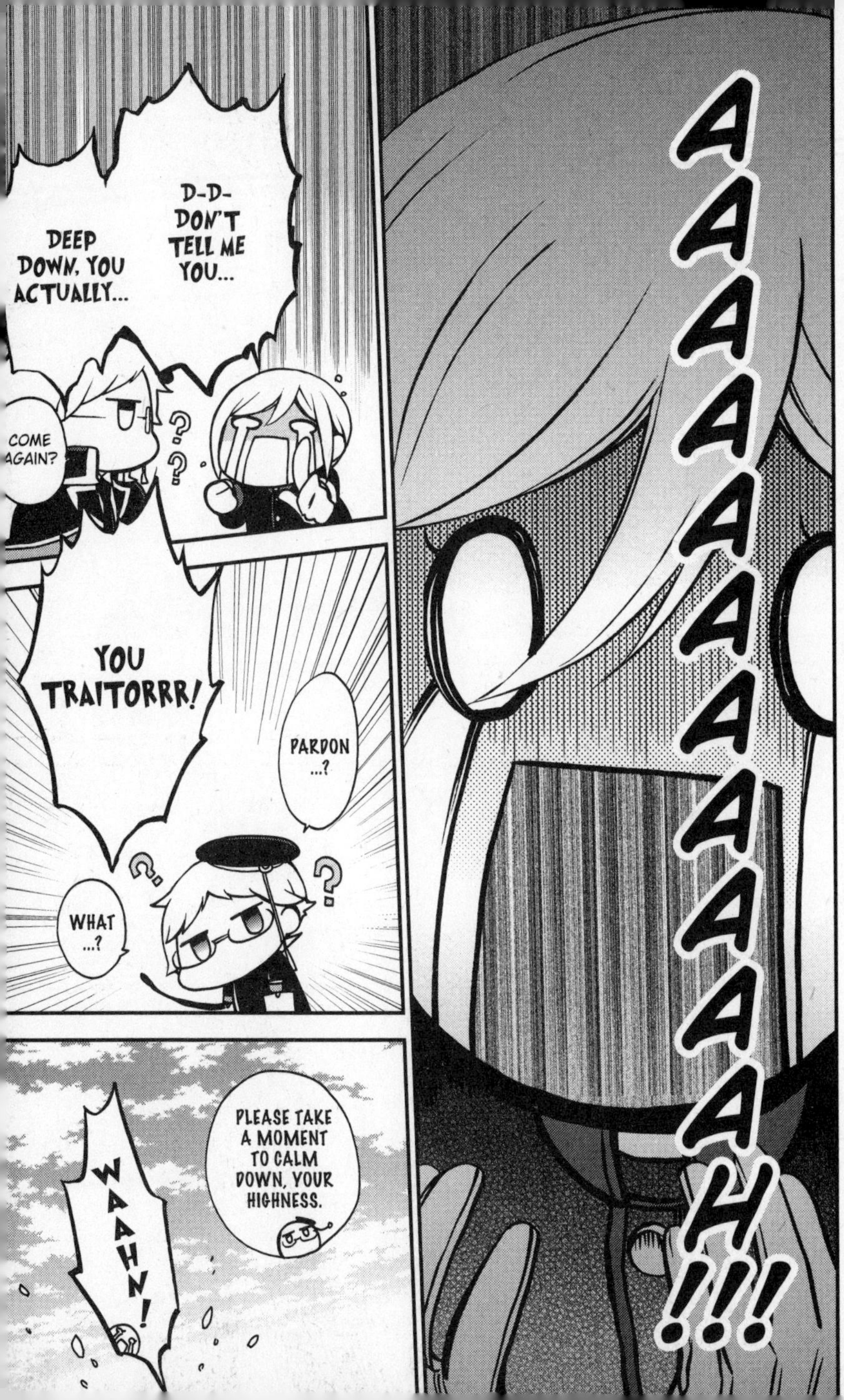
D-D-DON'T TELL ME YOU...
DEEP DOWN, YOU ACTUALLY...
COME AGAIN?
YOU TRAITORRR!
PARDON ...?
WHAT ...?
AAAAAAAAAAAAAH!!!
PLEASE TAKE A MOMENT TO CALM DOWN, YOUR HIGHNESS.
WAAHN!

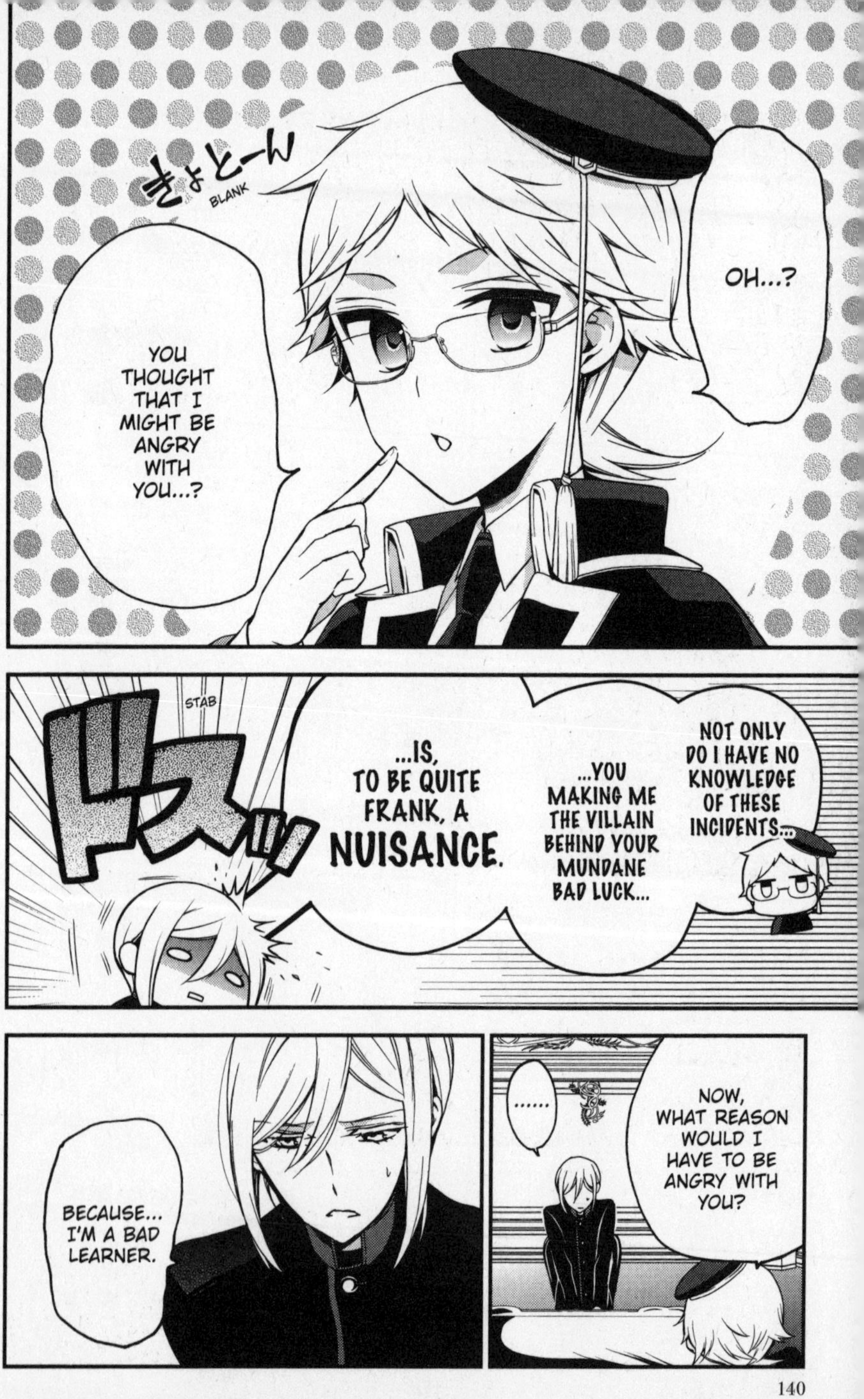
OH...?
きょとーん
BLANK
YOU THOUGHT THAT I MIGHT BE ANGRY WITH YOU...?
NOT ONLY DO I HAVE NO KNOWLEDGE OF THESE INCIDENTS...
...YOU MAKING ME THE VILLAIN BEHIND YOUR MUNDANE BAD LUCK...
...IS, TO BE QUITE FRANK, A NUISANCE.
ドス!!!
STAB
NOW, WHAT REASON WOULD I HAVE TO BE ANGRY WITH YOU?
......
BECAUSE... I'M A BAD LEARNER.

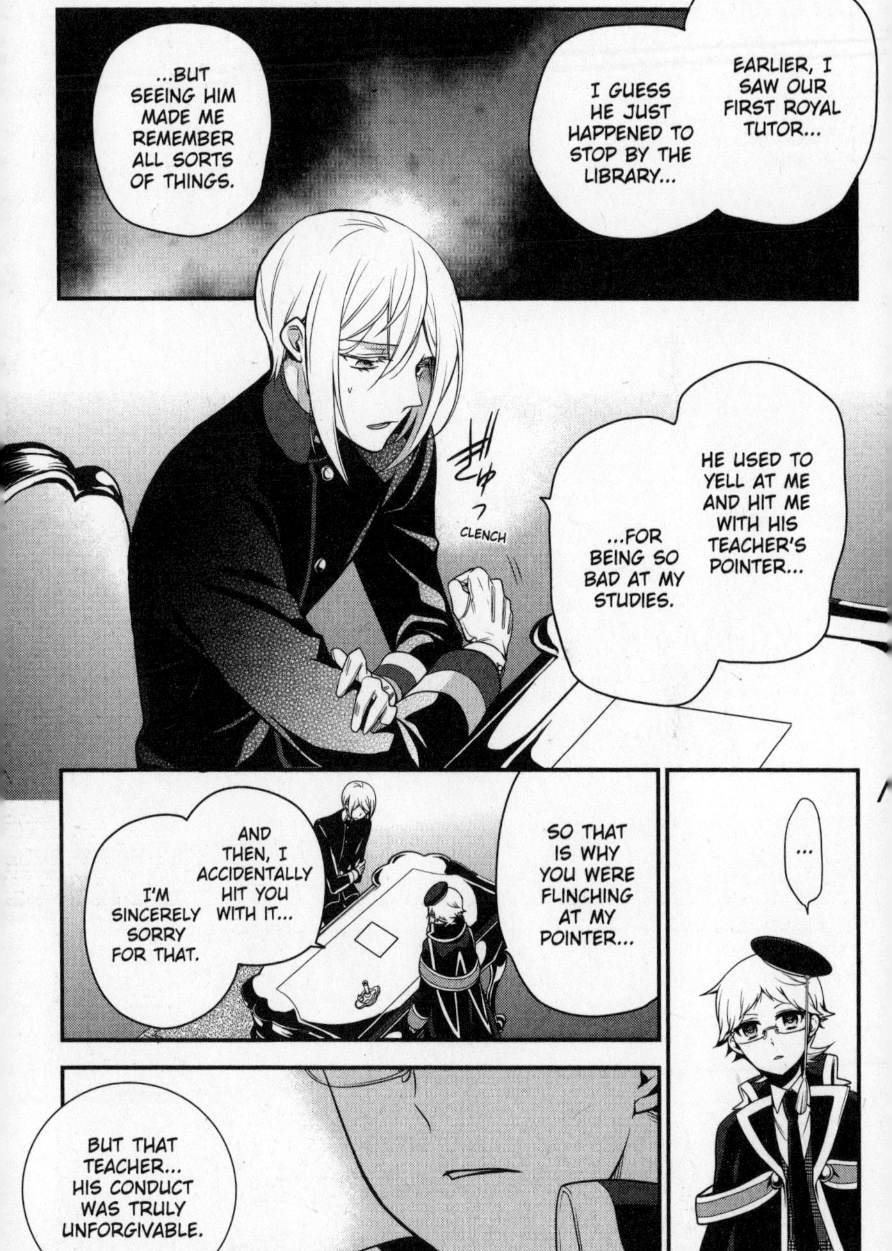
EARLIER, I SAW OUR FIRST ROYAL TUTOR...
I GUESS HE JUST HAPPENED TO STOP BY THE LIBRARY...
...BUT SEEING HIM MADE ME REMEMBER ALL SORTS OF THINGS.
HE USED TO YELL AT ME AND HIT ME WITH HIS TEACHER'S POINTER...
...FOR BEING SO BAD AT MY STUDIES.
CLENCH
SO THAT IS WHY YOU WERE FLINCHING AT MY POINTER...
AND THEN, I ACCIDENTALLY HIT YOU WITH IT...
I'M SINCERELY SORRY FOR THAT.
...
BUT THAT TEACHER... HIS CONDUCT WAS TRULY UNFORGIVABLE.

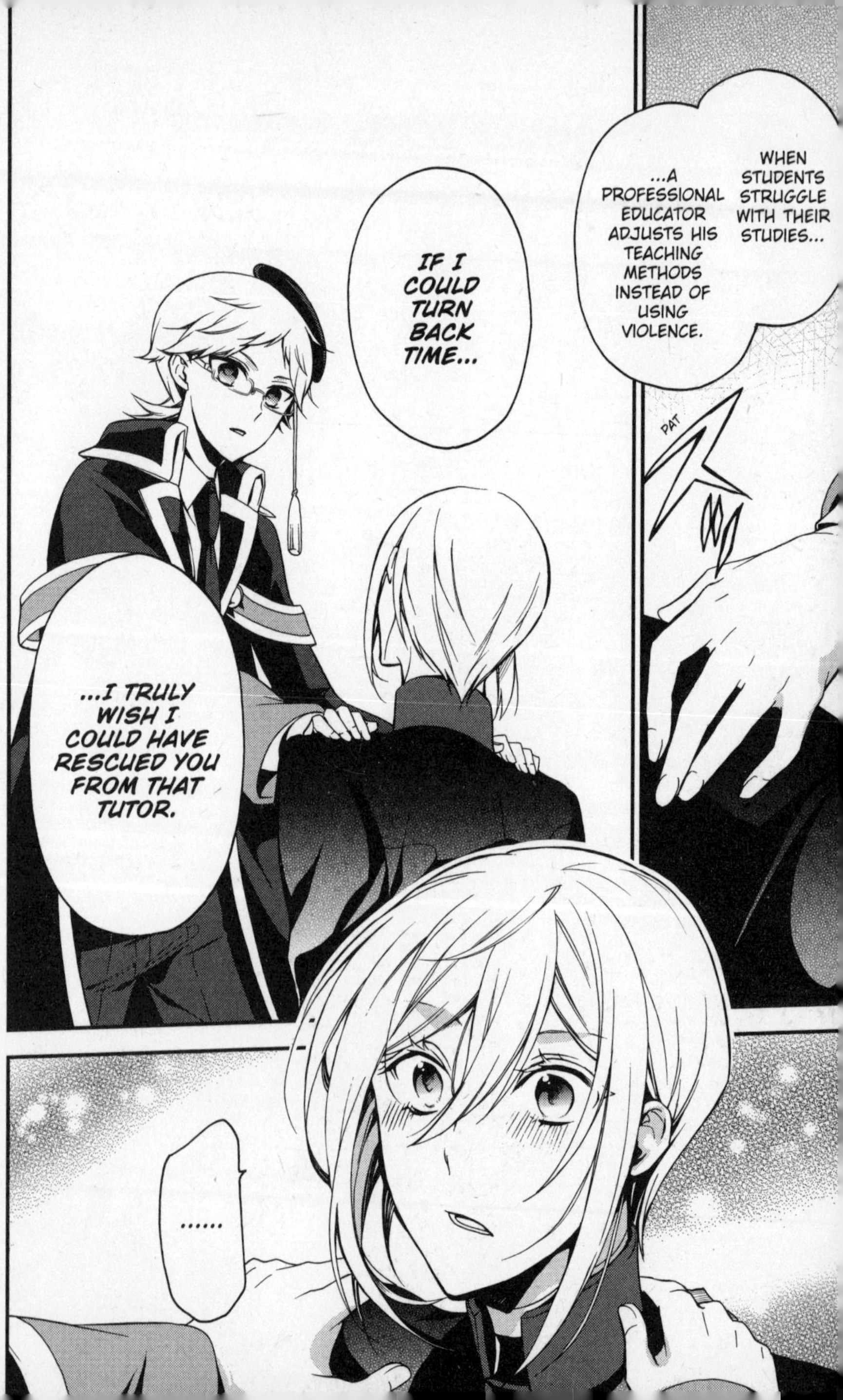
WHEN STUDENTS STRUGGLE WITH THEIR STUDIES...
...A PROFESSIONAL EDUCATOR ADJUSTS HIS TEACHING METHODS INSTEAD OF USING VIOLENCE.
PAT
IF I COULD TURN BACK TIME...
...I TRULY WISH I COULD HAVE RESCUED YOU FROM THAT TUTOR.
......

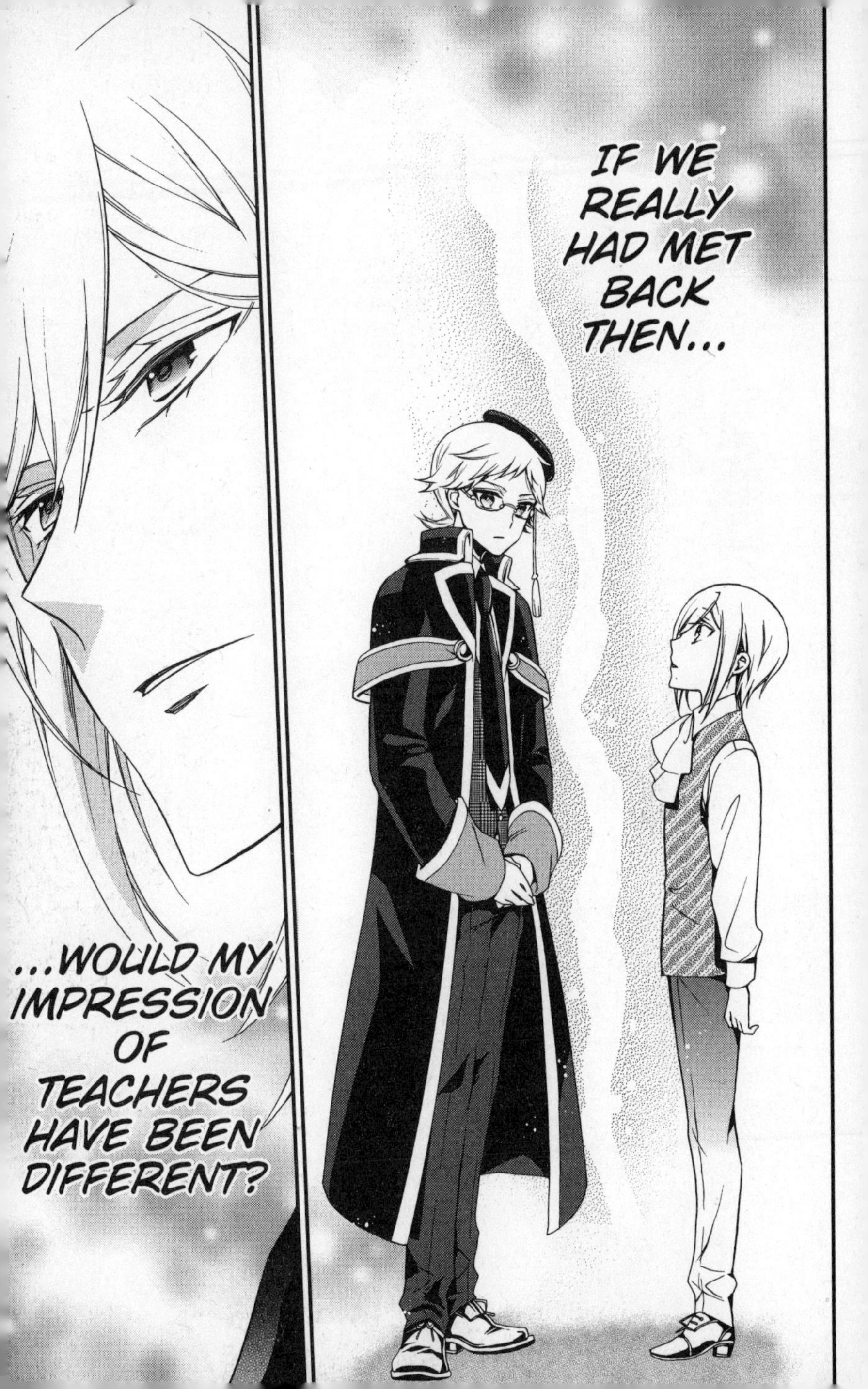
IF WE REALLY HAD MET BACK THEN...
...WOULD MY IMPRESSION OF TEACHERS HAVE BEEN DIFFERENT?

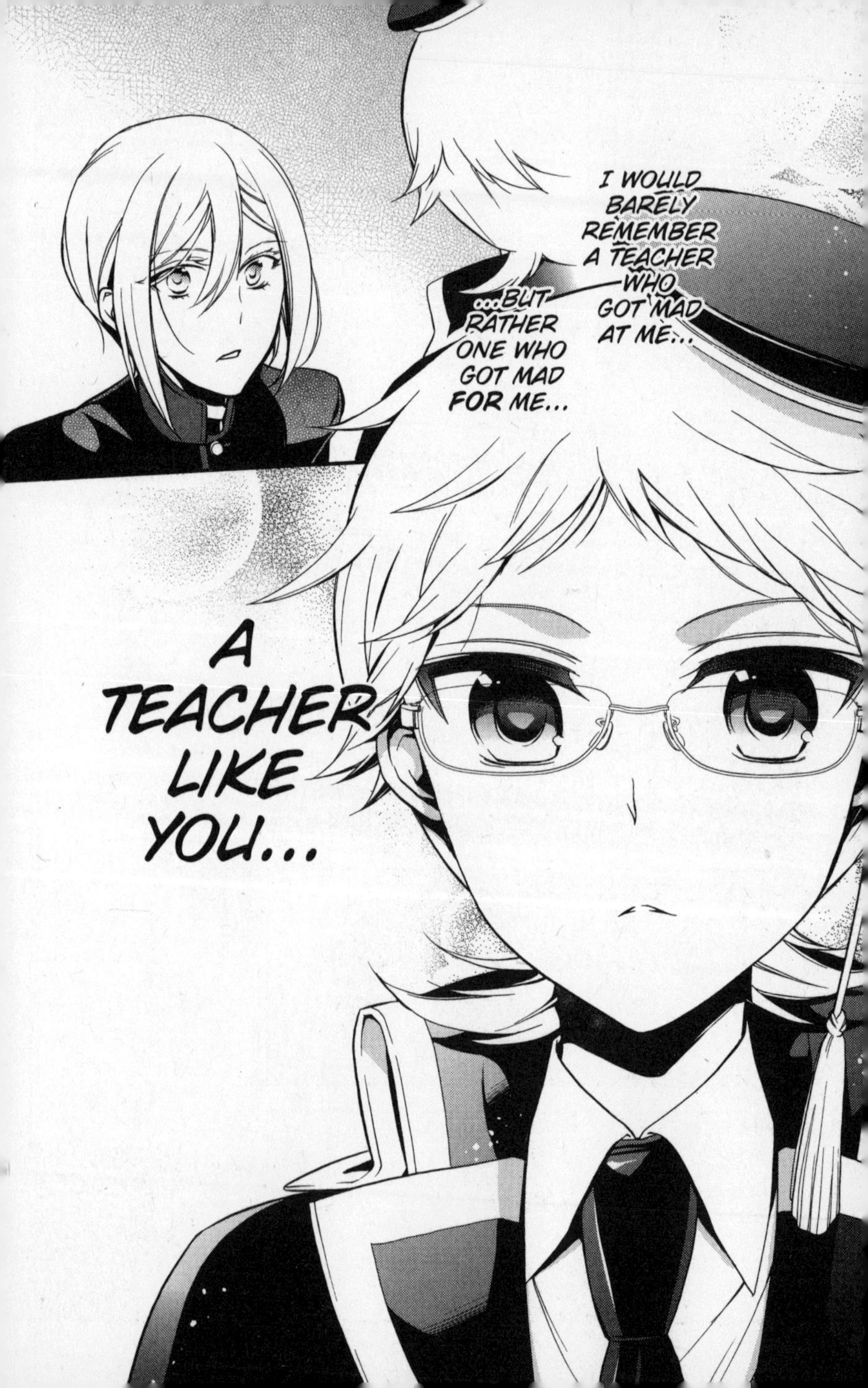
I WOULD BARELY REMEMBER A TEACHER WHO GOT MAD AT ME...
...BUT RATHER ONE WHO GOT MAD FOR ME...
A TEACHER LIKE YOU...

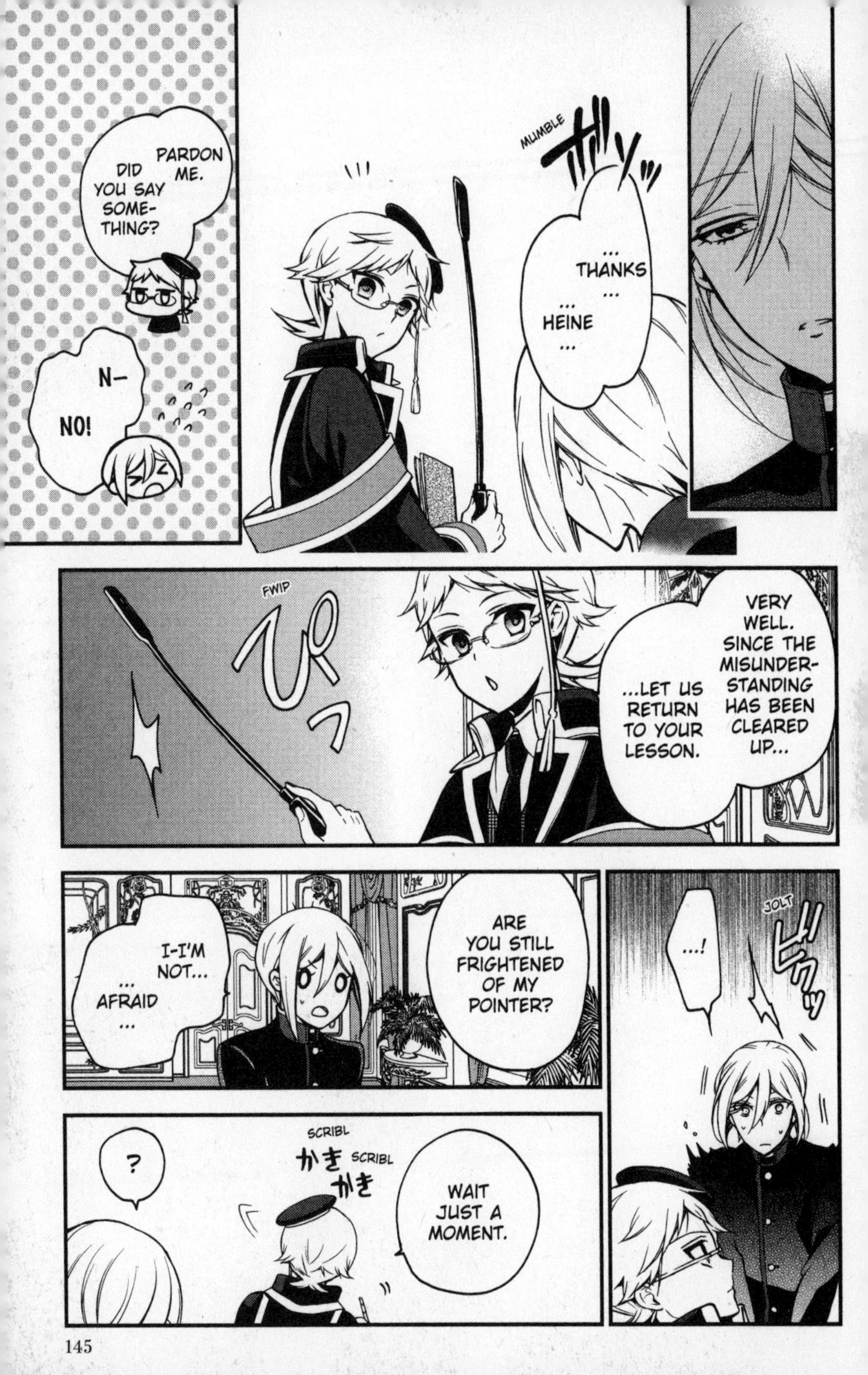
MUMBLE
... THANKS ... ... HEINE ...
PARDON ME. DID YOU SAY SOME-THING?
N- NO!
FWIP
VERY WELL. SINCE THE MISUNDER-STANDING HAS BEEN CLEARED UP...
...LET US RETURN TO YOUR LESSON.
JOLT
...!
ARE YOU STILL FRIGHTENED OF MY POINTER?
I-I'M NOT... ... AFRAID ...
SCRIBL
SCRIBL
WAIT JUST A MOMENT.
?

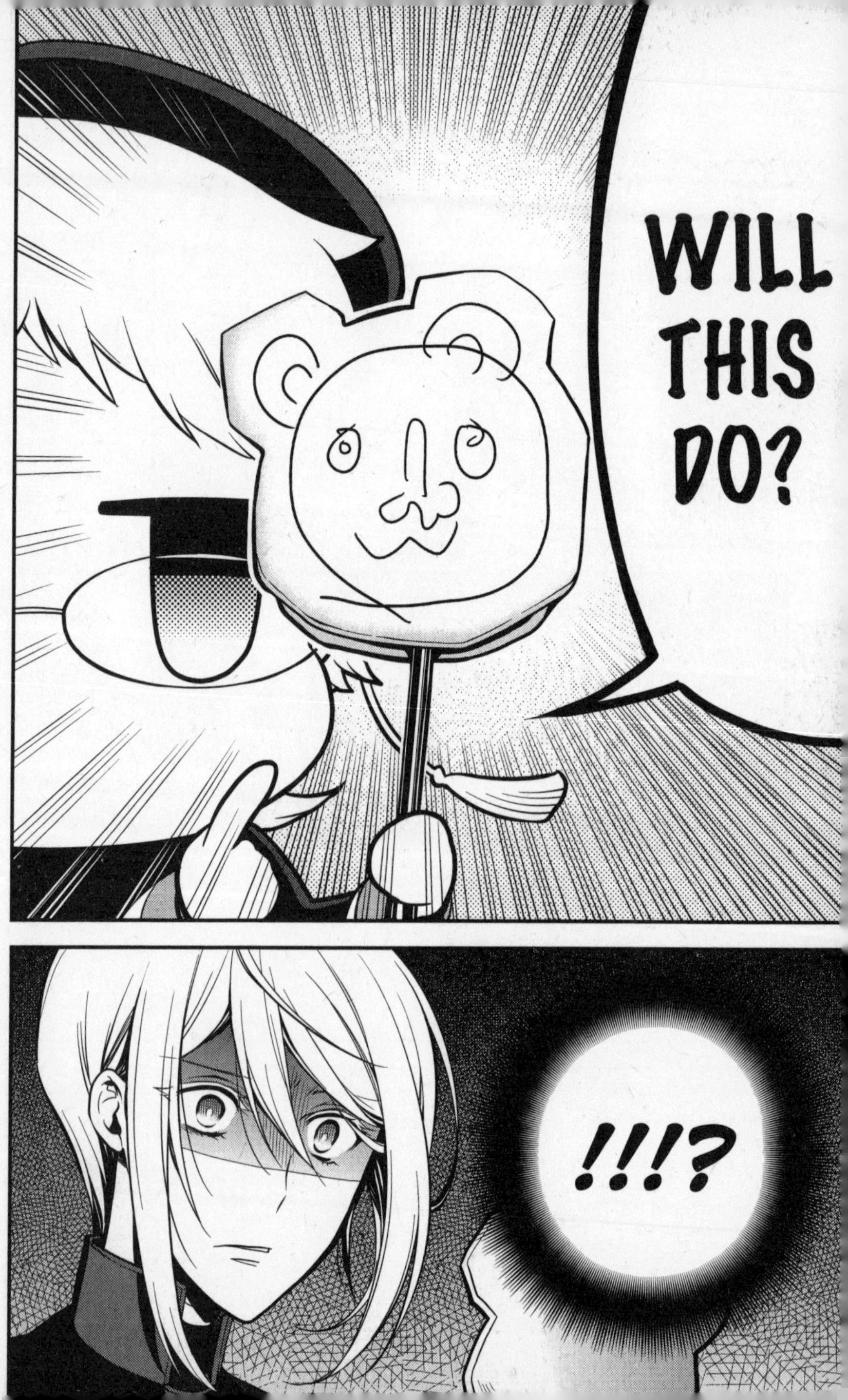
WILL THIS DO?
!!!?

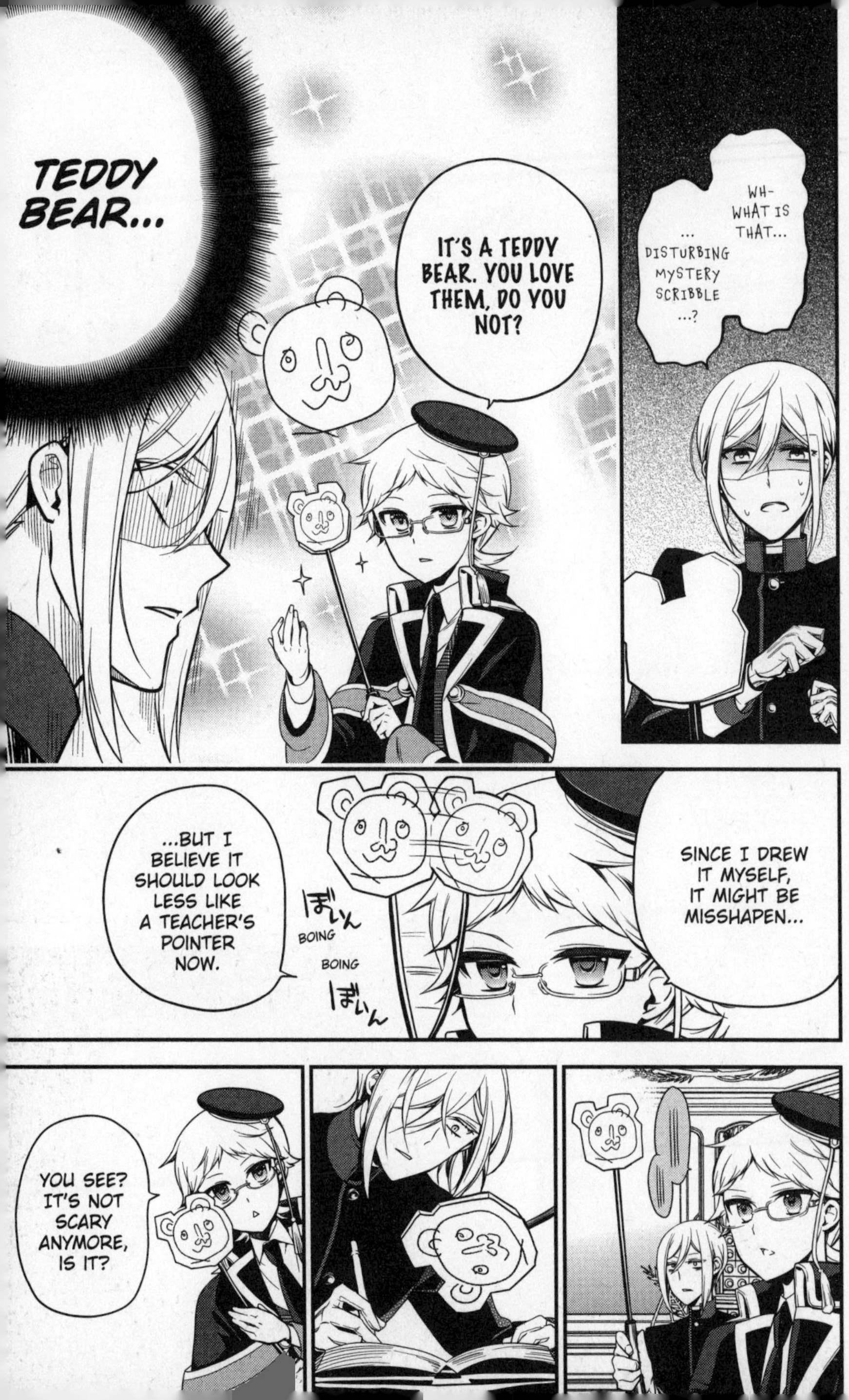

WH- WHAT IS THAT... ...DISTURBING MYSTERY SCRIBBLE ...?
IT'S A TEDDY BEAR. YOU LOVE THEM, DO YOU NOT?
TEDDY BEAR...
SINCE I DREW IT MYSELF, IT MIGHT BE MISSHAPEN...
ぼいん
BOING
BOING
ぼいん
...BUT I BELIEVE IT SHOULD LOOK LESS LIKE A TEACHER'S POINTER NOW.
YOU SEE? IT'S NOT SCARY ANYMORE, IS IT?

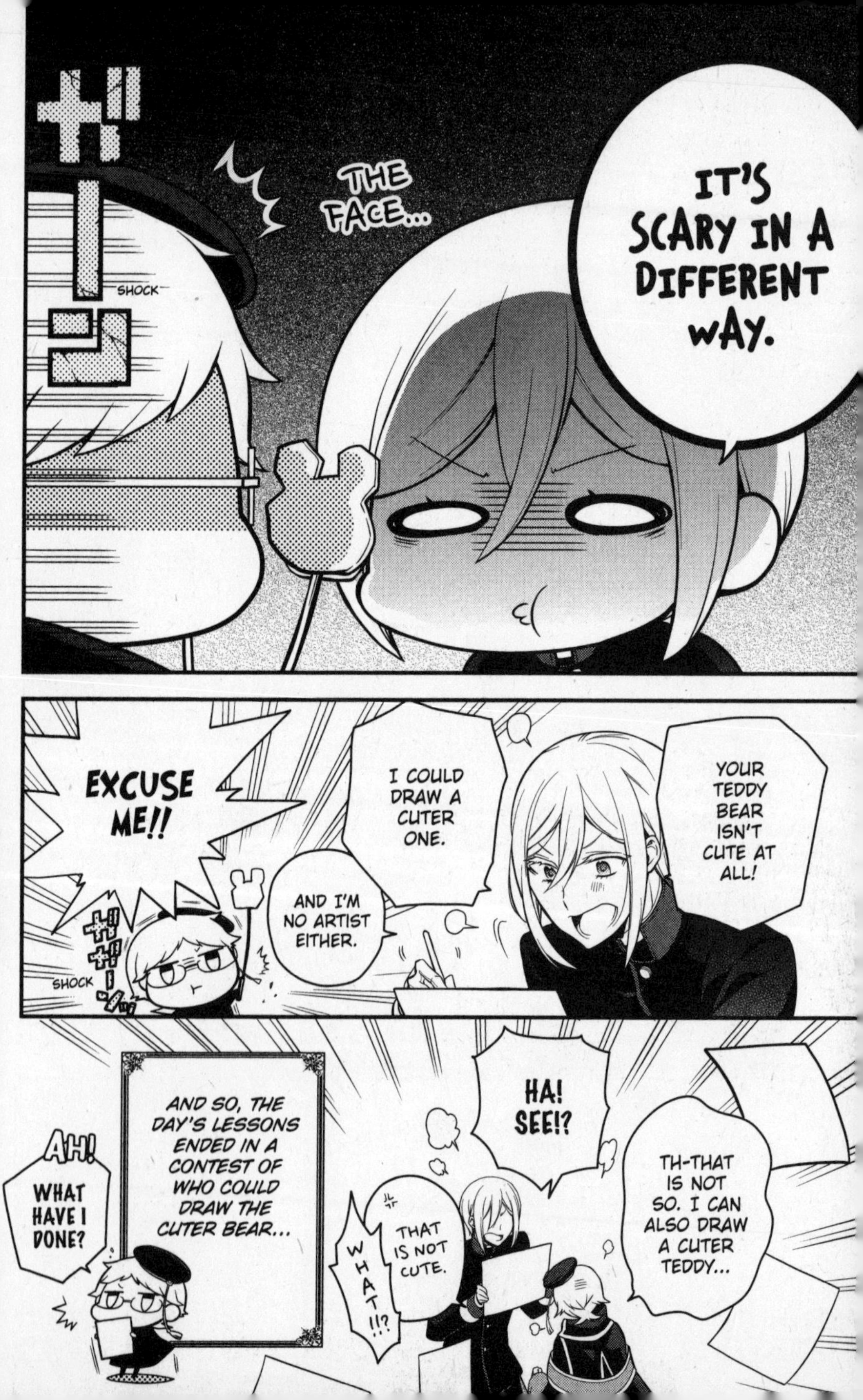
IT'S SCARY IN A DIFFERENT wAY.
THE FACE...
SHOCK
YOUR TEDDY BEAR ISN'T CUTE AT ALL!
I COULD DRAW A CUTER ONE.
AND I'M NO ARTIST EITHER.
EXCUSE ME!!
SHOCK
TH-THAT IS NOT SO. I CAN ALSO DRAW A CUTER TEDDY...
HA! SEE!?
THAT IS NOT CUTE.
WHAT!!?
AND SO, THE DAY'S LESSONS ENDED IN A CONTEST OF WHO COULD DRAW THE CUTER BEAR...
AH! WHAT HAVE I DONE?

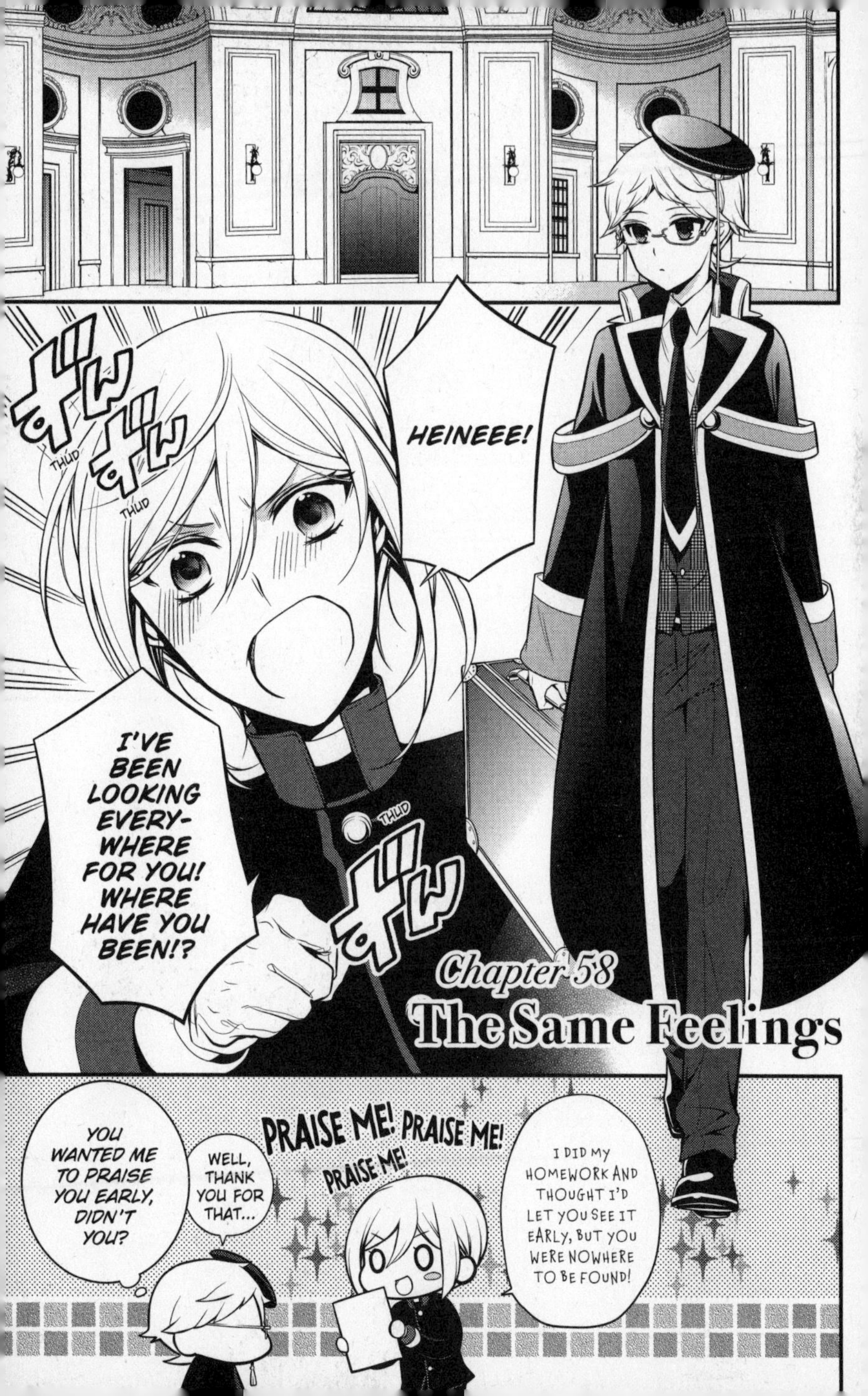
HEINEEE!
ずん THUD ずん THUD
I'VE BEEN LOOKING EVERY-WHERE FOR YOU! WHERE HAVE YOU BEEN!?
ずん THUD
Chapter 58
The Same Feelings
I DID MY HOMEWORK AND THOUGHT I'D LET YOU SEE IT EARLY, BUT YOU WERE NOWHERE TO BE FOUND!
PRAISE ME! PRAISE ME! PRAISE ME!
WELL, THANK YOU FOR THAT...
YOU WANTED ME TO PRAISE YOU EARLY, DIDN'T YOU?

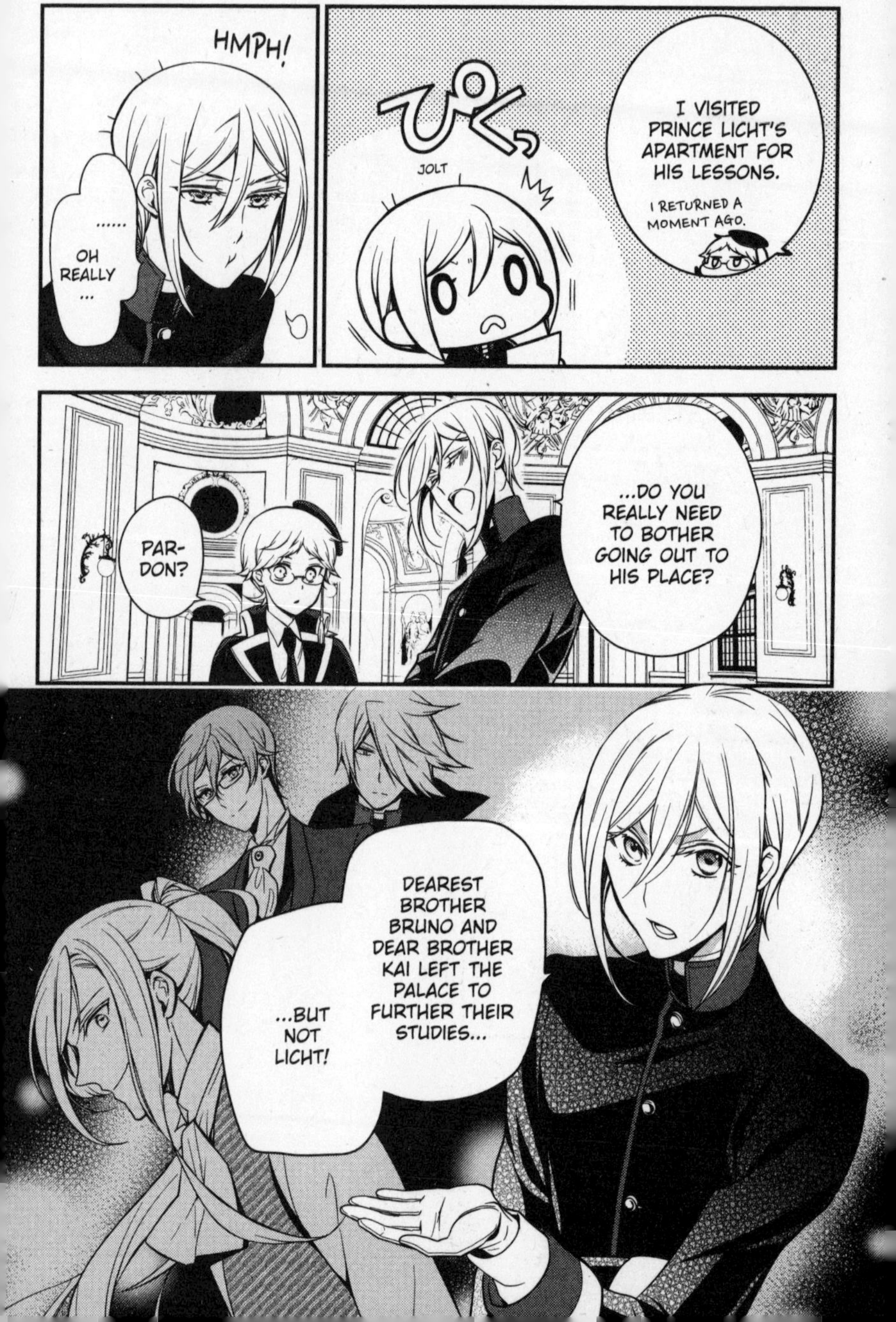
I VISITED PRINCE LICHT'S APARTMENT FOR HIS LESSONS.
I RETURNED A MOMENT AGO.
ぴくっ
JOLT
HMPH!
......
OH REALLY ...
...DO YOU REALLY NEED TO BOTHER GOING OUT TO HIS PLACE?
PAR-DON?
DEAREST BROTHER BRUNO AND DEAR BROTHER KAI LEFT THE PALACE TO FURTHER THEIR STUDIES...
...BUT NOT LICHT!

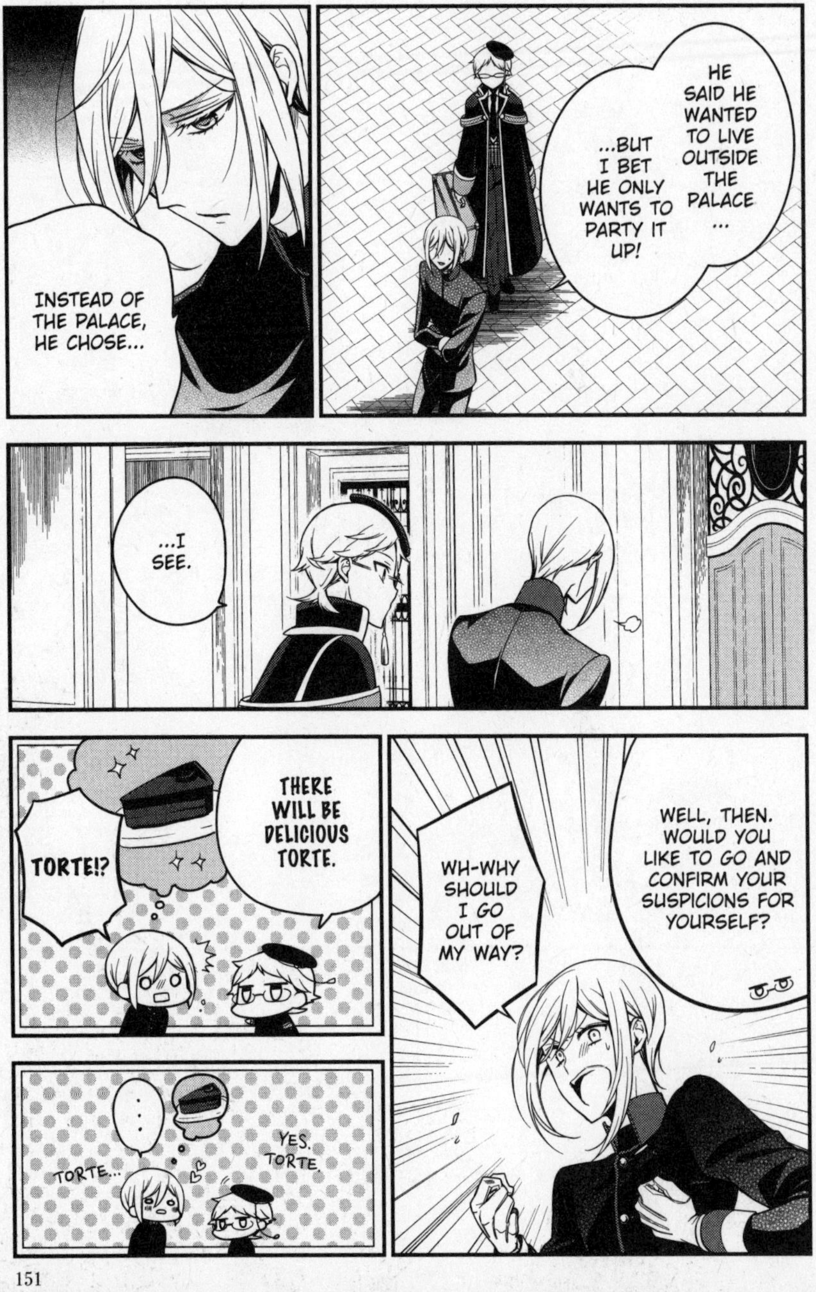
HE SAID HE WANTED TO LIVE OUTSIDE THE PALACE...
...BUT I BET HE ONLY WANTS TO PARTY IT UP!
INSTEAD OF THE PALACE, HE CHOSE...
...I SEE.
WELL, THEN. WOULD YOU LIKE TO GO AND CONFIRM YOUR SUSPICIONS FOR YOURSELF?
WH-WHY SHOULD I GO OUT OF MY WAY?
THERE WILL BE DELICIOUS TORTE.
TORTE!?
...
TORTE...
YES. TORTE.

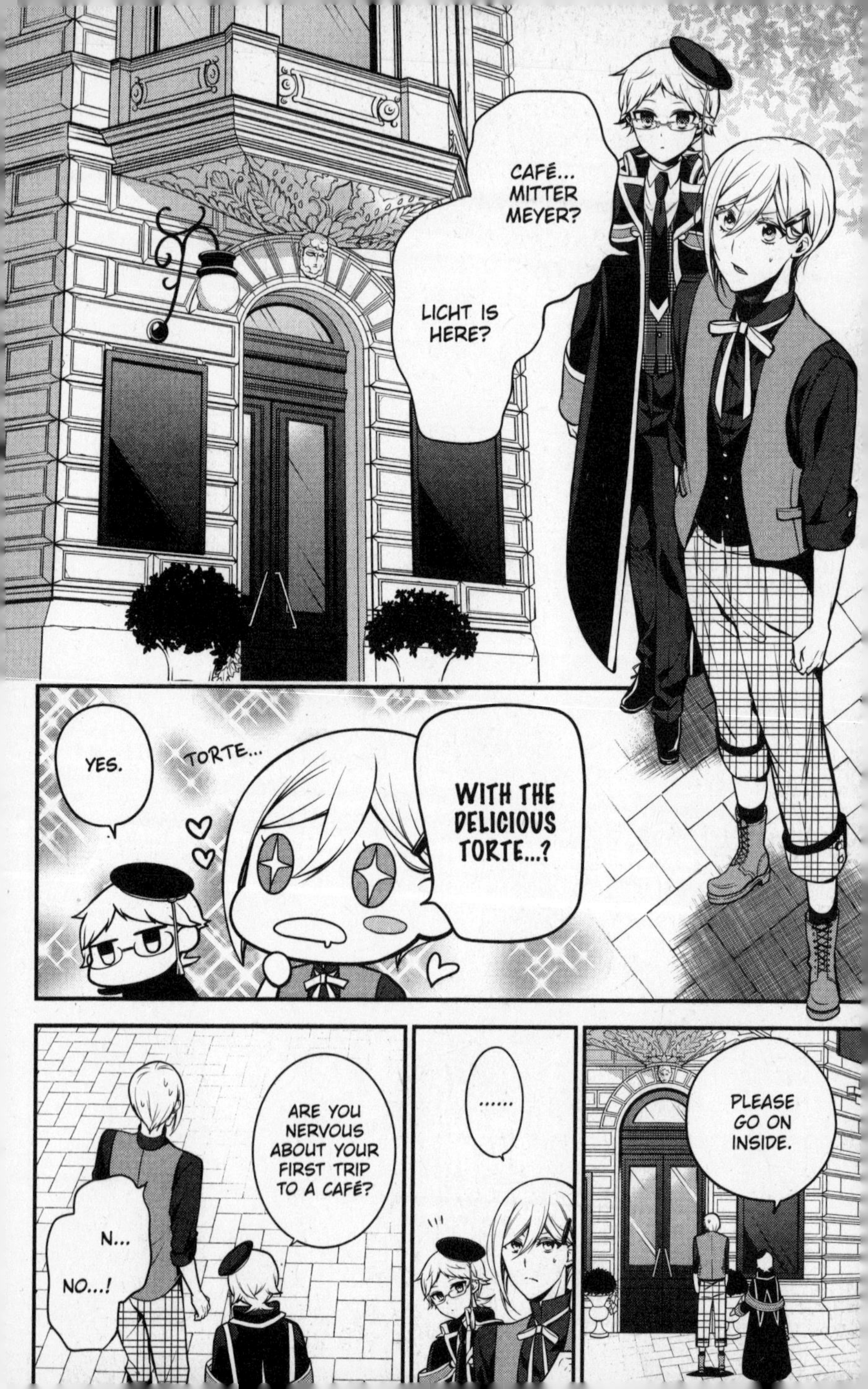
CAFÉ... MITTER MEYER?
LICHT IS HERE?
WITH THE DELICIOUS TORTE...?
TORTE...
YES.
PLEASE GO ON INSIDE.
......
ARE YOU NERVOUS ABOUT YOUR FIRST TRIP TO A CAFÉ?
N...
NO...!

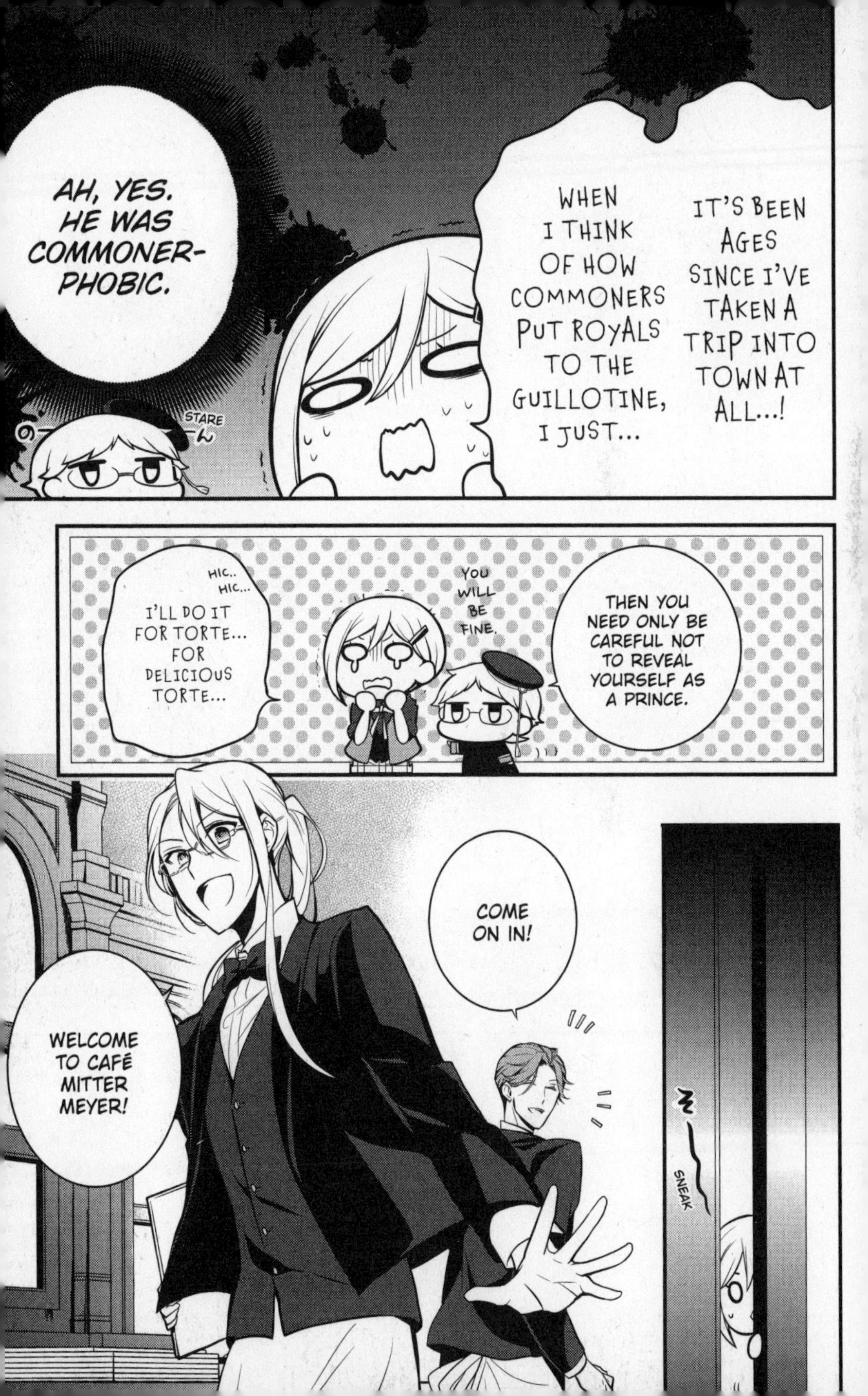
IT'S BEEN AGES SINCE I'VE TAKEN A TRIP INTO TOWN AT ALL...!
WHEN I THINK OF HOW COMMONERS PUT ROYALS TO THE GUILLOTINE, I JUST...
AH, YES. HE WAS COMMONER-PHOBIC.
STARE
THEN YOU NEED ONLY BE CAREFUL NOT TO REVEAL YOURSELF AS A PRINCE.
YOU WILL BE FINE.
HIC.. HIC...
I'LL DO IT FOR TORTE... FOR DELICIOUS TORTE...
SNEAK
COME ON IN!
WELCOME TO CAFÉ MITTER MEYER!

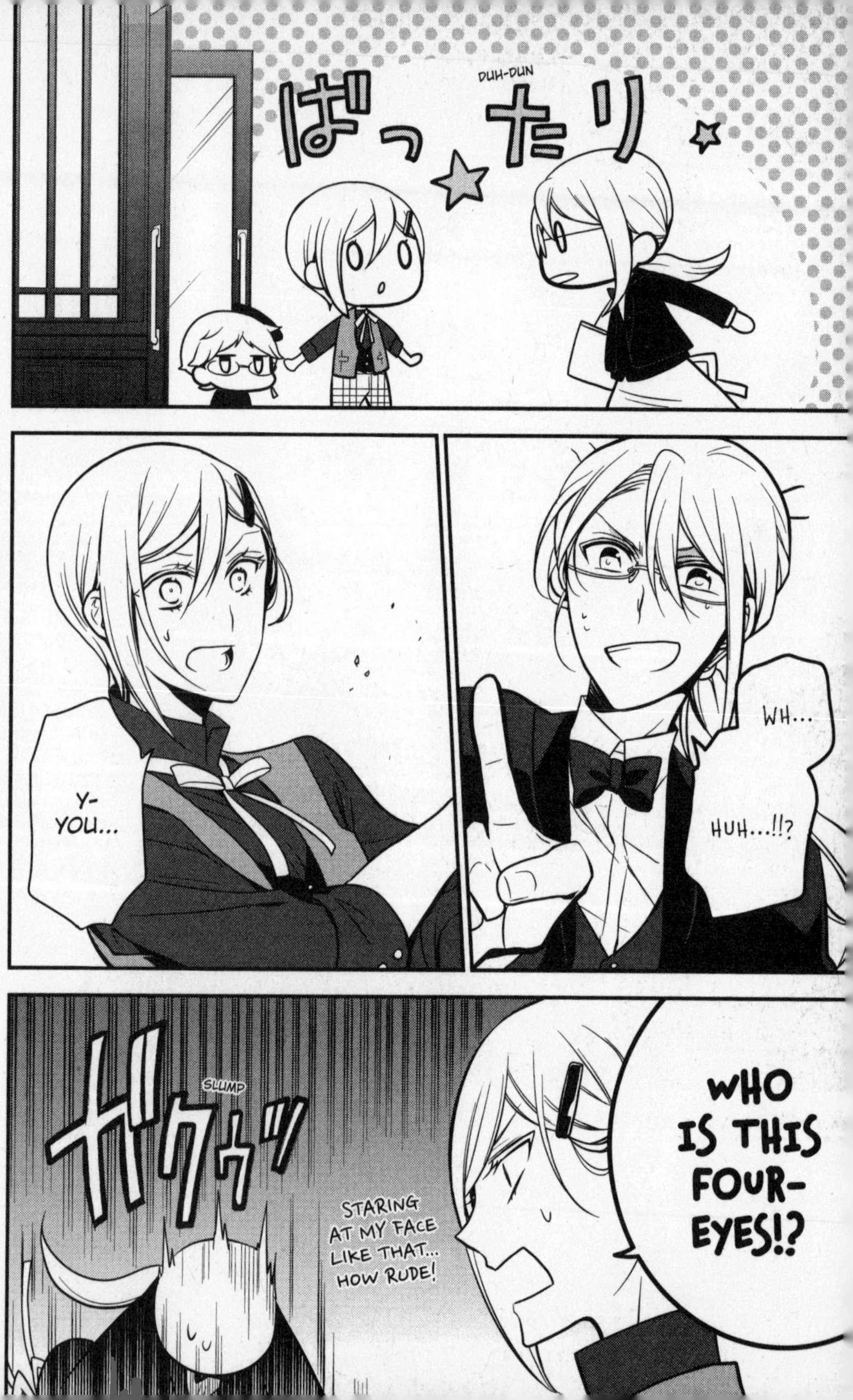
ばったり
DUH-DUN
WH... HUH...!!?
Y- YOU...
WHO IS THIS FOUR-EYES!?
STARING AT MY FACE LIKE THAT... HOW RUDE!
ガクゥッ
SLUMP

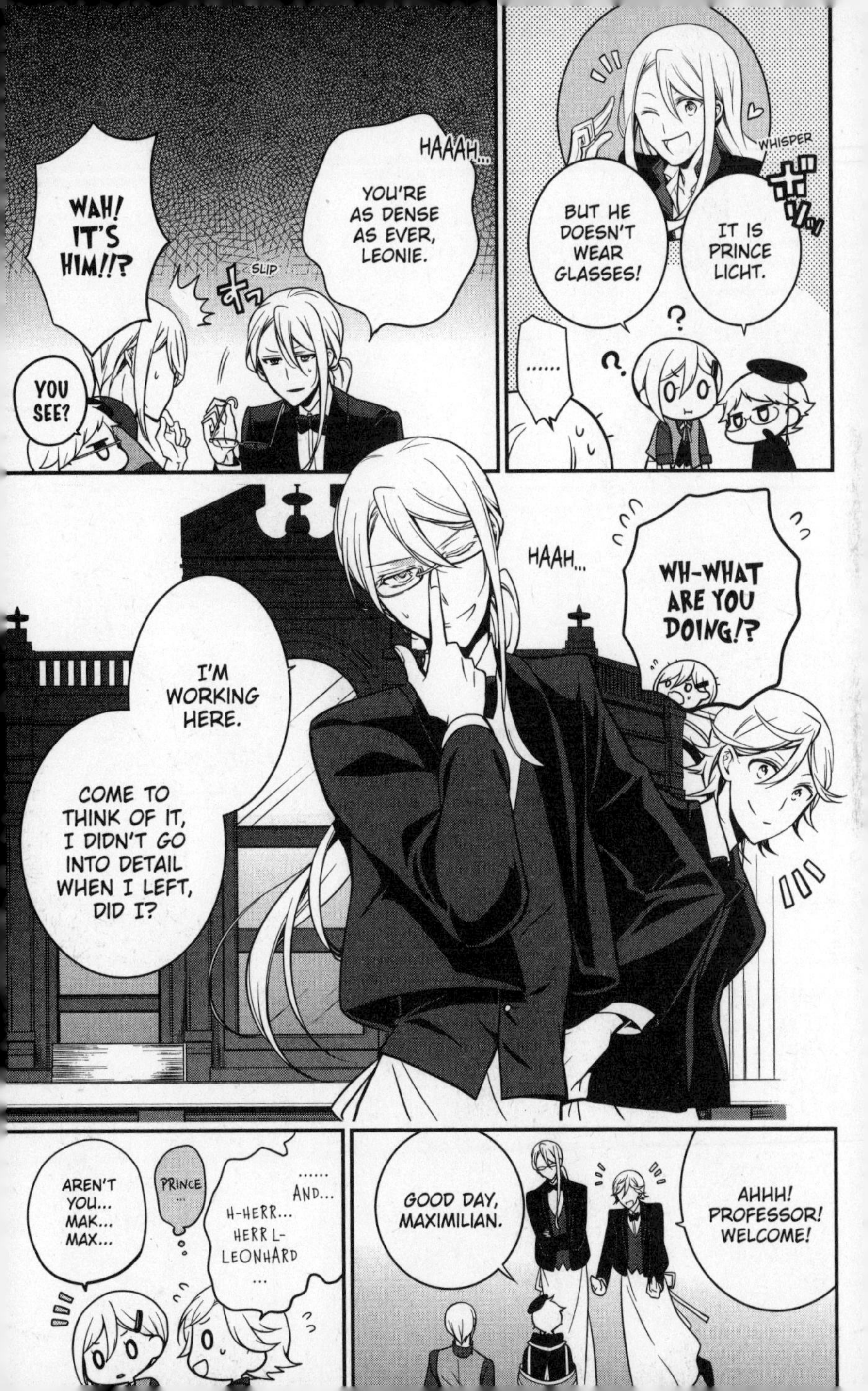
WHISPER
IT IS PRINCE LICHT.
BUT HE DOESN'T WEAR GLASSES!
......
HAAAH...
YOU'RE AS DENSE AS EVER, LEONIE.
SLIP
WAH! IT'S HIM!!?
YOU SEE?
WH-WHAT ARE YOU DOING!?
HAAH...
I'M WORKING HERE.
COME TO THINK OF IT, I DIDN'T GO INTO DETAIL WHEN I LEFT, DID I?
AHHH! PROFESSOR! WELCOME!
GOOD DAY, MAXIMILIAN.
...... AND...
H-HERR... HERR L-LEONHARD ...
PRINCE ...
AREN'T YOU... MAK... MAX...

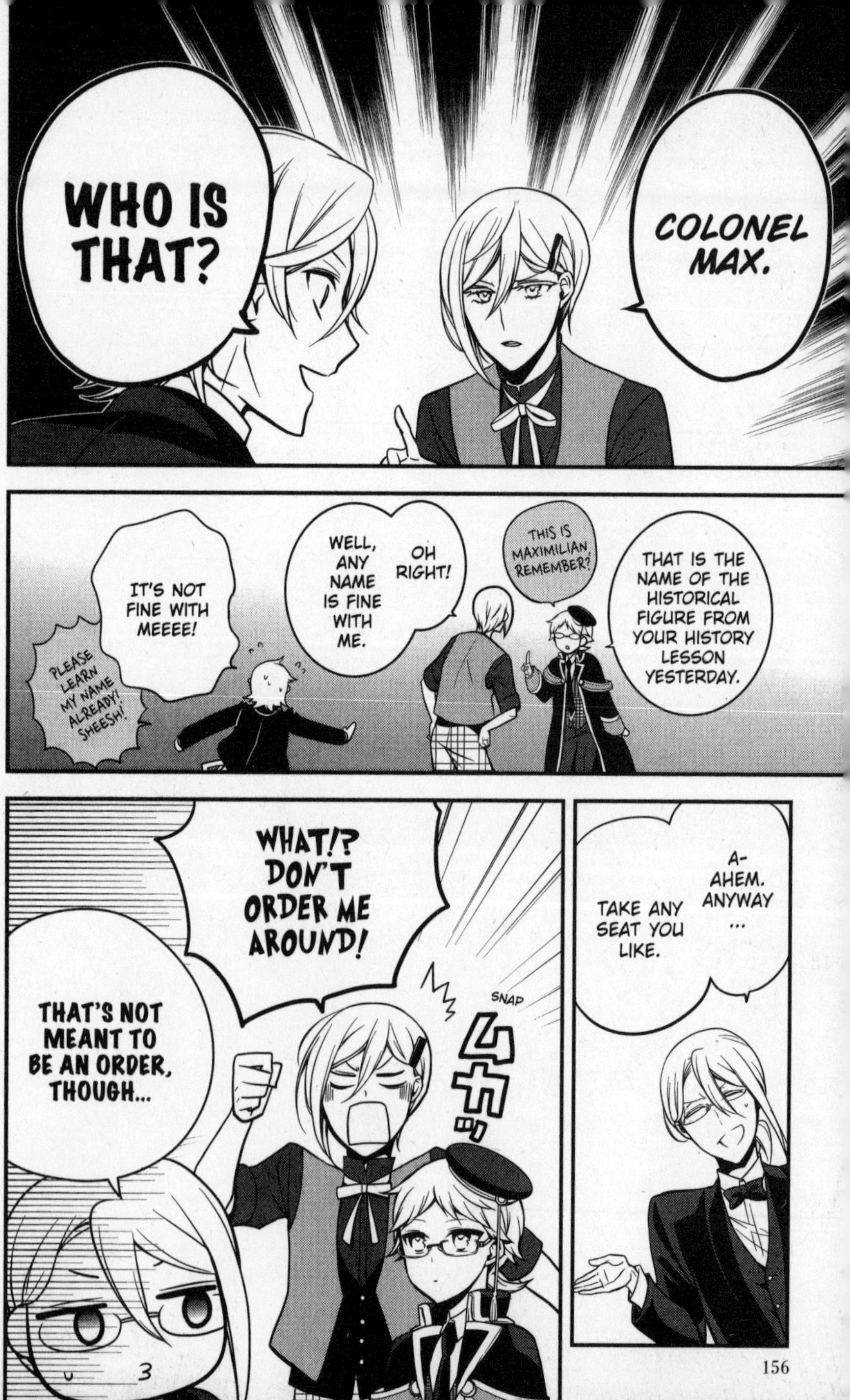
COLONEL MAX.
WHO IS THAT?
THAT IS THE NAME OF THE HISTORICAL FIGURE FROM YOUR HISTORY LESSON YESTERDAY.
THIS IS MAXIMILIAN REMEMBER?
OH RIGHT!
WELL, ANY NAME IS FINE WITH ME.
IT'S NOT FINE WITH MEEEE!
PLEASE LEARN MY NAME ALREADY! SHEESH!
A- AHEM. ANYWAY ...
TAKE ANY SEAT YOU LIKE.
WHAT!? DON'T ORDER ME AROUND!
SNAP
THAT'S NOT MEANT TO BE AN ORDER, THOUGH...

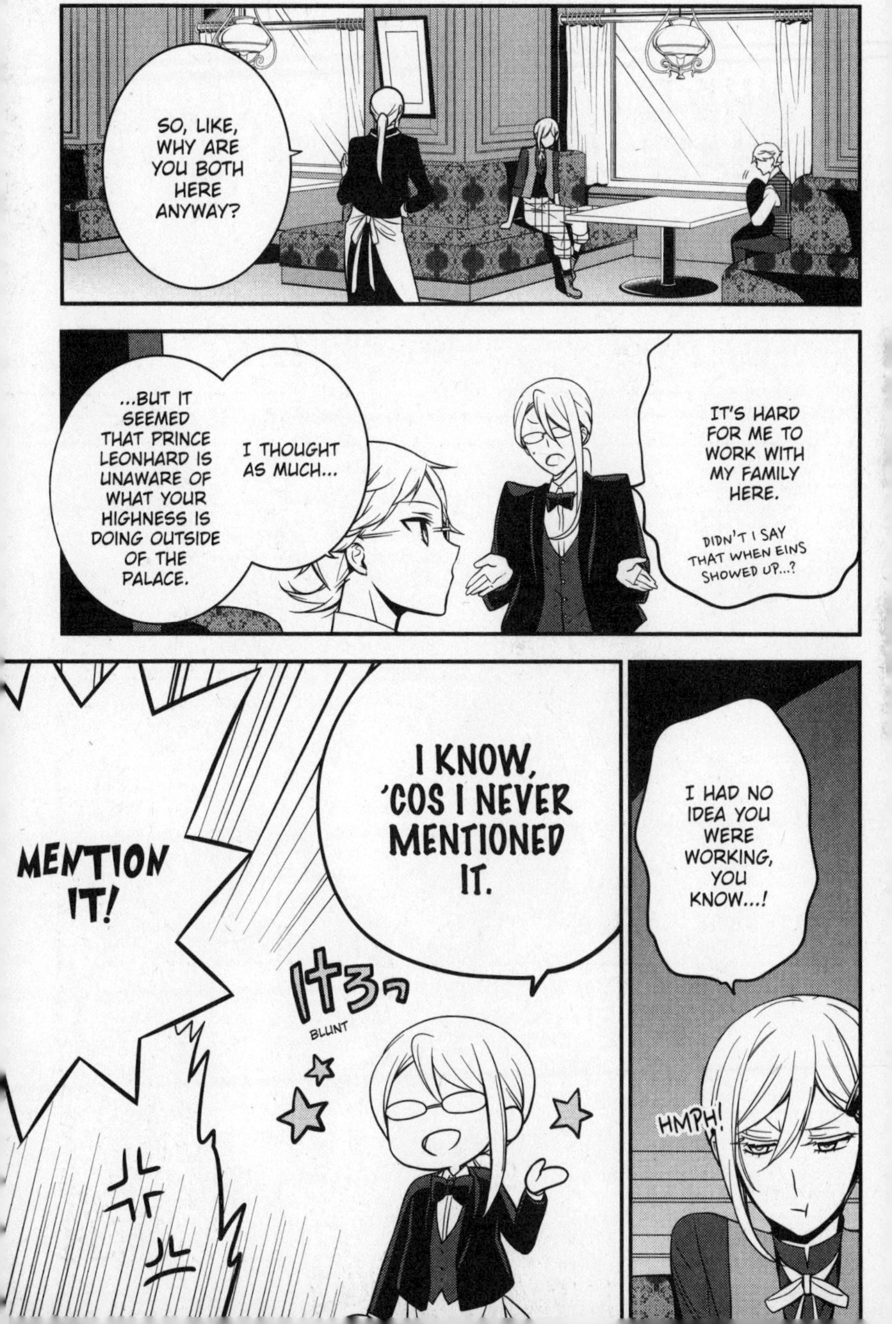
SO, LIKE, WHY ARE YOU BOTH HERE ANYWAY?
IT'S HARD FOR ME TO WORK WITH MY FAMILY HERE.
DIDN'T I SAY THAT WHEN EINS SHOWED UP...?
I THOUGHT AS MUCH...
...BUT IT SEEMED THAT PRINCE LEONHARD IS UNAWARE OF WHAT YOUR HIGHNESS IS DOING OUTSIDE OF THE PALACE.
I HAD NO IDEA YOU WERE WORKING, YOU KNOW...!
HMPH!
I KNOW, 'COS I NEVER MENTIONED IT.
けろっ
BLUNT
MENTION IT!

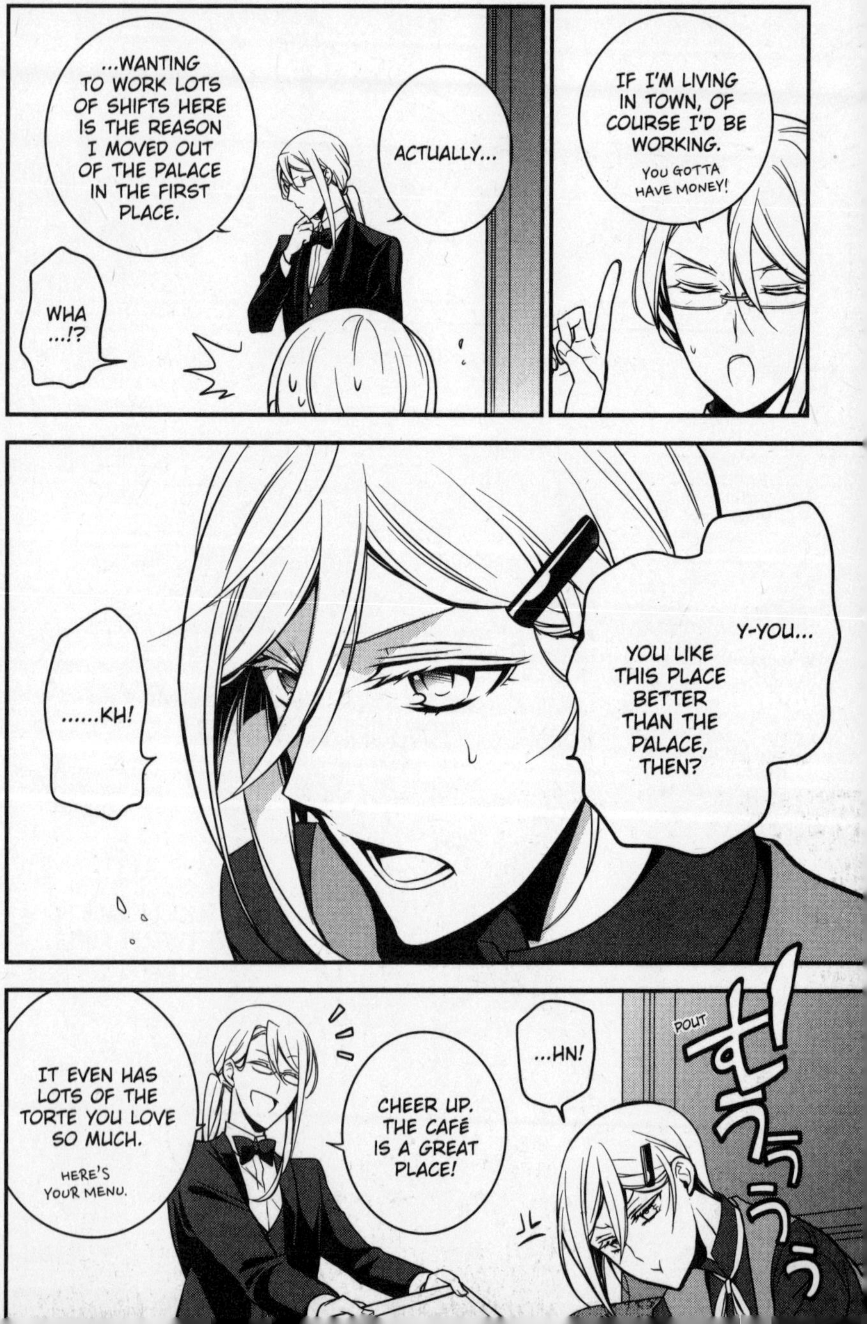
IF I'M LIVING IN TOWN, OF COURSE I'D BE WORKING.
YOU GOTTA HAVE MONEY!
ACTUALLY...
...WANTING TO WORK LOTS OF SHIFTS HERE IS THE REASON I MOVED OUT OF THE PALACE IN THE FIRST PLACE.
WHA ...!?
Y-YOU... YOU LIKE THIS PLACE BETTER THAN THE PALACE, THEN?
......KH!
POUT
...HN!
CHEER UP. THE CAFÉ IS A GREAT PLACE!
IT EVEN HAS LOTS OF THE TORTE YOU LOVE SO MUCH.
HERE'S YOUR MENU.

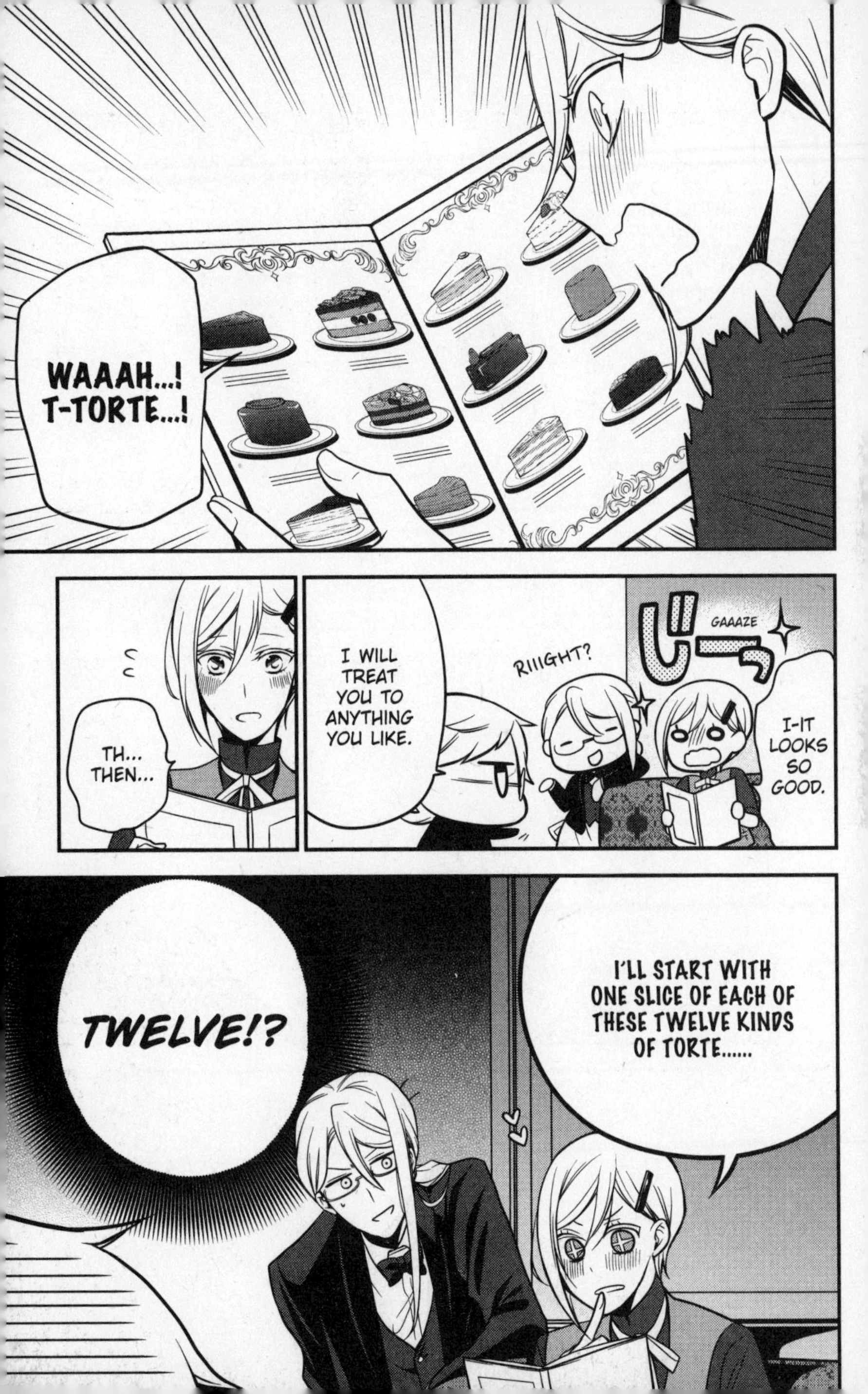
WAAAH...! T-TORTE...!
GAAAZE
I-IT LOOKS SO GOOD.
I WILL TREAT YOU TO ANYTHING YOU LIKE.
RIIIGHT?
TH... THEN...
I'LL START WITH ONE SLICE OF EACH OF THESE TWELVE KINDS OF TORTE......
TWELVE!?

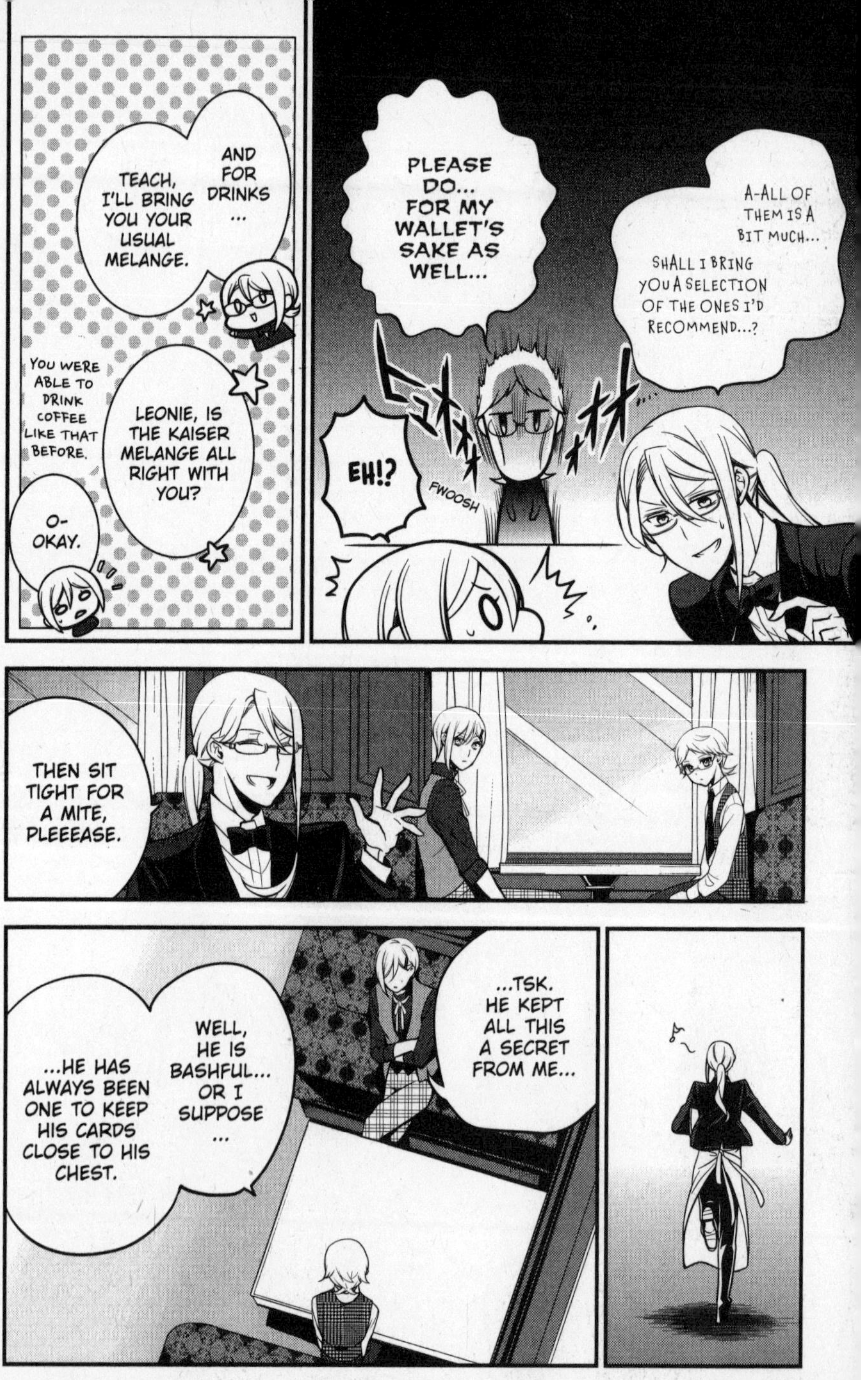
A-ALL OF THEM IS A BIT MUCH...
SHALL I BRING YOU A SELECTION OF THE ONES I'D RECOMMEND...?
PLEASE DO... FOR MY WALLET'S SAKE AS WELL...
EH!?
FWOOSH
AND FOR DRINKS...
TEACH, I'LL BRING YOU YOUR USUAL MELANGE.
LEONIE, IS THE KAISER MELANGE ALL RIGHT WITH YOU?
YOU WERE ABLE TO DRINK COFFEE LIKE THAT BEFORE.
O-OKAY.
THEN SIT TIGHT FOR A MITE, PLEEEASE.
...TSK. HE KEPT ALL THIS A SECRET FROM ME...
WELL, HE IS BASHFUL... OR I SUPPOSE...
...HE HAS ALWAYS BEEN ONE TO KEEP HIS CARDS CLOSE TO HIS CHEST.

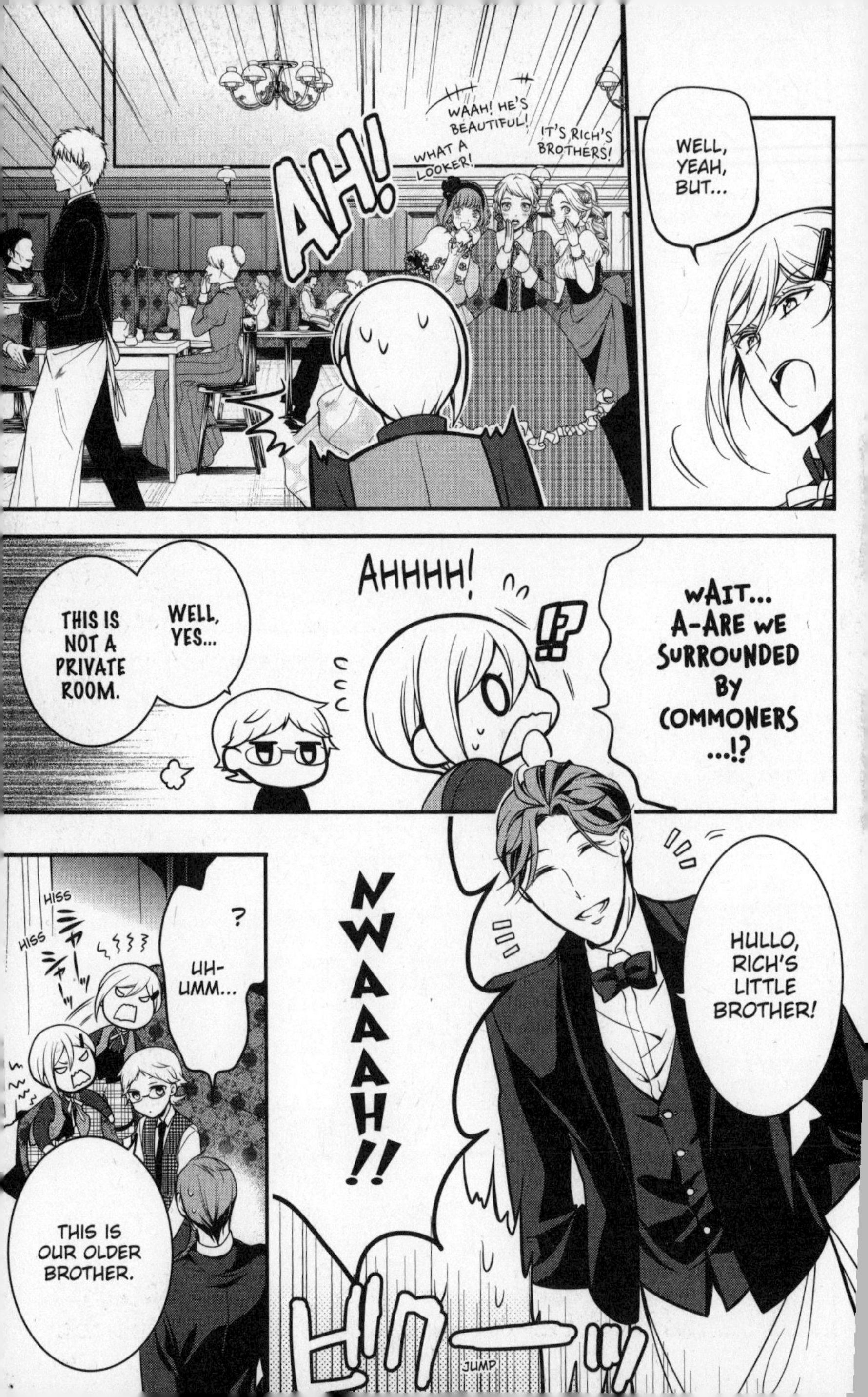
WELL, YEAH, BUT...
AH!
WAAH! HE'S BEAUTIFUL!
IT'S RICH'S BROTHERS!
WHAT A LOOKER!
WAIT... A-ARE WE SURROUNDED BY COMMONERS ...!?
AHHHH!
WELL, YES...
THIS IS NOT A PRIVATE ROOM.
HULLO, RICH'S LITTLE BROTHER!
NWAAAAH!!
JUMP
UH-UMM...
HISS
HISS
THIS IS OUR OLDER BROTHER.

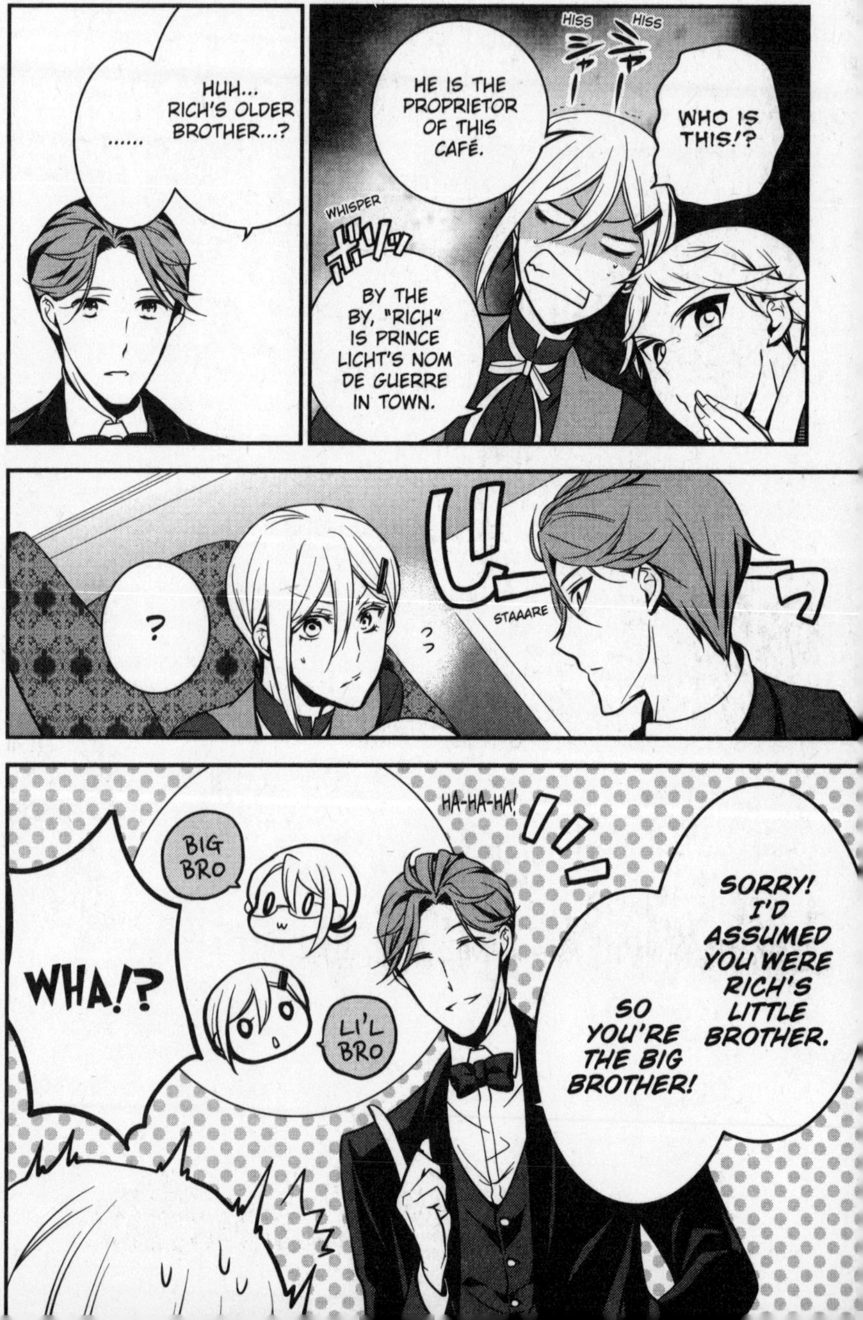
HISS
HISS
WHO IS THIS!?
HE IS THE PROPRIETOR OF THIS CAFÉ.
WHISPER
BY THE BY, "RICH" IS PRINCE LICHT'S NOM DE GUERRE IN TOWN.
HUH... RICH'S OLDER BROTHER...?
......
STAAARE
?
SORRY! I'D ASSUMED YOU WERE RICH'S LITTLE BROTHER.
SO YOU'RE THE BIG BROTHER!
HA-HA-HA!
BIG BRO
LI'L BRO
WHA!?

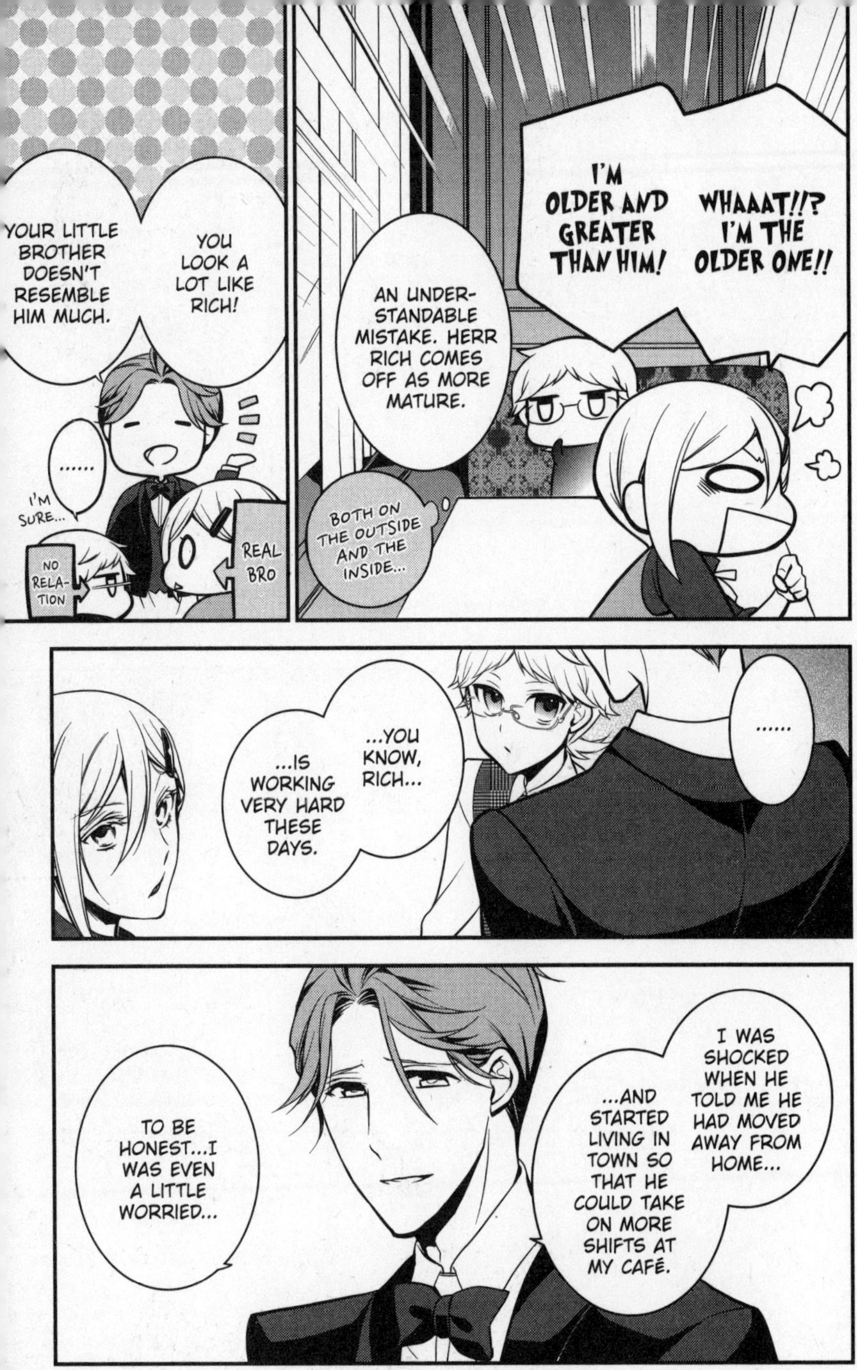
WHAAAT!!? I'M THE OLDER ONE!!
I'M OLDER AND GREATER THAN HIM!
AN UNDER-STANDABLE MISTAKE. HERR RICH COMES OFF AS MORE MATURE.
BOTH ON THE OUTSIDE AND THE INSIDE...
YOU LOOK A LOT LIKE RICH!
YOUR LITTLE BROTHER DOESN'T RESEMBLE HIM MUCH.
......
I'M SURE...
REAL BRO
NO RELA-TION
......
...YOU KNOW, RICH...
...IS WORKING VERY HARD THESE DAYS.
I WAS SHOCKED WHEN HE TOLD ME HE HAD MOVED AWAY FROM HOME...
...AND STARTED LIVING IN TOWN SO THAT HE COULD TAKE ON MORE SHIFTS AT MY CAFÉ.
TO BE HONEST...I WAS EVEN A LITTLE WORRIED...

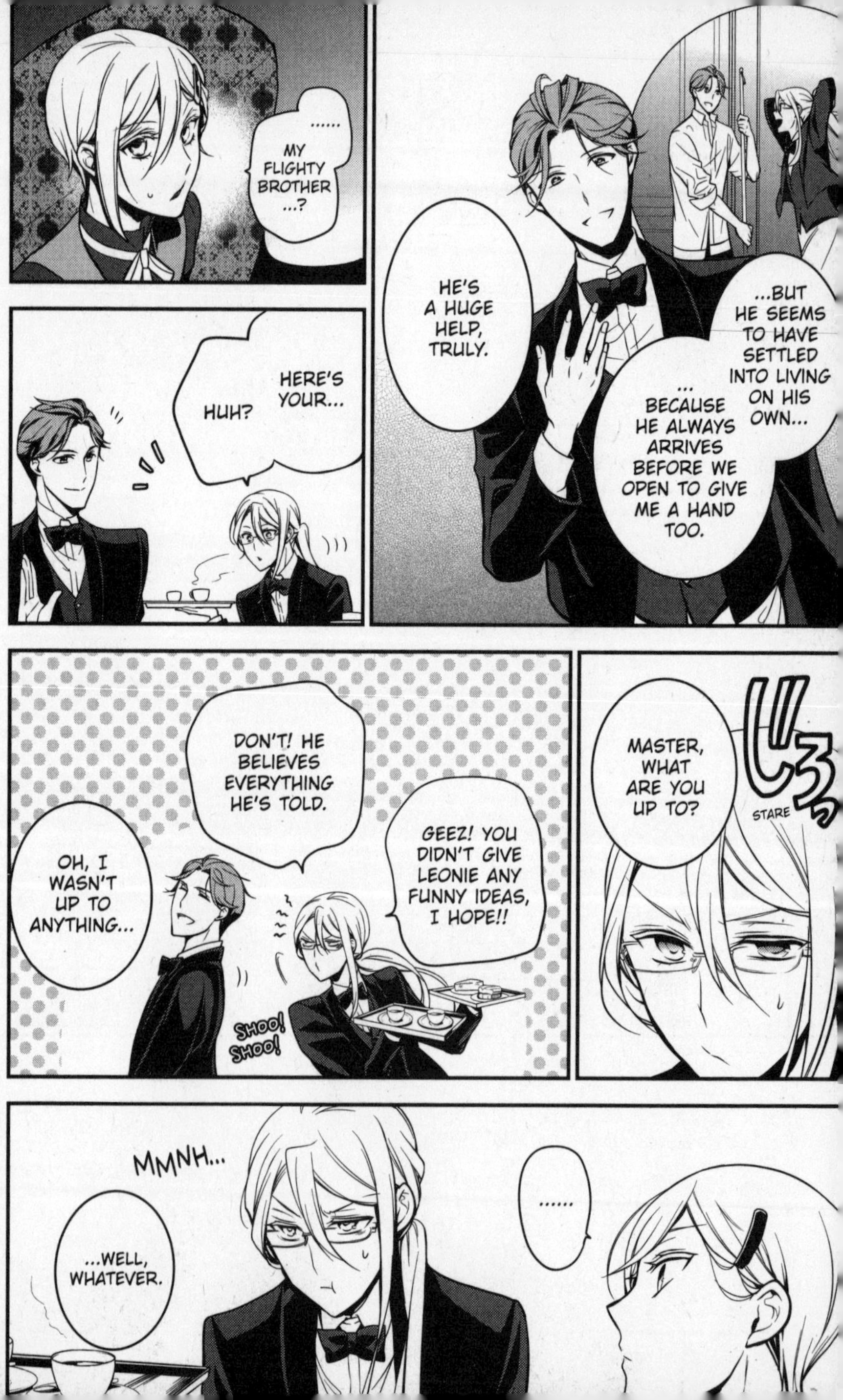
...BUT HE SEEMS TO HAVE SETTLED INTO LIVING ON HIS OWN...
HE'S A HUGE HELP, TRULY.
... BECAUSE HE ALWAYS ARRIVES BEFORE WE OPEN TO GIVE ME A HAND TOO.
...... MY FLIGHTY BROTHER ...?
HERE'S YOUR...
HUH?
MASTER, WHAT ARE YOU UP TO?
STARE
OH, I WASN'T UP TO ANYTHING...
GEEZ! YOU DIDN'T GIVE LEONIE ANY FUNNY IDEAS, I HOPE!!
DON'T! HE BELIEVES EVERYTHING HE'S TOLD.
SHOO! SHOO!
......
MMNH...
...WELL, WHATEVER.

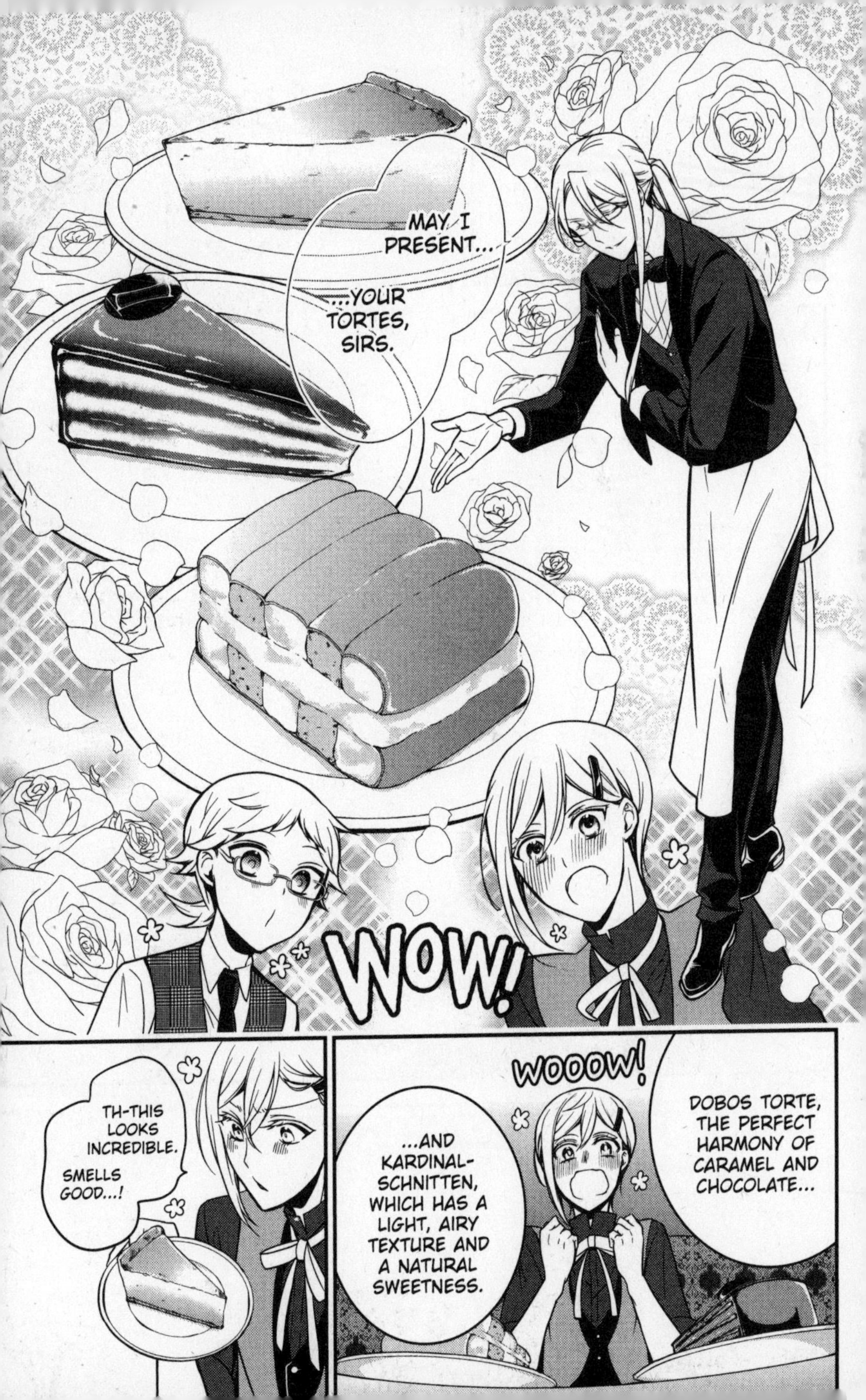
MAY I PRESENT...
...YOUR TORTES, SIRS.
WOW!
DOBOS TORTE, THE PERFECT HARMONY OF CARAMEL AND CHOCOLATE...
WOOOW!
...AND KARDINAL-SCHNITTEN, WHICH HAS A LIGHT, AIRY TEXTURE AND A NATURAL SWEETNESS.
TH-THIS LOOKS INCREDIBLE.
SMELLS GOOD...!

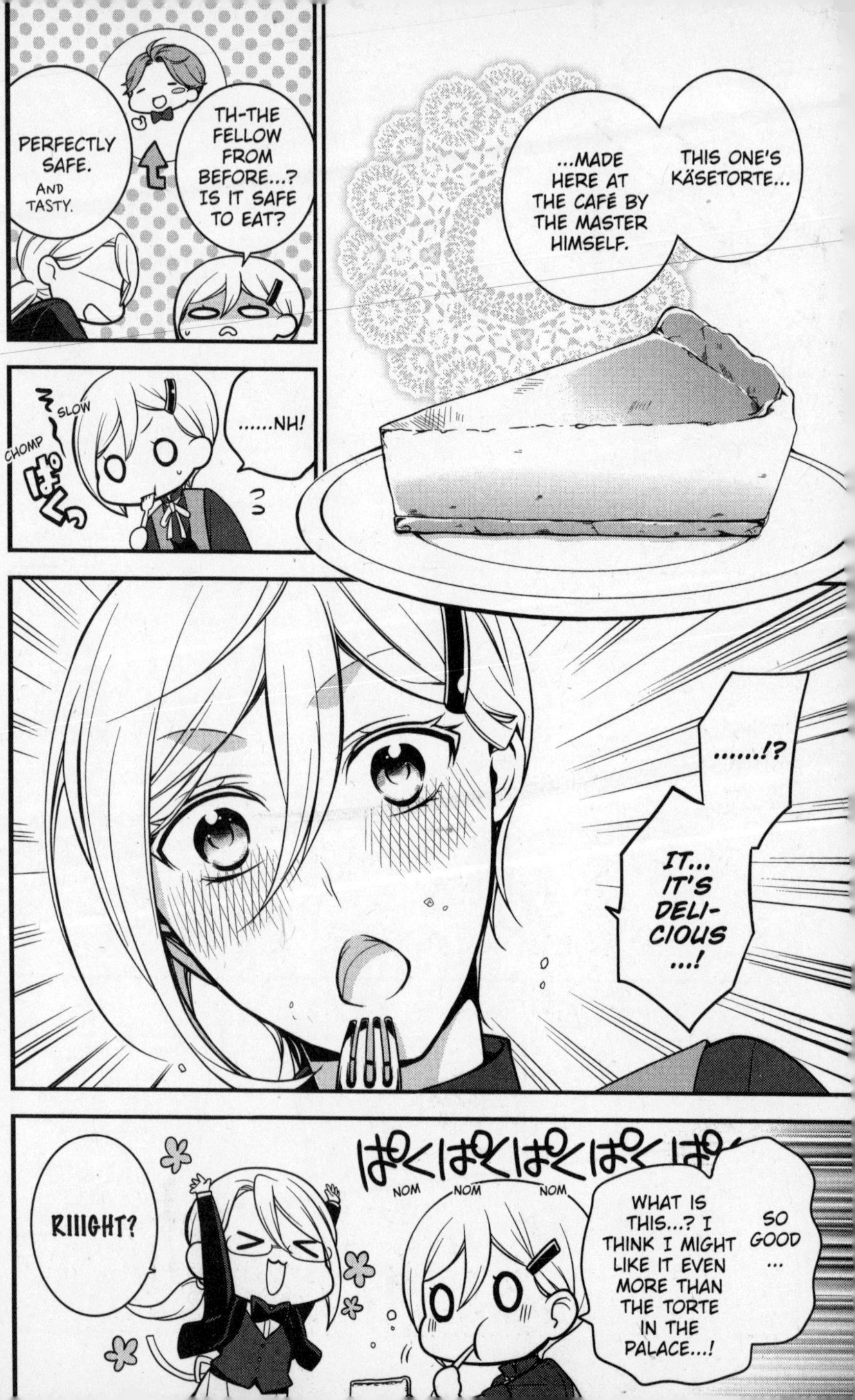
THIS ONE'S KÄSETORTE...
...MADE HERE AT THE CAFÉ BY THE MASTER HIMSELF.
TH-THE FELLOW FROM BEFORE...? IS IT SAFE TO EAT?
PERFECTLY SAFE.
AND TASTY.
......NH!
SLOW
CHOMP
ぱくっ
......!?
IT... IT'S DELICIOUS...!
SO GOOD...
WHAT IS THIS...? I THINK I MIGHT LIKE IT EVEN MORE THAN THE TORTE IN THE PALACE...!
NOM NOM NOM
RIIIGHT?

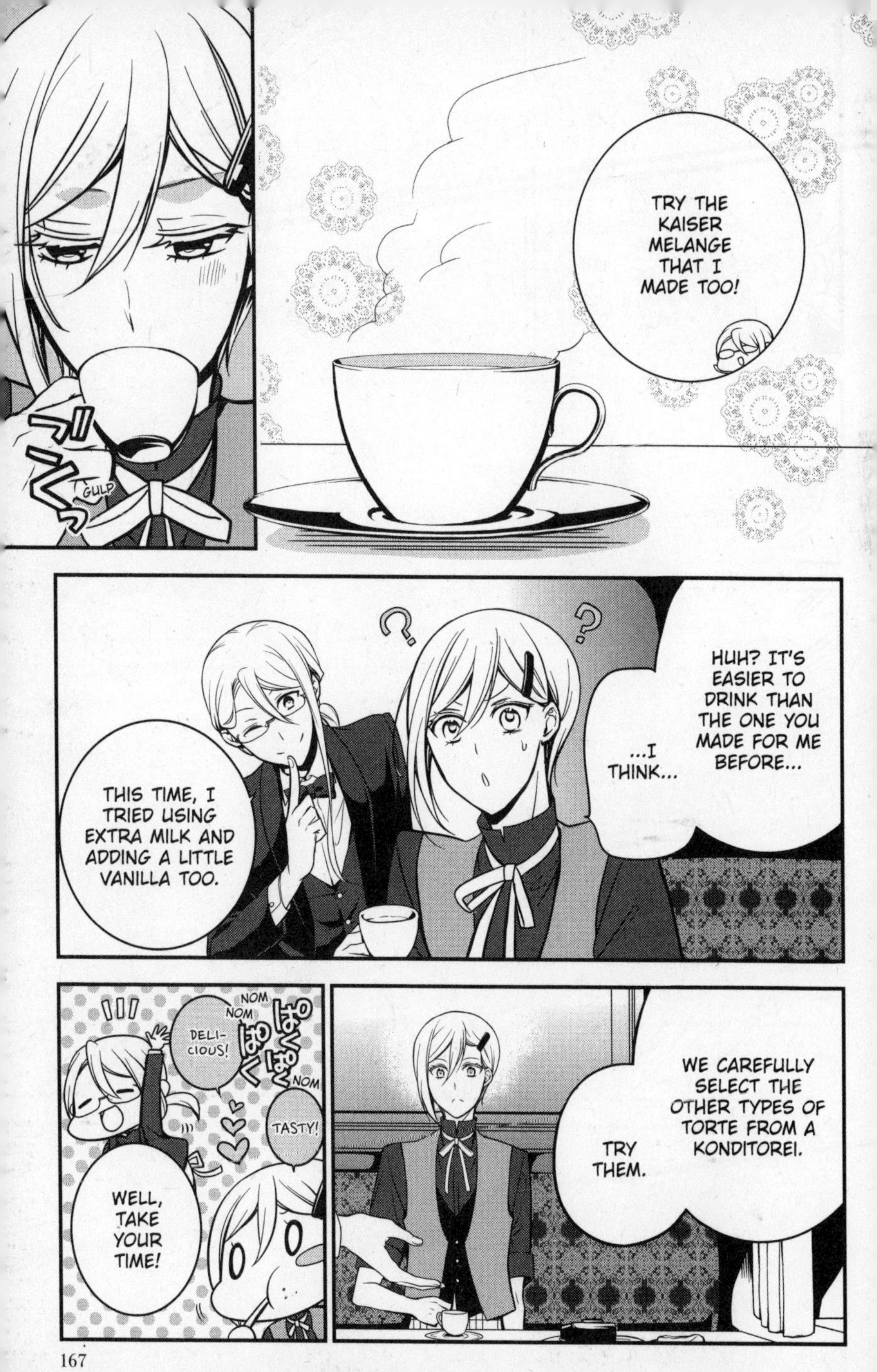
TRY THE KAISER MELANGE THAT I MADE TOO!
GULP
HUH? IT'S EASIER TO DRINK THAN THE ONE YOU MADE FOR ME BEFORE...
...I THINK...
THIS TIME, I TRIED USING EXTRA MILK AND ADDING A LITTLE VANILLA TOO.
WE CAREFULLY SELECT THE OTHER TYPES OF TORTE FROM A KONDITOREI.
TRY THEM.
NOM NOM
DELI-CIOUS!
NOM
TASTY!
WELL, TAKE YOUR TIME!

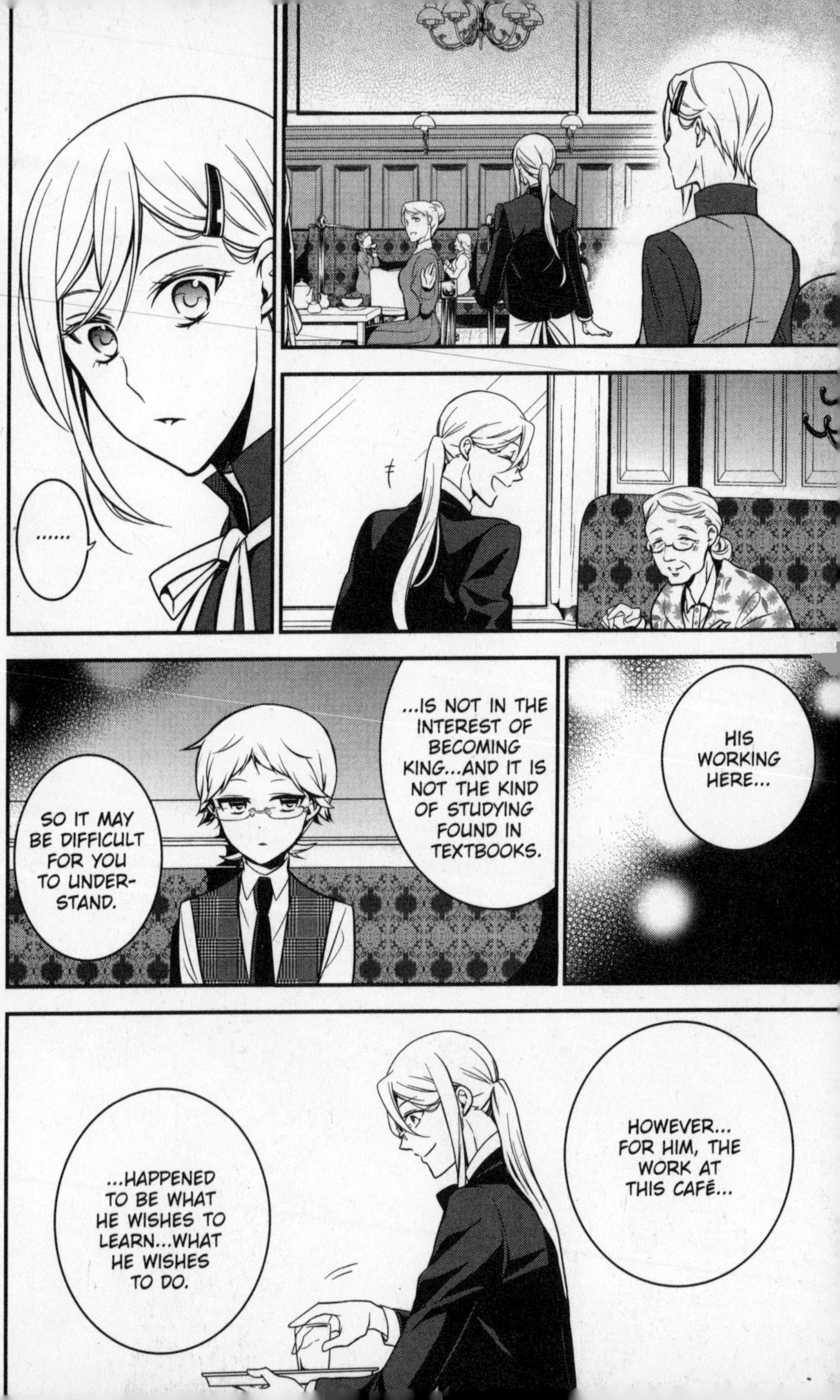
......
HIS WORKING HERE...
...IS NOT IN THE INTEREST OF BECOMING KING...AND IT IS NOT THE KIND OF STUDYING FOUND IN TEXTBOOKS.
SO IT MAY BE DIFFICULT FOR YOU TO UNDER-STAND.
HOWEVER... FOR HIM, THE WORK AT THIS CAFÉ...
...HAPPENED TO BE WHAT HE WISHES TO LEARN...WHAT HE WISHES TO DO.

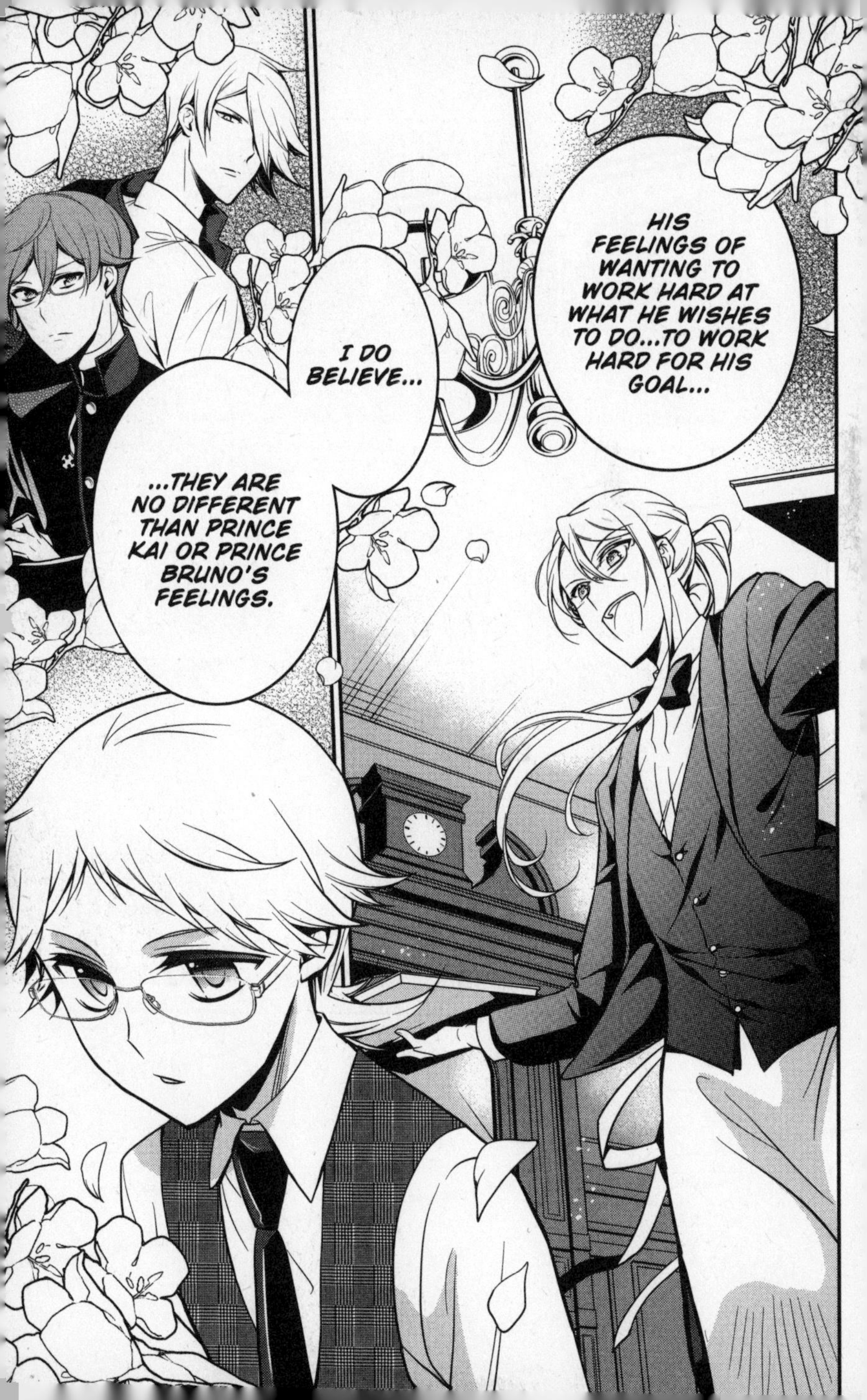
HIS FEELINGS OF WANTING TO WORK HARD AT WHAT HE WISHES TO DO...TO WORK HARD FOR HIS GOAL...
I DO BELIEVE...
...THEY ARE NO DIFFERENT THAN PRINCE KAI OR PRINCE BRUNO'S FEELINGS.

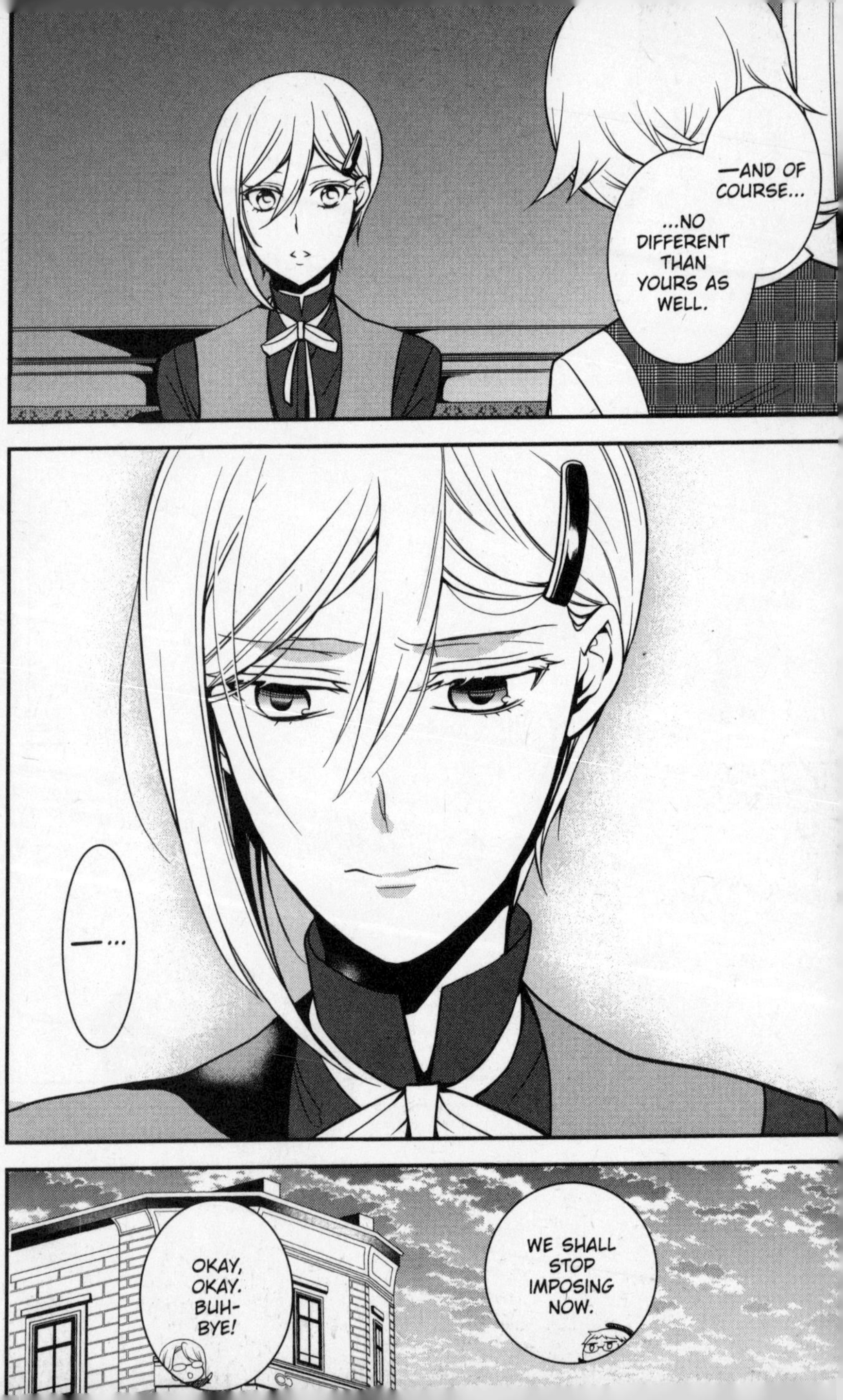
—AND OF COURSE...
...NO DIFFERENT THAN YOURS AS WELL.
—...
WE SHALL STOP IMPOSING NOW.
OKAY, OKAY. BUH-BYE!

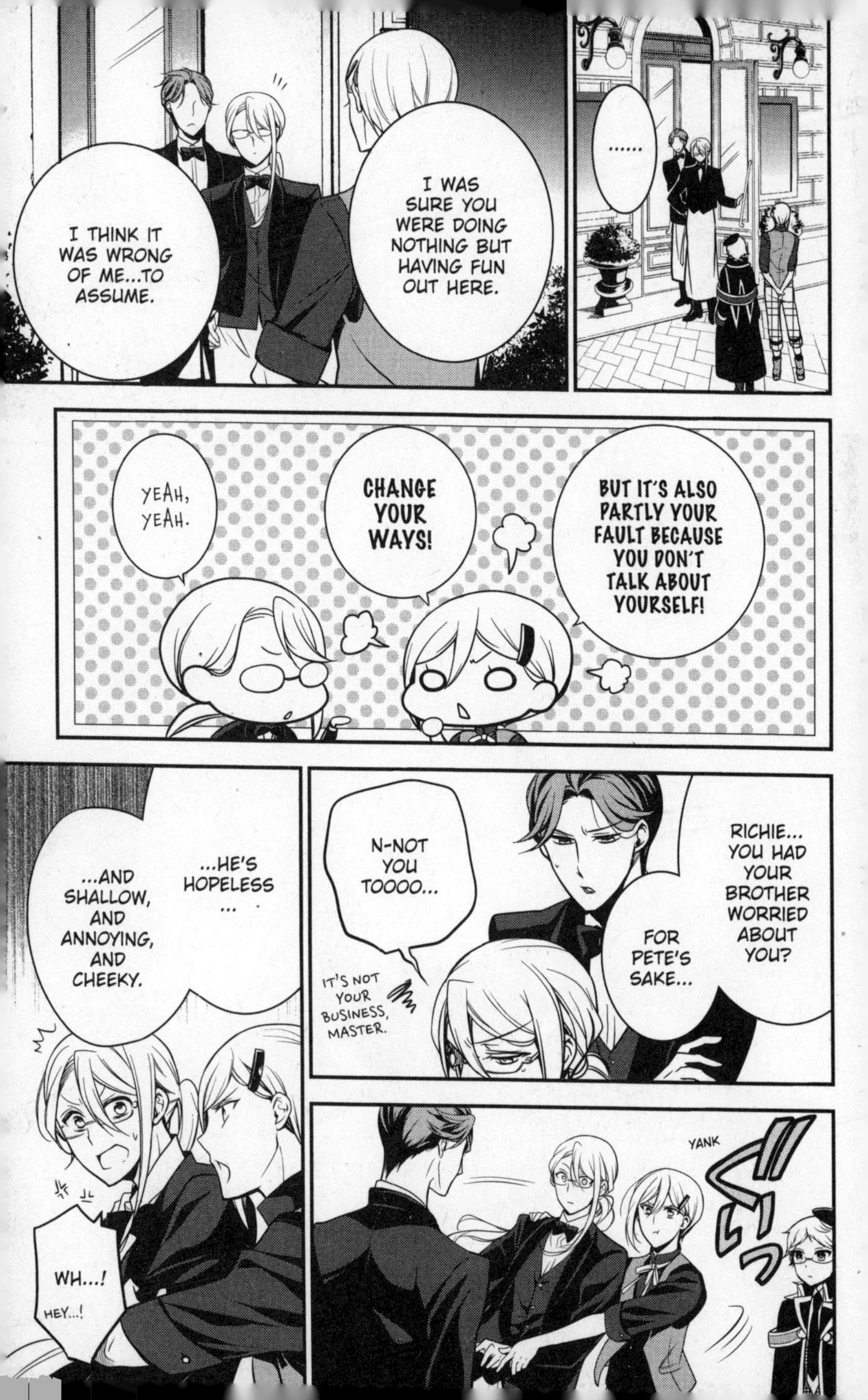
......
I WAS SURE YOU WERE DOING NOTHING BUT HAVING FUN OUT HERE.
I THINK IT WAS WRONG OF ME...TO ASSUME.
BUT IT'S ALSO PARTLY YOUR FAULT BECAUSE YOU DON'T TALK ABOUT YOURSELF!
CHANGE YOUR WAYS!
YEAH, YEAH.
RICHIE... YOU HAD YOUR BROTHER WORRIED ABOUT YOU?
FOR PETE'S SAKE...
N-NOT YOU TOOOO...
IT'S NOT YOUR BUSINESS, MASTER.
YANK
...HE'S HOPELESS ...
...AND SHALLOW, AND ANNOYING, AND CHEEKY.
WH...!
HEY...!

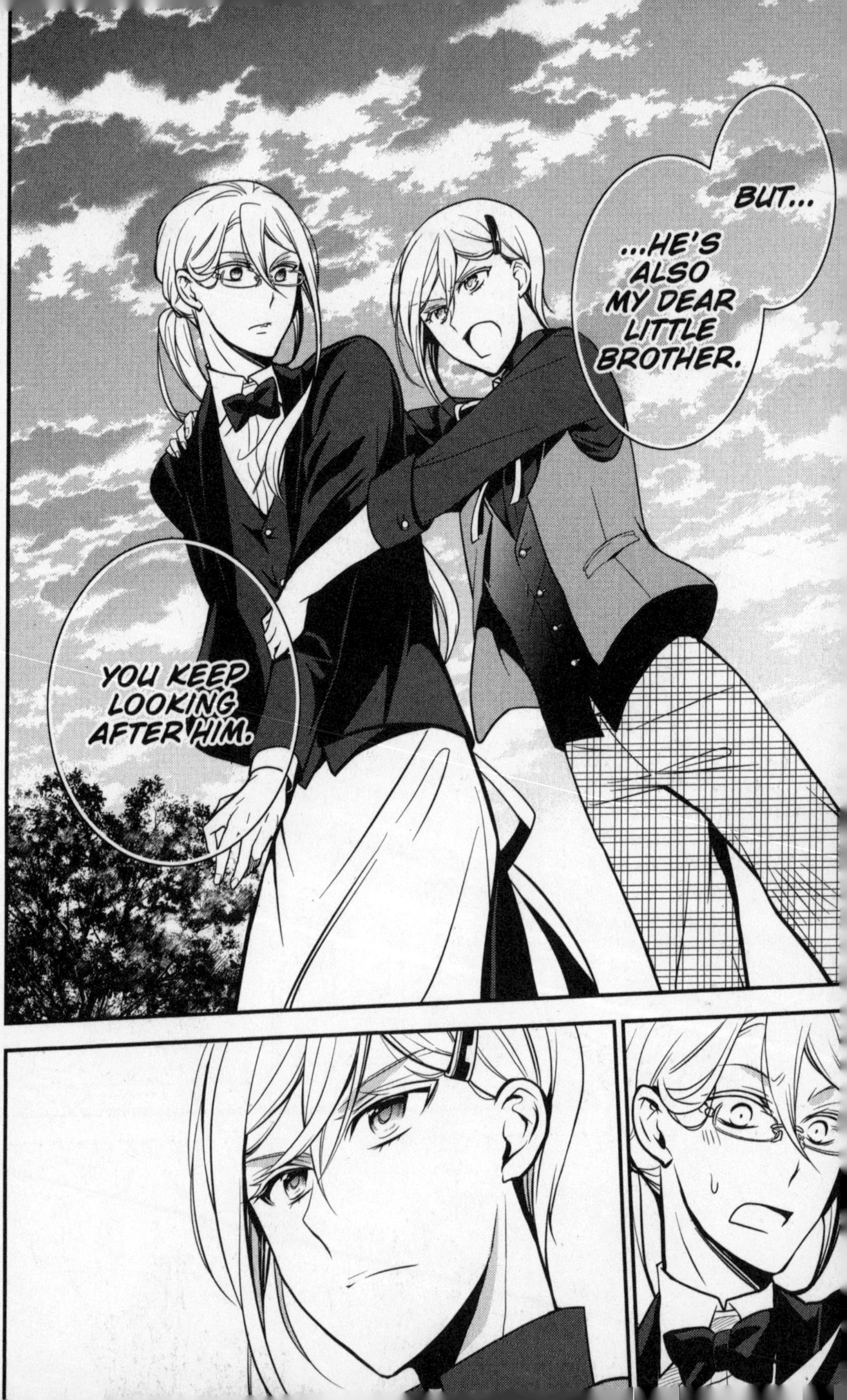
BUT...
...HE'S ALSO MY DEAR LITTLE BROTHER.
YOU KEEP LOOKING AFTER HIM.

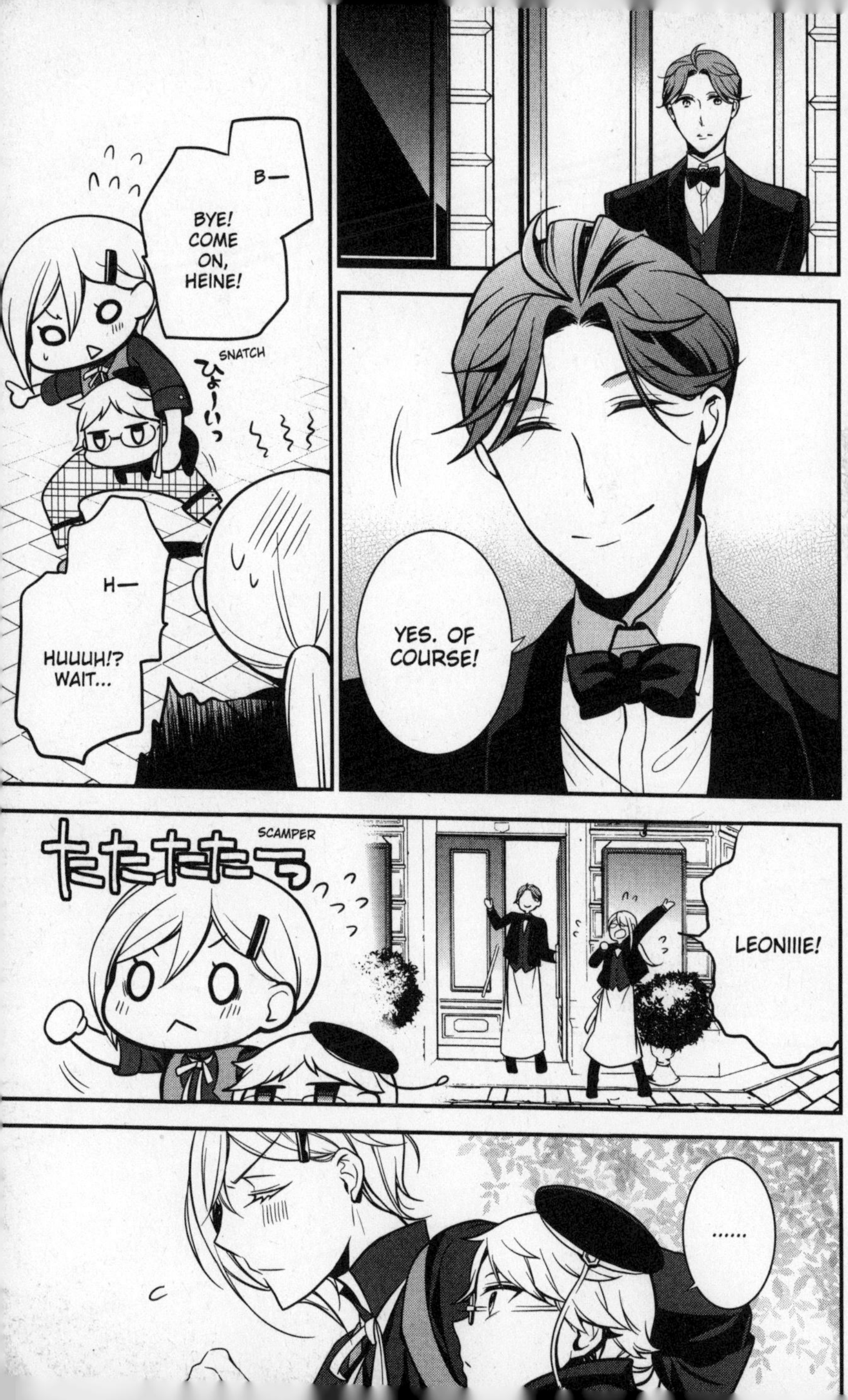
YES. OF COURSE!
B—
BYE! COME ON, HEINE!
SNATCH
ひょーいっ
H—
HUUUH!? WAIT...
LEONIIIE!
SCAMPER
たたたたっ
......

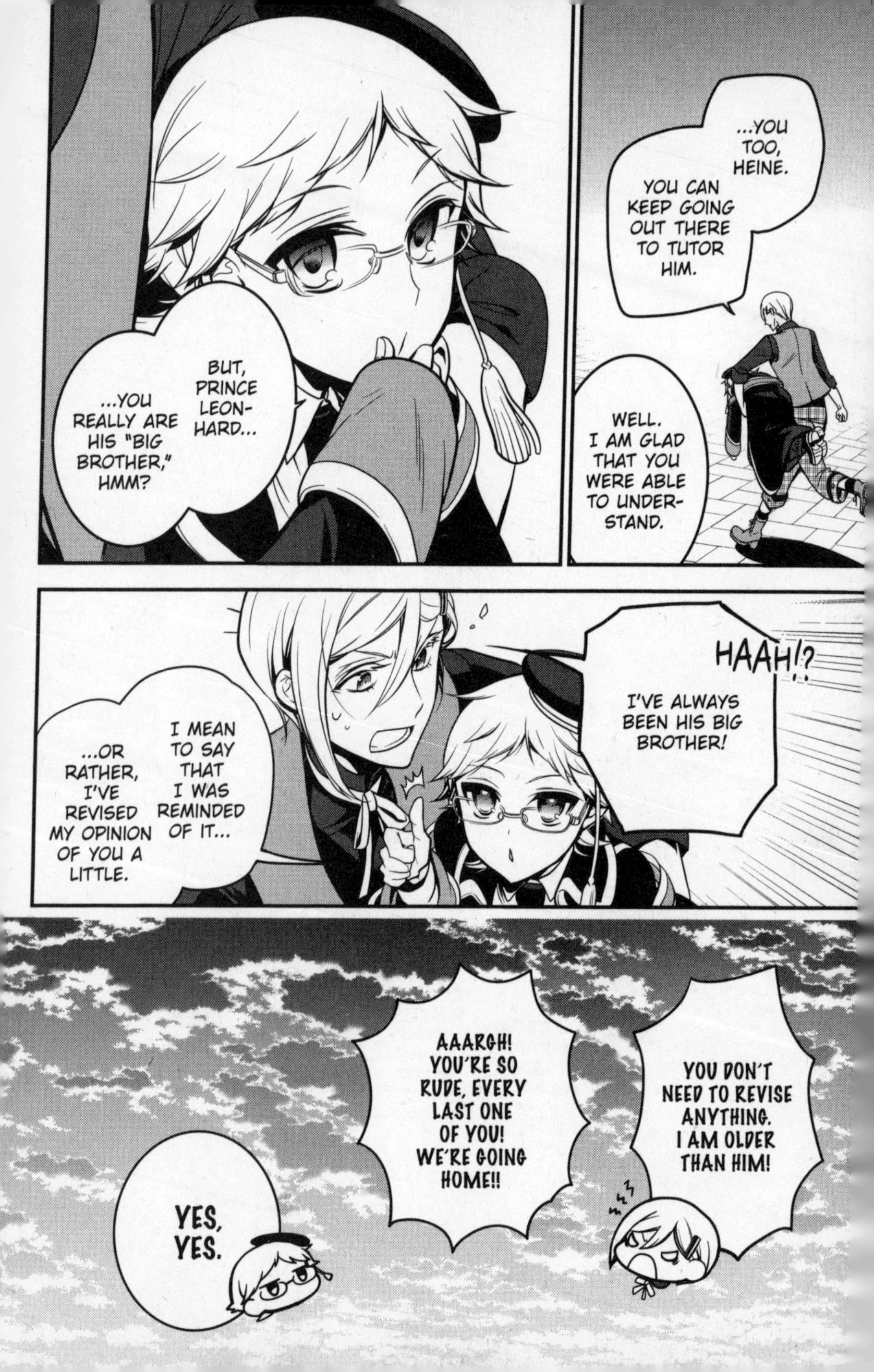
...YOU TOO, HEINE.
YOU CAN KEEP GOING OUT THERE TO TUTOR HIM.
WELL. I AM GLAD THAT YOU WERE ABLE TO UNDERSTAND.
BUT, PRINCE LEONHARD...
...YOU REALLY ARE HIS "BIG BROTHER," HMM?
HAAH!?
I'VE ALWAYS BEEN HIS BIG BROTHER!
I MEAN TO SAY THAT I WAS REMINDED OF IT...
...OR RATHER, I'VE REVISED MY OPINION OF YOU A LITTLE.
YOU DON'T NEED TO REVISE ANYTHING. I AM OLDER THAN HIM!
AAARGH! YOU'RE SO RUDE, EVERY LAST ONE OF YOU! WE'RE GOING HOME!!
YES, YES.

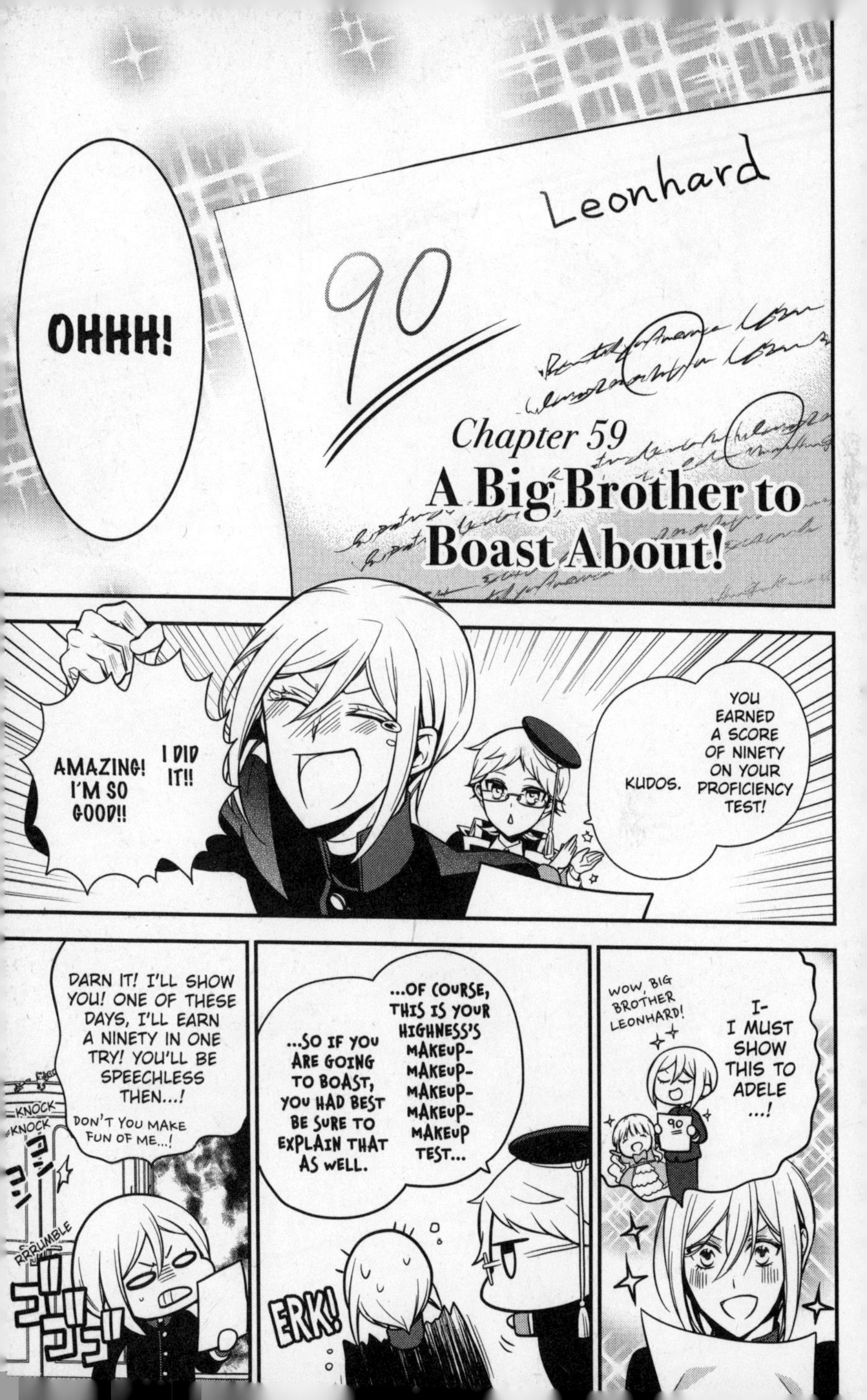
OHHH!
Leonhard
90
Chapter 59
A Big Brother to Boast About!
YOU EARNED A SCORE OF NINETY ON YOUR PROFICIENCY TEST!
KUDOS.
I DID IT!!
AMAZING! I'M SO GOOD!!
I- I MUST SHOW THIS TO ADELE...!
WOW, BIG BROTHER LEONHARD!
90
...OF COURSE, THIS IS YOUR HIGHNESS'S MAKEUP-MAKEUP-MAKEUP-MAKEUP-MAKEUP TEST...
...SO IF YOU ARE GOING TO BOAST, YOU HAD BEST BE SURE TO EXPLAIN THAT AS WELL.
ERK!
DARN IT! I'LL SHOW YOU! ONE OF THESE DAYS, I'LL EARN A NINETY IN ONE TRY! YOU'LL BE SPEECHLESS THEN...!
DON'T YOU MAKE FUN OF ME...!
KNOCK KNOCK
RRRUMBLE

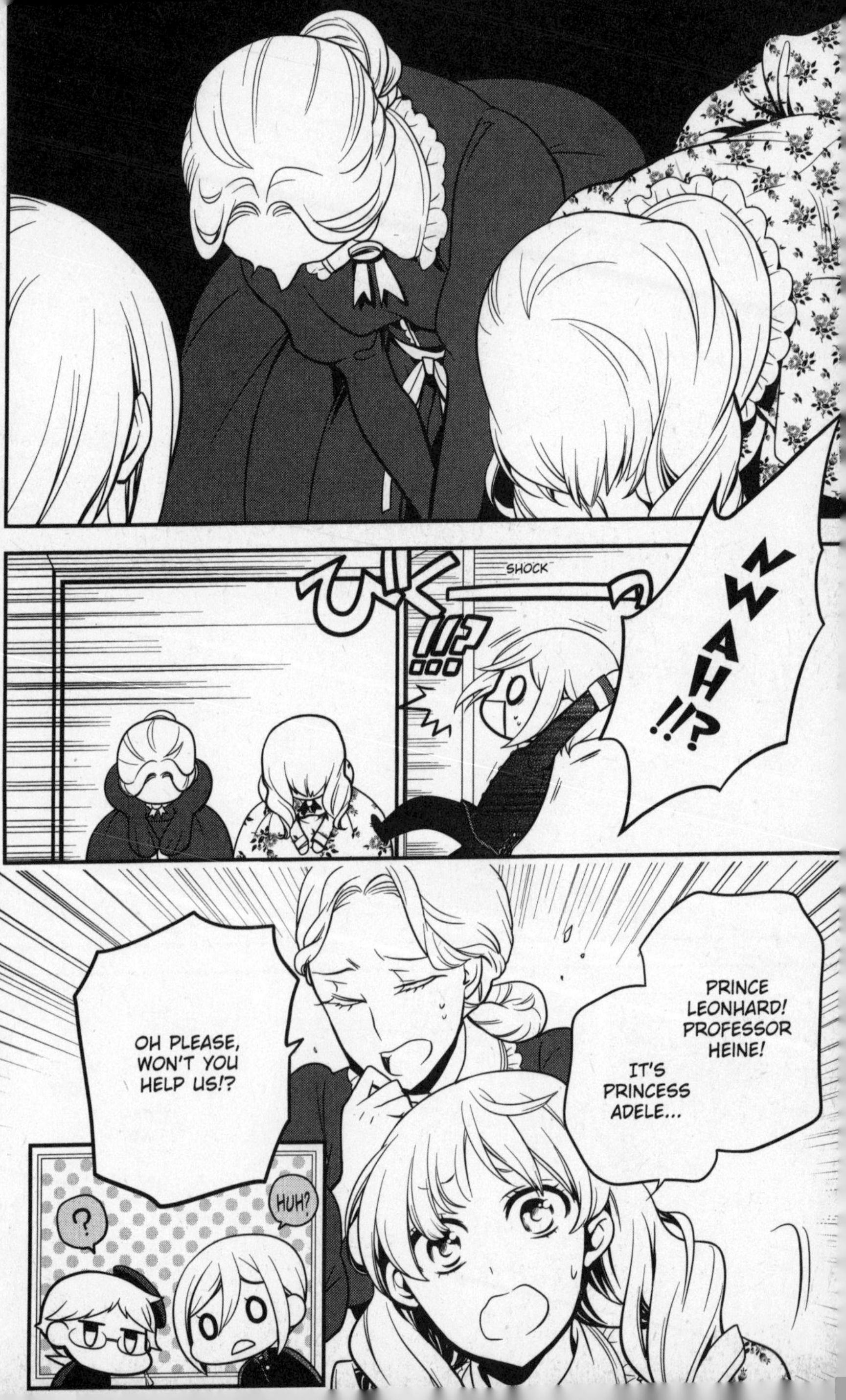
SHOCK
NWAH!!?
!!?
PRINCE LEONHARD! PROFESSOR HEINE!
IT'S PRINCESS ADELE...
OH PLEASE, WON'T YOU HELP US!?
HUH?
?

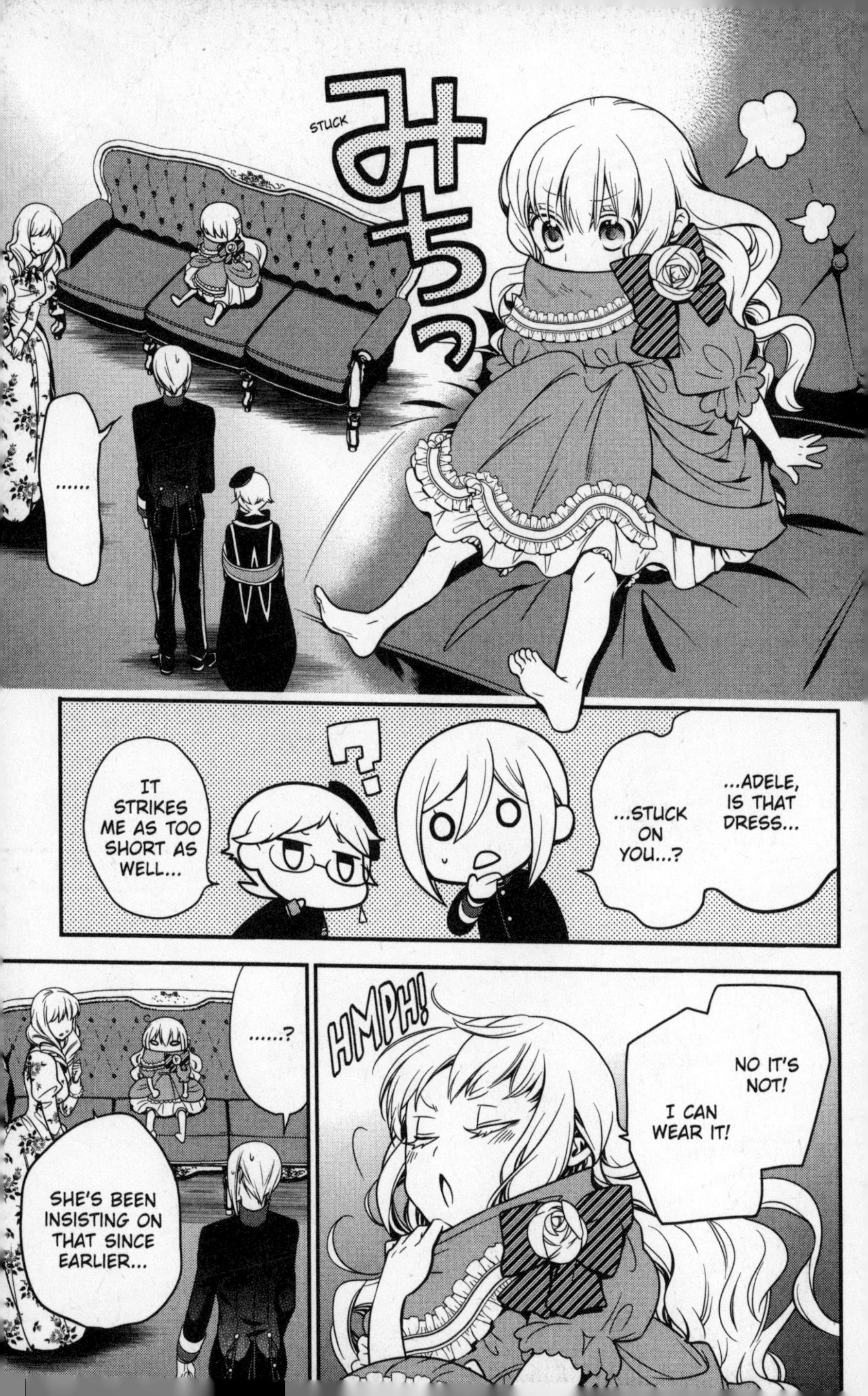
みちっ
STUCK
......
...ADELE, IS THAT DRESS...
...STUCK ON YOU...?
IT STRIKES ME AS TOO SHORT AS WELL...
HMPH!
NO IT'S NOT!
I CAN WEAR IT!
......?
SHE'S BEEN INSISTING ON THAT SINCE EARLIER...

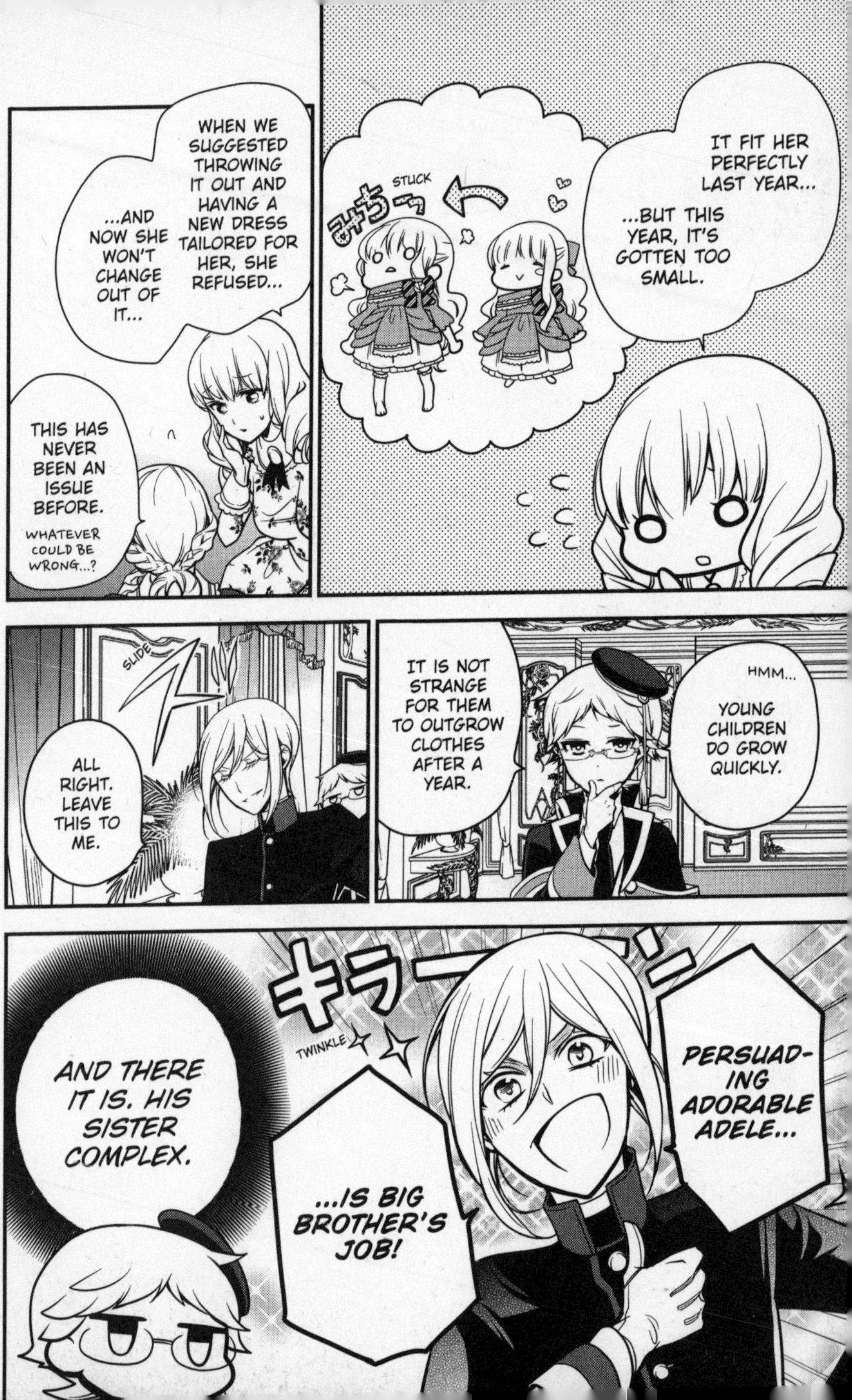
IT FIT HER PERFECTLY LAST YEAR...
...BUT THIS YEAR, IT'S GOTTEN TOO SMALL.
STUCK
みちっ
WHEN WE SUGGESTED THROWING IT OUT AND HAVING A NEW DRESS TAILORED FOR HER, SHE REFUSED...
...AND NOW SHE WON'T CHANGE OUT OF IT...
THIS HAS NEVER BEEN AN ISSUE BEFORE.
WHATEVER COULD BE WRONG...?
HMM...
YOUNG CHILDREN DO GROW QUICKLY.
IT IS NOT STRANGE FOR THEM TO OUTGROW CLOTHES AFTER A YEAR.
SLIDE
ALL RIGHT. LEAVE THIS TO ME.
キラー
TWINKLE
PERSUADING ADORABLE ADELE...
...IS BIG BROTHER'S JOB!
AND THERE IT IS. HIS SISTER COMPLEX.

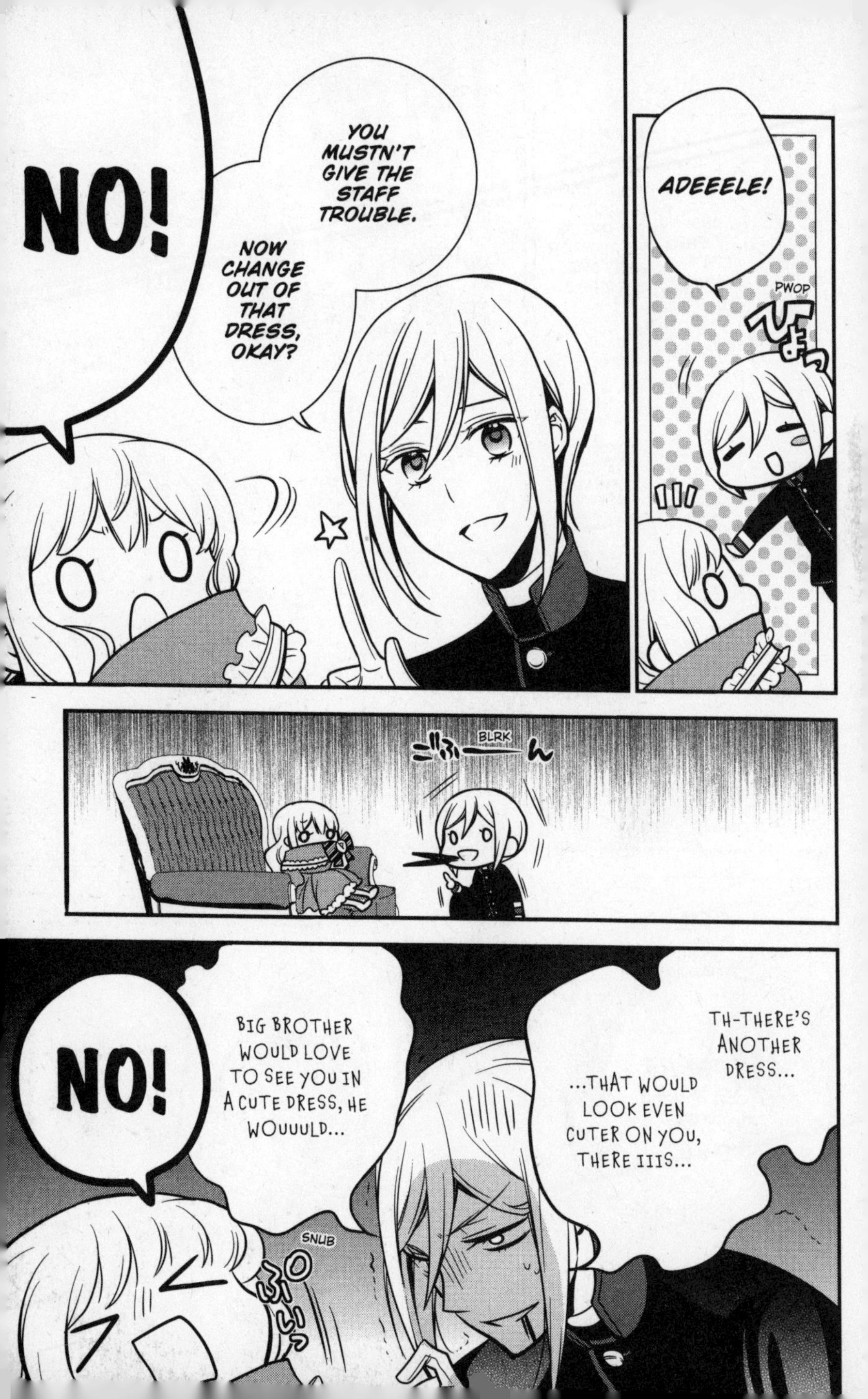
ADEEELE!
PWOP
YOU MUSTN'T GIVE THE STAFF TROUBLE.
NOW CHANGE OUT OF THAT DRESS, OKAY?
NO!
BLRK
TH-THERE'S ANOTHER DRESS...
...THAT WOULD LOOK EVEN CUTER ON YOU, THERE IIIS...
BIG BROTHER WOULD LOVE TO SEE YOU IN A CUTE DRESS, HE WOUUULD...
NO!
SNUB

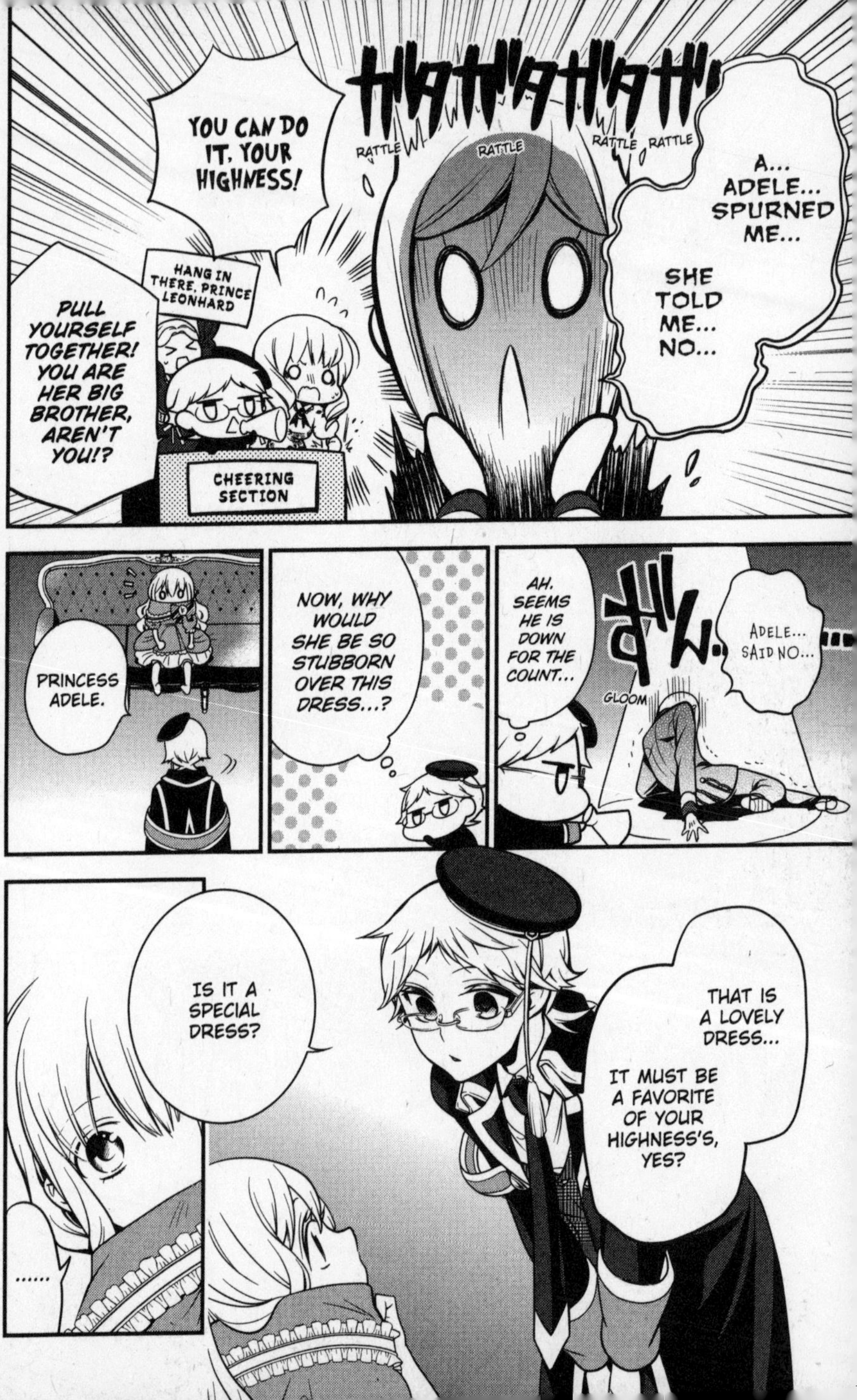
RATTLE
RATTLE
RATTLE
RATTLE
A... ADELE... SPURNED ME...
SHE TOLD ME... NO...
YOU CAN DO IT, YOUR HIGHNESS!
HANG IN THERE, PRINCE LEONHARD
PULL YOURSELF TOGETHER! YOU ARE HER BIG BROTHER, AREN'T YOU!?
CHEERING SECTION
ADELE... SAID NO...
GLOOM
AH. SEEMS HE IS DOWN FOR THE COUNT...
NOW, WHY WOULD SHE BE SO STUBBORN OVER THIS DRESS...?
PRINCESS ADELE.
THAT IS A LOVELY DRESS...
IT MUST BE A FAVORITE OF YOUR HIGHNESS'S, YES?
IS IT A SPECIAL DRESS?
......

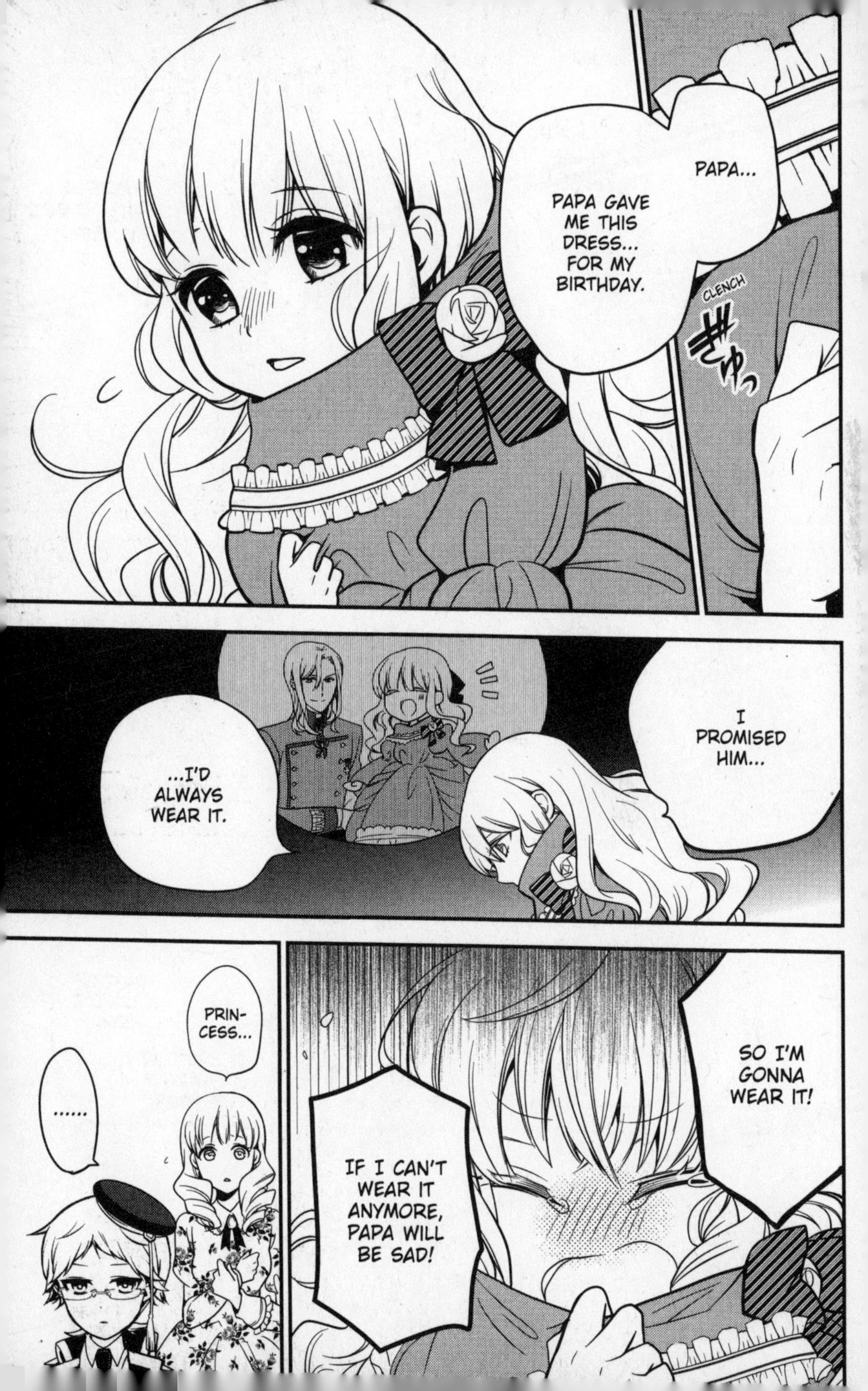
PAPA...
PAPA GAVE ME THIS DRESS... FOR MY BIRTHDAY.
CLENCH
ぎゅっ
I PROMISED HIM...
...I'D ALWAYS WEAR IT.
SO I'M GONNA WEAR IT!
IF I CAN'T WEAR IT ANYMORE, PAPA WILL BE SAD!
PRIN-CESS...
......

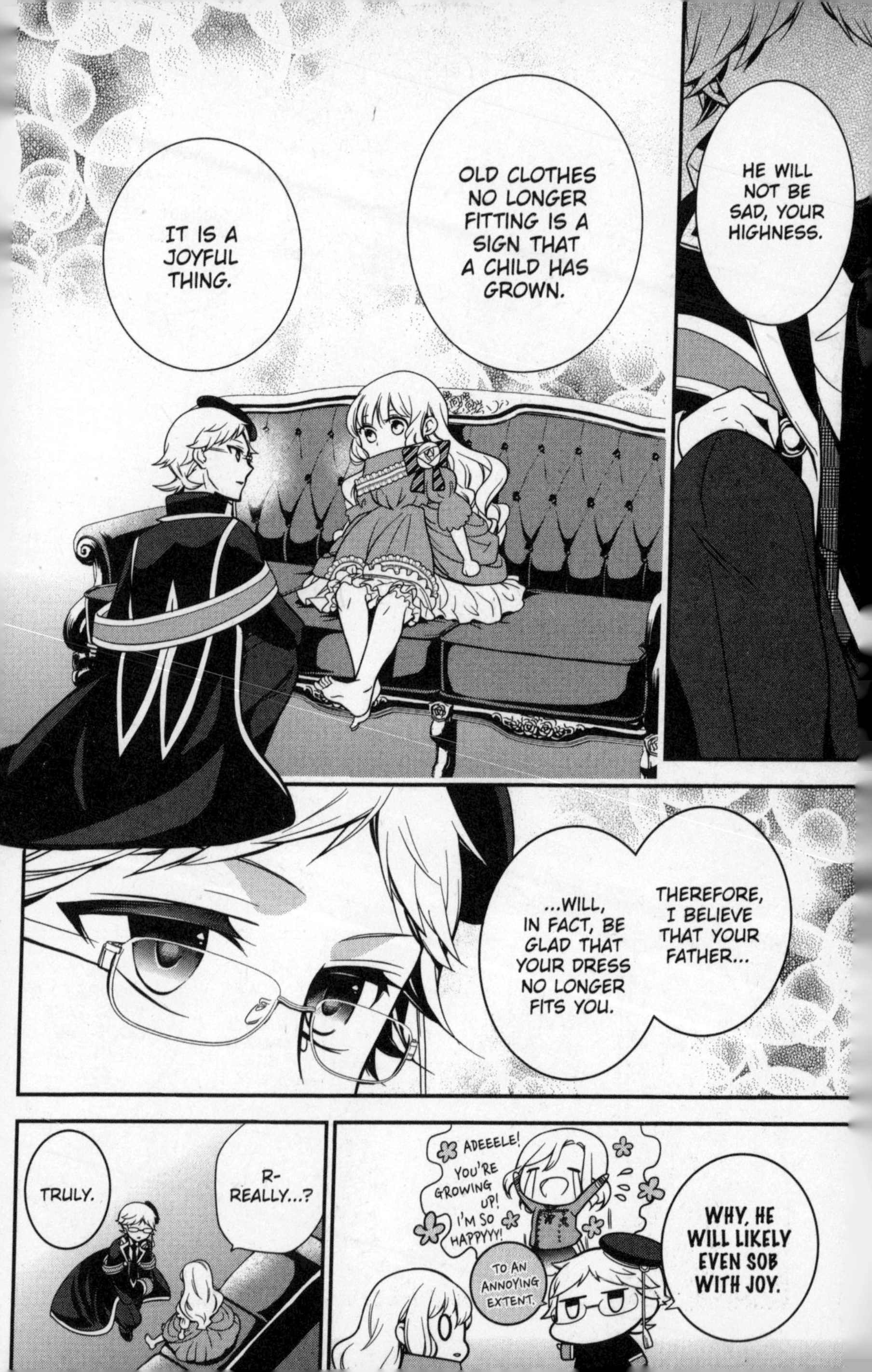
HE WILL NOT BE SAD, YOUR HIGHNESS.
OLD CLOTHES NO LONGER FITTING IS A SIGN THAT A CHILD HAS GROWN.
IT IS A JOYFUL THING.
THEREFORE, I BELIEVE THAT YOUR FATHER...
...WILL, IN FACT, BE GLAD THAT YOUR DRESS NO LONGER FITS YOU.
WHY, HE WILL LIKELY EVEN SOB WITH JOY.
ADEEELE! YOU'RE GROWING UP! I'M SO HAPPYYY!
TO AN ANNOYING EXTENT.
R- REALLY...?
TRULY.

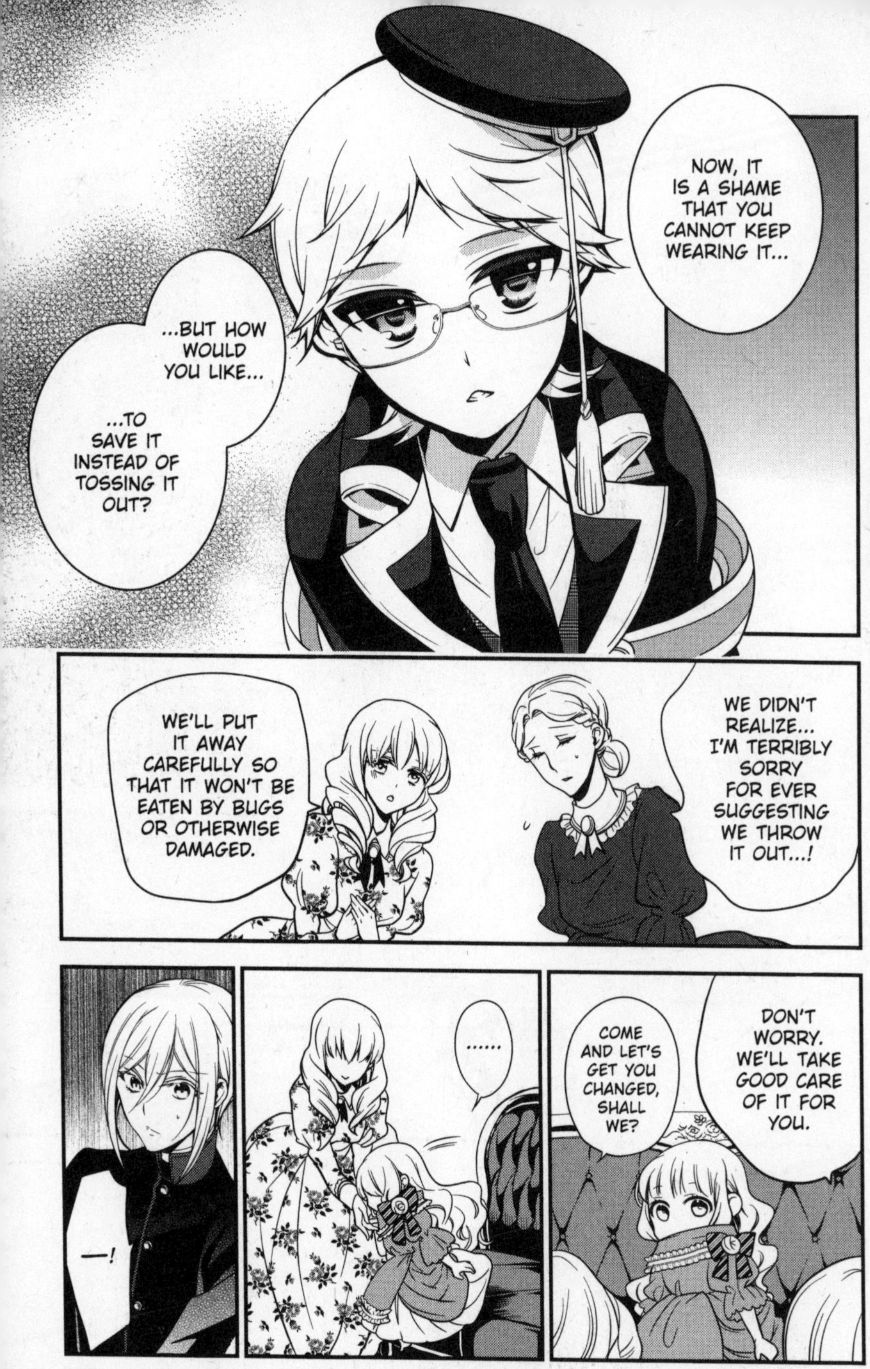
NOW, IT IS A SHAME THAT YOU CANNOT KEEP WEARING IT...
...BUT HOW WOULD YOU LIKE...
...TO SAVE IT INSTEAD OF TOSSING IT OUT?
WE DIDN'T REALIZE... I'M TERRIBLY SORRY FOR EVER SUGGESTING WE THROW IT OUT...!
WE'LL PUT IT AWAY CAREFULLY SO THAT IT WON'T BE EATEN BY BUGS OR OTHERWISE DAMAGED.
DON'T WORRY. WE'LL TAKE GOOD CARE OF IT FOR YOU.
COME AND LET'S GET YOU CHANGED, SHALL WE?
......
—!

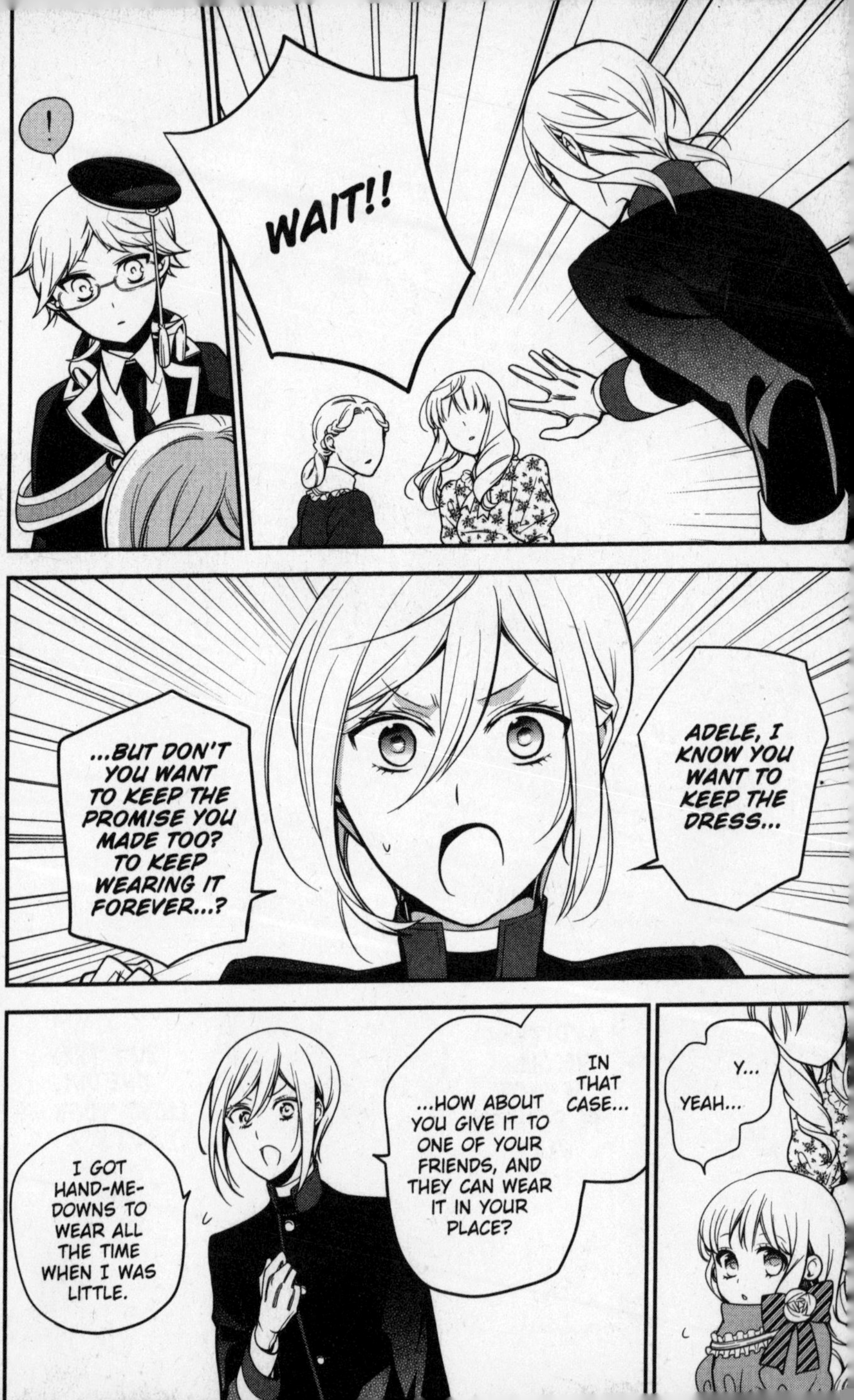
WAIT!!
!
ADELE, I KNOW YOU WANT TO KEEP THE DRESS...
...BUT DON'T YOU WANT TO KEEP THE PROMISE YOU MADE TOO? TO KEEP WEARING IT FOREVER...?
Y... YEAH...
IN THAT CASE...
...HOW ABOUT YOU GIVE IT TO ONE OF YOUR FRIENDS, AND THEY CAN WEAR IT IN YOUR PLACE?
I GOT HAND-ME-DOWNS TO WEAR ALL THE TIME WHEN I WAS LITTLE.

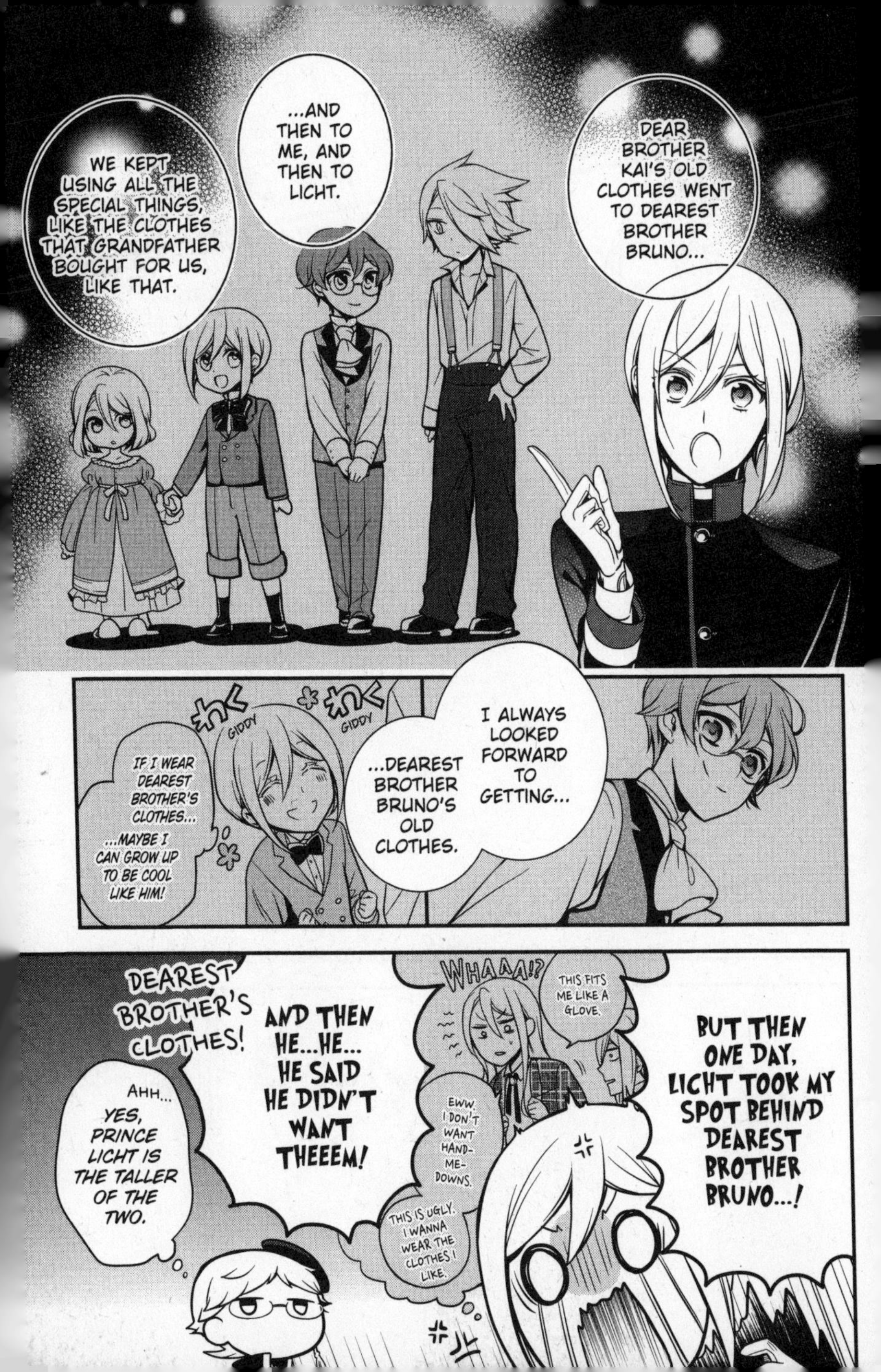
DEAR BROTHER KAI'S OLD CLOTHES WENT TO DEAREST BROTHER BRUNO...
...AND THEN TO ME, AND THEN TO LICHT.
WE KEPT USING ALL THE SPECIAL THINGS, LIKE THE CLOTHES THAT GRANDFATHER BOUGHT FOR US, LIKE THAT.
I ALWAYS LOOKED FORWARD TO GETTING...
...DEAREST BROTHER BRUNO'S OLD CLOTHES.
わく GIDDY
わく GIDDY
IF I WEAR DEAREST BROTHER'S CLOTHES...
...MAYBE I CAN GROW UP TO BE COOL LIKE HIM!
BUT THEN ONE DAY, LICHT TOOK MY SPOT BEHIND DEAREST BROTHER BRUNO...!
THIS FITS ME LIKE A GLOVE.
WHAAA!?
EWW. I DON'T WANT HAND-ME-DOWNS.
THIS IS UGLY. I WANNA WEAR THE CLOTHES I LIKE.
AND THEN HE...HE... HE SAID HE DIDN'T WANT THEEEM!
DEAREST BROTHER'S CLOTHES!
AHH... YES, PRINCE LICHT IS THE TALLER OF THE TWO.

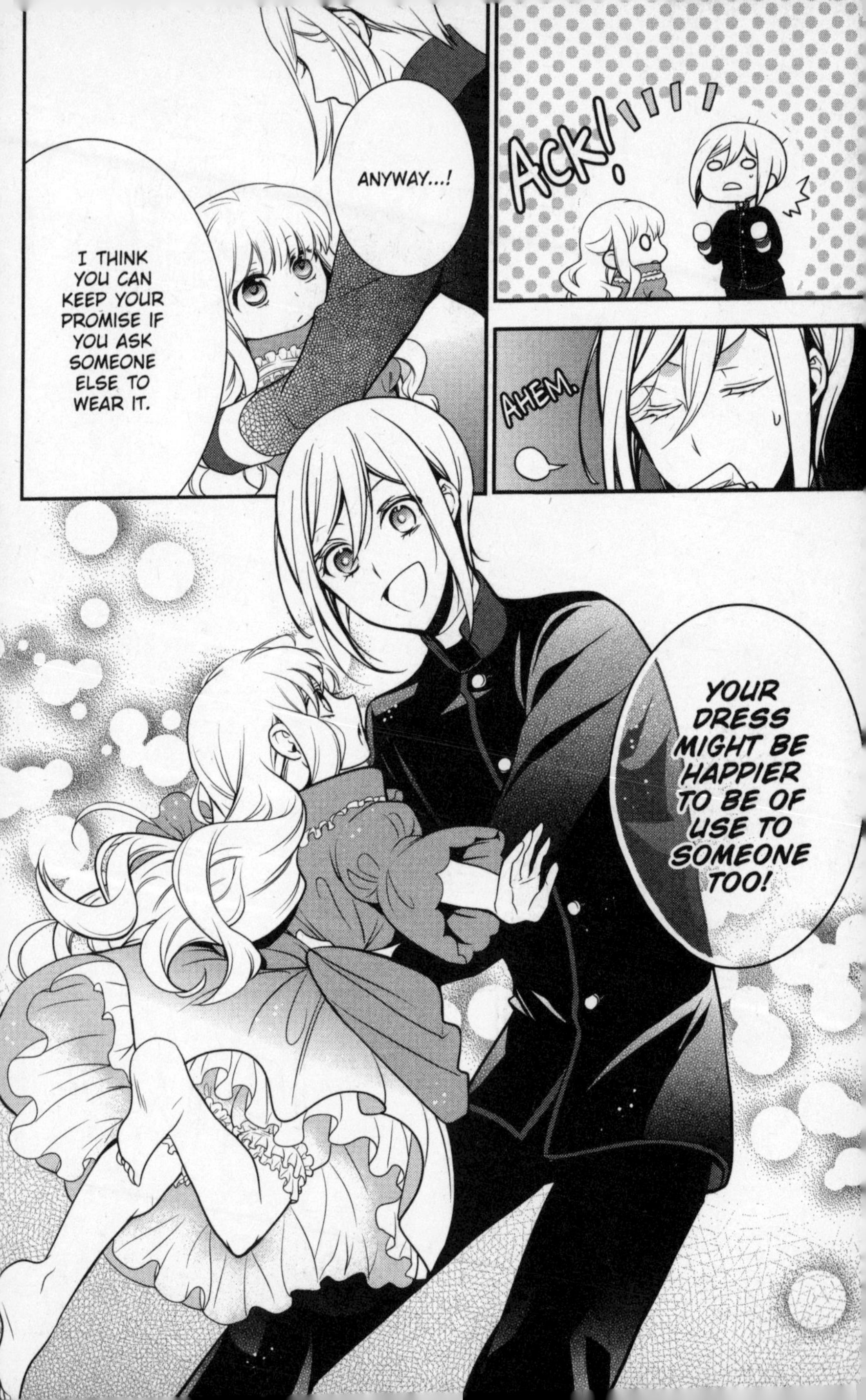
ACK!
AHEM.
ANYWAY...!
I THINK YOU CAN KEEP YOUR PROMISE IF YOU ASK SOMEONE ELSE TO WEAR IT.
YOUR DRESS MIGHT BE HAPPIER TO BE OF USE TO SOMEONE TOO!

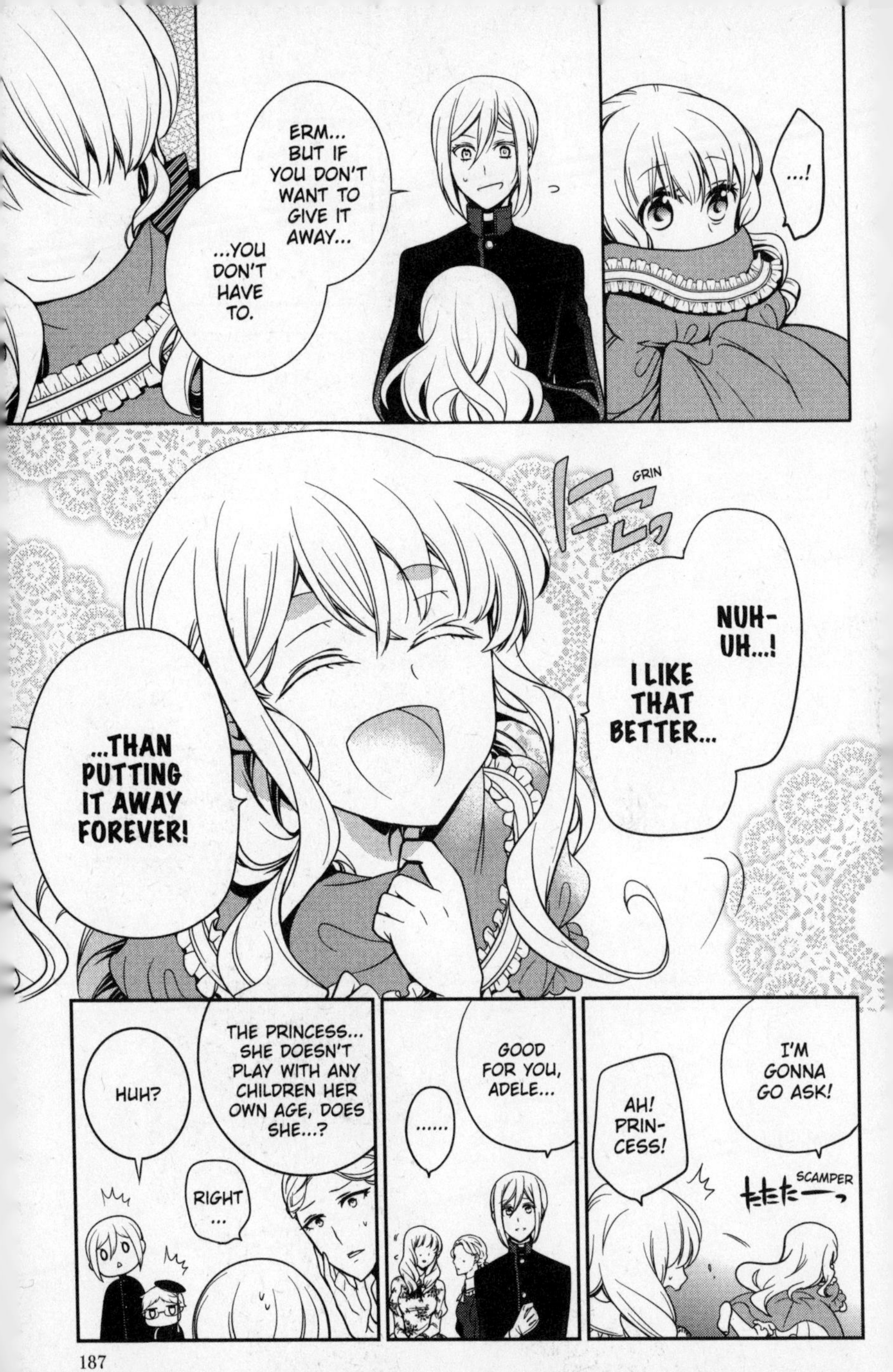
...!
ERM... BUT IF YOU DON'T WANT TO GIVE IT AWAY...
...YOU DON'T HAVE TO.
GRIN
NUH-UH...! I LIKE THAT BETTER...
...THAN PUTTING IT AWAY FOREVER!
I'M GONNA GO ASK!
AH! PRINCESS!
SCAMPER
GOOD FOR YOU, ADELE...
......
THE PRINCESS... SHE DOESN'T PLAY WITH ANY CHILDREN HER OWN AGE, DOES SHE...?
HUH?
RIGHT...

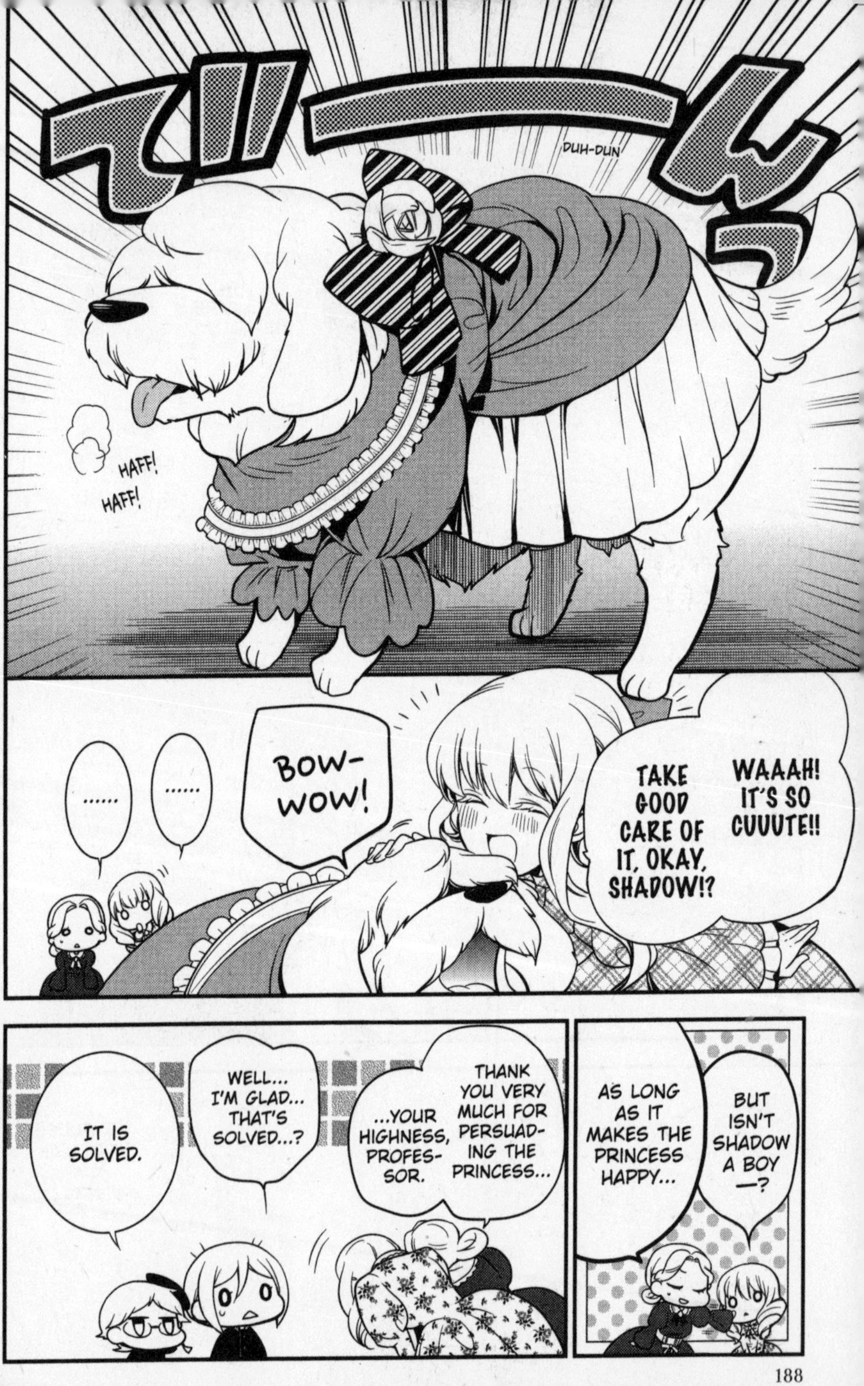
でーーん
DUH-DUN
HAFF! HAFF!
WAAAH! IT'S SO CUUUTE!!
TAKE GOOD CARE OF IT, OKAY, SHADOW!?
BOW-WOW!
......
......
BUT ISN'T SHADOW A BOY —?
AS LONG AS IT MAKES THE PRINCESS HAPPY...
THANK YOU VERY MUCH FOR PERSUADING THE PRINCESS...
...YOUR HIGHNESS, PROFESSOR.
WELL... I'M GLAD... THAT'S SOLVED...?
IT IS SOLVED.

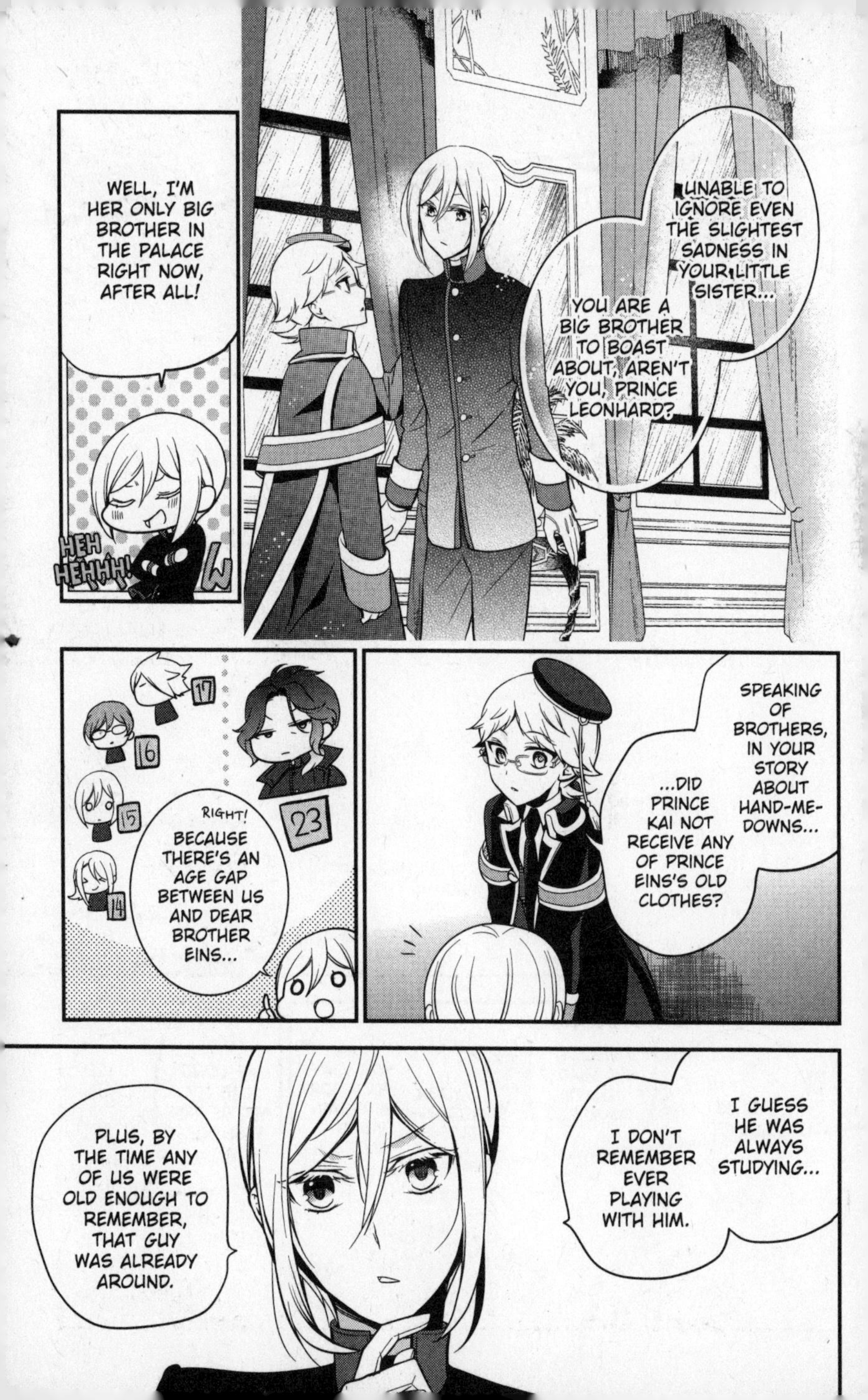
UNABLE TO IGNORE EVEN THE SLIGHTEST SADNESS IN YOUR LITTLE SISTER...
YOU ARE A BIG BROTHER TO BOAST ABOUT, AREN'T YOU, PRINCE LEONHARD?
WELL, I'M HER ONLY BIG BROTHER IN THE PALACE RIGHT NOW, AFTER ALL!
HEH HEHHH!
SPEAKING OF BROTHERS, IN YOUR STORY ABOUT HAND-ME-DOWNS...
...DID PRINCE KAI NOT RECEIVE ANY OF PRINCE EINS'S OLD CLOTHES?
17
16
15
14
23
RIGHT! BECAUSE THERE'S AN AGE GAP BETWEEN US AND DEAR BROTHER EINS...
I GUESS HE WAS ALWAYS STUDYING...
I DON'T REMEMBER EVER PLAYING WITH HIM.
PLUS, BY THE TIME ANY OF US WERE OLD ENOUGH TO REMEMBER, THAT GUY WAS ALREADY AROUND.

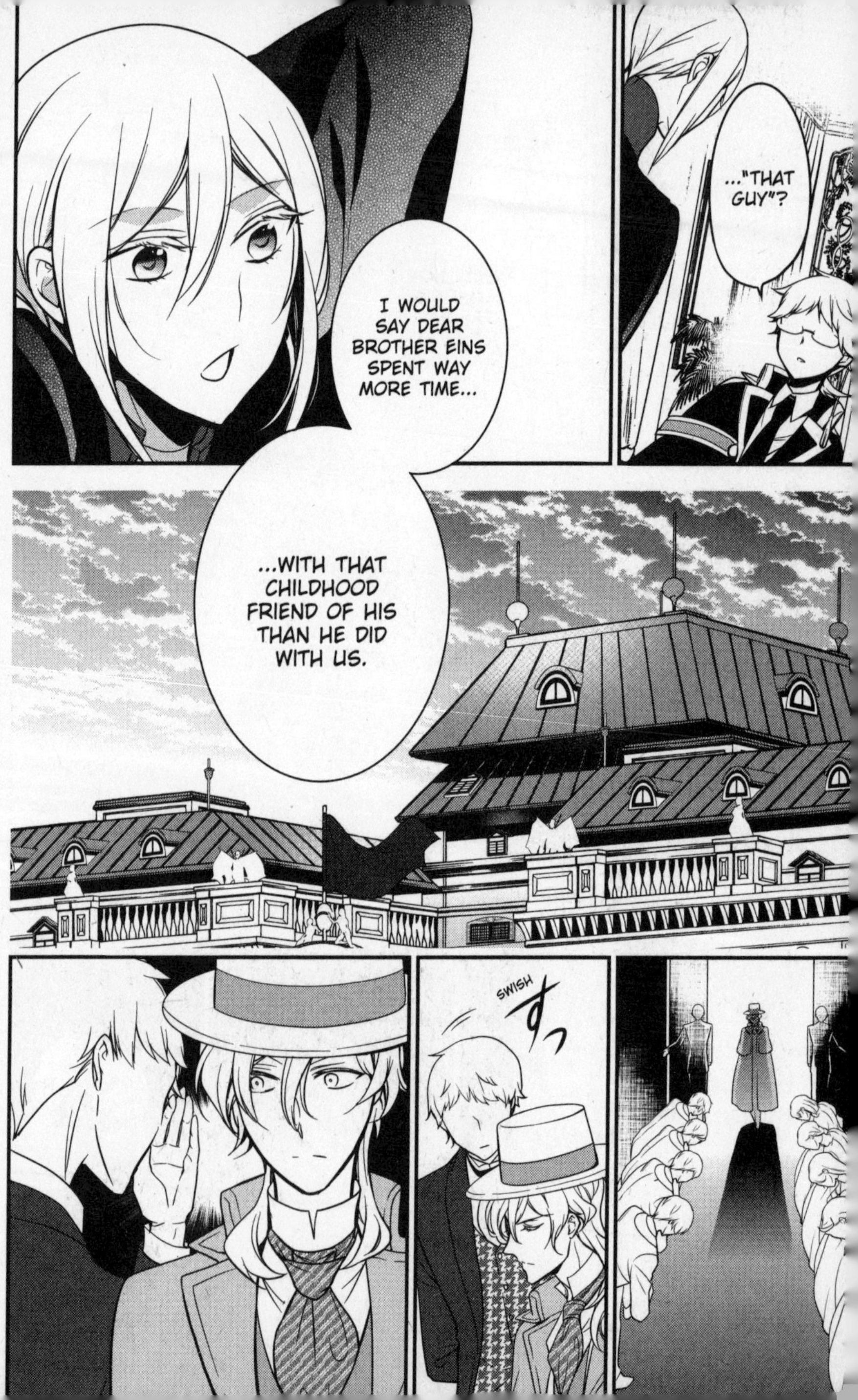
..."THAT GUY"?
I WOULD SAY DEAR BROTHER EINS SPENT WAY MORE TIME...
...WITH THAT CHILDHOOD FRIEND OF HIS THAN HE DID WITH US.
SWISH

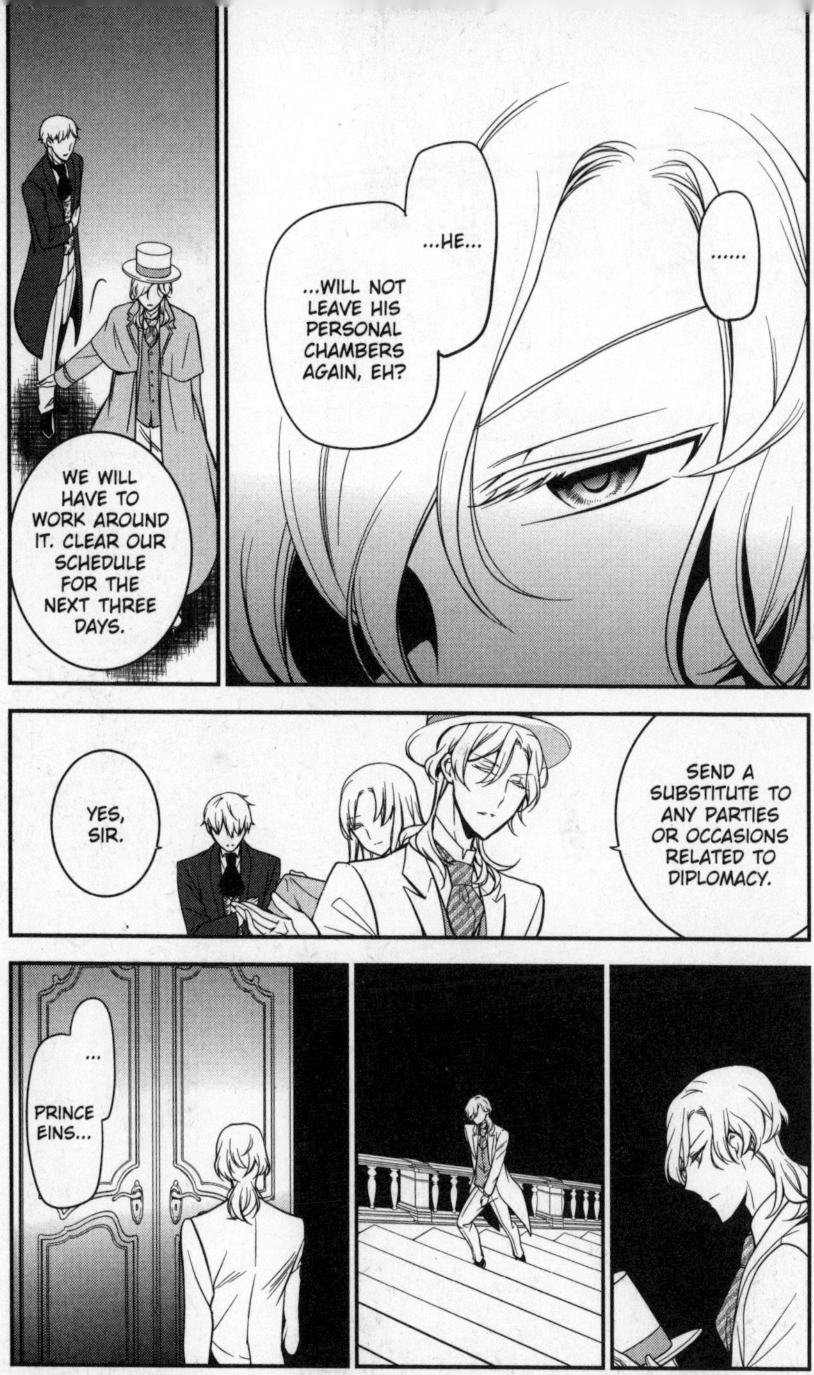
......
...HE...
...WILL NOT LEAVE HIS PERSONAL CHAMBERS AGAIN, EH?
WE WILL HAVE TO WORK AROUND IT. CLEAR OUR SCHEDULE FOR THE NEXT THREE DAYS.
SEND A SUBSTITUTE TO ANY PARTIES OR OCCASIONS RELATED TO DIPLOMACY.
YES, SIR.
... PRINCE EINS...

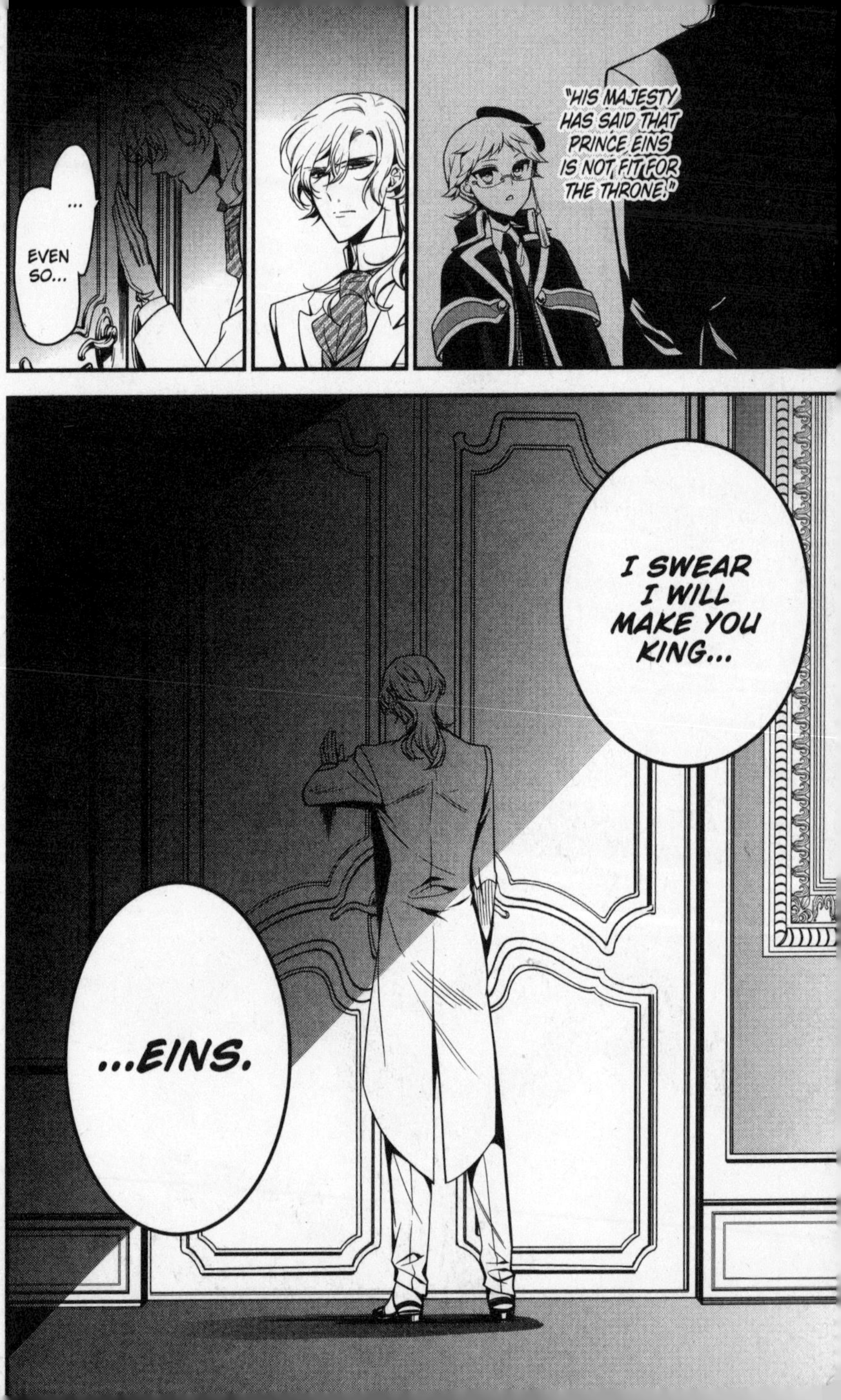
"HIS MAJESTY HAS SAID THAT PRINCE EINS IS NOT FIT FOR THE THRONE."
... EVEN SO...
I SWEAR I WILL MAKE YOU KING...
...EINS.

◆The Royal Tutor 10 End◆

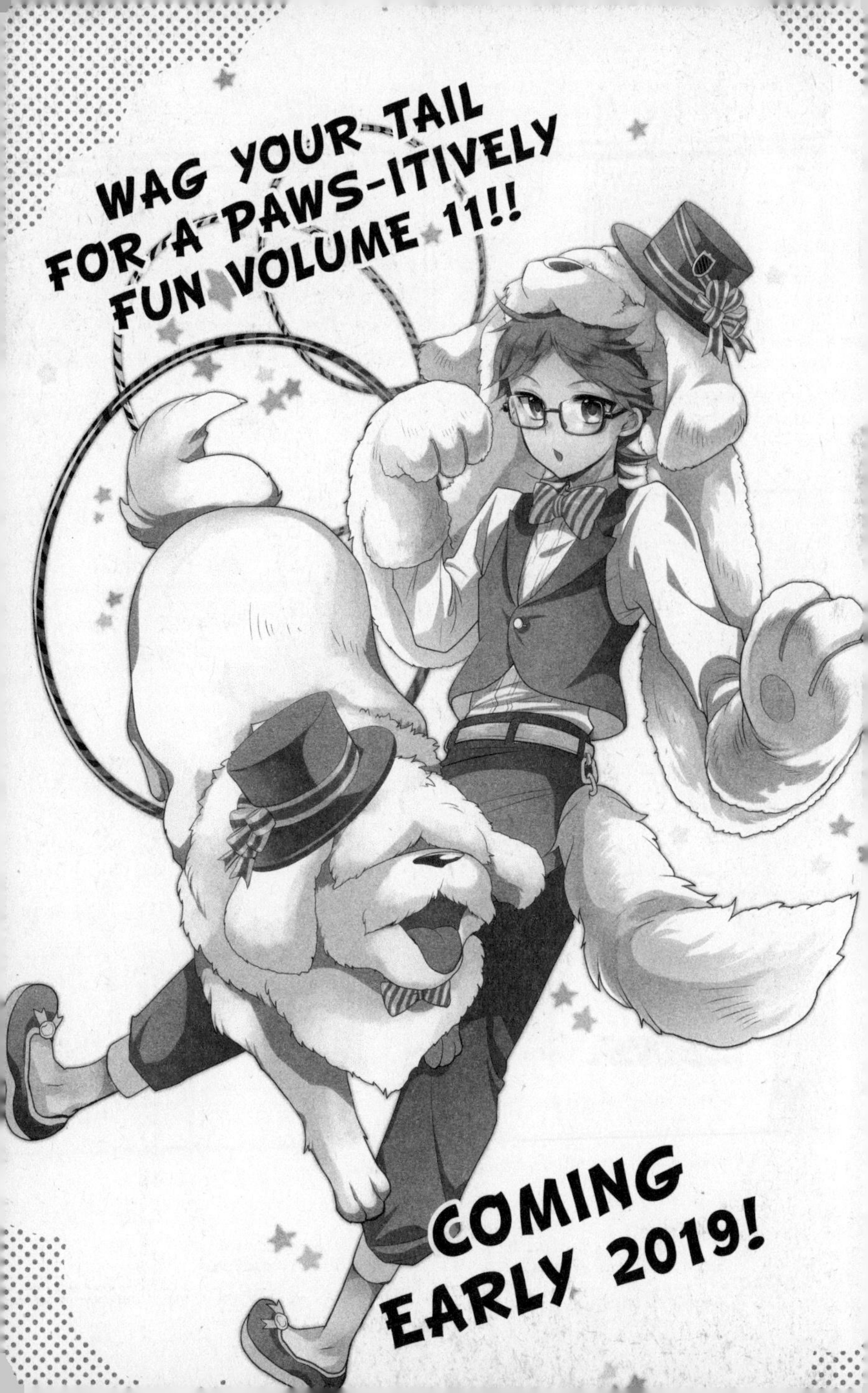
WAG YOUR TAIL FOR A PAWS-ITIVELY FUN VOLUME 11!!
COMING EARLY 2019!

The Royal Tutor ❿

Higasa Akai

Translation: Amanda Haley • Lettering: Abigail Blackman

THE ROYAL TUTOR Vol. 10 © 2018 Higasa Akai / SQUARE ENIX CO., LTD. First published in Japan in 2018 by SQUARE ENIX CO., LTD. English translation rights arranged with SQUARE ENIX CO., LTD. and Yen Press, LLC through Tuttle-Mori Agency, Inc., Tokyo.

English translation © 2018 by SQUARE ENIX CO., LTD.

Yen Press
1290 Avenue of the Americas
New York, NY 10104

Visit us at yenpress.com
facebook.com/yenpress
twitter.com/yenpress
yenpress.tumblr.com
instagram.com/yenpress

First Yen Press Edition: November 2018
The chapters in this volume were original published as ebooks by Yen Press.

Yen Press is an imprint of Yen Press, LLC.
The Yen Press name and logo are trademarks of Yen Press, LLC.

The publisher is not responsible for websites (or their content) that are not owned by the publisher.

Library of Congress Control Number: 2017938422

ISBNs: 978-1-9753-2815-3 (paperback)
       978-1-9753-2834-4 (ebook)

10 9 8 7 6 5 4 3 2 1

WOR

Printed in the United States of America